CW01303242

ELIZABETHAN PUBLISHING AND THE MAKINGS
OF LITERARY CULTURE

KIRK MELNIKOFF

Elizabethan Publishing and the Makings of Literary Culture

UNIVERSITY OF TORONTO PRESS
Toronto Buffalo London

© University of Toronto Press 2018
Toronto Buffalo London
utorontopress.com

ISBN 978-1-4875-0223-2

Library and Archives Canada Cataloguing in Publication

Melnikoff, Kirk, 1969–, author
Elizabethan publishing and the makings of literary culture / Kirk Melnikoff.

(Studies in book and print culture)
Includes bibliographical references and index.
ISBN 978-1-4875-0223-2 (cloth)

1. Book industries and trade – England – History – 16th century. 2. Publishers and publishing – England – History – 16th century. 3. Printing – England – History – 16th century. 4. Literature publishing – England – History – 16th century. 5. Transmission of texts – England – History – 16th century. 6. Literature and society – England – History – 16th century. 7. Early printed books – England – History – 16th century. 8. England – Intellectual life – 16th century. I. Title. II. Series: Studies in book and print culture

Z151.3.M45 2018   686.2094209'031   C2017-906091-0

University of Toronto Press acknowledges the financial assistance to its publishing program of the Canada Council for the Arts and the Ontario Arts Council, an agency of the Government of Ontario.

Canada Council for the Arts   Conseil des Arts du Canada

ONTARIO ARTS COUNCIL
CONSEIL DES ARTS DE L'ONTARIO
an Ontario government agency
un organisme du gouvernement de l'Ontario

Funded by the Government of Canada   Financé par le gouvernement du Canada

Contents

Tables and Figures   vii

Acknowledgments   ix

A Note on the Text   xiii

Introduction   3
    Book-Trade Publishing   7
    Collaborations, Obligations   12
    The Rise of the Publishing Bookseller   17
    Literary Makings   19

1 Geldings, "prettie inuentions," and "plaine knauery": Elizabethan Book-Trade Publishing Practices   27
    Acquiring   30
    Compiling   36
    Reissuing   57
    Altering   60
    Translating   66
    Specializing   70

2 Thomas Hacket, Translation, and the Wonders of the New World Travel Narrative   77
    The Career of Thomas Hacket   79
    Travelling in the Bookstalls   83
    Moving Travel Literature   89

3 Richard Smith's Browsables: *A Hundreth Sundry Flowers* (1573), *The Fabulous Tales of Aesop* (1577), and *Diana* (1592, 1594?)   99
    The Career of Richard Smith   101

    A Hundreth Sundry Flowers (1573)   108
    The Fabulous Tales of Aesop (1577)   117
    Diana (1592, 1594?)   125

4 Flasket and Linley's *The Tragedy of Dido Queen of Carthage* (1594): Reissuing the Elizabethan Epyllion   137
    Publishing at the Black Bear   138
    Reissuing Ovid   145

5 Reading *Hamlet* (1603): Nicholas Ling, Sententiae, and Republicanism   155
    Vending the Republic   158
    Speculating with *Hamlet* (1603)   170

Notes   183

Works Consulted   239

Index   281

Tables and Figures

Table 1   Dedications during the Elizabethan period   41
Table 2   Dedications by book-trade publishers during
           the Elizabethan period   41
Figure 1   Page headlines in Phillip Stubbes's *The anatomie
           of abuses* (1583)   50
Figure 2   The rebus emblem of Gregory Seton, from the title page
           of *A baite for Momus* (1589)   55
Figure 3   The rebus emblem of Thomas Woodcocke, from the title
           page of *The Bucoliks of Publius Virgilius Maro* (1589)   56
Figure 4   The printer's emblem of John Day, from the title page
           of *Reformatio legum ecclesiasticarum* (1571)   74
Figure 5   The printer's emblem of Thomas Millington, from the title
           page of *Deuoreux* (1597)   75
Figure 6   Printed marginalia in *The most wonderful and pleasaunt
           history of Titus and Gisippus* (1562)   91
Figure 7   Richard Smith's redesigned printer's emblem, from *Of
           prayer and meditation* (1596)   106
Figure 8   The title page of Thomas Bassandyne's *The moral fabillis
           of Esope* (1571)   121
Figure 9   The printer's emblem of Nicholas Ling, from the title page
           of *Rosalynde* (1596)   157
Figure 10 Gnomic markers in *The tragicall historie of Hamlet Prince
           of Denmarke* (1603)   172

Acknowledgments

Elizabethan Publishing and the Makings of Literary Culture is the culmination of work that began with my Boston University dissertation on Elizabethan clowning. Conducting research for a chapter on Marlowe, I first encountered Richard Jones's infamous *Tamburlaine* epistle and was made perpetually curious about the conditions, practices, and agents of publishing in an age of Shakespeare and the Stationers' Register. At that time, I was lucky that my dissertation advisers James R. Siemon and William C. Carroll ("Jim and Bill") were willing to see the relevance of Jones in a thesis about comic performance and authorship. What followed was a job in Charlotte, North Carolina; a research trajectory away from Tarlton, Kemp, and Armin; a series of articles and chapters on Jones and on his contemporaries Roger Ward and John Danter, Thomas Hacket, Nicholas Ling, and Thomas Millington; and this monograph.

Since beginning research on *Elizabethan Publishing and the Makings of Literary Culture* in earnest, I have been fortunate that my work on this book has been supported by a number of institutions and organizations. UNC Charlotte and its College of Liberal Arts and Sciences (CLAS) have been particularly generous. In 2006, the university granted my application for a Junior Faculty Reassignment of Duties in order to begin preliminary research. That year, CLAS also selected my project to receive a Francis Lumsden Gwynn Award. In 2011, CLAS underwrote a trip to the Huntington Library for work on my Flasket and Linley chapter, and UNC Charlotte funded my Faculty Research Grant for research at London's Drapers' Company on Smith and on Flasket. Much of my time during my reassignment-of-duties was spent in the reading rooms and stacks of the Folger Shakespeare

Library, and for the next few years, my name could regularly be found on the Folger Registrar's sign-in sheet. It was at the Folger that I had earlier completed two articles on the printer-publisher Richard Jones, and it was there too that I conducted research for my 2009 *Library* piece on the bookseller Thomas Hacket. I was particularly grateful to the Folger in 2008 when it awarded me a Short-Term Fellowship for work on Nicholas Ling's publication of *Hamlet*'s first quarto. In 2012, I was asked by The Centre for Early Modern Studies at the University of Aberdeen to present my research on Thomas Hacket, and in 2013, I was invited to Oxford University to present my chapter on Flasket and Linley as part of a *Performing Dido* conference at Christ Church College. Earlier that year, this chapter was co-recipient of The Calvin and Rose G. Hoffman Prize for a Distinguished Publication on Marlowe granted by The Calvin & Rose G Hoffman Marlowe Memorial Trust.

Institutions and organizations are only as good as the people who run them. At UNC Charlotte, I have benefited greatly from the support and encouragement of both my dean, Nancy Gutierrez, and my chair, Mark West. At the Folger, LuEllen DeHaven, Betsy Walsh, and Georgianna Ziegler have long managed to provide guidance even in the face of my inexperience and muddled thinking. I am indebted as well to Penny Fussell, archivist at the London Drapers' Company, for her generosity and assistance, and to Andy Gordan and Elisabeth Dutton respectively for invitations to present chapters at Aberdeen and Oxford.

Over the past decade, I have also been the beneficiary of the time and guidance of a number of individuals. Without their generosity, this book would never have been completed. The following have listened to my musings on Elizabethan publishing with sympathy and patience; others have read early drafts of this book's chapters or shared their work, namely Judith Bazler, Giles Bergel, Claire M.L. Bourne, Kent Brintnall, Sonya Brockman, William L. Carroll, Kent Cartwright, Kerry Cooke, James Daybell, Alan Farmer, Ed Gieskes, Andy Gordan, Andrew Hartley, Adam Hooks, Helen Hull, Tony Jackson, Eileen Jakeway, Laurie Johnson, Pete Kirwan, András Kiséry, Elizabeth Kolkovich, Zachary Lesser, Robert A. Logan, Stephen Longstaffe, Jeremy Lopez, Tara Lyons, David McInnis, Finley Melnikoff, Steve Mentz, Paul Menzer, Lucy Munro, Jennifer Munroe, Andrew Murphy, Sarah Neville, Aaron Pratt, Alan Rauch, Richard Schoch, James R. Siemon, Alan Stewart, Marta Straznicky, Garrett Sullivan, Holger Syme, Sarah Werner, Heather Wolfe, and Adam Zucker. I am especially indebted to Roslyn L. Knutson for her candour and unflagging support; to Peter Blayney for his wisdom and magnanimity; and to Adam Smyth for his incisiveness, confidence, and wit, and especially for his excellent advice. I would perhaps be most remiss if I did not thank my partner Lara Vetter. Over the past decade, she has happily listened to all of my research anecdotes and helped me wrestle with a number of thorny issues that a project like this inevitably raises. She is my most important adviser and my best friend.

Lastly, a section of chapter 2 appeared in "Thomas Hacket and the Ventures of an Elizabethan Publisher," *The Library*, 7th ser. 10.3 (2009): 257–71; and a shorter version of chapter 5 was published as "Nicholas Ling's Republican *Hamlet* (1603)," in *Shakespeare's Stationers*, ed. Marta Straznicky (Philadelphia: University of Pennsylvania Press, 2013), 95–111, 335–41. I am grateful to Oxford Journals, Oxford University Press, and the University of Pennsylvania Press for permission to republish this work.

A Note on the Text

All early modern English titles in this book's chapters have been modernized for spelling and capitalization; edition titles in the tables and figures and in the bibliography come from the ESTC. All parenthetical year references with early modern titles in this book's chapters refer to first editions unless otherwise indicated. Quotations from early modern books are in old spelling (with the descending *s* silently replaced with the round *s*), and they are derived from EEBO copies. Quotations taken from title pages are indicated by "tp"; line endings in these quotations are indicated with " | ". Abbreviations in early modern texts have been expanded, and capitalization and italicization have been retained. Variations between black letter and roman typefaces have not been indicated. Quotations from Arber's transcription of the Stationers' Register have been amended to remove italicization and all-cap renderings of proper nouns; years have been modernized to begin on 1 January. In the bibliography, entries for early-modern titles indicate place of publication and publisher(s).

ELIZABETHAN PUBLISHING AND THE MAKINGS
OF LITERARY CULTURE

Introduction

Sometime in the middle months of 1592, the London bookseller Cuthbert Burby ventured to publish the first English translation of *Axiochus*, a short dialogue "written in Greeke by *Plato* the Phy- | losopher" (1592a, tp).[1] This would be Burby's first publication since being made free of the Stationers' Company, and it advertised in a conspicuous space on its title page that the dialogue was translated "by | *Edw. Spenser*."[2] With this, Burby also "*annexed*" another work, "*a sweet speech or Oration, | spoken at the Tryumphe at White-hall before her | Maiestie, by the Page to the right noble Earle | of Oxenforde*" (1592a, tp), and above the imprint, he stamped the whole with his new printer's emblem: a phoenix rising from ashes to what was Elizabeth I's motto "SEMPER EADEM" ("always the same"). On the following leaves, the quarto's preliminaries featured a dedicatory epistle to the London alderman Benedict Barnam and a short address "To the Reader" that further praised "*Maister* Edward Spenser, *whose studies haue & doe carry no mean commendation, because their deserts are of so greate esteeme*" (sig. ¶4ʳ).

Like most Elizabethan first editions, Burby's composite *Axiochus* was never reprinted, and other than a number of speculative inquiries about its content in the eighteenth and nineteenth centuries, the quarto was lost for over three hundred years. In 1932, after a piece of the volume was happened upon, the title re-emerged to a groundswell of attention, not for its rumination on "the shortnesse and vncer- | tainty of this life" (1592a, tp), but for its attribution to Edmund Spenser.[3] Frederick Morgan Padelford in his 1934 facsimile edition lit a fire and fanned its flames by proclaiming *Axiochus* "one of Spenser's 'Lost Works'" (1934, vii). "It is hardly an exaggeration to say," wrote Padelford, "that [Spenser] transformed a rather uninspired dialogue into a prose poem of beauty and feeling, rapid, imaginative, and musical" (25). This attribution did not go unchallenged for long. In 1936, after a complete copy of Burby's volume was located, Bernard Freyd rejected Padelford's ascription, arguing that the translation's euphuistic passages were beneath the great Elizabethan poet and more likely by another writer.[4] "In brief," he concluded, "to meet the essential conditions of the problem, a 'Spenser' must be produced whose prose style was Euphuistic, who was attracted by sophistical paradoxes, who wrote 'triumphs,' who labored at translation without knowing Greek, and whose spelling was his own. He is not the Spenser whom we know; his name is Anthony Munday" (907–8). In 1944, Marshall S. Swan agreed, and he expanded upon Freyd's contention, arguing that both of the 1592 volume's titles – the dialogue *and* the oration – were undoubtedly by Munday.

Through all of this, Burby loomed large as a final piece in what Swan would call "as good a bibliographical romance as has ever been told" (161). Accounting for what he argued was the 1592 quarto's focus on Spenser with a cursory glance at Burby's publication history, Padelford characterized the bookseller as a social climber – as "so pushing a man" – willing to pursue any project to get ahead: "Sermons, ballads, handbooks, romances, plays, whatever would catch the public, Burbie was eager to print. He addressed himself to saints and sinners, Puritans and courtiers alike" (1934, 7). As Spenser's literary star was ascending in the early 1590s, argued Padelford, Burby thus "would have regarded the publication of the *Axiochus*, bearing the name of Spenser, as a veritable triumph" (1934, 8). Freyd concurred, but he recast the characterization of Burby. "Genuine or not," mused Freyd, "this publication was pirated by one who was eager to print 'whatever would catch the public'; and this being the case, we need not believe that it was the work of any Spenser, whether Edmund or Edward" (905). Echoing Freyd's assumptions about book-trade piracy, Swan not only indicted the bookseller as "poor and reckless" and a "questionable opportunist" (1944, 164) who was often in trouble with company authorities, but he added that the quarto's trade printers John Charlewood and John Danter were also known to be of "dubious integrity" (166). Assuming as well that Spenser's name was a prized print commodity in the early 1590s, Swan ultimately gave us a Munday and Burby that together "connived" (1944, 179) to bring out the whole under Spenser's name. What was for a few years understood to be an authoritative Spenser translation brought out by an opportunist was now an authoritative Munday volume brought out by a knave.[5]

It has now been 70-odd years since the dust first settled from this rediscovery and debate, and critical consensus – such as it is – has settled with Padelford; Spenser is now taken to be the translator of *Axiochus*, and its accompanying "*sweet speech or Oration*" has been set aside as written by somebody else.[6] In the end, like a rumoured sibling found, lost, and found again, authorial attribution has been taken to reveal all that was hidden, right all that was wrong. Except that it hasn't. Four hundred years after it first went to press, Burby's book has yet to be fully or even fairly glossed. In 1992, Gerald Johnson gave us the first measured overview of Burby's work as a publisher, considering his career without recourse to prejudicial terms, but almost no one has ventured the same for either John Charlewood or John Danter, the latter eternally damned by New Bibliography for his financing the first quarto of *Romeo and Juliet*.[7] But even though we now know something of Burby, questions remain about his 1592 publication. Why would the publisher intermingle a Socratic dialogue in prose on the inevitability of death with an allegorical speech originally delivered at a tilt held at Whitehall on 22 January 1581?[8] What sort of readership was Burby targeting with this composite volume in 1592? And was this the same audience that Burby was imagining when he commissioned his phoenix printer's emblem and published *The Third and Last Part of Conycatching*; *The Repentance of Robert Greene; A Discourse of the Great Overthrow Given by the French King*; *A Direction for Travelers*; *Gerileon of England*; *The First Sermon of Noah's Drunkeness*; *The Sinful Man's Search*; and *A Looking Glass for Drunkards*? One wonders as well whether Burby's clumsy attribution to "*Edw. Spenser*." should temper our sense of Spenser as a hot print-market commodity in the early 1590s, or whether Burby's couching of Spenser's works as "studies" at the very least suggests an agile approach to Spenser's marketability at that time.

Elizabethan Publishing and the Makings of Literary Culture is dedicated to answering questions like these, especially as they have to do with the publication of vernacular literature in the latter half of the sixteenth century. Inspired by D.F. McKenzie's groundbreaking *Bibliography and the Sociology of Texts* (1986), it tracks the full output – the "makings" – and imagined readership of a number of different publishers, and it uncovers a variety of intersections between their practices and products.[9] At issue throughout is Elizabethan literary culture. This book insists that neither its development nor its particularities – its norms, its idiosyncracies – can be fully appreciated without taking the activities of publishers into account. All book-trade publishers, be they printers, booksellers, and/or bookbinders, shared a dogged concern with the ins and outs of book financing, from acquisition to wholesaling and all practices in between. Of course, publishing then as it does now involves a number of common activities, but even so, as this book will stress, each Elizabethan publisher working in a London printing house or in a London bookshop held to his or her own distinct habits.

The Elizabethan book trade had no separate term for a person who took the lead in acquiring texts; preparing copy; financing the materials and process of print production; and wholesaling print titles.[10] Like an owner-operator of a printing house, this agent was called a "printer." In some cases, the agent who took responsibility for printing a title was also responsible for acquisition, preparation, financing, and distribution (hereafter, the "printer publisher" or "publishing printer"), but increasingly in the second half of the sixteenth century, the practices of publishing were carried out by a bookseller (hereafter, the "bookseller publisher" or a "bookselling publisher"). When procured by a bookseller publisher, copy was in due course commissioned out to a printing house where the printer (the "trade printer") would take responsibility for setting, inking, and proofing the edition. Finished sheets would then in most cases be returned to the bookseller publisher for wholesaling. While London book-trade publishing (by printer publishers and bookseller publishers alike) between 1558 and 1603 constitutes a general emphasis here, the activities and products of bookseller publishers like Burby are the main focus of these chapters. In this, this book looks past the rare literary project funded by an author or a patron (Bland 2010a, 208).[11] It does, however, consider Elizabethan publishers who were not formally affiliated with the Stationers' Company, these mostly the drapers and grocers who made much of their living retailing books and other commodities.

On its title page, Burby's 1592 quarto calls the annexed oration *"sweet"*; in its epistle "To the Reader," it refers to *"that worthy Scholler and Poet, Maister* Edward Spenser" along with *"the delightful pleasures* [his] *verses yeeldeth"* (sig. ¶4ʳ); and at the beginning of the dialogue, it calls *Axiochus* "both short *and very Elegant"* (sig. A1ʳ). With these, the volume signals its participation in what in the Elizabethan period was a burgeoning discourse having to do with the qualities of literary work in the vernacular. As it is difficult to imagine either Spenser or Munday making the mistake of "Edward," these words are in all likelihood Burby's, and they are part of a deliberate product wholesaled at "the middle shop in the Poultry, | vnder S. Mildreds Church." Elizabethan publishers were motivated readers of their merchandise. As Zachary Lesser wrote in 2004, "a publisher had to understand the text's position within all the relevant discourses, institutions, and practices, in order to speculate on the meanings his imagined customers might make of it" (36). Sweetness, delight, elegance, and "Spenser," in other words, were vendible qualities which Burby recognized and in which he invested. He also backed a pairing of texts that together explore the meaning of earthly existence, *Axiochus* finding it in "ouerlook[ing] that æternall and heauenly course of things" (sig. C1^v) and the oration in service to the transcendent Elizabeth I. Ultimately, *Elizabethan Publishing and the Makings of Literary Culture* both complements and counters recent accounts of vernacular literary culture that have turned back to authors and out to readers as essential participants in literary development and change in the second half of the sixteenth century.[12] Its chapters together consider dozens upon dozens of overlooked early-modern texts, recounting the early rise – the "makings" – of a number of vernacular genres during the Elizabethan period from a different perspective and demonstrating that book-trade publishers made substantial interventions in what were developing literary forms.

Book-Trade Publishing

In associating Burby with piratical and fraudulent practices, Freyd and Swan were quick to assume that the publishing side of the book trade – printers and booksellers alike – was fraught with disobedience and misconduct. While it is undeniable that there existed a few publishers like John Wolfe and Roger Ward who made a habit of violating Stationers' Company rules during their long careers, the vast majority of London's publishing grocers, drapers, printers, booksellers, and bookbinders actually appear to have been relatively upstanding and compliant. This, however, is not an impression that one always derives from R.B. McKerrow's collaborative *A Dictionary of Printers and Booksellers in England, Scotland and Ireland, and of Foreign Printers of English Books 1557–1640* (1910), an unrevised tome that still stands – even after the revision and expansion of the Oxford *DNB* in 2004 –

8   Elizabethan Publishing

as a central resource for information about the Elizabethan book trade.[13] McKerrow's *Dictionary* consists of hundreds of short biographical entries, each providing select details about company achievements, places of occupation, involvement with significant titles (especially Shakespeare), probate negotiations, and company violations and imprisonments. Infractions populate a lesser but significant proportion of entries, and in a number of cases they are included even when only a small fraction of other incidences and activities are glossed. Given this, it is sometimes the case that a publishing bookman's life and career is unduly characterized as one of flimflam and malfeasance. Thus, Danter's ten-year career which consisted of over two dozen published titles and as many trade printing jobs is recounted as a linked sequence of seized presses and "trouble" with an interspersed smattering of poor-quality printing and publishing (83–4). Robert Robinson's prolific work as a publishing printer over two decades is similarly summed up as consisting of a patent dispute, of his acquisition of a printing-house, and of his "frequent … fine[s]" for "disorderly printing," levies that in fact only occurred four times over fourteen years (231). In some cases, the *Dictionary* is even more unduly damning. The bookseller Thomas Cadman is described as "constantly in trouble for disorderly conduct and for quarrelling with other stationers," even though misdemeanours were only recorded for five of his thirty years as a freeman (61).[14] In a related vein, Valentine Simmes's extensive and varied endeavours as a publishing printer over 30 years are prefaced with condemnation: "From the outset of his career he was constantly in trouble for printing books that were obnoxious to the authorities, or were the property of other men" (245). And the bookseller and printer Garrat Dewes is called "a disorderly member of the company" because in thirty years he was fined by the Stationers' Company around a half-dozen times (91). Dewes is so decried even as he was elected into the Stationers' Company livery, serving both as Renter Warden and Under Warden.[15]

To some extent, the emphasis on malfeasance in the *Dictionary* is an understandable product of what was a limited availability of evidence about the Elizabethan book trade. Aside from that which could be found in early print editions themselves, much of the information that McKerrow and his contributors relied upon came from Edward Arber's late-nineteenth-century transcription of Stationers' Company records.[16] Dedicated to "the daily running of the organization" along with "[securing the company's] legal position and [protecting] its landed and literary property" (Myers 1990, xvii), these records are instrumental in purpose; as such, they paint a narrow portrait of book-trade activity as consisting mainly of title entry, apprentice enrollment, and fines. What they do not offer is information about the innumerable day-by-day transactions between publishing bookmen like Danter, Cadman, Simmes, Robinson, and Dewes, transactions that would have been set down in now-lost account books, bonds, commonplace volumes, diaries, letters, and probate records. Also not included in Arber's transcript are entries from the Court of the Stationers' Company.[17] Further documenting the array of misdemeanours and disputes among a broad majority of Stationers' Company members, these make it amply clear that infractions and conflict were not an exception – confined to a disorderly few – but a widespread albeit relatively small part of the everyday reality of the book trade.

Still, the McKerrow *Dictionary*'s good apple–bad apple book trade was not simply a skewed product of the readily available, early-twentieth-century evidence; it reflected as well the theories of textual transmission being newly proposed by McKerrow, Pollard, and Greg at the beginning of the twentieth century. In the late nineteenth century, most literary scholars and historians imagined the transmission of texts – from quill to press – to have been driven by publisher greed and characterized by theft. In Heminge and Condell's famed allusion to "diuerse stolne, and surreptitious copies," (Shakespeare 1623, sig. A3ʳ) they found specifically a warrant to decry all single editions of Shakespeare's plays before the First Folio and more generally a brush to paint the finance side of early-modern book publishing. For Sidney Lee, second editor of the Oxford *DNB*, the majority of publishers working during Shakespeare's day were knavish "adventurers" (1904) who used any "unscrupulous method" (*Passionate Pilgrim* 1905, 9) to procure copy at the expense of authors, translators, playing companies, and the like. Not only was surreptitious publishing the "common practice of the age" (1904, 1.xlii), insisted Lee, but more often than not, the agents engaged in book financing were wholly lacking in "natural sentiment" (qtd. in Kirschbaum 1955, 6). Looking to redeem most early Shakespeare quartos as authoritative authorial texts, New Bibliography (as it is today called) offered instead a submissive book trade, one cowed by state and social authority and populated by mostly upright artisans.[18] Only on its desperate fringe did the trade have a problem with agents like Cadman and Danter who were willing to risk involvement with a patented title or with what Pollard and Greg would first describe as a "bad quarto." According to Pollard in his 1909 *Shakespeare's Folios and Quartos*, "the printers and publishers [of Shakespeare's day] seem as a rule to have been honest men, though there were black sheep among them" (1909, v). "They were," he adds, "prudent, careful tradesmen, with a wholesome fear of colliding with authority" (1909, 4). New Bibliography, then, pulled the financing side of the book trade almost fully out the muck, but it only did so to suggest a more streamlined process of textual transmission. As a man of "common sense" and "English character" (Pollard 1909, 13), the English publisher became either the deferential textual agent or – as McKerrow and Greg would rejoin – the disinterested, profit-oriented capitalist, absently passing copy either to trade printer (if a bookseller or bookbinder); to compositor; and then to corrector (if a printer).[19] No longer a meddling, greedy knave, he was now a "Robin Hood" (4) or a broker.

The result of these competing accounts – publisher as sinner, saint, or small-scale venture capitalist – was that the acquisition and distribution side of the book trade was either ignored or impugned for much of the twentieth century. This proved especially true for the large numbers of book-trade publishers that were not printers, agents that are a central focus of this book. At the same time, the printing house – newly imagined as a potential root of textual maladies engendered in transcription, casting off, setting, and correcting – became the obsession of historians, scholars, and editors alike.[20] But even as the flawed theories of New Bibliography – good quartos, bad quartos, blocking entries, etc. – have been more and more discredited over the last three decades, the assumptions about publishers underlying the ideas of Pollard, Greg, McKerrow, and their predecessors have only just begun to be challenged. Today, one still encounters editions, articles, and books suggesting that most book-trade publishers – especially those at the bottom of the socio-economic ladder – were ethically suspect or – even more damning – interested in making a profit.[21] Publishing, of course, has long been a profit-oriented endeavour. This book, though, treats this functionalist observation as the beginning point of a discussion not as an end, maintaining that there's more to know about a given merchant beyond whether he or she is trying to make a living through buying and selling.[22] It insists that the orientation towards profit tells us nothing useful about the particular business practices or products of publisher addresses in Lombard

Street under the Pope's Head, at the corner shop at the Northwest door of Paul's Church, or at the Black Bear in Paul's Churchyard. Nor does it reveal anything about the surrounding economic, social, and creative networks that helped give us two very different versions of Constable's *Diana* or the first edition of Shakespeare's *Hamlet*.

Publishing may not have been a profession during the Elizabethan period (Blayney 1997, 391), but it was an essential and regular practice that had – as this book's first chapter will show – its own set of characteristic endeavours from specialization, copy acquisition, and compiling to reissuing and wholesaling. Just as the quality, type and ornaments, number of workmen, and number of presses varied across London printing houses, publishing practice differed significantly from publisher to publisher. John Day, for example, relied on the profits from his printing patents for small, cheap titles to bankroll his many larger projects like Foxe's *Acts and Monuments*. He also invested much time, energy, and resources in book illustration throughout his career.[23] Likewise, the bookseller Edward Aggas not only specialized in the acquisition and publication of French news pamphlets in the 1580s and early 1590s, but he also spent a good part of his career translating these and other French-language titles.[24] Chapters 2–5 together provide a new survey of book-trade publishing in the second half of the sixteenth century, outlining the diverse practices and products of Thomas Hacket, Richard Smith, Paul Linley and John Flasket, and Nicholas Ling respectively.

Driven almost solely by the aforementioned Gerald D. Johnson in the 1980s, the identification of the distinctive agency of specific publishers was given two shots in the arm in the last twenty years, first by Blayney's foundational "The Publication of Playbooks" in 1997 and then by Lesser's *Renaissance Drama and the Politics of Publication* in 2004. Blayney's essay provided the first detailed account of the course and costs of playbook publication in the Elizabethan period. Along the way it makes the essential point that

> if we want to investigate the text of a play – the relationship between what the typesetter saw in the manuscript and what appears on the printed page – we need to study the printer. But if our concern is the source of the manuscript, the reasons why *that* play was published *then*, or the supposed attitude of the players or the playwright to the fact of publication, we must focus not on the printer but on the publisher. (391)

Lesser's book underscores the economic importance of specialization for some early-modern publishers while at the same time stressing the significance of reading and speculation as early-modern publishing practices; it also provides exemplary case studies of the seventeenth-century publishers Walter Burre, Nicholas Vavasour, Thomas Archer, and Thomas Walkley. Taking its cue from Blayney, this book focuses on the varying motives and conditions that drove book financing during the Elizabethan period – on the "whys" and the "whens" – careful all the while to distinguish between the work of a publisher and the work of a trade printer. Like *Renaissance Drama and the Politics of Publication*, it insists that publishers be understood as uniquely invested readers of the manuscripts that they brought to press. It, though, focuses its attention on the Elizabethan period and considers not just plays but the publication of travel narratives, lyric poetry, literary anthologies, and erotic verse. In this, *Elizabethan Publishing and the Makings of Literary Culture* contends that the Elizabethan book trade routinely initiated a process of print commodification in a wide variety of early-modern cultural spheres; it grants that authors, compilers, and translators were often involved in these activities, but demonstrates that in many cases they were not understood necessarily to authorize a title's meaning. Crucially, this book sees specialization as just one among many publishing practices; it also pays close attention to the many sustained connections that drove the Elizabethan book trade – connections between publishers, editors, collectors, translators, and authors; between publishers and patrons; between publishers and trade printers; and especially between publishers.

Collaborations, Obligations

The agents who laboured in the printing houses and bookshops around London routinely worked with one another in a variety of different ways to bring their projects to fruition. In the 1970s and 1980s, McKenzie and then Blayney established once and for all that shared printing "was *extremely* common" (Blayney 1973, 440) in the late sixteenth and early seventeenth centuries. This joint work on a project was sometimes prearranged, sometimes decided upon on the fly, and it occurred either simultaneously or consecutively at two or more printing houses.[25] As this book will stress in its first chapter and track in those that follow, project sharing was not just habitual in the industrial side of London's print trade, it was also a regular and essential practice for book-trade publishers. Charted here then are not just the particular courses of individual publishers – their careers, their cultural interventions, and their commitments – but also their collaborative networks. In some cases, particular tasks were farmed out. The acquisition of copy, for example, could be managed by agents who ultimately had no stake in the publishing projects that they helped initiate.[26] Once copy was printed, wholesaling could also be subcontracted out to printers and booksellers with warehouse space to spare. Publishing bookmen and bookwomen could turn as well to their peers for paratextual material and for translating work.[27] In other cases, publishing projects could be fully collaborative, risk and profit shared between more than one publisher from beginning to end.[28] And such collaboration could continue for years on a number of different projects. Traces of partnerships between Lucas Harrison and George Bishop in the 1570s; between William Broome and Thomas Man in the 1580s; between John Busby and Nicholas Ling in the early 1590s; and – as chapter 4 will track – between John Flasket and Paul Linley in the late 1590s can be seen both in Stationers' Register entries and in imprints and colophons.

Imprints and colophons disclose as well working relationships between trade printers and publishers, and in many instances, these arrangements lasted years, even decades. Though he conveyed *Axiochus* to Charlewood and Danter, from 1592 to 1594 Burby ferried almost all of his copy to the printer Thomas Scarlet. From 1578 to 1584, the bookseller Thomas Woodcock took close to two-dozen different jobs to Thomas Dawson at the Three Cranes in the Vintry. Likewise, from 1594 to 1596, the bookseller Thomas Adams brought all of his print work to Valentine Simmes (Ferguson 1968, 12).[29] What these and the many other extended business relationships between publishers and trade printers like them suggest is that the line in the book trade between a paid job and a collaboration/partnership was likely much thinner than has usually been imagined.[30] More generally, the ubiquity of shared work and collaboration – creating as it must have done a web of sustained bonds between printers, booksellers, and bookbinders – would certainly have tempered – at the very least complicated – the stakes of competition in the Elizabethan book trade.

Shared work and collaboration were ubiquitous in the book trade not just because they made good fiscal sense – allowing individual agents to accelerate work and/or distribute risk – but because they were an offshoot of what Craig Muldrew has described as the period's "economy of obligation." Emergent in the early sixteenth century and peaking around 1580 as a result of increased household consumption, rising inflation, and limited coinage, this system of exchange was characterized by carried debt between merchants, between merchants and producers, and between merchants and consumers.[31] Only rarely would accounts between bookmen and bookwomen have been settled through a process called "reckoning" (Muldrew, 108–9). This economy was facilitated by credit or trust, and, argues Muldrew, "such trust was interpersonal and underpinned by emotional relations between individuals communicated in the form of reputation" (5). In working regularly with their peers in the trade, Elizabethan bookmen and bookwomen galvanized credit and – when these dealings went smoothly – they bolstered their reputations, and this in turn translated to more credit. Regular working arrangements then between publishers, between publishers and trade printers, between publishers and wholesalers, and between publishers and producers (authors, translators, and collectors) affirmed the financial credibility of the parties involved even as they extended debt entries in account books.

Debt was almost assuredly widespread in the Elizabethan book trade, not just between booksellers and consumers, between the Stationers' Company and its members, but between bookmen and bookwomen. Of course, a number of the stationer wills that we possess contain the conventional directive that all debts be duly and truly paid by their executors, but some of these wills mention debts to specific men and women in the trade.[32] In his 1602 will, the bookseller Francis Coldock, for example, alluded to the "somme of fortie and eight poundes more in money that my sonne in lawe William Ponsonby hath heretofore had and received of me" (Plomer 1903, 36).[33] Five years later, the bookseller Ralph Newbery took a different course in dealing with outstanding obligations, offering to give "all my bookes remayninge and beinge in my shoppe" if his former servants Roger Jackson and John North "paie ... such severall somes of money and in such manner and forme as the same are lymitted appointed or agreed to be paide by a noate and agreement under their handes" (Plomer 1903, 40). It is not known whether the two took Newbery's bait. Debt is often alluded to in the proceedings of the Stationers' Court as well. On 8 January 1577, the court presided over the transfer of two titles from the bookseller

Thomas Hacket to the bookseller John Wight. As part of this arrangement, it dictated that the "said Ihon and Thomas doo discharge either to other all man' of debte duties and matters from the begynnynge of the world to this day" (Greg and Boswell 1930, 1). In other instances, the court served as an arbitrator in disputes involving unpaid dept. Ten months after the Hacket-Wight arbitration, the court was called upon to settle debt owed by the printer bookseller Hugh Singleton to James Askell (2). In one of these cases in 1587, it supported the bookseller Robert Waley's plea for a past unpaid "Reckoninge betwene [Augustine Lawton] & Iohn walley father of the said Robert" (22).[34]

It stands to reason that debt relations like these sometimes led to profit-sharing collaborations – stakes in publishing projects being exchanged for money owed. Potential traces of the intermixing of debt, credit, and collaboration in the publishing side of the book trade can be gleaned from a combination of sources. Though it is impossible to know for sure, some of the controversies having to do with rights to copy in the recorded proceedings of the Stationers' Court appear to have been the product of these kinds of arrangements gone awry.[35] In one instance on 5 December 1598, the court arbitrated a disagreement over the now-lost title *The Mirror of Man's Miseries* between the bookseller William Blackwall and the printer Edward Allde. Four years earlier, on 21 November 1594, Allde had entered the title in the Stationers' Register, and he seems to have printed a now-lost edition sometime before 1598 (Arber, 3.665). Even so, the court decreed that while Allde "shall enioy the said booke as his own copie," it also directed that he should pay Blackwall 20 shillings and that "at the next printing of the said booke the said Edward shall frely gyve to the said william One hundred pfect Booke ... all clere and free both paper & printing" (Greg and Boswell 1930, 66). From 1594 to 1596, Allde and Blackwall had worked together on as many as five separate publication projects, and it seems likely that *The Mirror of Man's Miseries* may have originally been part of a continued arrangement – collaboration and/or carried over debt – between the two bookmen.[36]

Whatever the terms of Blackwall's engagement with Allde, his career, like those of a large majority of publishing booksellers working during the Elizabethan period, has yet to be examined in any detail. *Elizabethan Publishing and the Makings of Literary Culture* is in part dedicated to recognizing and redressing this "scholarly ignorance."[37] These ends are worth pursuing because, as Gerald D. Johnson wrote in 1985 about early-modern publishers in general, "what can be discovered about their habits and practices may throw additional light on the process by which manuscripts were procured, transmitted to the printing house, and thence to the bookstall" (2). They are vital too because the careers of bookselling publishers have much to tell us about the titles and trends that did much to shape the cultural sphere in the final decades of the sixteenth century. The booksellers of Elizabethan London – whether they were managing shops in St Paul's, near the new Royal Exchange, or along Fleet Street near the Inns of Court – were uniquely positioned to respond with their publications to the demands of buyers. Bookshops, though, were not simply sites of commodity exchange. Many early accounts describe them as popular meeting places where customers gathered both to learn the latest news and to discuss what was on their minds, be it the newest gossip or books that they had just read.[38] Moreover, in an age when book advertising was essentially limited to word-of-mouth, to the occasional printed blurb, and to title pages glued to walls, bookshop proprietors needed to function as on-the-ground promoters of new titles and on-hand authorities over the quality and kind of their wares if they wanted to be successful.[39] In essence, London's booksellers were the book market's front line.[40] If it is true then as Lesser has argued that publishers, "more than any other stationers, must ... *speculate* on the meanings of texts" (2004, 28), it follows that publishing booksellers – surrounded as they were by books and readers – were in the best possible position to do so.

Beyond responding to demand and possessing knowledge of a large subset of titles, London's publishing booksellers were also uniquely able to assess and measure the ever changing supply of books in the English book trade – folio, quarto, octavo, duodecimo; domestic and foreign; new and used. Since an essential part of their business involved purchases and exchanges with London's large number of wholesalers in order to stock and restock their shops, these men and women were regularly faced with the latest reams and dusty remnants of their peers' endeavours. This was an insider's knowledge to be sure, and it distinguished the publishing bookseller from the publishing printer. As much as the conventional practices and financial realities of publishing titles were shared by these two sets of bookmen and bookwomen, the publishing bookseller, in being fully invested in both the wholesale and retail side of the trade, enjoyed a distinct advantage in gauging the past, present, and immediate future of the book market.[41]

The Rise of the Publishing Bookseller

After incorporation, booksellers would become the dominant force behind book financing. During the Elizabethan period, London saw a significant increase in book publishing among London's many booksellers, a development part and parcel with a significant increase in trade or "job" printing among printing houses. It was during the second half of the sixteenth century, in other words, that the cultural work of publishing came to be dominated by bookmen and bookwomen who were not directly involved with the industrial side of the trade. As Blayney has recently outlined in *The Stationers' Company and the Printers of London 1501–1557*, a division among those engaged in book-trade publishing emerged most clearly in the 1520s and 1530s, when London for the first time saw publishers who never learned to print, booksellers like John Butler at the sign of St John the Evangelist and John Gough at Paul's Gate in Cheapside. The number of titles brought out by non-printers continued to increase into the 1540s, though more than 80 per cent of these were printed by a master printer who was also publisher.[42] During the reign of Edward VI, however, more than one quarter of print titles produced in London were produced by printers for other publishers who were mostly booksellers.[43] From 1575 until 1588, this figure again increased until one half of all titles were printed by master printers working as trade printers for others (Blayney 2003, 20). This trend continued into the 1590s, at least for vernacular, speculative titles.[44] In 1593, roughly 57 per cent of these titles were produced by printers like John Windet, Richard Field, and the Orwins (Thomas and his widow Joan) working for other publishers. Six years later in 1599, roughly seven out of ten vernacular titles were trade printed by master printers like Simon Stafford in Black Raven Alley, Peter Short at the Star, and Edward Allde in Aldersgate over against the pump.

With hindsight, this dramatic shift in publishing work during the Elizabethan period – moving as it did from printing houses to bookshops, from producers to distributors – has an air of inevitability. Decades before the Stationers' Company received its charter from Queen Mary in 1557, few avenues existed where publishers could protect their investments from opportunistic rivals.[45] From the time of Henry VIII, the crown had granted exclusive rights to certain books and then to certain classes of books, but only a few men, mostly master printers like Richard Jugge, John Day, William Seres, and Richard

Tottel, were fortunate enough to obtain them.[46] These conditions essentially dictated that early publishing in England was dominated by a set of wealthy printers. Ever-increasing demand appears to have helped offset risk after the 1520s, but it wasn't until 1557 that practices were changed to encourage a wide swathe of non-printing publishers. Of these changes, by far the most important was the establishment of a mostly unrestricted system of copyright within the new Stationers' Company that guaranteed the significant fiscal outlay required to publish titles.[47] With the financial risk of publishing lessened, demand coupled with an increased supply of vernacular writers eventually led in the 1570s both to a considerable increase in the number of titles published by non-printers and to an unprecedented jump in published London titles – from 1392 in the 1560s to 1908 in the 1570s.[48]

Along with an increase in titles and trade printing, the late 1570s also saw raised tensions in the Stationers' Company between master printers holding printing patents and the many printers, journeymen printers, and booksellers who did not.[49] Like incorporation, these disputes helped to precipitate a shift in the landscape of London publishing. Complaints about patents were initially filed with the Privy Council in 1577 and twice more in 1582.[50] The initial rumblings included a petition apparently submitted to Lord Burghley in August 1577 entitled "The griefes of the printers glasse sellers and Cutlers sustained by reson of priuilidges granted to priuatt persons" which included the names of forty-five plaintiffs (Arber, 1.111). These ultimately generated a series of concessions from the patent-holding master printers and led to the appointment by the Privy Council in 1582 of a special commission to look into the matter. This in turn led to the 1586 Star Chamber *Decrees for the Order of Printing* that limited the number of master printers and apprentices, and put a moratorium on new printing presses. The Stationers' Company followed the next year with "orders" of their own, among these directives that "no formes of letters be kept standinge to the preiudice of Woorkemen at any tyme"; and "no booke to be printed excede the number of 1250 or 1500 at one ympression" (Arber, 2.43). Though they were precipitated by dissension from journeymen, lesser printers, and booksellers, the 1586 *Decrees for Orders in Printing* and the subsequent 1587 Stationers' Company *Orders Concerning Printing* (Arber, 2.43–4) ended up offering economic incentives for trade printing. Their limitations on master printers, printing presses, and print runs all worked to dismantle printing-house monopolies and thereby constrain printing-house competition.[51] This in turn increased competition for printing-house work among publishing booksellers and others. Ultimately, in the face of increased internal resistance to printing patents, the decrees guaranteed an unchanging industrial capacity, this in a print environment of ever-increasing vernacular copy and demand. In effect, the profitability of trade printing was assured (what Christopher Barker called the necessity of printers being "well mayntayned" [Arber, 1.115]); this also allowed master printers to eschew wholesaling with its requirements of warehouse space and commodity exchange.[52]

Between the 1550s and the early 1600s, then, fewer and fewer master printers were regularly involved with the ins and outs of book-trade publishing, with – as my first chapter will track – copy acquisition, commissioning, compiling, marketing, editing, and reissuing. In effect, it was during the Elizabethan period that the active cultural work of the book trade became predominantly driven by booksellers.[53]

Literary Makings

A significant part of this book's focus has to do with the various endeavours of publishers in furthering a native literary culture during the second half of the sixteenth century. The Elizabethan period has long been identified as an age of unprecedented growth in vernacular literature. As Richard Helgerson and a host of others have laid out, it was during these decades that "a large number of the brightest and most energetic young Englishmen ... [were] drawn to the collective project of creating a national literature" (1983, 15), and as part of this effort, England witnessed more and more attempts to categorize and delineate the various manifestations of an English literary tradition.[54] In the 1580s, Sidney in his *Defense of Poesy* simultaneously extolled the "poeticall sinnewes" (1595a, sig. I4^v) of Chaucer's *Troilus and Cresseyde* and Spenser's *Shepheardes Calendar*, while at the same time energetically berating most English "play matter" for being "like an vnmannerly Daughter, shewing a bad education, [that] causeth her mother Poesies honesty, to bee called in question" (1595a, sig. K3^v). In a divergent mode a few years later, George Puttenham in his *Art of English Poesy* singled out Chaucer and then Gower, Lydgate, and Harding above all "for their antiquitie" (1589, sig. I1^r) at the same time as he praised Vaux, Sidney, Raleigh, "and that other Gentleman who wrate the late sheapherdes Callender" (sig. I1^v).[55] He draws to an end by coyly admitting that "Others haue also written with much facillitie, but more commendably perchance if they had not written so much nor so popularly" (sig. I2ʳ). Understood in terms of its form and decorous subject matter, in terms of its limited, elite reception, or in a variety of other ways during the period, vernacular literature – both as a mushrooming product and as an object of a burgeoning discourse – played a significant role in England's continued rise as a self-conscious nation state during the sixteenth century.[56]

To point out that authors like Sidney and Puttenham were active participants in England's early conceptualizations of vernacular literature breaks no new ground; to contend that their publishers put their own mark on this cultural enterprise ventures into what has mostly been unchartered territory. When Henry Olney brought out what is thought to have been the first edition of *The Defense of Poesy* in 1595, he prefaced Sidney's above musings with both an endorsement and an invitation.[57] "The stormie Winter," he writes in his "*To the Reader*," "which hath so long held backe the glorious Sun-shine of diuine Poesie, is heere by the sacred pen-breathing words of diuine Sir *Philip Sidney*, not onely chased from our fame-inuiting Clyme, but vtterly for euer banisht eternitie: then graciously regreet the perpetuall spring of euer-growing inuention, and like kinde Babes, either enabled by wit or power, help to support me poore Mid-wife." Espousing a canonization of Sidney as the epitome of the English poet that had been ongoing in the years following his death in 1586, Olney echoes as well the *Defense*'s nationalist sense of England's "fame-inuiting Clyme."[58] In doing so, he proclaims the 1590s the springtime of England's "diuine Poesie" and pledges his own willingness to support the "inuention" of his babe readers.[59] Prefacing *The Art of English Poesy* with a dedicatory epistle to William Cecil, Richard Field offered a far less effusive account of Puttenham's comparable efforts. "*Perceyuing besides the title to purport so slender a subject*," he admits, "*I thought it no condigne gratification, nor scarce any good satisfaction for such a person as you*" (sig. AB3ʳ).[60] Field would go on twice to praise the "*noueltie*" of Puttenham's efforts, but his rationale for publication would ultimately rest with the treatise's "*tending to the most worthy prayses of her Maiesties most excellent name*" (sig. AB3ᵛ). Howsoever Sidney's, Puttenham's, and Olney's words might be taken to suggest widespread enthusiasm for what was perceived to be a nascent literary movement in England, Field's reveal an alternative perspective that assumed English poetry to be a novel albeit "*slender ... subject*," one not automatically of interest to readers at the top of the social scale.

Such book-trade appraisals of the literary in England were not unusual in the Elizabethan period. As this book will show, the publishers of works like Gascoigne's *A Hundreth Sundry Flowers*, Marlowe's *Dido Queen of Carthage*, and Constable's *Diana* actively participated with authors, translators, collectors, and editors in what was a broad effort in the second half of the sixteenth century to identify and conceptualize literary works in the vernacular. In some cases, the cultural assumptions behind these endeavours are only indirectly suggested by these men and women in their title-page blurbs and prefatory matter. Such is the case with the reticence of printer-publisher Valentine Simmes in introducing Robert Tofte's poetry collection *Laura* in 1597: "To censure of this worke, is for better wittes than mine ovvne; it is for Poets, not for Printers, to giue iudgement of this matter" (sig. A4[r]). Book-trade publishers, though, were not always so deferent. In title-page blurbs, dedicatory epistles, reader addresses, and commendatory poems, a number of these men and women actively contributed to an emergent discourse surrounding vernacular literature in the Elizabethan period.[61] In some cases, they echoed the sentiments of their authors, translators, or collectors; in others, they fashioned distinct perspectives on the literary merits of the work at hand, offering critical commentary that was sometimes prosaic, sometimes contradictory, sometimes inventive. Whatever their particularities, these responses are treated as invaluable by this book in that they afford access to the earliest reception of England's nascent literary tradition, this by men and women of the middling sort.

As we have already seen, Burby, in publishing his amalgamate *Axiochus*, deemed elegance, sweetness, delight, and learnedness to be his book's most attractive qualities. In similar fashion, the printer-publisher Richard Jones frequently "gave judgment" on the vernacular poetry that he published in the 1590s.[62] Together, these paratextual appraisals registered not simply his intellectual investment in works like *Breton's Bower of Delights* (1591) and *The Arbor of Amorous Devices* (1597) but also what was his own particular deployment of the Horatian binary of profit and delight to endorse his creative offerings.[63] In *Breton's Bower of Delights*, Jones praises his poetry compilation's balance of "worthines" and "wantonnes": "GENTLEMEN: I present you here, in the Authours absence, with sundrie fine Deuices, and rare conceytes, in English verse: by the names of Epitaphes, Poems, Pastorals and Sonets: some of worthines, and some of wantonnes, yet (all in my poore censure) wittie, pleasant, & commendable." Seven years later, after financing five further collections of poetry, Jones essentially reiterates this rationale in a translation of the medieval song *Phillis and Flora*: "*COurtuous Gentlemen, according to my accustomed maner, which is, to acquaint you with any Booke, or matter I print, that beareth some likelihood to be of worth, or might seeme pleasing or acceptable in your favorable censures*" (Map: sig. A3ʳ).[64] Jones's penchant for forms of "*worth*" over profit is telling. Distanced from what Robert Matz has described as Elyot's humanist, Sidney's Protestant, and Spenser's subordinate understanding of profit, Jones's "*worth*" betrays his own gravitation towards an aristocratic courtly audience – those invested in the worthy and "*pleasing*." That he deploys a version of the Horatian binary, however, can be seen too as a vague gesture at an upwardly mobile middling-sort readership – those responsive to promises of profit. Jones's sense of the literary then was inflected by his understanding of the market conditions that he was looking to exploit with his courtesy manuals and poetry collections.

Book-trade publishers did not just contribute to a developing discourse about vernacular literature in the second half of the sixteenth century; they also actively participated in the institutionalization of vernacular literary genres in a number of ways.[65] To begin with, genre was regularly added by publishers to title pages as part of their marketing strategies. Large-type titles frequently highlighted novel generic formulations like *A Pleasant Poesy, or Sweet Nosegay of Fragrant Smelling Flowers* (1572); *A Moral and Pitiful Comedy, Entitled, All for Money* (1578); *The Honorable, Pleasant and Rare Conceited History of Palmendos* (1589); or *The Lamentable and True Tragedy of M. Arden of Feversham* (1592).[66] Title-page blurbs routinely tendered genre as well. As part of his 1578 collection of George Whetstone's narrative poems *The Rock of Regard*, the bookseller Robert Waley promised "diuers other mo- | rall, natural, & tragical discourses: | *documents and admonitions: be* | ing all the inuention, collec- | tion and translation of *George Whetstons* | Gent." Similarly, the bookseller Edward White in his 1588 edition of Robert Greene's *Perimedes the Blacksmith* outlined that "*Heerein are interlaced three merrie and necessarie* | discourses fit for our time: with certaine | *pleasant Histories and tragicall tales, which* | *may breed delight to all, and offence* | *to none.*" And after entering the two parts of *Tamburlaine* in the Stationers' Register as "The twooe commicall discourses of Tomberlein the Cithian shepparde" (Arber: 2.558), Richard Jones titled his 1590 volume "Tamburlaine the

Great" with a blurb down the title page adding that the whole was "*Deuided into two Tragicall Dis- | courses.*"

Though not as direct and conspicuous as these title-page formulations, genre was also codified by multi-volume packaging wherein titles were suggestively juxtaposed by book-trade publishers. The most familiar of these volumes are those that contain title sequences linked by author like Richard Jones's two-part *The Right Excellent and Famous History, of Promos and Cassandra: Divided into Two Comical Discourses* (1578) by George Whetstone or Edward White's two-part *Morando the Tritameron of Love: the First and Second Part. Wherein Certain Pleasant Conceits, Uttered by Diverse Worthy Personages, are Perfectly Discoursed* (1587) by Robert Greene. Less known are the Elizabethan volumes that bring together separate titles under what the publisher suggests are shared properties. In 1590, for example, the bookseller John Perrin "*annexed*" (tp) the Inns-of-Court tragedy *Gorboduc* with John Lydgate's *The Serpent of Division*.[67] Lydgate's prose tract headlines the volume, and what is implicit is that the titles are meant to be understood under the generic terms of *The Serpent of Division*'s subtitle, as both offering a "true Histo | ry ... of ... ouerthrowe, go- | uerned by Auarice, Enuye, and Pride, the | decaye of empires be they ne- | uer so sure" (tp).[68] Whereas Perrin was vending "true Histo | ry," the bookseller William Jaggard, in a publication project nine years later, was marketing authorship and the sonnet form when he coupled *The Passionate Pilgrim by W. Shakespeare* with *Sonnets to Sundry Notes of Music* in a four-sheet octavo. As has been emphasized in a number of recent commentaries, Jaggard's highlighting of "*W. Shakespeare*" in the first title may attest to the growing value of Shakespeare's name for the book trade.[69] More than this, though, Jaggard's coupling of a group of "*Passionate*" sonnets with another of "*Sundry Notes of Music*" suggests an inherent link between love and the sonnet. If Katherine Duncan-Jones is right, Jaggard's octavo may have inspired the bookseller Eleazar Edgar to publish a related volume of poetry the following year (2010: 2–5). Entered in the Stationers' Register as "A booke called Amours by J D. with certen oyr [other] sonnetes by W S." (Arber: 3.153), the work apparently was never brought to press, but its proposed title implies another genre-oriented project, this one again connecting amatory content with the sonnet form.

Ultimately, the moves of Jaggard and Edgar matched up with what has come down to us as an orthodoxy of literary history, namely, that the sonnet was principally understood to be a love poem during Shakespeare's day.[70] Perrin's grouping, though, gives us access to an alternative history of Elizabethan literary genres, one in which plays could be received not as tragedies or comedies but as histories, as courtesy manuals, or even – as chapter 4 will show – as Ovidian narratives. *Elizabethan Publishing and the Makings of Literary Culture* then builds upon Hans Robert Jauss's understanding of literary genres as "historical families," careful to pay attention to the bastards, distant cousins, and in-laws.[71] In so doing, it eschews a teleological account of the literary. Instead, it concerns itself with emergent and dead-end concepts of vernacular literature and of literary genres, particularly with how these were articulated by some of the first men to finance, print, and sell some of the earliest trappings of an English literary tradition.

Because the activities of the printing house have wholly overshadowed those of the publisher and publishing house, *Elizabethan Publishing and the Makings of Literary Culture* begins with what is an unprecedented overview of the various practices that constituted book-trade publishing during the second half of the sixteenth century. Some of these practices like acquisition and reissuing have usually been understood as essential activities of a publisher's vocation, but many of them have been routinely (and many times wrongly) attributed to authors, collectors, translators, editors, or trade printers without a second thought. This first chapter, "Geldings, 'prettie inuentions,' and 'plaine knauery': Elizabethan Book-Trade Publishing Practices," then, situates acquisition, translating, compiling (adding titles, prefatory material, textual apparatuses, ornamentation, indices, and errata lists), altering, reissuing, commissioning, and strategizing as constitutive activities of Elizabethan publishers. Recasting these, the chapter lays the groundwork for the chapters that follow, suggesting both the shape and extent of an Elizabethan publisher's cultural work and the potential span of his or her affiliations with patrons, authors, and other men and women working in the book trade.

Amplifying and focusing chapter one's audit of the various practices of Elizabethan publishers, this book's second chapter, "Thomas Hacket, Translation, and the Wonders of the New World Travel Narrative," considers the career of the London bookseller Thomas Hacket and his significant contributions to the rise of the travel account as a literary genre in the 1560s and 1570s. Hacket financed many ground-breaking titles during his three decades as a stationer: among them, the first

English translation of Ovid's Narcissus myth, the earliest edition of an English comedy, and Thomas Nashe's initial foray into print. He also not only published some of the first vernacular accounts of the Americas, he also cast a number of them into English. In translating and marketing titles like *The Whole and True Discovery of Terra Florida* (1563) and *The New Found World or Antarctic* (1568), Hacket fashioned the travel narrative for a broader audience, reshaping it as enjoyable and elevating reading material for a Protestant England. Hacket's career underscores the mediating potential – as translators, as compilers, as editors, and as patrons – of many early-modern bookselling publishers. It also affords insight into specialization and collaboration as fundamental practices in the speculative side of the early-modern book trade.

Looking into the almost entirely ignored career of the first English publisher of Henryson's Aesop, Gascoigne, and Constable's poetry, chapter 3, "Richard Smith's Browsables: *A Hundreth Sundry Flowers* (1573), *The Fabulous Tales of Aesop* (1577), and *Diana* (1592, 1594?)," offers a different picture of the growth of vernacular lyric poetry. Motivated by his experiences as a bookseller in the bookstalls of Elizabethan London, the London draper Richard Smith fashioned his publications between 1567 and 1597 as browsable, multivocal literary objects. Instead of moving more and more towards coherent titles authorized by author figures, in other words, throughout his career he actively fashioned unstable, capricious texts. Like many of his publishing contemporaries Smith's work was characterized by market speculation and collaboration; it also involved a significant amount of interventive energy and creativity. His publication efforts culminated in two early versions of Henry Constable's sonnet sequence *Diana* in 1592 and 1594(?), sequential editions with a wholly different trajectory than the first two editions of *Astrophel and Stella*. Together, *Diana*'s early editions speak to Smith's flexible, consumer-driven conception of textuality, authorship, reading, and the literary sphere.

The Elizabethan publishing-house practice of reissuing informs this book's fourth chapter, "Flasket and Linley's *The Tragedy of Dido Queen of Carthage* (1594): Reissuing the Elizabethan Epyllion." This chapter traces the print history of Christopher Marlowe's *Dido, Queen of Carthage* from its initial publication by the bookseller Thomas Woodcock in 1594 to what appears to have been a planned reissue with John Dickenson's *Arisbas, Euphues amidst his Slumbers* by the bookselling partnership of John Flasket and Paul Linley in the late

1590s. As the chapter demonstrates, this multi-title reissue would have been an apt amalgamation, one anchored by a shared debt to the wit and sexual licence of the Ovidian narrative poem. *Dido*'s early reception by the Elizabethan book trade, then, underscores the cultural sophistication of book-trade publishers. It also uncovers the makings of what today might look like an eccentric constellation of thematically related texts, one delimited by neither mode nor genre.

The final chapter of *Elizabethan Publishing and the Makings of Literary Culture*, "Reading *Hamlet* (1603): Nicholas Ling, Sententiae, and Republicanism" returns to specialization as a defining practice of Elizabethan publishing. Nicholas Ling worked as a London bookseller between 1579 and 1607, collaborating during this time on a variety of different publishing ventures with fellow stationers like Cuthbert Burby and John Busby. He is best known, though, as the publisher of the first two editions of *Hamlet* in 1603 and 1604. In the 1590s, Ling began to specialize in two types of publications: sententiae collections and republican-themed works – literary and otherwise – having to do with governance, counsel, and political virtue. As this chapter shows, the first edition of *Hamlet* correlates well with Ling's slate of republican publications and its gnomic markers also bear witness to Ling's interest in sententiae as commodities for his readers interested both in literary pastimes and in republican forms of governance. Ling's engagement with the first edition of *Hamlet*, then, can be seen as an instance of how this print title was read during the uneasy final months of Elizabeth's reign. It can be understood as well as the culmination of a republican book-trade specialization, one discernible through its editing practices, titles, reprints, procurements, and marketing strategies.

Chapter One

Geldings, "prettie inuentions," and "plaine knauery": Elizabethan Book-Trade Publishing Practices

if I haue not gelded to mutch, I think I haue deserued the lesse blame.
　　　　　　　　Richard Watkins, *A Petite Palace of Pettie his Pleasure* (1576)

for that they are tending vnto vertue and prettie inuentions full of wittie sentences, I haue thought good to adde ...
　　　　　　　　　　　　　　John Proctor, *Golden Mirror* (1589)

[the sequel] is a cosenage and plaine knauery of him that sels it.
　　　　　　　　　　　　　　Thomas Nashe, *Pierce Penniless* (1592)

Though they tend to be glossed in the abstract as discrete, single-authored entities, the print titles available in the book markets of Elizabethan London were almost always disseminated as part of multifarious, multivocal books. When published singly, they were still routinely surrounded with dedicatory epistles, commendatory poems, tables of content, errata lists, arguments, illustrations, marginalia, and indexes along with title-page blurbs, epigraphs, and printers' emblems. Published en masse with an arrangement of these paratextual elements, they could be highlighted on busy title pages as main texts or located within a secondary framework of annexed titles. Indeed, the average book browser making his or her way through the crowded bookstalls around St Pauls in 1580 would not have had to look far to discover unbound stacks of volumes like:

> Ioyfull newes out of the newfound world ... Wherevnto are added three other boo[kes tre]ating of the Bezaar stone, the herbe es[cuer conera], the properties of yron and steele, in medicine and the benefite of snowe.

> A floorish vpon fancie. As gallant a glose vpon so triflinge a text, as euer was written. Compiled by N.B. Gent. To which are annexed, manie pretie pamphlets, for pleasant heads to passe away idle time withal. By the same authour.
>
> A regiment for the sea conteining very necessary matters, for all sorts of sea-men and trauailers ... Where-vnto is added a hidrographicall discourse to goe vnto Cattay, fiue seuerall wayes Written by VVilliam Bourne

In some instances, the entirety of one of these Elizabethan books – be they collections of titles or no – was fully assembled by a collecting reader, by a translator, or by an author. Once put together, it then was sold to a book-trade publisher, sometimes for a few shillings, sometimes for a few-dozen unbound copies.[1] Frequently, though, these projects were imagined, mustered, and/or assembled by publishers.[2] In 1582, for example, the printer Henry Denham brought out a further edition of Francis Segar's *The School of Virtue*, this with the addition of what is advertised as "*certaine Praiers and Gra- | ces compiled by R*[obert]. *C*[rowley]" (tp). Denham was the assignee of the title's previous publisher William Seres; he had either commissioned Crowley's work or had obtained it on its own. Either way, as owner of *The School of Virtue*'s right to copy, it was his decision to expand the title, making it a more extensive – and thereby more marketable – guide for the godly behaviour of youth. Four years earlier in 1578, the printer Henry Bynneman paid John Poleman "*to collect, and translate out of sundrie approued Authors*" a volume that he ultimately published under the title *All the Famous Battles that Have Been Fought in Our Age throughout the World*. Taken together, assures Bynneman in his dedicatory epistle to Christopher Hatton, "*it coulde not but generally delight all Noblemen and Gentlemen of this Realme*" (sig. A2r). Having recently financed a number of titles about the world without England, Bynneman was in an excellent position to know.

This chapter is dedicated to the heterogeneous arrangement that is the Elizabethan book, particularly to how its textual and paratextual elements speak to the publishing practices of the men and women responsible for its financing. While underscoring the essential distinction between the work of a book-trade publisher – be he a master printer, a bookseller, or a bookbinder – and a trade printer, this book draws attention to the various activities that could both precede and follow an Elizabethan publisher's acquisition of a copy – be it in English or no, be it in manuscript or no. In some instances, abetted by a winsome manuscript and an accommodating author, translator, or collector, a publisher could play the aloof foster father in streamlining a title's journey from its original parent(s) into print. Often, though, such publishing-house rearing was not so absent. Gauging the immediate print market (its recent trends in buying and publishing), Elizabethan book-trade publishers chose their copy accordingly. They also frequently commissioned the copy that they intended to ink, often turning, as we shall see in this chapter, to a familiar network of writers to complete jobs.[3] As discussed above in the Introduction, these networks were bound together not simply by familial, vocational, and local ties; they were also linked by extensive bonds of trust and informal credit.[4] But procured, commissioned, or purchased, copy was routinely moulded – either through the regular processes of compiling, repackaging, and/ or altering – by a publisher before it was brought to press.

In stressing the ubiquity of mediation in the transmission of texts, this chapter listens closely to what Elizabethan book-trade publishers have had to tell us about their own practices. By this, I mean not just that it attends to the subtle implications of form and content but more basically that it actively dissects the words of these bookmen and bookwomen. Unlike trade printers, the stationers who financed book publication routinely spoke in title-page blurbs and epigraphs, in dedicatory epistles, in epistles to readers, in commendatory verse, in marginalia, in tables of content, in indices, and in emblems. Too often, these articulations have often been ignored, distorted, reascribed, even dismissed by editors and critics alike, usually in an attempt to establish or defend some edition by the likes of Sidney, Spenser, or especially Shakespeare as authorial through and through.[5] Here, the assumption has been that these publisher pronouncements – unless there are compelling reasons to think otherwise – are rarely knavish ruses or authorial ventriloquizings; rather, they are essential – albeit sometimes obscure – guides to the particularities of textual transmission and to the nuances of Elizabethan print culture. To be sure, as Margreta de Grazia has pointed out with respect to the First Folio, these assertions can "encode ... events in a form that ... give[s] viability to the book they are in the process of constituting" (1991, 29), but this does not mean that they have nothing significant to reveal about a book's making.

While this book's larger interests have to do with literary production in England during the second half of the sixteenth century, this chapter is concerned with a large swath of books in the vernacular published between 1512 and 1652 – from broadsheet ballads to bibles in folio, from travel narratives in quarto to octavo news pamphlets. This chapter recognizes, in other words, both that many Elizabethan publishing practices were carried over from earlier decades and continued into the seventeenth century and that they were usually not genre-specific, that the complex textual negotiations that led to Foxe's *Book of Martyrs* in 1563 may have much in common with those in 1591 that gave us Sidney's *Astrophel and Stella*. Ultimately, in its focus upon compiling and textual alteration, this chapter insists upon the idiosyncracies of Elizabethan books as essential evidence of publishing practices. In thinking about these practices, materiality matters, as does composite packaging, title discrepancies, paratextual material, the provenance of woodcut illustrations, and specialization along with the expansions, alterations, and corrections of reprinted editions. Together, this evidence establishes the pervasive role that book-trade publishers could and did play in the ever-expanding Elizabethan book market. These men and women helped finance an English revolution in information and culture, and they had much to do with what were its particularities.

Acquiring

Gauged according to the author complaints that from time to time appeared in print during the early-modern period, the acquisition of copy by members of the book trade can readily appear to have been fraught with shady backroom dealings or knavery. In such accounts, manuscripts are underhandedly obtained, roughly handled, and incompetently set to press by "printers" who are at best indiscreet, at worst menacing. Thus, Michael Drayton wrote in a corrected and augmented edition of his works in 1596: "GEntlemen, since my first publishing of these tragicall complaints of *Piers Gaveston* and *Matilda* it is not vnknowne to any which traffique with Poetry, how by the sinister dealing of some vnskilfull Printer, *Piers Gaveston* hath been lately put forth contrary to my will, with as manie faults as there be lynes in the same" (sig. A3^r).[6] Eight years later in 1604, Samuel Daniel offered a more puffed-up rant after an account of one of his royal masques appeared without his knowledge in the London bookstalls. "IN respect of the vnmannerly presumption of an indiscreet Printer," he bemoans, "who without warrant hath divulged the late shewe at

Court, ... by the Queenes Maiestie and her Ladies, and the same verie disorderly set forth: I thought it not amisse seeing it would otherwise passe abroad, to the preiudice both of the Maske and the inuention, to describe the whole forme thereof" (sig. A3r).[7] Too much attention given to protestations like these along with a shared misunderstanding of the prehistory of authorial copyright helped form the basis of many a late-nineteenth-century condemnation of early-modern book financing, especially of bookselling publishers. This bias is still with us today.

In practice, though, copy was usually offered directly to a publisher by a collector, translator, editor, or author.[8] After establishing that rights to the manuscript were not owned by a peer (Blayney 1997: 394), this bookman or bookwoman would then negotiate a price. The only unambiguous evidence that we have for prices comes from a manuscript account left by the translator and editor Richard Robinson. There, in nineteen transactions, Robinson records not publisher payments of ready coin but instead exchanges of manuscript copy for print-run shares, each share amounting to twenty-six books (Vogt 1924). Once printed, one book was given to its named patron in hope of reward while the rest were given or sold to family, friends, and acquaintances. Robinson's manuscript has often been taken to be the last word on acquisition payments to authors, translators, collectors, editors, and third parties, but it is unlikely that it tells the full story. For starters, a collation of Stationers' Register entries against ESTC entries makes it clear that it was a common practice for publishers to acquire titles that they never brought to press. On these occasions, it would have been impossible for a publisher to pay in books, and as such, in these instances, copy must have been exchanged for money (or its equivalent in credit or debt). Indeed, scattered references to acquisition payments in coin do exist. In his 1598 collection of epigrams, the Anglican clergyman Thomas Bastard contemptuously refers to the low price that the bookseller Joan Broome paid for his work: "I reade an hundred pamphlets; for my life/Could I finde matter for two verses there?/.../And yet the Printer thinkes that he shall leese, /Which buyes my Epigrams at pence a peece" (sig. L2v). Bastard's collection contains 290 epigrams, which means – if we take Bastard's quip for truth – that Broome paid him around one pound, four shillings for the eleven-sheet work. Three decades later, in his description of "A Pot Poet," John Earle similarly describes the exchange of copy for pence. "The Presse is his Mint," he writes, "and stamps him now and then a sixe pence or two in reward of the baser coyne his Pamphlet. His Workes would scarce sell for three halfe-pence, though they are giuen oft for three Shillings, but for the pretty Title that allures the Country Gentleman: and for which the Printer maintaines him in Ale a fortnight" (sig. E9ᵛ).[9] If we assume that most ballads and cheap pamphlets required around one sheet, Earle's pot-poet earned at most less than half of what Bastard earned per sheet. Bastard, though, appears to have earned less than Robinson, who records eventually earning 35 shillings for his ten-sheet translation *A Dial of Daily Contemplation* (1578) and 37 shillings for his ten-sheet translation *A Godly and Learned Exposition, upon the XXV. Psalm of David* (1580) (Vogt, 632–3). Given this, it may be that Robinson opted for the exchange of copy for books as it had the potential of being more lucrative than a quick, one-time payment of coin.[10] For Earle, as it was for many other producers, a shilling in hand was worth more than two in the bush.

As is vaguely suggested by the above author complaints, copy was also regularly brought to publishers by third parties. Ensured in part by what was still a vigorous manuscript culture and in part by an absence of authorial copyright guarantees, the reality of copy acquisition in Elizabethan England was that it remained a wide-open affair, even after some semblance of order was brought to the larger process of textual transmission after incorporation in 1557. It was to this form of copy acquisition, that the vague publisher disclosures of "happening upon" a manuscript, obtaining a title "by chance" likely refer. For every case of a manuscript being acquired from a third party by a publisher against an author's wishes, however, there were many, many more that were straightforward victimless transactions. As they were already bought and sold by London's various professional playing companies, play titles appear to have been frequently sold (either as foul or fair papers) to members of the book trade from the 1590s on. The sale of other forms of copy – from sermons and religious treatises to maritime manuals to narrative poems – was often arranged by family, friend, or acquaintance, many times after an author had died or after he or she had left the country. The former appears to have been the case in the immediate years after the Anglican clergyman Henry Smith died in 1591, when his sermons were published by a number of different publishers.[11] For writers like Thomas Lodge, George Whetstone, Henry Constable, and Edmund Spenser, third-party arrangements were an inevitable function of their time spent abroad.

Though copy was more often than not initially offered up by authors, collectors, translators, or third parties, an abundance of evidence demonstrates that acquisition was frequently instigated by publishers. These projects highlight the lengths to which publishers could go to secure marketable titles; they also underscore publisher agency in dictating the kinds of products available in London's bookshops. In some cases, book-trade publishers pursued available copy that they believed they could sell. It stands to reason that a significant subset of the large numbers of copyright transfers recorded in the Stationers' Register was driven by this kind of inter-company venturing.[12] New copy was also often secured in this fashion. As Blayney and others have surmised, in the late 1580s and 1590s blockbuster plays like *Tamburlaine* and *The Spanish Tragedy* may have drawn the interest of publishers with extra pounds to invest. Work by popular print authors also encouraged book-trade speculation. In the 1591 first edition of Spenser's *Complaints*, for example, the bookseller William Ponsonby cites "the fauorable passage" of the recently published *Faerie Queene* as motivating him to "get into [his] handes such smale Poemes of the same Authors; as I heard were disperst abroad in sundrie hands, and not easie to bee come by, by himselfe" (sig. A2ʳ).[13] Two decades before, in the early 1570s, the bookseller and printer Richard Jugge pursued copy for another reason when he approached the former exchequer teller and scholar William Patten about a glossary of proper names in the Bible that he had translated out of Latin. At this time, Jugge was sole Royal Printer to the Queen. In the immediate years after the death of his partner John Cawood in 1572, he had undertaken a new edition of the English Bible. Addressing potential buyers in his 1575 *Calendar of Scripture*'s "The Printer unto the gentle Reader," Jugge describes how he came to understand that Patten's calendar was the perfect compliment for this project. "The commoditie of the Calender consydering with my self, how pleasaunt for varietee, and profitable for knowledge it mought be unto all," he writes, "and thearwith how aptly it mought square with the trauayle I haue in hand in the reprintyng of oour English Byble: I could not stay me, but to use the diligens and cunning I could, to get the copy soon into my hand" (sig. A3ʳ).[14] Given that Patten was at that time still reeling from a financial scandal which left him thousands of pounds in debt to the queen, it is not hard to imagine different kinds of "diligence and cunning" that Jugge may have employed to acquire his copy.[15]

In other cases, book-trade publishers commissioned the copy that they brought to press. This course was especially common when it came to untranslated titles in French, Spanish, Italian, Dutch, and German. Though we have almost no evidence of translator fees, we know that Adam Islip paid Philemon Holland four pounds for his 500+ page translation *Roman History ... of Ammianus Marcellinus* (1609).[16] Often offered up by a third-party patron, friend, or acquaintance, untranslated material was perused, purchased, and then sent out for translation.[17] Ponsonby recounts such a procedure in his dedicatory epistle to *A Treatise Paraenetical, ... the Right Way & True Means to Resist the Violence of the Castilian King*. There he explains how the treatise was "imparted & commended vnto [him] by a Gentleman my friend, who ... thought it would be neither vnfit nor vnpleasing in these times, if it were made knowne in our English tongue" (Anon. 1598a, sig. *2ʳ). Holding his friend's judgment in the highest regard, Ponsonby then "cause[d] the same to be translated, & ... imprinted in our owne language" (sig. *2ʳ). That same year, a similar account is given by John Wolfe in his dedicatory epistle to Julius Caesar where he explains how he came to acquire the travel narrative *John Huygen Van Linschoten. His Discourse of Voyages into the East & West* and then commission it out for translation with William Phillip. According to Wolfe, the work was first brought to him in the Dutch by one who "wished [it] might be translated into our Language, because hee thought that it would be not onely delightfull, but also very commodious for our *English Nation*. Vpon this commendation and opinion, I procured the Translation thereof accordingly, and so thought good to publish the same in Print, to the ende it might bee made common and knowen to euerybody" (1598, sig. A1ᵛ).[18] At the beginning of Elizabeth's reign in 1559, John Day paid the Oxford Fellow Peter Wormen to translate the Swiss naturalist Conrad Gesner's *The Treasure of Euonymus*. In his reader's epistle, Day makes it clear that it was he who "caused this precious treasure to be translated into oure usuall, and natiue language" (sig. ✚2ʳ). A year earlier, Richard Jugge commissioned Morwen to produce the translation *A Compendious and Most Marvelous History of the Latter Times of the Jews Commonweal* out of Latin. Morwen documents Jugge's commission in his epistle to the reader. "Being moued and requested," writes Morwen, "of a certayne honest master prynter of London, studiousse in his vocation of the commoditie of this our cuntrey, that I wold take in hand to translate this part of the history of the Iewes" (sig. ✚2ʳ).

Just as they sought out vernacular copy, publishers also pursued untranslated copy on their own, thereafter identifying a translator to do the job. In his dedicatory epistle to Sir Henry Clinton in *The Noble Art of Venery or Hunting* (1575), the printer Christopher Barker speaks of "*with some charge caus*[ing] *the same to be collected and translated out of sundry good authorities*" (sig. A1ʳ); he also credits Gascoigne with identifying Clinton as a possible patron.[19] For his own part, Gascoigne, in his translator's epistle, refers to Barker as his "*friend*" and heaps much praise upon the publisher "*who to his great costs hath sought out as muche as is written and extant in any language, concerning the noble Artes of Venerie & Falconrie: and to gratifie the Nobilitie and Gentlemen of this land, hath disbursed great summes for the Copies, translations, pictures, and impressions of the same. I will not say that he hath spared neither English, Frenche, Latine, Italian, not Dutche Author to search (as it were in the bowels of the same) an exquisite tradition & methode of those two Artes*" (sigs. A2ʳ⁻ᵛ).[20] Towards the end of the same decade, Henry Bynneman describes a slightly different process in bringing John Poleman's *All the Famous Battles That Have Been Fought in Our Age* to press. In his dedicatory epistle to Julius Caesar, the printer speaks of "*caus*[ing his] *friende to collect, and translate out of sundrie approued Authors*" (sig. A2ʳ). Here Bynneman may have come up with the idea for the project, but he relied entirely on Poleman as both collector and translator.

To obtain works to be translated, publishers seem to have developed a number of working strategies. For prolific publishers like John Wolfe, predictable streams of copy were acquired as a result of establishing direct ties to the many Continental book markets and book fairs.[21] In other cases, the process was less rationalized. Publishers were sometimes offered foreign copy by other publishers, by merchants, by diplomats, or by religious officials recently returned from abroad.[22] St Paul's Churchyard itself was also a common source of material to be translated. As I consider extensively in chapter 3, Richard Smith in his 1577 translation of Henryson's Aesop pens a prefatory poem that recounts "*late passing thorowe Paules Churchyarde, /aside I cast mine eye, /And ere I wist, to me appearde/ Sir* Esope *by and by, /Apparelled both braue and fine, /after the Scottish guise*" (sig. ¶3ʳ). Finally, there also presumably must have been cases where bookmen acted as literary agents, obtaining copy on their own trips abroad.[23]

Compiling

After acquiring, authorizing, licensing, and entering copy in the Stationers' Register, it was the rare Elizabethan publisher who did not involve him or herself at some point with the design and content of his or her title pages, these being one of the important, relatively new features of the printed book.[24] Oft chocked full with some combination of title, subtitle, epitaph, blurb, printers' emblem, and imprint – in various type sizes and fonts – the Elizabethan title page was more often than not a busy, semantically rich affair. Its most basic function was to provide booksellers with information about the location where a book could be obtained wholesale.[25] Plastered across the streets of London on posts, on walls, on the book stalls surrounding St Paul's and its environs, title pages at the same time were frequently used to announce new titles, giving book buyers information about their content.[26] As Nashe complains in his *The Terrors of the Night* (1594), a posted title page was frequently the beginning and end of a browser's engagement with a particular title: "*A number of you there bee, who consider neither premisses nor conclusion, but piteouslie torment Title Pages on euerie poast: neuer reading farther of anie Booke, than Imprinted by* Simeon *such a signe*" (sig. A4ʳ).[27]

While it has been often assumed that the titles of early English printed books seamlessly originated with authors, the reality undergirding these titles often had more to do with book-trade pragmatics than with authorial designs.[28] Along with patrons and literary agents, book-trade publishers often bore much responsibility for the titles of publications. This should not be surprising. Titles remain essential marketing tools in the print trade; they are vanguards that contribute to the overall commercial success or failure of a printed book. They also have a powerful impact on a text's reception, establishing for readers what Hans Robert Jauss described as a "horizon of expectations."[29] In this day and age, it is the rare author who does not have a litany of anecdotes involving his or her original titles being cut down, revised, even rejected by a callous publishing house. Working more than a century before authorial copyright in a milieu with varying pathways of textual transmission and unstable notions of authorship and intellectual property, Elizabethan publishers had little to keep them from tweaking, revising, even conjuring titles for their publications.[30] In a number of cases, the titles that they sent to press reveal much about these agents' speculative engagement with their copies at hand.

In some instances, titles were born when publishers acted to provide titles for untitled copy.[31] In 1550, for example, having obtained a long untitled "prolog" by John Purvey to Wycliffe's translation of the Bible, Robert Crowley – in this instance working as a printer – felt compelled to provide the text with what he believed would be a provocative "name."[32] "After I had perused this prolog," Crowley writes in "To the Redear," "I thought it mete to geue such a name to it, as myght declare the fruite that springeth therof, that thee by the gredy studentis of gods boke might be stirred (euen when they do but heare it named) wyth the desyre to reade it, kepe it in memorie, and applie it to the use it seruith fore." Crowley appended his new title *The Pathway to Perfect Knowledge* to the first page of the book's second gathering, to the beginning of the text (sig. B1ʳ); he also made it the running header throughout. The bookseller William Welby found himself with a more pressing dilemma after obtaining a sermon by the Church of England clergyman William Crashaw. In a short note included with the 1610 publication, "L.D." – the agent responsible for obtaining Crashaw's sermon *"without his leaue"* – instructs Welby *"to giue it what Title you will."* That Welby obliged with the title *A Sermon Preached in London before the Right Honorable the Lord La Warr, Lord Governor and Captain General of Virginia, and Others of his Majesty's Counsel for that Kingdom, and the Rest of the Adventurers in that Plantation* clearly articulates the publisher's stress upon the sermon's original audience over its content. A more contentious exchange having to do with unauthorized, untitled copy occurred 15 years earlier in 1595, when the bookseller John Drawater published *A Discourse of the Usage of the English Fugitives*, a sensational account by Lewis Lewkenor of his treatment as a captive at the hands of the Spanish.[33] Later that same year, a revised and expanded edition of the text appeared (apparently first financed by the bookseller William Ponsonby), this with an added epistle to the reader by Lewkenor.[34] In it, Lewkenor denounces Drawater's previous edition, complaining that it is "in the whole so falsified and chaunged, aswell in matter as words, & ignorantly entermixed with fictions of the publisher, that ... those that are of farther reach and insight, cannot but condemne it as a thing fabulous, grossely handled and full of absurdities" (sig. 2ᵛ). In his first edition of the quarto, Drawater's "fictions" abound, the text differing in a large number of details from Lewkenor's second approved edition. Moreover, the work's initial title was apparently part of what Drawater "grossely handled," the second edition appearing under the new title *The Estate of English Fugitives under the King of Spain and his Ministers*.

Along with being the result of a wide-open early-modern milieu of textual transmission, untitled copy was also a facet of particular kinds of Elizabethan texts. Poetic miscellanies, for example, could come to publishers as untitled books or as disparate sets of loose papers in need of compiling.[35] This appears to have been the case with lyric collections like Richard Tottel's *Songs and Sonnets* (1557); Richard Jones's *A Handful of Pleasant Delights* (1566); Henry Disle's *The Paradise of Dainty Devices* (1576); Richard Jones's *Breton's Bower of Delights* (1591); and William Jaggard's *The Passionate Pilgrim* (1599).[36] Stressing ephemeral pleasure rather than acculturation or enlightenment, a majority of these titles speak to the early history of the vernacular lyric in the Tudor book trade. Even when a poetry collection was brought by its author to a publisher, this was apparently no guarantee that the bookman would not come up with his own title. In 1615, George Wither – never one to mince words when it came to book-trade practices – wryly attributed the title of his pastoral poetry collection *The Shepherd's Hunting* to his publisher George Norton: "If you thinke [the included poetry] hath not vvell answered the Title of the *Shepheards Hunting*, goe quarrell with the *Stationer*, who bid himselfe God-father, and imposed the *Name* according to his owne liking" (sigs. H6ᵛ–H7ʳ).

Sermons also seem to have come to press with titles added by publishers. This was in part because, with the rise of shorthand ("characterie" as it was called in the period) in the second half of the sixteenth century, publishers were often on the receiving end of unauthorized, hurriedly produced rough transcriptions.[37] As the second half of the sixteenth century progressed, publishers increasingly put together small collections of sermons under an added general title in order to best exploit what apparently was burgeoning market demand.[38] Most of these volume titles are practical and straightforward, listing the number of sermons offered and by whom they were written. Others are more creative, like John Day's 1560 collection of Roger Hutchinson's sermons entitled *A Faithful Declaration of Christ's Holy Supper*; Roland Hall's 1561 volume of Calvin's sermons entitled *Four Godly Sermons against the Pollution of Idolatries Comforting Men in Persecutions, and Teaching Them What Commodities They Shall Find in Christ's Church*; and Richard Smith's unauthorized collection of Launcelot Andrewes's sermons entitled *The Wonderful Combat (for God's Glory and Man's Salvation) between Christ and Satan* (1592).[39] The godly clergyman Henry Smith complained of such unauthorized transcriptions in *The Wedding Garment* (1590), the authorized edition of his sermon on Romans 13:14. There, Smith explains that he supported the new edition "[t]*o controll those false coppies of this Sermon, whiche were printed without my knowledge (patched as it seemeth) out of some borrowed notes*" (sig. A2r). To what must have been Smith's continued annoyance, Nicholas Ling brought out another "*false coppie*" that same year with the added title *A Fruitul Sermon Upon part of the 5th Chapter of the First Epistle of Saint Paul to the Thessalonians*.[40] In his authorized collection *The Sermons of Master Henry Smith* (1593), Smith dressed up the title, dubbing it *The True Trial of the Spirits*.

In some cases, however, Elizabethan book-trade publishers went so far as to amend, expand, even entirely revise the given titles of their copy.[41] Evidence of these interventions comes both from paratextual material and from the Stationers' Register.[42] *Tamburlaine the Great* (1590), for example, was originally entered in the Stationers' Register by the printer Richard Jones on 14 August 1590 as "The twooe commicall discourses of Tomberlein the Cithian shepparde" (Arber, 2.558). That Jones apparently cut what he describes as the copy's "fond an friuolous Iestures" (1590, sig. A2r) indicates that he was the agent responsible for the plays' more stately general title.[43] It was a publisher, then, that first propagated *Tamburlaine*'s author – now taken to be Christopher Marlowe – as serious and literary-minded. A year later in 1591, the booksellers Thomas Nelson and Edward White appear to have been responsible for a revision to the original title of Robert Greene's first cony-catching pamphlet. Nelson and White entered the pamphlet in the Stationers' Register as "The arte of Connye katchinge" (Arber: 2.600), and this is the title that Greene himself assumes in the quarto's epistle "To the Reader" when he laments that "*Cardes ... is grown to a preiudiciall practice, and most high degree of coosenage, as shall be discouered in my Arte of Cunny-catching*" (1591, sig. A3). When Nelson and White brought the tract to press later that same year, however, the title had been changed to *A Notable Discovery of Cozenage*, the duo marketing the quarto as true-crime exposé rather than as anatomizing manual. This, of course, could have been a last-second change instigated by Greene, but we have little evidence that Greene's relationship with publishers ever extended further than an exchange of copy for printed copies and/or shillings.[44]

Along with titles and title pages, prefatory material constitutes conspicuous evidence of Elizabethan book-trade publishers taking active roles in the compiling of their offerings. What seems clear is that by the 1570s, these men and women had started to see real value in such prefatory material and were willing to foot the extra costs that went along with it. Bookmen and bookwomen not only commissioned such material from what was a growing population of professional writers in Elizabethan London, but they also routinely added their own prefatory epistles, dedicatory epistles, commendatory verses, and dedicatory poems to their publications.[45] The publishers William Barley, Robert Crowley, John Day, Thomas East, Thomas Hacket, Richard Jones, and John Wolfe all penned a significant amount of such material for their books; and dozens more like James Rowbotham, Edward Blount, Thomas Newman, William Ponsonby, Richard Smith, and Thomas Purfoot also appended publications with dedicatory epistles and poems of their own.[46]

Much of this material was directed at potential patrons. In this, book-trade publishers directly participated in what was a significant expansion in dedicatory writing in Elizabethan print publications.[47] In 1557, the year of the Stationers' Company's incorporation, around 12 per cent of the total number of English-language titles were printed with dedicatory epistles or poems in their first few leaves (see table 1). In the 1570s, however, this percentage doubled; the majority of these – as the print market was still characterized by what remained a strong demand for classical and Continental works – were translations. This marked increase continued into the 1580s, when more than 30 per cent of published titles included dedications.[48]

With prolific authors like William Perkins and Robert Greene, Elizabethan publishers also penned dedicatory epistles and poems. During Elizabeth's reign, the printers Thomas East, Richard Jones, Henry Bynneman, and John Wolfe along with the booksellers Thomas Hacket, Richard Smith, William Barley, and Thomas Newman together penned dozens of dedicatory pieces (see table 2).[49] In 1592, for example, shortly after the passing of Robert Greene, Newman dedicated his quarto *Greene's Vision* to his "*good friend*" Nicholas Saunders of Ewell. In his dedicatory epistle, Newman assures Saunders that even though "Manie haue published repentaunces vnder his name, ... none [are] more vnfeigned then this, being euerie word of his owne: his own phrase, his own method." He then calls the patron "an especiall *Mecenas*, and supporter of learning in these her despised latter daies" and maintains that he himself has "no interest in knowledge, but the inseperate loue that I beare to them that professe it" (sigs. A3[r–v]). It is

Table 1 Dedications during the Elizabethan period[50]

Year	Titles	Dedications	Translators	Collectors	Authors	Publishers	Other	%
1557	93	11	3	3	3	–	2	11.8
1562	145	25	9	2	8	3	3	17.2
1567	157	24	11	4	7	1	1	15.2
1572	154	33	16	5	8	2	2	21.4
1577	210	55	26	6	17	3	3	26.2
1582	195	64	16	8	36	1	3	32.8
1587	210	77	19	6	47	4	1	36.7
1592	252	66	10	4	45	7	–	26.2
1597	233	85	14	5	60	5	1	36.4
1602	268	84	12	8	61	2	1	31.3

Table 2 Dedications by book-trade publishers during the Elizabethan period[51]

Years	Titles	Dedicatory epistles	Dedicatory poems	%
1560–4	689	5	1	0.87
1565–9	703	3	–	0.42
1570–4	854	3	–	0.35
1575–9	1054	16	1	1.61
1580–4	1227	5	–	0.40
1585–9	1146	12	1	1.13
1590–4	1218	15	1	1.31
1595–9	1331	27	–	2.03
1600–3	1125	11	–	0.98

unknown whether Saunders was sufficiently flattered to reciprocate with a reward.

By the early 1590s, dedicatory gushings like Newman's were anything but rare.[52] For the printer Thomas East in the mid-1580s, the practice had already come to be irrevocably linked to a title's success. "Now," he writes in his 1585 dedication to Thomas Powell, "sithens custome hath made it to bee as a lawe in mens hearts obserued, that they account bookes published not to haue sufficient warrant, except they be dedicated to some worthie personage of authoritie, I am bolde to present vnto your Worship this Booke" (Ortúñez, sigs. A3^{r-v}).

Thirteen years later, the "custome" had not abated. Dedicating the travel narrative *John Huygen Van Linschoten. His Discourse of Voyages into the East & West* to Julius Caesar, John Wolfe too refers to the conventionality of the practice: "And calling to minde the vsuall custome of *Writers* and *Printers* in these daies, who do commonly shelter and shrowde their works vnder the credit of some such as are able to Patronize the same, your Worship represented it selfe before mee, and did (as it were of right) challenge the *Patronage* hereof, as being a Matter that appertaineth to your *Iurisdiction*" (sig. A1ᵛ). Wolfe, however, was less concerned with providing the "warrant" of "some worthie personage" for his publication than with selecting a suitable patron.

Potential buyers bore much publisher attention as well, inspiring pages upon pages of prefatory addresses both in prose and in verse. Frequently taking the form of "The Printer to the Reader," these prefatory epistles could offer summaries of the book at hand, apologies about the shape and content of a book, and/or information about a book's particular path to publication.[53] In his "Printer to the reader," William Seres confined himself to the latter. In his first English edition of Castiglione's *The Courtier* (1561), he attributed the long delay in bringing the title to press to its being initially "*misliked of some, that had the perusing of it*" (sig. A2ʳ). Predicting the potential for a different kind of negative response, the bookseller Robert Waley composed a short "Printer to the Reader" prefatory poem in ballad metre for his first edition of *Rich his Farewell to the Military Profession* (1581). "*And for suche faultes,*" writes Waley, "*as scaped are, /the presse, whereof thers store./Reproue the Printer for his haste, /blame not the booke therefore./But as by mirthe tis meant to moue, /thy mynde to some delight:/Reward his paine with praise, whiche did/these pleasaunt Stories wright*" (Rich, sig. C2ᵛ). As the popular romance collection's publisher and not its printer, Waley may not have been apologizing for his own "haste"; he might instead have been deflecting potential criticism onto John Kingston the volume's trade printer.

As Newbery did in citing Greene's "own phrase ... own method," these prefatory addresses could offer informed and discerning perspectives on the work at hand. For publishers like Christopher Barker, William Ponsonby, and Edward Blount, an acculturated judgment was in part a function of the educated and elite company that they kept, but for all publishers discrimination constituted a requirement of their occupation. As Lesser has argued, an ability to read prospective copy with a discriminating eye was an essential element of effective practice for those engaged in print financing. Traces of such publisher speculation can be found throughout early-modern books, but they are perhaps most clearly apparent in the prefatory material composed by publishers. In 1563, the draper James Rowbotham offered a range of speculative rationales in publishing *The Most Ancient and Learned Play, Called the Philosopher's Game*, a user's guide for the two-player medieval board game also called "Rithmomachia." Presenting the work to Robert Dudley, Rowbotham, in his thirty-seven-stanza dedicatory poem, argues not simply that "The body it doth styrre and moue, /to lightsomnes and ioye": but that the game "practiseth Arithmeticke"; "In Geometrie it truly vvades"; "Proportion also musicall, /it ioynes with thother tvvayne:/So that therin three noble artes, /are exercisde certayne" (Lever, sig. A4ᵛ). Music was a publishing specialty of Rowbotham, and this explains his making "Proportion also musicall" a selling point. But the draper also understood the need to appeal to buyers well versed in the ethics of Christian humanism, wherein all reading needed to be noble and productive exercise. Two and one half decades later in 1588, the bookseller John Harrison similarly speculated upon the meaning that Dudley and buyers like him might make. In his extensive dedicatory epistle, Harrison reasons that the noble icon would be most interested in reading his *Three Books of Colloquies Concerning the Art of Shooting* as a "storehouse" of "diuers ... deuices." "What rather than this martiall booke," contends Harrison, "may I offer for a present in these martiall times? Seeing it is not onely a rich storehouse gathered by the forenamed Master Cyprian Lucar out of the famous Nicholas Tart[a]glia and diuers other Authors in diuers languages, but also by diuers of Master Lucar his deuices greatly furnished and enriched" (Tartaglia, sig. ∴3ʳ).

When not providing his or her own prefatory material, the publisher could instead take the lead in obtaining a commendatory blurb for his or her publication.[54] As this material was usually printed last as part of the first gathering, publishers would have had extra time to solicit such contributions. Nashe, in a letter to the printer in the second edition of *Pierce Penniless*, assumes such commissioning when he rails against unauthorized sequels to his satire, advising his publisher John Busby "to get some body to write an Epistle before it, ere you set it to sale againe, importing thus much; that if any such lewd deuise intrude it selfe to their handes, [the sequel] is a cosenage and plaine knauery of him that sels it" (sig. ¶2ᵛ). Book-trade publishers would even going so far as to request prefatory epistles from writers who had not even read the work at hand. In his epistle prefacing *The Queen of Navarre's Tales* (1597), for example, A.B. describes receiving such a request from the book's publisher John Oxenbridge, a man he calls "his assured good friend": "Sir, you hauing manie times beene in hand with me about a booke intituled, *The Queene of Navarres Tales*; which (as you say) you haue caused to be translated out of French, at your proper charges, on mind to Print it, and you haue seuerall times bin in hand with me to write you a Preface. You know I neuer read the Booke, and therefore I am not able to say what argument it holdeth … But the Title is enough … whereby any man may coniecture that the contentes are some pithie Discourses, written for pleasure and recreation" (Margarite, sig. A2^r). Undeterred by his unfamiliarity with the work, A.B. goes on to fill out the epistle with a short story recounting Nature's conjuring of a beautiful man only to be rebuffed for not making him an Englishman, the anecdote meant to prepare Oxenbridge for the inevitable criticisms to come from "perillous conceited fellowes" (Margarite, sig. A4^v).

Elizabethan publishers were particularly zealous in obtaining commendatory verses for their publications. Prefatory poems praising a printed work and/or its author – what Franklin B. Williams calls "puffs" – initially appeared in late-fifteenth-century Continental books with the rise of Renaissance humanism.[55] In England, such verse also made its way into the publications of Caxton and his peers, but it was only after 1570 that the practice really took off, with more commendatory poems being appended to English books between 1571 and 1580 than were added in the previous ninety years (Williams 1966, 3). In some cases, poems of praise were written at the request of an author. Thomas Lodge, for example, in 1589 was in all likelihood personally asked by Robert Greene to contribute an eight-line commendatory poem to Greene's anti-Catholic pamphlet *The Spanish Masquerado*. Lodge, after all, had for some years been Greene's friend, and it was around this time that two had even collaborated on a play.[56] Three years later, Greene returned the favour, and contributed both a dedicatory epistle and a commendatory blurb to Lodge's *Euphues Shadow*. In the former letter to Robert Radcliffe, Greene writes, "By his last letters, [Lodge] gaue straight charge, that I should not onely haue the care for his sake of the impression therof, but also in his absence to bestowe it on some man of Honor, whose worthye vertues might bee a patronage to his worke" (Lodge, sig. A3^r). By 1592, Radcliffe and his wife Bridget had gained a reputation as literary patrons, and along with his epistle in *Euphues Shadow*, Greene that same year dedicated his novella *Philomela* to the Lady Radcliffe.

In a number of cases, though, commendatory poems were procured by publishers. John Allde, for example, obtained poems from "W.M.," "Anthony Munday," "Thomas Proctor," and "Iohn Peeterhouse" for his *News from the North*, a satiric pamphlet on contemporary legal-system abuses (T.F. 1579, sigs. A3^v–B1^r).[57] Nicholas Ling similarly secured commendatory poems by Robert Allot, Anthony Munday, and Michael Drayton for the second edition of his wise-saying collection *Politeuphuia* in 1598 (sigs. A3^v–A4^r). And two decades earlier, Christopher Barker obtained a commendatory poem for his *The Noble Art of Venery or Hunting* (1575), this after commissioning George Gascoigne to "*collect*" and translate the same (sig. A1^r). In his commendations, "T.M.Q." ends by underscoring – in terms no doubt much appreciated by Barker – the value of the book: "Wherefore my Muse, must recommend the same, /As worthy prayse, and better worth the price, / ... /A Booke well bought, God graunt it to be solde, /For sure such Bookes, are better worth than golde" (sig. A4^v). By "Stuart times," writes Williams, "it is clear from scattered evidence, the task of soliciting puffs was frequently, if not customarily, assumed by the publisher or stationer" (Williams 1966: 7). Solicitation was so common by the middle of the seventeenth century that William Shirley could assure Richard Brome that his play *The Jovial Crew*, new come to press in 1652, "will raise/It self a Monument, without a Praise/Beg'd by the *Stationer*; who, with strength of Purse/And Pens, takes care, to make his *Book* sell worse" (sig. A4^r).

Shirley's ironic comment imagines "Praise" to be an overdetermined product, both "Beg'd" by a publisher and at the same time readily supplied by his paid arsenal of "Pens." The reality behind the "puff" was likely less desperate. Book-trade publishers appear to have obtained commendatory verses by commission or – in a number of cases – through some obligatory arrangement with London's ever-growing cadre of professional and amateur writers.[58] It was to the covert reality of penning commendatory verse that Nashe refers in commenting upon the dedicatory epistle in *Pierce's Supererogation* (1593), where Gabriel Harvey thanks Barnabe Barnes, Anthony Chute, and John Thorius for "the rich largesse" of their accompanying commendations. "*Oh ho*," taunts Nashe in *Have with You to Saffron-Walden*, "*those whom hee calls the three orient wits. ... It is to thanke them for their courteous Letters and commendatorie Sonnets, writ to him from a farre, as namely out of the hall in the kitchin at* Wolfes, *where altogether at one time they lodged and boorded*" (1596, sig. Q2r). For Nashe, Wolfe acted not simply as publisher of Harvey's 1593 pamphlet; he also drew upon his "*kitchin*" of writers for paratextual endorsements of the publication. Like the commendations in *Pierce's Supererogation, Politeuphiua*'s aforementioned commendatory poems were obtained as part of an ongoing and mutually beneficial business relationship between Ling and the writers Allot, Munday, and Drayton. In the same way, Thomas Hacket seems to have established a collaborative acquaintance with the translator and poet John Partridge (fl. 1566–82).[59] In 1566, Hacket entered and then published two long poems by Partridge: *The Worthy History of the Most Noble and Valiant Knight Plasidas* and *The Notable History of Two Famous Princes, Astianax and Polixena*. Hacket's entry for the *The Worthy History* (Arber, 1.308) immediately precedes his entry for *The Notable History* (Arber, 1.309), indicating that Hacket procured the manuscripts at the same time. Hacket might even have commissioned *The Worthy History*, as Partridge admits in the title's dedicatory epistle that he wrote the poem "at the request of a speciall friend of mine" (sigs. ¶4r–v). That same year, Partridge provided accompanying poems for Hacket's publications *The Government of all Estates* and *The Great Wonders that are Chanced in the Realm of Naples*. These poems are respectively "To Babes and Sucklings" (Schottennius, sigs. A3v–A4v) and "An admonition or Warning to England" (I.A. 1566, sigs. A5r–A6v). Conceivably, this series of exchanges was obligatory, possibly driven by carried-over debt between the publisher and the poet.

A similar yet longer-lived working arrangement seems to have been struck in the early 1560s between the stationer Thomas Marshe (c. 1554–87) and the soldier-writer Thomas Churchyard (1523?–1604). Marshe had for a short time worked as a bookseller and publisher at the sign of the Prince's Arms in Fleet Street before the Stationers' Company was incorporated in 1557.[60] Over his long career, he printed and published a large number of books in a variety of genres; he also enjoyed a monopoly on Latin schoolbooks (Arber, 1.116) and had risen to a position of distinction among his stationer peers.[61] Churchyard began his military career in the early 1540s, either in Ireland or Flanders, and he continued to serve – as both an English and a mercenary soldier – in a series of Protestant campaigns up until the early 1580s.[62] Listed by Meres with the likes of Spenser, Daniel, and Shakespeare as "the most passionate among vs to bewaile and bemoane the perplexities of Loue" (sig. Oo4ʳ), Churchyard, in his half century of writing, produced translations, poems, ballads, verse satires, tragedies, royal progresses, and prose pamphlets. Evidence of Churchyard's association with Marshe comes first from the publisher's 1563 expanded edition of *A Mirror for Magistrates*. Included there is what would be one of Churchyard's best-known works, a seven-leaf poem on the tragic life of Jane Shore.[63] In a later text, Churchyard claims that he first penned the poem during the reign of Edward VI, but it was during his relatively long stint in London between 1560 and 1566 that he may have offered it to Marshe's new edition. Before serving in a military campaign in the Low Countries in late 1568, Churchyard penned a long commendatory poem for *Pithy Pleasant and Profitable Works of Master Skelton, Poet Laureate*, Marshe's octavo monument to Skelton. By 1573, Churchyard would not only publish a translation of Ovid – *The Three First Books of Ovid's De Tristibus* (1572) – with Marshe, but he would also contribute three more prefatory pieces to Marshe publications: a dedicatory poem to *Huloet's Dictionary* (1572); and a dedicatory epistle and poem to *Cardanus Comfort Translated into English* (1573). The *Cardanus* epistle is particularly revealing in that it suggests that Churchyard was working as a literary agent for Marshe in the early 1570s before he again returned to the Low Countries for a military campaign in 1572. According to Churchyard, *Cardanus*'s translator showed him the work, and shortly thereafter Churchyard "perswaded … the publishing of this precious present." As part of the arrangement, Churchyard also then penned his dedicatory poem, this making an already valuable title even more to its potential readership's "lykinge": "The person that puts it out, I tel you may a little (yea & very much) leade you to good lykinge: My Verses thoughe simple they are, somewhat shall tel you of the nature of the booke" (Cardano, sig. A5ᵛ). Churchyard's association with Marshe seems ultimately to have led to the publication of the first two editions of *The First Part of Churchyard's Chips* (1575, 1578), a heterogeneous collection of Churchyard's early poetry and prose. This volume was apparently in the works for a number of years, Churchyard detailing a recent delay in its publication in his 1572 *de Tristibus* epistle: "*My booke being vnredye, considering I was commaunded (by a great and mighty parsonage) to write the same againe, I am forced in the meane while to occupye your iudgmente with the reading of an other mans worke. … The rest of that worke which as yet is not come forth, I purpose to pen and set out, crauinge a little leasure for the same*" (Ovid). That Churchyard advertises this coming volume in a Marshe publication may indicate that he and the printer had already agreed to terms on its future printing.

Books like *The First Part of Churchyard's Chips* fashion their texts with more than prefatory apparatuses; they append a litany of marginal notes as well. Printed marginalia were not simply ubiquitous but highly regarded in the sixteenth century, so much so that Shakespeare could imagine Lady Capulet swooning over Paris as "a faire volume" whose mysteries are revealed in "the margeant of his eyes," and render Lucrece's innocence in terms of her not being able to "read the subtle shining secrecies/VVrit in the glassie margents of such bookes [as Tarquin]."[64] Nashe too, in his prefatory epistle to the 1591 first edition of *Astrophel and Stella*, assumes that his "witles youth may be taxt with a margent note of presumption, for offering to put vp any motion of applause in the behalfe of so excellent a Poet [as Sidney]" (sig. A3r). Not surprisingly, for the 1590s satirist, such marginalia proves more corrective than enlightening. As has been well established by William Slights, Evelyn Tribble, and others, these sentences and phrases were important spaces for the management of reader response in early-modern print culture, they reveal speculations about reception, and they could often prove a shifting "territory of contestation [where] ... issues of political, religious, social or literary authority [is] fought" (Tribble 1993, 2). While often provided by authors working in printing houses or off-site with proofs, marginalia was at times provided by publishers as well.[65] In 1559, for example, the grocer-turned-printer John Kingston contributed a set of marginal references to his new edition of Robert Fabyan's *Chronicle* both to indicate its borrowing from Geoffrey of Monmouth and to signal sites of "varieties." "Al through the storie of the Britons, wherein he followeth Geoffrey of Monmouth," he writes in his printer's epistle, "I haue caused, his storie to be conferred with Geffries and noted the chapiters in the margine ... And because the controuersie and varieties, is greate among writers, aboute the number of yeres, from Adams creation, to Christes incarnation ... So haue I in the margine, added the accompt of Ihon Functius, and other" (sig. A1v). In indicating points of "controuersie" in the margin, Kingston modelled the history on a number of biblical texts that had been appearing in the stalls of St Paul's from the late 1530s; he was appealing to buyers familiar with these texts, comfortable with the reading practices figured therein. A more general assessment of the place of marginalia in publishing practice is provided by the aforementioned bookseller John Harrison. In his 1573 printer's epistle for *A Plain Description of the Ancient Pedigree of Dame Slander*, Harrison apologizes that he, at the request of the author, has not "coated in the margent al such cotations and notes of the principal matters whereof the booke specifieth, with the confirmation of such scriptures as the matter well requireth ... Which together with thee, I confesse to be profitable in all bookes" (Anon. 1573, sig. A6ᵛ).⁶⁶ Compelled to apologize for the shape of his publication, Harrison brings to light what was the common practice of publisher margin additions; he also divulges what was a latent tension between an author's and a publisher's sense of "profitable ... bookes."

Along with adding the more standard marginal cues in the left and right margins, publishers also stamped their texts with less orthodox kinds of marginalia. Richard Jones, for example, deployed what have been described as "page headlines" in his editions of Phillip Stubbes's *The Anatomy of Abuses*, published between 1583 and 1594 (see figure 1).⁶⁷ Though a recurring feature of sixteenth-century English Bibles, the headlines in Stubbes's text were unusual in the 1570s and 1580s.⁶⁸ Appearing in all of the first four editions of *The Anatomy*, these begin after the text's prefatory material, are on average three to four words long, and can be found on either side of the running header "The Anatomie of Abuses" for almost the entirety of the remaining pages. All told, they run to over two hundred different headlines.⁶⁹ Jones would ultimately show a penchant for this textual feature, over the next four years producing similar headlines in four more of his publications: William Fiston's compilation of conceits *The Wellspring of Witty Conceits* (1584d); John Norden's *A Sinful Man's Solace* (1585); Angel Day's *The English Secretary* (1586); and George Whetstone's *The Censure of a Loyal Subject* (1587). In the decade or so leading up to *The Anatomy of Abuses*, page headlines most frequently appear in the printed catechism, particularly the five editions of *A Catechism or First Instruction and Learning of Christian Religion* and the six editions of *A Catechism or Institiution of Christian Religion*. Written as dialogues with headlines at the top of their pages, these texts appear likely models for Jones's decision to add headlines to *The Anatomy of Abuses*, and as such they suggest new reception contexts for Stubbes's work.

Along with adding title pages, prefatory material, and differing kinds of printed marginalia, Elizabethan book-trade publishers also frequently took it upon themselves to provide other sorts of apparatii for their publications like chapter headings, tables of contents, and indexes.⁷⁰ Taking responsibility for this material, they undertook work that was often the domain of in-house correctors in the great printing

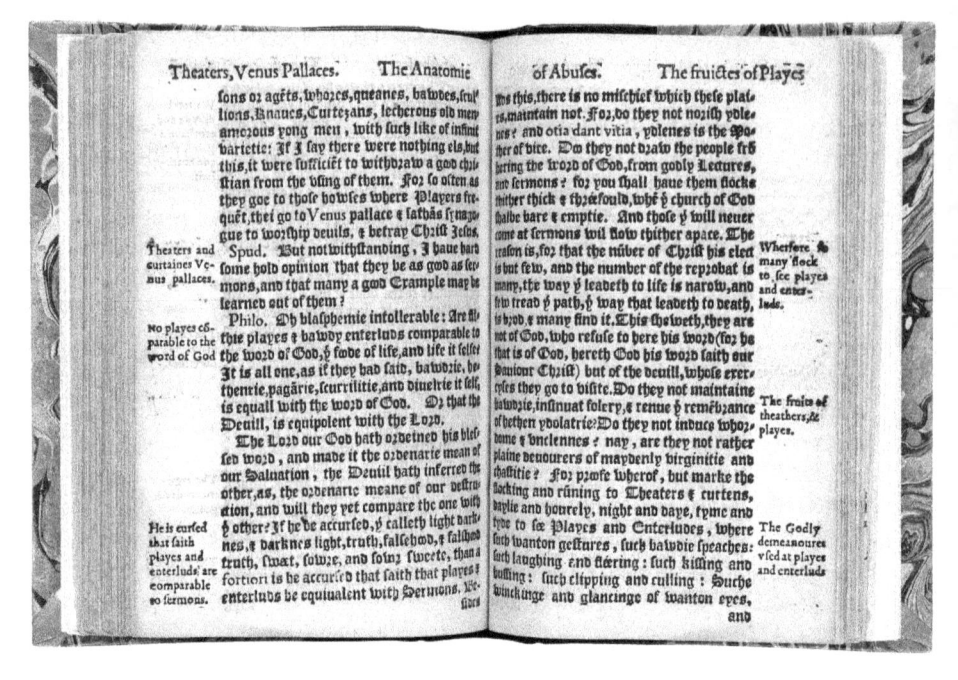

Figure 1 Page headlines in Phillip Stubbes's *The anatomie of abuses* (1583). By permission of the Folger Shakespeare Library.

houses on the Continent.[71] These textual additions helped manage readers' engagement with texts, providing telling instances of publishers predicting potential modes of reception. At the same time, though, this material could offer competing conceptions of the texts at hand.

In 1576, the bookseller and printer Richard Watkins added "Arguments" to the beginning of each "history" in his first edition of George Pettie's *A Petite Palace of Pettie his Pleasure*.[72] Apologizing for what he has "left undoone, and doone, whatsoeuer [he has] doone in this behalfe," Watkins boasts in his "The Printer to all Readers of this Booke," that the book's twelve "arguments" were "added" by him: "I haue also of my selfe added an argument to euery history, that the effect of the discourse may bee the more easily caryed away" (sig. A4ʳ). Ten-to-fifteen-line summaries of the tales at hand, Watkins's arguments are straightforward and short, and thus "easily caryed away," but they also compete for readerly attention with the particularities of Pettie's euphuistic narratives, elements consisting of extended scenes of dialogue rendered through overtly stylized language. Watkins peddles Pettie's euphuisms – his title page promising "pretie Hystories | ... set foorth in comely colours" – but with his added arguments he also markets easily obtained "effect[s]" to his readers. The printer Edward Allde provided similar apparatuses in his aforementioned *News from the North*. There, in his own "*Printer to the* READER," Allde describes a collaborative process between him and the author "T.F." in which Allde was ultimately responsible for the organization of the whole. According to Allde, "[The author's] care was greter to couch the matter truly in substance then to parte or to deuide or otherwise to digest the same. Which hee referred vnto mee, & which also I haue doon as the shortnes of the time gaue me leaue. Bothe which excuses, if it please thee to admit; thou maist in time to come receive it in more perfection aswel for his part being the matter in substance ... and also for the diuision beeing mine" (sig. A3ʳ). Allde's "parte"ing and "digest"ions take the form both of book and chapter divisions, and of a series of extended chapter headings such as chapter 16's "*An other tale by the Hoast of a yong Gentleman that had morgaged his Land, comming to an other great Officer of the Lavv to whome hee offered to sell his land of vvhome hee had great comfort*" (sig. G4ᵛ).[73] Though reminscent of Watkins's arguments, Allde's headings are offered not as autonomous add-ons but as necessary contributions towards what he assumes is a readerly ideal of book "perfection."

Longer Elizabethan printed books also frequently feature tables of contents or headings lists (or as they were called during the period "tables"). Found both in the introductory sections of print volumes or sometimes at their tail end, these apparatuses run from a half-page to many leaves, and in their assorted manifestations during the period frequently blur boundaries between list and argument.[74] Abundant in varying forms within twelfth-century Bibles and thirteenth-century scholastic manuscripts, such tables were to be seen three centuries later too in mystical texts and anonymous devotional volumes.[75] As Walter J. Ong and Michel de Certeau have each suggested, the emergence of textual guides like these should be seen as part and parcel of new communal practices and new ways of seeing at the end of the medieval period. Caxton, himself a late medieval product, modelled his own print productions upon manuscript books, frequently including such tables – what in his *The Mirror of the World* (1481) he calls "the table of the rubrices of this presente volume" (Caxton, sig. A1ʳ)

– within his publications.[76] Following Caxton, Elizabethan publishers were often the agents that provided tables of contents for their more extensive volumes, either producing them themselves or in some cases – when not straightforward gleanings from chapter headings – commissioning them out.[77] In 1563, for example, the printer Roland Hall provided a seven-leaf "Table" of contents at the beginning of *A Brief and Pithy Sum of the Christian Faith* for the reader's "profit." "After I had read this confession," Hall writes, "and sene the greate riches of spirituall doctrine which is therein conteined, I thought I shoulde doe a thing acceptable and also profitable if for your comforte I did make a table setting in order the principall matters conteind herein, the which thinge I did for your commoditie & easenes" (Beza, sig. A7ʳ).[78] Hall's table is a relatively straightforward transcribed list of *A Brief and Pithy Sum*'s subchapter headings; it does, however, still encourage a more piecemeal, more "commoditie"-oriented engagement with the text at hand.

Also common in longer Elizabethan books were indexes or "tables" as they were also commonly called. These finding aids can be found in printed English books as early as the 1480s, and they could appear at the beginning or end of print volumes (Blair 2000, 77). Like tables of contents, in the second half of the sixteenth century, they were routinely advertised on title pages as desirable textual features.[79] For Conrad Gessner, the mid-sixteenth-century Swiss naturalist who has been called "the father of bibliography," indices were essential as both aids to memory and research guides. "Truly," wrote Gessner in 1548, "it seems to me that, life being so short, indexes to books should be considered as absolutely necessary by those who are engaged in a variety of studies, … whether one will be reminded of something one had read before, or so that one might find something new for the first time."[80] Though systematic and rational in his approach (calling for the alphabeticizing of indexes), Gessner ultimately left it up to the indexer to decide upon an index's "desired order." Such freedom with an index's ordering was not uncommon in Elizabethan print indexes. These tables of the "Principal Matters" or "most notable thinges, matters, and wordes" appear sometimes alphabeticized, sometimes haphazardly organized.[81] Ultimately, though, as Ann Blair has tracked, the trend during the period was more and more towards alphabeticization and coherence (Blair 2000, 82). As they were more difficult and time-consuming to produce, indexes seem to have been either provided by titles' authors, translators, or collectors; or they were commissioned by a publisher after a title was acquired. In 1576, Ralph Newbery published the fourth edition of *The Zodiac of Life*, a translation of Palingenius Stellato's philosophical poem by Barnaby Googe. For this reprinting, Newbery commisioned Abraham Fleming to produce what Newbery advertises as "*a large Table, as well of | wordes as of matters menti- | oned in this whole worke*" (tp).[82] Running to ten leaves, Newbery's table is organized in lettered groupings (e.g., "A"; "B"; "C") by "matters" such as historical personages, places, virtues, and vices, and – most prevalently – aphorisms like "Age the next neighbour to death" (sig. Q2^v), "Friendship of the vnthankfull, faileth" (sig. R1^r), and "Night, a meete season for deceites" (sig. R4^v). In this, Fleming appealed to commonplacing readers accustomed to and interested in reading for sententiae.

Just as Elizabethan bookbuyers read for pithy bits of aphoristic wisdom, they also were accustomed through the varying forms of the printed errata list to read for error. Introduced into English books by a third generation of printers at the beginning of the sixteenth century, errata lists were a common feature in printed books during Elizabeth's reign with as many as one in twenty titles including them in 1560, one in thirteen in 1580, and one in fourteen in 1600.[83] These corrections usually appeared on a final page or at the end of a first gathering, and they were compiled at some point after an edition was fully printed. Printing houses most often fitted errata into the empty spaces of undistributed copies, but they also appended them in added sheets. As Ann Blair has shown, errata lists were generally inserted by printing houses to appease unhappy authors and "to forestall … criticism" (2010, 113). These lists of "faultes" and "errors," though, functioned as more than just appeasements or disclaimers. They worked too as cues for a particular kind of material interaction with printed texts, one where readers themselves played correctors. This is the engagement explicitly encouraged by *The Most Excellent and Learned Work of Surgery*, an Italian surgical manual published in 1565. "[S]*ith* [error] *is destinate, /And none can clerely it withstande,*" it concludes in a short poem prefacing three pages of errata, "*with loue and with most friendly rate, /Before to rede thou take in hande/ This worke, let all the faultes be scande, /And by this rule the same redresse, /Leste faultes good frutes to muche opresse*" (Lanfranco, sig. Fff2^v). And it is further encouraged by a significant number of Elizabethan titles like *A Plain Confutation of a Treatise of Brownism* (1590), where in an epistle directly preceding his own added errata list, Richard Alison directs, "And also before [the reader] beginne to read this treatise, to amend such faultes as by default in the printing were committed" (sig. A4ᵛ).[84] Late-sixteenth-century copies frequently bear witness to this practice as their printed lines bear manuscript corrections jotted above and over their printed mistakes.[85]

Though errata lists seem to have been mostly produced by authors, translators, collectors, and in some cases trade printers, they were also compiled by book-trade publishers – either by master printers financing, printing, and distributing their own copies or by publishing booksellers. Richard Jones, for example, twice produced errata for his own publications. In 1578, he added a short list of corrections to his expanded edition of Edward Hake's *A Commemoration of the Most Prosperous and Peaceable Reign of our Gracious and Dear Sovereign Lady Elizabeth*, this, he writes, after too closely "following of the old [1575] copy" (sig. A4ᵛ) and not updating the years of Elizabeth's reign with Hake's text. Jones again asks for his reader's "pardon" in *Breton's Bower of Delights* (1591). "Where you happen to find any fault," he entreats in his reader's epistle, "impute it to bee committed by the Printers negligence, then (otherwise) by any ignorance in the Author: and especially in **A3**, about the middest of the page, for **lime or lead**, I pray you read it **line or lead.** So shall your poore Printer haue iust cause hereafter to be more carefull."[86] Just as Jones took extra pains to look over his publications after they had been fully printed, Christopher Barker went to the extra pains of both perusing and preparing an errata sheet for his first edition of George Tuberville's *Book of Falconry or Hawking* (1575) after he had its leaves back from the printer Henry Bynneman. In this added errata page at the end of the volume, Barker admits that "sundry faultes" were "escaped in printyng ... contrarye to the Authors meaning and myne," averring that the mistakes were unavoidable because "the copie [was] obscurely penned and not legible in sundrie places, for that it was the translaters originall." He then advises his readers "to runne ouer to the Errata, where thou shalte be satisfyed in euery pointe." When he republished the title thirty-six years later in 1611, the master printer Thomas Purfoot prepared his second edition according to Barker's errata sheet, advertising on his title page that the book was "now newly reuiued, corrected, and augmented."[87]

The Elizabethan book trade relied on finding aids and errata lists to make their books more predictable and perfectable; they turned to visual material to make them more alluring. Akin to the textual augmentations that appeared in books like the second edition of Turberville's

Figure 2 The rebus emblem of Gregory Seton, from the title page of *A baite for Momus* (1589). By permission of the Folger Shakespeare Library.

Book of Falconry or Hawking, the illustrated page in the Elizabethan period – in woodcuts and then, towards the end of the seventeenth century, in metalcuts too – was also in part driven by publishing printers and publishing booksellers.[88] Of course, most bookmen – be they involved in the financing of new titles or no – possessed an extensive and versatile set of ornamental and pictorial cuts which they used to decorate their pages. But book-trade publishers also commissioned and owned sets of cuts to illustrate the texts that they financed.[89] The most obvious examples of these publisher-owned cuts are the dozens upon dozens of printers' emblems that routinely graced the title pages of Elizabethan books (see figures 2 and 3).[90] In most cases, these emblems advertise publishers, not trade printers. Master printers like John Day, Henry Bynneman, and John Charlewood also commissioned illustrations for their own publications that they printed themselves.[91] They then reused these in titles that they printed for other publishers.[92] In 1588, in one of many examples, Charlewood commissioned a

Figure 3 The rebus emblem of Thomas Woodcock, from the title page of *The Bucoliks of Publius Maro* (1589). By permission of the Folger Shakespeare Library.

woodcut of a youthful Queen Elizabeth for his first edition of Henry Lite's *The Light of Britain*; he then reused the woodcut three years later in the quarto *The Approved Order of Martial Discipline* that he printed for the publisher Abraham Kitson (Luborsky and Ingram 1998, 557).

In some cases, publishers commissioned woodcuts for their own titles. In what was a costly publication project in 1575, Christopher Barker commissioned over two dozen woodcuts for the previously mentioned *The Noble Art of Venery or Hunting*. Gascoigne, in his translator's epistle, gives credit to Barker for having "*disbursed great summes, for the Copies, translations, pictures, and impressions of the same*" (sigs. A2^{r-v}).[93] Evidence of publisher-owned cuts can be found too when a new woodcut or set of woodcuts migrates with a publisher either from edition to edition (trade printer to trade printer) or from title to title (trade printer to trade printer). Ponsonby, for example, appears to have commissioned and maintained ownership of two sets of woodcuts, each of which appearing in the editions inked by different trade printers:

the 1598 and 1603 editions of Sir Richard Barckley's *A Discourse of the Felicity of Man*; and the 1590 and 1596 editions of Spenser's *The Faerie Queene*.[94] Similarly, in 1571, Richard Jones sent *The Excellent Comedy of ... Damon and Pithias* to William Williamson for printing. In the next few years, woodcuts that first appeared in this quarto reappeared in two titles both published and printed by Jones: William Turner's *The Catechism* (1572) and Arthur Bourchier's *A Worthy Mirror* (1577?).[95]

Reissuing

From time to time, Elizabethan publishers assumed an active role in repackaging their on-hand stock in order to stimulate or expand market interest.[96] Such repackaging usually took the form either of a "reissue" or of a "nonce collection." The definitive work upon the bibliographic categories of "issue" and "reissue" was undertaken first in 1927 by Ronald B. McKerrow, who defined an "issue" as "some special form of the book in which, for the most part, the original printed sheets are used but which differs from the earlier or normal form by the addition of new matter or by some difference in arrangement."[97] Left with stacks of unsold sheets, publishers would reissue an edition either "to make some correction or alteration in the preliminary matter which was thought desirable" or "to make an old book appear a new one" (McKerrow 1927, 177). In either case, a new title and a new title page routinely indicated the change.[98] In some instances, publishers would repackage old stock into a trade "nonce collection."[99] First codified by W.W. Greg in *A Bibliography of the English Printed Drama to the Restoration* (1939–59), a "nonce collection" is "a group of independent books designed for separate sale ... formed for issue as a collection under a general title-page" (Bowers 1986, 501). Bringing together work by the same author, on a shared theme, or in a shared genre, such volumes were not always composed entirely out of old material; they could also combine newly published editions with old editions. Whether reissuing editions or collecting previously printed editions together under a general title, a publisher's motivation in these cases was as McKerrow described it, "to give a new life to the old sheets" (1927, 177).[100]

Enlivened sheets conjured out of the dust of a publisher's stockroom appear to have constituted a significant number of titles available on an Elizabethan bookseller's stalls.[101] In the 1560s, for example, at least three vernacular texts were reissued by Elizabethan publishers: two almanacs and a religious treatise by Nicholas Sander. In the 1580s, four works were repackaged: a political treatise by George Whetstone, a conduct pamphlet, an interlude, and a medical treatise.[102] Publishing-house nonce collections were apparently more common. In the Elizabethan period, a number of volumes were published with general title pages that included older editions with their own separately dated titles pages.[103] Together, these trade collections may have initially emerged out of the flexible marketing and distribution practices of England's earliest publishers and booksellers – out of what Alexandra Gillespie has described as "a mobility that enhanced marketability" (205) – when print editions were routinely understood as fodder for *Sammelbände*.[104] Whatever their print genealogy, nonce collections afforded Elizabethan publishers a practical method for marketing anew multiple editions of unsold stock. Such a rationale helped drive John Flasket and Paul Linley's repackaging of Marlowe's *Dido* and Dickinson's *Arisbas* in a nonce collection sometime during the 1590s, a project that I consider at length in this book's fourth chapter.

Repackaged editions are significant not simply because they can provide evidence of a particular text's fortunes (or misfortunes) in the developing Elizabethan print market; they – like expanded editions – also can document some of the earliest cultural negotiations involving the text(s) at hand. In 1586, for example, Richard Jones reissued the conduct pamphlet *Civil and Uncivil Life* under the new title *The English Courtier, and the Country Gentleman*. In its initial manifestation in 1579, Jones had underscored the utility and pleasure of the thirteen-sheet quarto. His title page stressed the pamphlet's applicability to *"the quiet, and | cumlynesse of* [the reader's] *owne priuate estate | and callinge,"* and he also contributed a dedicatory epistle that, in the popular euphuistic prose of the late 1570s, downplayed its substance. "[A] *silly Subiet substantially handled,"* he writes, *"is not onely passable, but also praiseable. A little flower well sauored is worthy smelling: a trifling stone set by a cunning craftesman, deserueth to be worne: A poore Pamphlet perfitly handled, asketh the reading"* (Anon. 1586, sig. A2ʳ). Jones's 1586 reissue retains his epistle, but the title page expands the potential utility of the text, marketing it even more as a potential tool for the aspiring reader. There, his new title advertises the social capital of the speakers. His revised title-page blurbs describe the pamphlet as a *"learned Disputation"* and newly insist that it is "ne- | cessarie to be read." Gone is the previous reference to the reader's "priuate estate and callinge," the advertisement this time ending with the promise that the text will "make [the reader] a | person fytte for the publique seruice of his Prince and | Countrey." Fifteen years later, the draper-turned-stationer Simon Stafford was apparently less patient with the initial market fortunes of one of his publications.[105] In 1601, just one year after he first put it to press, Stafford offered the cartographer John Norden's *Vicissitudo Rerum, an Elegaical Poem* for wholesale under a new title and with a new title page. Released as *A Storehouse of Varieties*, the 1601 text purged the title page of all Latin (in the title and in the title-page preliminaries), of a printer's emblem, and of any reference to the work being the first part of a poem. In their place is a relatively plain sheet advertising the text as a brief discourse of the "Change | *and Alteration of things* | in this world." Stafford's repackaging of the six-sheet pamphlet suggests a limited market for elite, philosophical verse at the turn of sixteenth century. It at the same time may show Stafford looking to capitalize upon what was a vibrant market for sententiae collections at the end of the 1590s, his "*Storehouse*" competing with the *Garden*s, *Commonwealth*s, *Treasury*s, and *Theatre*s of the Bodenham circle.[106]

Nonce collections can be similarly revealing. In 1570, the master printer John Day grouped five of Thomas Norton's political pamphlets with Norton's collaborative play *Ferrex and Porrex* (better known as *Gorboduc*) under a new title, *All Such Treatises as Have Been Lately Published by T. Norton*. Day's project fashioned a new author-ensured commodity that helped the publisher move a large number of his unsold copies. As Tara L. Lyons has recently argued, it may also have given the godly stationer Day a more extensive vehicle "to persuade English readers to unite against their Catholic foes after the 1569 Northern Rebellion."[107] Thomas Hacket produced a nonce collection of his own in 1588 when he combined unsold copies of *The Householder's Philosophy* with Barthlomew Dowe's *A Dairy Book for Good Housewives* under a new general title page.[108] A translation of Tasso's dialogue *Il padre di famiglia* by Thomas Kyd, *The Householder's Philosophy* was originally advertised as the "true Oeconomia and forme of | Housekeeping" by "*that excellent Orator and Poet | Signior Torquato Tasso*," formulations directed at an audience of "Father[s], … Husband[s], and Maister[s]" (sig. B4ᵛ) interested in edifying advice. In combining the tract with a more practical dialogue directed at "all good huswiues," Hacket seems to have hedged his bets and targeted a broader swathe of the domestic sphere.

A repackaged edition, then, along with signalling a work's market fortunes, can also tell us something about the Elizabethan market for cultural goods. Predating a number of rationalized mechanisms of control that we now associate with the modern state, this market was versatile and fluid. Moreover, even while a reissue's impetus was most often profit, it still represented a particularly proactive form of print-market speculation requiring not just reading but rereading on the publisher's part and a command of the contemporary trends in book buying and book publishing. As Benedict Robinson has suggested about nonce collections, "The crucial point ... is not the pragmatic motivation behind the manufacture of these books, but the judgment underlying it" (2002: 371). The additions to and/or new arrangements of these texts can provide, in other words, evidence of a work's earliest reception, its perceived contours in terms of meaning, genre, genealogy, audience, and/or cultural import.

Altering

Along with compiling and repackaging their offerings, Elizabethan publishers at times made significant alterations to their copy, putting them to press in what were – in comparison to their manuscript or extant print states – new forms.[109] Book-trade publishers undertook these changes either on their own or through commission, and their interventions commonly involved expansion, censorship, or editing.[110] Frequently, these alterations were advertised as enhancing an edition's value, title-page blurbs touting texts that had been newly "augmented," "expanded," "corrected," or "compiled." John Kingston, at the same time that he added marginalia to his aforementioned 1559 edition of Robert Fabyan's *Chronicle of Fabyan*, also expanded Fabyan's narrative to the middle of the sixteenth century. "I haue also continued the storie from Fabians tyme," writes Kingston, "till the ende of our late soueraigne quene Maries. Briefly touchyng the speciall matters, that haue happened therein" (sig. A1ᵛ). Fifteen years later in 1574, the printer Thomas Marshe published *The First Part of the Mirror for Magistrates*. This volume was intended as a prequel to William Baldwin's *A Mirror for Magistrates* (1559) and was written by the Oxford scholar John Higgins. In it were sixteen *de casibus* tales, from the fall of Brutus to the valiant deeds of Nennius. Thirteen years later in 1587, Marshe's son then combined Higgins's work with Baldwin's under the general title *A Mirror for Magistrates*. On the expanded collection's title page, Henry Marshe advertises only that it is *"Newly imprinted, and with the addition of di- | uers Tragedies enlarged."*[111]

Particularly subject to publishers' penchants for augmented texts were the many volumes of vernacular poetry that appeared in the wake of Richard Tottel's landmark 1557 lyric miscellany. In a number of cases, book-trade publishers augmented copy – be it a longer narrative poem or a collection of poetry – with poems taken from other acquired manuscripts. In some instances, these poems came from the same authors.[112] In 1589, after what he describes as two years of "deliberation" over the "end and purpose of the vvriter" (sig. A2ʳ), the bookseller John Proctor proceeded to finance the first edition of Richard Robinson's *A Golden Mirror*, a series of three allegorical poems prognosticating England's future good fortune. Robinson being absent, possibly deceased, Proctor informs his readers that he added – possibly to expand the quarto from three to eight edition sheets – a further series of etymological poems by Robinson on various Chester County noblemen and noblewomen: "Hereto bee adioyned of the foresayd Authours doyng also, certaine Verses penned vpon the name of my Lord Straunge, and sundry others, vpon the names of diuers worshipfull, whiche, for that they are tending vnto vertue and prettie inuentions full of wittie sentences, I haue thought good to adde vnto the former Treatise" (sig. A2ᵛ). Tellingly, even though his added "Verses" were by Robinson, Proctor still felt compelled to justify his additions along thematic, ethical, and aesthetic lines. Shared authorship, it seems, was not enough to justify the additions.

In other instances, added poems chosen by book-trade publishers were derived from manuscripts or printed books containing work by other authors.[113] Never a publisher to baulk at author authority, Richard Jones not only augmented poetry by Nicholas Breton with poems by a variety of other poets in *Breton's Bower of Delights* (1591), but also published the collection without Breton's knowledge.[114] A year later, in a note prefacing *The Pilgrimage to Paradise*, Breton cried foul on both counts. "Gentlemen," Breton complains, "there hath beene of late printed in london by one Richarde Ioanes, a printer, a booke of english verses, entituled *Bretons bower of delights*: I protest it was donne altogether without my consent or knowledge, & many things of other mens mingled with few of mine … which I know not how he vnhappily came by" (sig. ¶3ʳ).[115] In 1595, Ponsonby published *Colin Clout's Come Home Again*, continuing what had been his specialization in Spenser's works over the previous four years. Even though the collection's title page advertises that the whole was "*By Ed. Spencer*," Ponsonby concludes the volume by adding seven elegies on the death of Sidney, two of which by Mary Sidney and Fulke Greville.[116] As I discuss in more detail in chapter 3, the draper Richard Smith's publication of the second edition of Henry Constable's *Diana* (1594?) provides one of the more forthright examples of these augmented titles. Adding as many as four dozen sonnets to his first edition of *Diana*, Smith also divides the whole into eight decades and draws no clear distinctions between the poems by Constable and those by other "honorable and | lerned personages" (tp). Having left for exile in France three years earlier, Constable was in no position to complain about Smith's alterations. Such was not the case with Francis Davison and his poetry collection *A Poetical Rhapsody* (1602). In his reader's epistle, Davison complains of "the mixing ... of diuerse thinges written by great and learned Personages, with our meane and worthles Scriblings." "I vtterly disclaime it, as being done by the Printer," he writes, "either to grace the forefront with Sir *Ph. Sidneys*, and others names, or to make the booke grovv to a competent volume." As Arthur Marotti points out (1995, 234–5), Davison's protest was more likely an authorizing strategy – highlighting as it does the volume's juxtaposition of his and his brother's poetry with Sidney's – than a serious complaint against the publisher John Bailey. Davison's epistle after all appears in *A Poetical Rhapsody*'s first edition. Straightforward or no, though, it presumes an interceding publisher.

Not all alterations by Elizabethan book-trade publishers were undertaken to expand copy; some were undertaken to suppress particular material. During the Elizabethan period, the Stationers' Company had two formal mechanisms in place through which potentially offensive material was identified and censored: "authority" and "license."[117] First, in accordance with Elizabeth's 1559 *Injunctions*, all titles had to be authorized in writing by a church or state representative. Second, all titles had be licensed for printing by the Company (through its elected Master and/or Wardens). As Blayney has explained, licensing had primarily to do with establishing a publisher's right to print a particular title (i.e., that it did not infringe upon another licensed title), but it also certified that – from the perspective of the company – sufficient authority had been secured. In some cases, a title was licensed by the company with the understanding either that it would not be printed until further or better authority had been found or that it would be printed at its publisher's "owne peril."[118]

Habituated to a routine of authorization and licence, Elizabethan bookmen and bookwomen conducted their print ventures within a pervasive albeit unpredictable climate of censorship, attuned all the while to the potential peril of financing an offensive volume.[119] Severe punishment loomed as a real possibility. In 1568, the printer John Allde was sentenced to time in the Counter for publishing a pamphlet about the Duke of Alva; in 1580, the printer Henry Bynneman was imprisoned for printing a libelous letter; in January 1584, the London printer William Carter was hanged at Tyburn for publishing the treasonous title *A Treatise of Schism*; and in 1586, the printer Robert Waldegrave was imprisoned by the Archbishop of Canterbury for printing a series of radical Prostestant pamphlets.[120] Wary of such fates, some booksellers and printers went so far as to take the extra step of cutting potentially objectionable material from their copy. Richard Watkins, for example, along with adding the aforementioned arguments to *A Petite Palace of Pettie his Pleasure*, also acted the moral censor in preparing the collection of euphuistic romances for the press. In his prefatory address, Watkins assures his readers that he had used "discretion in omitting sutch matter as in the Aucthours iudgement might seeme offenciue, and yet I trust not leauing imperfection in the discourse, whereof if I haue not gelded to mutch, I thinke I haue deserued the lesse blame. And consideryng that in matters of pleasure, the Prynter may sooner offende in printyng to mutch, then in publishying to litle" (1576, sig. A4^r). The extent and quality of Watkins's gelding – strained metaphor notwithstanding – remains a mystery, even as the collection's popularity – six editions by 1613 – is indisputable. Two years later, working with a copy of *The True Discourses of the Late Voyages of Discovery*, the printer Henry Bynneman felt compelled to "alter" an account of Frobisher's Arctic voyages by his lieutenant George Best. He did so in order presumably to respect the economic interests and thereby avoid the ire of the Muscovy Company that underwrote the ventures. "I haue in a fevv places," confesses Bynneman, "somewhat altered from my Coppie, and wronged thereby the Authoure, and haue sought to conceale vpon good causes some secretes, not fitte to be published or reuealed to the world (as the degrees of Longitude and Latitude, the distance, and true position of places, and the variation of the compasse)" (sigs. B3^v–B4^r).

Elizabethan book-trade publishers altered their copy not simply to avoid offence or objections from high places. They also modified their copy according to generic, aesthetic, linguistic, or authorly ideals, editing their manuscripts through deletions, additions, and reorganizations in order to create authoritative texts.[121] It was to such editorial work – undertaken by publishers themselves or by editors commissioned by publishers – that title-page assurances of "corrected" and "perfected" texts many times referred.[122] In this, the Elizabethan print market vaguely followed earlier developments on the Continent, where the humanist ideal of readable, annotated, correct, and complete texts – ensured by scholarly editors – came more and more to be expected by publishers, authors, and buyers alike.[123] Throughout the period, vernacular texts in a wide range of genres were edited and distributed by publishers. In 1591, the bookseller William Wright published Henry Smith's sermons on *The Pride of King Nebuchadnezzer*, after he had "*caused them to bee examined by the best Copies, and to bee corrected accordingly*" (sig. A2r). Sometime after acquiring the right to copy Thomas Fitzherbert's popular *Book of Husbandry* in 1594, the printer James Roberts "*corrected, amended, and | reduced, into a more pleasing forme | of English then before*" (tp). He then published it, promising his readers that if they appreciate his "paynes taken" that he will "worke thy further delight with the like worke" (1598, sig. A4v).[124] The printers Thomas Creede and Valentine Simmes also concerned themselves with the quality of English in preparing Caxton's translation *The Ancient History of the Destruction of Troy* for publication in mid-1590s, commissioning the London translator William Phiston to edit the text in order "to bee made plainer English" (1597, sig. A4r). During that same period, the bookseller Edward White prepared the third edition of Peter Levens's *A Right Profitable Book for All Diseases* for publication by correcting and augmenting its content.

Publishers also often ensured that Elizabethan poetry was edited before being brought to press. As his modern editor Hyder Rollins has shown, Tottel was not simply the financial backer and wholesaler of *Songs and Sonnets* (1557); he also edited its poems, regularizing metre and providing titles.[125] While Tottel does not directly recount his methods on his sparse title page or in his short prefatory epistle, he does underscore "the statelinesse of stile" (sig. A1v) of his included poems, vaguely pointing to this as his editorial goal. Richard Jones appears also to have been an active editor of the numerous poetry collections that he published in the 1560s, 1570s, and 1590s.[126] In his third edition of *A Handful of Pleasant Delights* (1584), Jones advertises poems linked with "the newest tunes | that are now in vse" (tp), matching "Meeter" (tp) to music "as Ladies may wel like" (Robinson, sig. A1v). In his epistle "To the Gentlemen *Readers*" in the aforementioned *Breton's Bower of Delights* (1591), he boasts of his "labour" in preparing the work for the press, of the collection as ultimately being "wel compiled." While Jones was marketing edited poetry to young inns-of-court gentlemen, the bookseller Thomas Newman was riding the first wave of what would become a flood of Sidney's work in print in the 1590s. In his 1591 first edition of *Astrophel and Stella*, he is careful to describe the multi-poet volume as "restoring" an uncorrupted originary form.[127] "I haue beene very carefull in the Printing of it," assures Newman, "and where as being spred abroade in written Coppies, it had gathered much corruption by ill Writers: I haue vsed their helpe and aduice in correcting & restoring it to his first dignitie" (sig. A2^v).[128] Within the year – possibly under pressure from members of the Sidney family – Newman published a new second edition, one which excised the poems by other authors and which was based on a collation of the first quarto against a different manuscript of Sidney's poems.[129]

Elizabethan drama was also corrected by book-trade publishers or by agents working for these publishers. As Sonia Massai has argued, the practice of editing English plays for print dates from the earliest decades of the sixteenth century.[130] At that time, the printers John and William Rastell were influenced by the editorial practice of Sir Thomas More and his circle (which was in turn influenced by Erasmus). Motivated by the humanist concern with textual accuracy, the Rastells edited their play publications like *Fulgens and Lucrece* (1512–16?) and *The Nature of the Four Elements* (1520?) for pedagogical purposes. Decades later in the Elizabethan period, John Wolfe and Richard Jones continued this practice of playbook correction. Undergoing his earliest book-trade training in Italy, Wolfe was directly influenced by contemporary Italian editorial practices that placed a premium on scholarly editors and that generated prefatory material detailing the circumstances surrounding publication, "corrected" divisions, speech prefixes, and stage directions. Jones, argues Massai, was in turn influenced by Wolfe in the late 1570s, Jones's edition of *Promos and Cassandra* (1578) bearing traces of Italianate corrections.

It was in the 1590s that a substantial corpus of printed professional plays was first brought to press by book-trade publishers; a number of these plays are corrected editions produced by publishers (Farmer and Lesser 2005). In 1590, Jones published the first of three octavo editions of *Tamburlaine*. These, like his *Promos and Cassandra* editions, are shaped by the above Italian editorial practices; they also bear traces of non-authorial correcting annotations by Jones (Massai 2007, 86). As mentioned above, Jones's prefatory epistle announces that the publisher cut "fond and friuolous Iestures" (sig. A2ʳ) from his first edition of *Tamburlaine*. Jones appears to have done this in order to fashion his octavo as an ideal piece of chivalric literature to be read, attractive to his book buyers who tended to come from the Inns of Court. In addition, "Jones's intervention," writes Massai, "was prompted by a wish 'to perfect' the text rather than by a programmatic attempt to restore the author's 'true reading'" (2007, 87).[131] Following Jones's 1590 *Tamburlaine*, a number of printed professional plays advertise their being "newly corrected": Thomas Creede's first edition of *Locrine* (1595); Edward White's second edition of *The Spanish Tragedy* (1592) and second edition of *Soliman and Perseda* (1599); Cuthbert Burby's second edition of *Romeo and Juliet* (1599) and second edition of *Love's Labour's Lost* (1598); and Andrew Wise's second edition of *The History of Henry the Fourth* (1599).[132] For the majority of these seven editions, it remains unclear whether they were corrected by authors, publishers, or by editors commissioned by publishers. In the case of Wise's *The History of Henry the Fourth*, for example, the edition's substantive variants do not establish whether corrections were undertaken by Wise or by Shakespeare (Massai 102–5).[133] It also remains impossible to know exactly what kind of authoritative edition each of these editions was supposed to offer.

Translating

Unlike English plays in the vernacular, translations – particularly of French titles – constituted a significant portion of books published during the Elizabethan period. In a large number of cases, book-trade publishers frequently played a significant role in these projects.[134] H.S. Bennett focuses almost entirely upon professional translators in his chapter on Elizabethan translations in *English Books and Readers, 1558–1603*, suggesting that it was these men – sometimes with the "backing" of publishers – who conceived of and drove most of the translation projects in the second half of the sixteenth century (1965, 110–11). Elizabethan publishers, however, routinely did more than simply underwrite pre-existing translation projects. In a substantial number of instances, they played an active role in the earliest stages of such ventures.[135] Indeed, one could go so far as to say that the book trade was a significant source of "agencies, actions, influences, and decisions" in what one recent volume has described as England's early-modern "culture of translation" (Demetriou and Tomlinson 2015, 13).

As the aforementioned translation projects produced by Day-Morwen and Barker-Gascoigne demonstrate, relationships between publishers and translators could be close, extending over years, even decades.[136] These extended collaborations might have been the product of personal or professional affinities; they might also have been the consequence of carried-over fiscal obligations. Wolfe and Phillip, for example, had worked together a year before they collaborated on *John Huygen van Linschoten*, producing in 1598 the much more modest travel narrative *The Description of a Voyage Made by Certain Ships of Holland into the East Indies*. After that, for reasons that are unclear, the two did not work together again. The renowned translator Arthur Golding, by contrast, produced eight separate translations for the booksellers Lukas Harrison and George Bishop between 1569 and 1577, Harrison and Bishop first reaching out to Golding to translate a text by Lutheran theologian Niels Hemmingsen.[137] Two years after Harrison's death in 1578, Golding then translated three works for Bishop and Thomas Woodcock. Between 1569 and 1581, the Oxbridge-graduate-turned-deacon Thomas Newman sold a series of his translations to the then printer Thomas Marshe, among these English renderings of works by Cicero, Seneca, and Lemnius. Marshe also published an original work by Newman in 1580. Newman continued to do business with Marshe even though the stationer was, according to Newman, responsible in 1569 for "*shufling vp of* [his first translation of Cicero], *without my presence, consent, and knowledge*" (Cicero 1577, sig. A2r).

Elizabethan bookmen and bookwomen were not always dependent upon men like Golding, Phillip, Gascoigne, and Wormen for translation work. A small but not insignificant number of publishers translated their own copy. On the face of it, this was anything but a new development within the Stationers' Company. From the earliest days of England's print trade, bookmen commonly translated and published poetry and prose originally in Latin, French, Spanish, Dutch, etc. Like William Caxton, the early-sixteenth-century printer-publishers Wynkyn de Worde, Robert Copland, and Robert Wyer devoted much of their labour to translation.[138] Two elements of book-trade translating, however, were different in the Elizabethan period. First, most of these translations were undertaken by booksellers and not printers. Such a development seems well in line with what was the increased division of labour between printers and booksellers as the sixteenth century progressed, with printers more and more restricting themselves to the industrial side of the trade. At the same time, translation work seems to have been less common among stationers in the Elizabethan period. Part of this may simply have been due to an upsurge of available labor in London after the mid-sixteenth century, the result of an overly productive humanist education system. It might also have been the product of a steadily increasing supply of written material in the vernacular, this too an offshoot of the humanist schools. A final explanation has to do with changes in the culture of the Stationers' Company, where incorporation, rationalization, and expansion seem to have gradually undermined the Continental norm of the printer scholar.[139]

During the Elizabethan period, more than a dozen men in the book trade translated their own copy. For men like William Barley, Nicholas Bourman, Miles Jennings, Nicholas Ling, and Richard Smith, translation appears to have been a secondary occupation at best, undertaken once or twice in response to a particular circumstance or opportunity. In 1577, the draper bookseller Richard Smith explained his decision to work for two years to produce a verse translation of Henryson's Aesop in terms of the work's broad appeal and useful knowledge. Smith, in his dedicatory epistle to Richard Stonley, assures his patron that "there is learning for all sorts of people worthy the memorie" and hopes Stonley "shall finde doctrine both pleasant and profitable" (sigs. ¶2^{r-v}). Miles Jennings undertook the "paynes, trauaile, and charges" of translating what would be *The Galant, Delectable and Pleasant History of Gerileon of England* only after he "by chaunce" ended up with partially and poorly translated copy. "Whereupon," writes Jennings in his dedicatory epistle, "I was driuen to sustaine a double labour: One in perfectyng [its] imperfections: The other in finishying and supplying that parte of the Booke, where [the translator] had abruptly broken of, and absurdlie skipped ouer" (Maisonneufve 1578, sig. *1^r). The bookseller Nicholas Ling describes a less pragmatic impetus for the labour of translation. In his translator's epistle to *A Sum or a Brief Collection of Holy Signs, Sacrifices and Sacraments*, he claims that he originally undertook the translation of the French-language copy both because of the "worthynes of the matter" and for "myne owne exercise in that tongue" (1563, sig. A3^r). According to Ling, only after being "earnestly moued thervnto by diuers godly persons" (1563, sig. A3^r), did he then decide to bring the pamphlet to press.

For a handful of Elizabethan bookmen, however, translation constituted a significant part of their vocation. The most prolific of these translators was undoubtedly the London bookseller Edward Aggas. During the course of his five decades as a freeman, Aggas translated more than three dozen French works, most of these short news pamphlets propagandizing the Protestant side in the French Wars of Religion. With these, he also financed a number of religious texts, many of these Anglican sermons. Having apprenticed with Humphrey Toy, an active importer of Continental Protestant books, Aggas laboured within the religious specialization of his master. He also would have been familiar with Toy's text network.[140] Approximately half of his own translations Aggas published himself. The other half was brought to press and wholesaled by the prolific printer and publisher John Wolfe – probably in collaboration with Aggas. Unlike most of his book-trade translating peers, Aggas remained for the most part silent about his work as a translator. In two of his earliest translations, however, he does contribute prefatory pieces that display some degree of self-consciousness about the quality of his endeavours. To his translation of Phillipe de Mornay's *The Defense of Death* (1576), Aggas adds a dedicatory epistle to Margaret Stanley, Countess of Darby, in which he asks the patroness to "*sheelde and defend asvvel the rudenesse of the translation, as also the raggidnes of the stile thereof, from the bitter tants and biting scofs of cruel reprehension*" (sigs. A2ᵛ–A3ʳ).[141] Ten years later in his English rendering of François de la Noue's *The Politic and Military Discourses of the Lord de La Noue* (1587), Aggas again appends a dedicatory epistle, this time to George Clifford, Earl of Cumberland. In it, Aggas is less apologetic about his work, saying only that it is "*faithfullie and trulie translated out of the French*" (sig. A2ᵛ).

As I explore in more detail in chapter 2, the bookseller Thomas Hacket also translated and then published travel narratives from French sources.[142] In the 1560s, Hacket was one of the first English publishers to market travel narratives and cosmographies, offering them as reading material for a Protestant nation with world ambitions. Hacket's fluency with French is apparent not just in the polish of his translations but also in his familiarity with French source material translated by others. Such conversance comes through in *The Treasury of Amadis of France* (1572?), where he opines that the extensive work "yeld[s] not so pleasant a grace in the Englishe toung as it dothe in the Frenche, the vvhiche it vvas written in" (sig. ¶3ʳ). All told, three French titles appear to have been translated by Hacket himself: *The Whole and True Discovery of Terra Florida* (1563); *A True and Perfect Description, of the Last Voyage Attempted by Captain John Ribaut, into Terra Florida* (1566); and *The New Found World or Antarctic* (1568).

Edward Blount also produced his own translations during the course of his bookselling career. Best known for his extensive involvement with Shakespeare's First Folio, Blount first cut his teeth in the book trade with the bookseller Ponsonby. As we have seen, Ponsonby achieved fame for his financing of a number of works by Spenser and Sidney, and as a result has long been understood as a publisher of "literary taste and discrimination" (Brennan 1983). Before apprenticing with Ponsonby, Blount, as the son of a merchant tailor, likely was enrolled in the Merchant Taylors' School, where he would have mastered the syntax and grammar of Latin (Taylor 2004). Eventually working as a bookseller at the "Great North Door" in St Paul's Churchyard after being freed of the company in the late 1580s (Arber, 2.702), Blount published his first title in 1594: *The Profit of Imprisonment*, a verse translation by Joshua Sylvester of Odet de la Noue's *Paradoxe que les adversitez sont plus necessaires que les prosperités*. Translations would come to make up a significant portion of Blount's publications during his career, him financing more than two dozen separate titles before his death in 1632. In 1600, Blount published *The Hospital of Incurable Fools*, the first of three lengthy translations from his own pen. Advertised as "Erected in English, as neer the first | Italian modell and platforme, as | the vnskillfull, hand of an igno- | rant Architect could | deuise" (tp), the twenty-two-sheet quarto includes a short epistle to the reader in which Blount wryly apologizes for the shortcomings of his work. "*Yet consider what pattence you haue with the wine you drink in Tauernes, and beleeue me (as a poore Traueller) it is all exceedingly bastardiz'd from his originall purity: and euen your Phisicall drams, that are so greedily sought after, suffer a little sophistication by the hands of the Apothecarie. Thinke not much therefore, if so fickle and foolish a commoditie as this is, be somewhat endamaged by the transportation of it out of Italy*" (sig. a2ʳ). In the Jacobean period, Blount translated and brought two further texts to press: *Ars aulica* in 1607 and *Christian Policy* in 1632.

Specializing

Like their Tudor forbearers and their Jacobean heirs, Elizabethan book-trade publishers would sometimes specialize in one or more particular kind of books. As I have shown, for Blount and Wolfe, works in translation constituted a publishing specialty (Lievsay 1969, 14–23); for Aggas and Wolfe, foreign news. The publishing specialties

Geldings, "prettie inuentions," and "plaine knauery" 71

of other bookmen can also be identified within the growing range of Elizabethan offerings.[143] Working in tense conjunction with the patent holders William Byrd and Thomas Morley, the printer Thomas East, the draper James Rowbotham, and the draper-turned-stationer William Barley all specialized in music. The master printer and patent holder John Day specialized in Protestant books, particularly by John Foxe. Richard Tottel specialized in law books; the printers Richard Jugge and Thomas Dawson (one of Jugge's apprentices), and the printer John Windet in maritime navigational guides; the bookseller Thomas Man, senior in godly titles (Green, 16); the bookseller William Ponsonby in vernacular literature connected to the Sidney circle; the bookseller John Trundle in sensational news; the bookseller Thomas Millington in pamphlets and plays having to do with civil conflict; the printer John Danter in play ballads; and the printer Thomas Creede in professional drama.[144] This list should also include the bookseller Thomas Hacket, who specialized in travel narratives and cosmographies in translation; the printer Richard Jones, who also specialized in ballads (Tessa Watt calls him "the closest thing the Elizabethans had to a broadside tycoon" [1998, 65]); and the bookseller Nicholas Ling, who specialized in collections of sententiae and in works with republican themes.[145] As Lesser argued in *Drama and the Politics of Publication* (2004), publishers specialized not necessarily because they had a personal interest in works of a particular kind or of a particular political or religious bent – although, in some instances, this *was* the case – but because it was in best their economic interest to do so. This economic advantage, contends Lesser, was the product both of consumer society's emergence in early-modern England and of practices within the English book trade itself, namely, those having to do (1) with the right to copy; (2) with title-page imprints; and (3) with relationships between publishers and authors.[146]

Identifying publishing specialties can be useful because they tell us something about the demand for particular kinds of books in the early-modern English print market. Book-trade publishers invested in familiar kinds of copy because they were in the advantageous position of being able to monitor the positive stockroom trajectories of related titles. Risk was reduced, in other words, by investing in texts with predictable track records. The range of specialties during a given year can be correlated with demand. In order to best take advantage of the market, specializing publishers were also some of the most interested readers of copy. As Lesser pointed out, "Because publishers, as capitalists, must *speculate* on the future sales of their books, they, more than any other stationers, must also *speculate* on the meanings of texts" (2004, 28). No one would have known better than Hacket, for example, that his translation of Thevet's *The New Found World or Antarctic* needed to be made to appeal to a wide array of readers, from mariners and patrons of exploration to the average Protestant, middling-sort book buyer interested in titillation, to be successful. No one would have known better than Ling that the first edition of *Hamlet* would be more saleable if it was also made to look like a readily digested resource of aphoristic wisdom. Publishing specialties would have been most lucrative when they were widely recognized – by publishers, by booksellers, by printers, by book agents, by book buyers, and by authors alike. Wolfe's considerable specialization in translated foreign news, for example, was apparently so well known that Gabriel Harvey could wryly allude to it at the start of his *New Letter of Notable Contents*: "Mr. Wolfe, *Good Newes* was euer a welcome guest vnto me: and you do well in the current of your businesse, to remember the Italian Prouerbe; *Good Tidings* would be dispatched to ride post, as *Ill Tidings* may haue good leaue to be a footeman" (1593a, sig. A2ʳ).[147] The year before, Wolfe had published as many as nine news pamphlets reporting events across the channel in the French Wars of Religion. For supporters of King Henry IV and the Protestant cause in France, a number of these would have been better left to footmen.

Trace evidence of specialization can be gleaned not only from contemporary allusions to book-trade publishers; it can be culled as well from the aforementioned publisher's devices that adorned books printed during the Elizabethan period. Initially connected to the sign adjacent to a publisher's bookshop, a printer's device, writes McKerrow, was "any picture, design or ornament … found on the title-page, final leaf, or in any other conspicuous place in a book, and having an obvious reference to the sign at which the printer or publisher of the book carried on business, or to the name of either of them, or including the arms or crest of either of them."[148] Often positioned in the dead centre of a title page and taking up half of the page's space, printers' devices were designed to attract a buyer's attention and were – at least in some cases – deployed by publishers as what might best be described as "brands." After incorporation in 1557, devices referring to a publisher's name began to dominate over those that referred to a publisher's or printer's sign, and between 1574 and 1581, more new devices appeared than had ever appeared before (McKerrow 1913, xli–xlii).[149] Together, devices could take the form of a rebus or pun; initials; a heraldic device; a portrait; or an emblem.

In surveying the many printers' devices in early-modern volumes, McKerrow concluded that in the Elizabethan period most were likely "based upon emblems," and he was able to trace a number of these back to their sources in emblem books or in Continental publishing houses. Ultimately, he was convinced that "the emblem chosen evidently depended on the mere fancy of the printer or publisher who chose it" (1913, xiii). In most cases, because it is impossible to determine the motivation behind a particular emblem, McKerrow's "mere fancy" remains the best explanation for what clearly was the variable tastes of a large number of merchants and artisans. In some cases, though, the emblems chosen appear to be more than the product of indiscriminate desire; they seem instead to be strongly resonant with the publishing specialties of their owners. In the 1570s and 1580s, for example, John Day frequently employed an emblem showing a heart being purified by fire in a crucible. The fire emerges from a tile reading "CHRISTUS," under which is a scroll with the words "HORUM CHARITAS" ("To Charity"), and attached below this with a chain is a sphere above the sun (see figure 4). Framing the emblem are Day's initials "J.D." Day had obtained the emblem from the printer Thomas Gibson, and he had replaced Gibson's initials with his own.[150] Applied to editions of the Psalms, Latimer's sermons, and Nowell's catechisms, Day's Protestant emblem underscores what was his sustained commitment to publishing godly books.[151] A decade later, the bookseller Thomas Millington had two of his 1590s publications printed with an emblem showing bending reeds and a tree being broken by the wind (see figure 5).[152] In a frame surrounding the image, Millington's initials "T" and "M" appear on either side. As McKerrow has shown (1913, 118), the emblem seems to have been drawn from Whitney's *A Choice of Emblems, and Other Devices* (1586) which explains it thus: "The mightie oke, that shrinkes not with a blaste, /But stiflie standes, when Boreas moste doth blowe, /With rage thereof, is broken downe at laste, /When bending reeds, that couche in tempestes lowe/With yeelding still, doe safe, and sounde appeare:/…/When Enuie, Hate, Contempte, and Slaunder rage:/Which are the stormes, and tempestes of this life;/With patience then, wee must the combat wage, /And not with force resist their deadlie strife" (sig. e2ᵛ). "Strife" – especially that of civil strife – was the pervasive theme in most of Millington's offerings during his short ten-year career, so much so that it constituted a specialty for the bookseller.

74 Elizabethan Publishing

Figure 4 The printer's emblem of John Day, from the title page of *Reformatio legum ecclesiasticarum* (1571). By permission of the Folger Shakespeare Library.

Millington published three further professional plays on the subject including *The Most Lamentable Roman Tragedy of Titus Andronicus* (1594) and *The First Part of the Contention betwixt the Two Famous Houses of York and Lancaster* (1594) along with a series of ballads and pamphlets on the French Wars of Religion. Millington's investment in this particular emblem, then, was more than "mere fancy"; it was fashioned to reflect the thematic outlines of most of his publications.[153]

Ultimately, it is the contention of this book that, just as they can be distinguished by their specialties, Elizabethan publishers can also be differentiated by the particularities of their practice. While it has routinely been assumed by bibliographers and editors alike that earlymodern publishing practice was essentially straightforward and homogeneous due to it being mostly driven by a profit motive, the reality was that publishers pursued profit in a variety of different ways.[154] In some cases, these methods could themselves help determine the

Figure 5 The printer's emblem of Thomas Millington, from the title page of *Deuoreux* (1597). By permission of the Huntington Library, San Marino, California.

shape and timing of publications. In the early 1590s, the bookseller Millington routinely seeded the market for news – for sensational local happenings and news of the French Wars of Religion across the Channel – with relatively cheap fare before acquiring more substantial copy (Melnikoff 2013b). From time to time, he appears to have collaborated with company peers in offering related fare. During the years 1594 and 1595, he would three times pursue this strategy, publishing first a set of titles recounting the recent grisly murder of the London chandler Robert Beech and his boy Thomas Winchester by his neighbour, the food and beer vendor Thomas Merry; one set of titles pertaining to Sir John Norris's victories in Britanny; and another to an assassination attempt upon the French king by the Jesuit scholar Jean Chastel.[155] In flooding London's bookstalls in the late summer of 1594 with sets of relatively cheap publications, Millington simultaneously tested the market, manufactured buzz, and protected his investments. It was during this period as well that Millington acquired with

Nicholas Ling a copy of *The Jew of Malta*.[156] They entered the play in the Stationers' Register two days after Danter entered the now-lost ballad "the murtherous life and terrible death of the riche Jew of Malta" (Arber, 2.649). Such synchronicity was likely inspired by new performances of the play at the Rose Theatre, and it may have been a further manifestation of Millington's strategy of publishing in series.

The career of the aforementioned Cuthbert Burby, who worked as a bookseller at a number of different shops in London between 1592 and 1608, gives us an example of a particularly successful set of publishing practices.[157] Burby died with a net worth of approximately £2500, a truly impressive figure for the son of a farmer, in the top 3 per cent of London freemen as recorded in the Common Serjeant's books. Burby's success was evidently a combination of his holding as a liveryman shares in the company's original offering of English Stock (established in 1603), of his acquiring already successful copyrights (either through reassignment or negotiated joint ownership), and of his frequently entering into collaborative publishing arrangements with other stationers like Thomas Man, William Leake, and George Bishop. Burby was most interested in religious titles, specifically in sermons by Henry Smith and Richard Greenham, and religious pamphlets by William Perkins. Between 1598 and 1599, Burby capitalized upon his ownership of Smith copyrights by publishing his copies together as collected volumes; he did the same with his Greenham copies in 1604. With his stationer peers, he published editions of *Basilicon Doron* in 1603 and of John Rider's English-Latin dictionary in 1606. Together, Burby's practices translate to habits of minimizing risk by (1) investing in titles with proven market records – both individually and as a group – and (2) pooling investment capital when venturing upon new titles.

The chapters that follow outline the distinct publishing activities of Millington's and Burby's Elizabethan forebearers and contemporaries, from Thomas Hacket in the 1560s, to Richard Smith in the 1570s and 1590s, to John Flasket and Paul Linley in the 1590s, to Nicholas Ling in the 1590s and early 1600s. Together, they show how different sets of practices – having to do with acquisition, reissuing, and everything in between – served to distinguish the publishing side of these bookmens' businesses. They also demonstrate that particular practices helped contribute to the distinct characteristics of these bookmen's cultural products – translation to travel literature; compiling to collected vernacular poetry; reissuing to erotic literature; and specialization to professional plays in quarto.

Chapter Two

Thomas Hacket, Translation, and the Wonders of the New World Travel Narrative

In 1576, the London draper and bookseller Henry Disle made literary history with the publication of *The Paradise of Dainty Devices*, a twelve-sheet verse miscellany compiled by the Chapel Royal Master Richard Edwards.[1] With Tottel's *Songs and Sonnets*, *The Paradise* would become the most popular poetry miscellany of its era, reaching a ninth edition in 1606.[2] Together, the ninety-nine poems by Edwards, Thomas Vaux, William Hunnis, and others sing of what were the conventional themes of friendship, love and loss, religion, and death. They also offer recurring images of travel. Most of these are straightforward Petrarchan fare – ships as forlorn lovers, unpredictable weather as fortune, ports as consummated love, etc.[3] Others, however, belong to what was an emergent vernacular discourse of world exploration in the 1550s and 1560s, one that preceded the first beginnings of English colonial exploration in the late 1570s. These images include Jasper Heywood's rejected explorers' bounties of "treasure great of golde or precious stone" (sig. A4ᵛ) in his poem "*Who mindes to bring his shippe to happy shore*" and William Hunnis's opening picture of "the Shipman hoise[ning] saile, in hope of passage good" in his "*Hope well and haue well*" (sig. H1ʳ).[4] Contemporary images of travel can be found too in Edwards's own twenty-two-line poem in iambic fourteeners "*He requesteth some frendly comfort affirmyng his constancie.*" There, in imagining the many works of nature that will ultimately "by trackt of tyme decaie," Edwards begins by speaking of geological features, again from a maritime perspective idealizing "free passage": "mountaines hie whose loftie topps, doeth mete the hautie sky" and "The craggie rocke that to the sea, free passage doeth deny." At the end of the poem, in admitting his own special limitations as an Englishman,

Edward also invokes the wondrous and the strange. "I am not myne," he writes, "but thine I vowe, thy hests I will obeye, / And serue thee as a seruaunt ought, in pleasyng if I maie: / And sith I haue no fliyng wings, to see thee as I wishe, / Ne finnes to cut the siluer streames, as doeth the glidyng fishe. / Wherefore leaue now forgetfulnesse, and sende againe to me / And straine thy azured vaines to write, that I maie greetyng see" (sig. H1ᵛ). To be sure, Edwards's negative allusions to "wing[ed]" and "finne[d]" men summon what was the late medieval fantastic world of Sir John Mandeville's *Travels*. Popular enough to be reprinted by the printer Thomas East in 1568, this collection of wondrous descriptions was England's earliest and most popular print travel narrative. Edward's poem, though, with its list of daunting geography ("loftie topps" and "craggie rocke[s]"), pervasive flora ("the aged Oke" and "the pleasaunt herbe"), and salient fauna (the "Lyon," "Eagle," "Serpent" and "loathsome Tode"), also echoes accounts by the Spanish and the Portuguese, by famed explorers like Peter Martyr and Gonzalo Fernández de Oviedo. These offered their own lists of sublime geography, plants, and animals.

Edwards's *Paradise* registers, then, some of the first traces of English concern with global exploration and maritime ventures, its poems demonstrating that this interest was sufficiently widespread to shape a burgeoning literary culture. Granted, as colonial artefacts go, these poems are at best nascent productions, works setting out conventional themes through contemporary imagery of travel; none of them are explorations of travel – its own themes, its own politics, its own consequences – through the literary. Years away, in other words, are Sidney's lyrical entanglements with the other in *Astrophel and Stella*, Spenser's Protestant allegories of English settlements abroad in *The Faerie Queene* ("Of fruitfullest *Virginia* who did euer vew?" [sig. M6ᵛ]), and Shakespeare's portrait of the colonialist in *The Tempest*.[5] Still, Edwards's miscellany of poems attests to new patterns of book buying and to new habits of reading. Together, these would ultimately help inspire literary engagements with "wordes ... of *Indian* ware" (Sidney 1591a, sig. F3ᵛ) and "the still-vext *Bermoothes*" (Shakespeare 1623, sig. A2ʳ).

England's mid-century interest in worlds without Europe does in fact correlate directly with what was the appearance in the 1550s of Continental travel literature in translation in the bookstalls of St Pauls and other areas of London. As this chapter will show, these texts – translated by Richard Eden and others – were directed at a specialized audience and had the stated purpose of motivating what they saw as England's idle denizens to undertake expeditions of their own. These works in turn inspired a new wave of travel narratives in translation, a current both fashioned and driven in large part by the London bookseller Thomas Hacket. Like his peers Richard Jugge, Thomas Dawson, and Henry Bynneman, Hacket did much to identify, commission, and finance texts in this genre.[6] Hacket emerged as an active publisher in the 1560s, and over his thirty-year career, he put his stamp on the early Elizabethan print market not simply as a compiler, marketer, and wholesaler but as a translator fully engaged with the cultural work of his makings. He was the first bookman to target a broad readership for contemporary accounts of exploration in translation beyond mariners, explorers, and venture capitalists. In these 1560s and 1570s publications, he emphasized and advertised the wondrous in such reports as facilitating a visceral experience of the divine, in effect devising an aesthetic ground for engagement where there had strictly been only utility before. Building upon Eden's groundbreaking translations in the 1550s, Hacket would stand at the forefront of a newly invigorated print market for travel narratives of all kinds, vending them as both pleasurable and elevating reading material for a Protestant nation slowly talking its place on the world stage.

The Career of Thomas Hacket

The son of a French bookbinder, Hacket worked as a bookseller and a publisher in London for more than three and one half decades.[7] He died in the first week of August 1590.[8] Arber has suggested that he, along with John Wayland and Hugh Singleton, was "probably of the Brotherhood, and yet ... not named in the [Stationers' Company] Charter" of 1557 (Arber, 1.xxxiv). Evidence of Hacket and his work as a stationer before the Charter comes both from his paying a mandatory company contribution to "the howse of brydewell" in the spring of 1556 (Arber, 1.48) and his presenting the apprentice "Thomas foster" on 8 March 1557 (Arber, 1.43).[9] During his lifetime, Hacket at some point seems to have married and had at least one daughter "Joan" and one son "Ambrose," the latter being admitted to the Stationers' Company "per patronagium" on 14 June 1582 (Arber, 2.686).[10] That same year, the London Subsidy Roll lists Hacket as an "Englishm[a]n" living in the St Olave, Hart Street parish of southeastern London and an assessment of three shillings on a three-pound valuation. Such an assessment is relatively low and may indicate the small size of Hacket's business at this point in his career.[11] After her husband's death in 1590, "Mistres Hackett" is recorded as representing the apprentice "Andrewe Harris" when he is made free of the company on 25 February 1595 (Arber, 2.715); she seems to have died a year later in September 1596.[12]

The greater part of Hacket's living as a stationer appears to have been derived from his bookselling business, with sporadic publishing, as it was for most booksellers, undertaken to supplement his regular income.[13] Early on, this business was successful enough for Hacket to be taken into the livery in 1568/9 (Arber, 1.391) and to be working with Francis Coldock as Senior Renter Warden in 1575/6 (Arber, 1.471).[14] It was around this time in the middle of the 1570s, however, that Hacket ceased publishing for almost a decade, assigning two of his rights to copy to the draper-bookseller John Wight.[15] These actions may have had something to do with a downturn in Hacket's finances. In 1585, Hacket alludes to these past problems when he laments in a dedication to "*his very good friend Maister* Richard Candler" that up until that time "welth and abilitie [were] lacking to accomplish [his] desired pretence" (Pliny 1585). Whatever occurred in the mid-1570s, Hacket's fortunes seem to have rebounded in the early 1580s. He is elected to the Court of Assistants sometime between 1581 and 1583,[16] and in 1584 he restarts the publishing side of his business, financing on average approximately three editions and thirty edition sheets per year for what would be his last seven years.[17]

During what we can glean of his career as a bookseller, Hacket appears to have sold from as many as five different bookshops, most of which were located in and around Lombard Street and the Royal Exchange. Before the completion of neighbouring Cornhill's Royal Exchange in 1568, Lombard Street was, according to John Stow, the preferred meeting place for "*Longo*bards, and other merchantes, straungers of diuers nations assembling there twise euery day (1598, sigs. L6ᵛ–L7ʳ)."[18] It was also arguably "one of the major centres of the London book trade" (Worms 1997, 209).[19] Such a location helps to explain what was Hacket's career-long penchant for publishing translations and travel narratives.[20] Not only did it provide Hacket with a ready market of merchants, eager for "news of landfalls and fresh discoveries" (Worms 1997, 218), but it also gave him access to London's large population of merchant strangers, from whom he would have been able to obtain and gather news of recent foreign publications.

Identified in the imprint to *The Fable of Ovid Treating of Narcissus* (1560), the first of Hacket's recorded shops was located immediately south of Lombard Street "in Cannynge strete, ouer agaynste the thre Cranes." "Cannynge Strete" ("Cannon Street," or "Candlewicke Street" in Stow) was the main road in the Candlewright street ward, a thoroughfare lined with "rich Drapers, sellers of woollen cloth, &c" (1598, sig. M6r). Two years later in 1562, Hacket's publications advertise that they may be bought wholesale at "hys shop in Lumbarde streete" (Boccaccio 1562, sig. C3r). Hacket seems to have worked out of this location until as late as 1568, when he appears to have again moved his centre of operations to Paul's Churchyard "at the signe of the Key" (Polybius 1568, tp).[21] Whatever his reasons for shifting to Paul's, Hacket likely did not stay long. When the Royal Exchange was officially opened in 1570, Hacket was one of its first vendors.[22] *The Treasury of Amadis of France* (1572?), the first title Hacket published after 1568, advertises in its imprint a "shoppe in the | Royall Exchaunge. At the signe | of the greene Dragon."[23] By the final years of his career, Hacket had moved south of the Exchange, this time across Cornhill Street to a location on the Lombard Street side of Pope's Head Alley "vnder the Popes | head" (1584c, tp). Hacket's final relocation might have been driven by economy. Elizabeth's famed 1571 visit had provided a much-needed boon for the Exchange, allowing Gresham quickly to raise shop rents in 1572 and thereafter (Saunders, 45). Whatever its impetus, it was from this site that Hacket wholesaled what turned out to be the majority of his publications until his death in 1590.

At its start, Hacket's career as a publisher was marked by collaborative ventures. Of his eight editions published between 1560 and 1562, four appear to have been the product of Hacket sharing financial risk. As discussed in "Acquiring" in chapter 1, this was not an uncommon practice.[24] Publishers would share in the entrance of copy, collaborate in the procurement of manuscripts, and negotiate special arrangements with their printers, all with the goal of stretching their investment capital.[25] That such collaboration was limited to his initial publishing ventures suggests Hacket's early caution with his own funds. In 1561, Hacket published *A New Interlude ... of Godly Queen Hester* with William Pickering. Pickering entered and likely printed the text (Arber, 1.154), and he and Hacket jointly distributed it from their shops in Lombard Street.[26] That same year, Hacket seems also to have entered into a similar arrangement with the printer-bookseller

John Tisdale in order to publish *An Apology Made by the Reverend Father J. Hooper*.[27] A year later in 1562, Hacket and Tisdale reprinted Hooper's *Apology* with the Protestant martyr's *An Exposition upon the 23 Psalm*. Like the previous edition, this text was likely printed by Tisdale and was jointly distributed from his and Hacket's "shoppes in Lombarde strete" (1562a, sig. D4ʳ). During 1562, Hacket published as well *The Laws and Statutes of Geneva* with Roland Hall. In this venture, Hall provided the copy for, printed, and wholesaled this octavo text; Hacket's role seems to have been limited to the contribution of capital and possibly materials.[28]

After 1562, none of his imprints suggests Hacket's involvement in collaborative publishing ventures. They at the same time together indicate a habit of working almost exclusively with a particular printing house, this possibly indicating a penchant for carried-over debt between Hacket and his trade printers.[29] In 1566, the year of his move to Paul's Churchyard, Hacket took at least eight texts to Henry Denham for printing. In the twenty-six years that he operated a printing house, Denham would become one of London's busiest printers, operating four presses in 1583 (Arber, 1.248); he would also come to have a reputation for high standards of craftsmanship (Blayney 1997, 405).[30] By 1567, though, Hacket had left Denham and had established a regular business arrangement with another of London's busiest printers, the printer-bookseller Henry Bynneman.[31] In seven years until 1574, Bynneman printed a number of different texts for Hacket (mostly at his Knightrider Street printing shop), including *The New Found World or Antarctic* and *The Treasury of Amadis of France*. After his eight-year hiatus from publishing between 1575 and 1583, Hacket worked almost exclusively with the printer John Charlewood. It was Charlewood who set Hacket's late publications like Rankins's antitheatrical tract *A Mirror of Monsters* (1587) and Nashe's *The Anatomy of Absurdity* (1589).

Unlike fellow publishers George Cawood (who reprinted John Lyly's *Euphues* at least ten times) and John Day (who reprinted Thomas Becon's *The Sick Man's Salve* at least eleven times), Hacket never proved to have exceptional market acumen when it came to his publishing ventures. Few of his publications were reprinted during his lifetime, and they also did not attract much interest from other investors.[32] The first of Hacket's publications to reach another edition was *Theatrum mundi* (1566?) in 1574.[33] A translation by John Alday of Pierre Boaistuau's *Le théâtre du monde* (Paris, 1558), *Theatrum mundi* offers an encyclopedic account of the miseries of man drawn from patristic, medical, philosophical, and literary authorities.[34] In it, writes Hacket in his 1574 edition, "thou maist see & behold all the vniversall world; thou maist first see thy selfe what thou art, and what miseries al humaine creatures are subiect to" (sig. ¶3ᵛ). Other Hacket publications reaching subsequent editions in his lifetime were *A Watch-Word to England to Beware of Traitors* (1584) in 1584; *A Summary of the Antiquities and Wonders of the World* (1566) in 1585 and 1587; *The Work of P. Mela. The Cosmographer* (1585) in an enlarged edition in 1590; and *A Dial for Dainty Darlings, Rocked in the Cradle of Security* (1584) in an enlarged edition in 1590. Perhaps not surprisingly given their unremarkable sales, few of Hacket's publications ended up being transferred to other publishers.[35] As referred to above, in 1577 the Court of Stationers oversaw the transfer of Hacket's publishing rights for *A Regiment for the Sea* and *Theatrum mundi* to John Wight. After his death in 1590, the Stationers' Register has no record of his publications being bought and transferred to another stationer.

By the end of his bookselling career, works-in-translation had become one of Hacket's specialities.[36] In three decades, Hacket published at least twenty different translations, adding up to half of his extant publications. All told, they amounted to around two thirds of the edition sheets that he financed. Hacket appears to have gone so far as to commission certain of his translations. This seems to have been the case with his 1572(?) publication *The Treasury of Amadis of France*. In his epistle "*To the gentle Reader*," the translator Thomas Paynell reveals that "[a] VERY frend of myne (most gentle reader) instantly desired me, to English him this french booke" (sig. ¶3ᵛ).[37] In his preceding dedicatory epistle to Thomas Gresham, Hacket appears to be this particular "frend"; not only does he prove very familiar with the work but he also apologizes for "it yeld[ing] not so pleasant a grace in the Englishe toung as it dothe in the Frenche, the vvhiche it vvas vvritten in" (sig. ¶3ʳ). As a commissioner of translations and distributor of translated material, Hacket capitalized on the extensive resource of Continental, scholastic, and classical material, a ready labour market of translators, and an ever-growing number of middling-sort readers.[38]

Traveling in the Bookstalls

Travel literature made up a significant subset of Hacket's specialty in translations, as it did for his stationer contemporaries John Wolfe, John

Denham, and Henry Bynneman.[39] Indeed, Hacket seems to have been one of the first booksellers to specialize in this area of the book trade.[40] Beginning in 1561/2 with his entry of "the unyversall Cossemographe Apyane in Englesshe" (Arber, 1.175), books describing the world without England would be a mainstay of Hacket's publishing. Hacket financed at least eleven of these titles, and together they accounted for more than a third of the edition sheets that he published during his career. Hacket himself was responsible for three of these translations and possibly a section of a fourth, demonstrating a personal investment on his part going beyond the financial. Some of Hacket's travel narratives were collections of geography and natural history written by ancient authorities. Among them were *A Summary of the Antiquities and Wonders of the World*, *The Work of P. Mela. The Cosmographer*, and *The Worthy Work of Julius Solinus Polyhistor* (1587). Together, these collections advertise the "vncredible" (Pliny 1566, sig. A2^r) and the "secretes" (Solinus 1587, tp) of the world. Mariners in particular were the mark of the 1574(?) aid to navigation *A Regiment for the Sea*, wherein Hacket in a dedicatory poem advises: "So now thou Seaman eke, that spredst abroad thy sayle/be thankfull for thy Author here, whiche is for thy auayle" (Bourne, sig. B1^v).[41]

Hacket's publications also included a number of New-World travel narratives, those in the 1560s being some of the first to be published in England.[42] In 1563, Hacket both translated and published *The Whole and True Discovery of Terra Florida*, a "true" account by the French mariner John Ribault of his 1562 journey to North America. In his dedicatory epistle to the London alderman Sir Martin Bowes, Hacket assures his patron, apparently in light of the present French travel narrative, that he "cannot but amongst the rest [of great voyages] reioyce to see the forwardness in these later yeares of Englishmen."[43] Three years later in 1566, Hacket published the *True Discovery*'s sequel: *A True and Perfect Description, of the Last Voyage Attempted by Captain John Ribaut into Terra Florida*. A translation of Nicolas Le Challeux's *Histoire memorable du dernier voyage aux Indes* (Lyon, 1566), *The Last Voyage* describes Ribault and his companions' brutal encounter with the Spanish at their return to the Americas, an encounter resulting in Ribault's own death. Following the apocalyptic *The Great Wonders that are Chanced in the Realm of Naples* (1566), Hacket published and likely translated *The New Found World or Antarctic* (1568), French Royal Cosmographer André Thevet's 1557 narrative of his recent expedition to Brazil, the return journey taking him past Cuba and Florida, and almost to Canada.[44] In 1587, Hacket would publish his last travel narrative, Thomas Greepe's verse celebration *The True and Perfect News of the Exploits Performed by Sir F. Drake at Santo Domingo*. In his epistle "To the Reader," Hacket praises Drake "for hys good successe, to the great terror and feare of the enemie" (sig. A3ʳ).[45]

In intimately involving himself with these early New World travel narratives, Hacket laboured among a small group of pre-Hakluyt translators, men who often shared similar ideological motivations, similar senses of audience, and similar approaches to their craft. Most notable was the cosmographer and alchemist Richard Eden, and he was joined by the Bristol merchant trader John Frampton, the shipowner Thomas Nicholas ("Thomas Nicholls"), and the famed author and language teacher John Florio.[46] As Andrew Hadfield has observed, English travel writing in the second half of the sixteenth century – penned by English travellers and translators alike – was routinely driven by a desire "to participate in current pressing debates about the nature of society."[47] Appearing in the half-century following Sir Thomas More's *Utopia*, English-language works in this genre – in their overdetermined content and their paratextual material – frequently forwarded explicit religious, economic, and political agendas.[48]

As much as anything else, early English translators of New World travel writing endorsed aggressive nationalist programs, pushing for an English wave of colonialism, one that could rival, even surpass, that of Spain and Portugal.[49] Such nationalism frames the earliest New World travel narrative in the vernacular to appear in the bookstalls of London: Eden's 1553 translation of selections from Sebastian Münster's Latin *Cosmographia* (first compiled in Germany in 1544), entitled *A Treatise of the New India*. For Eden, England's present inferiority as a colonial power was a failure of testosterone. "Manlye courage," he contends in his dedicatory epistle to the Duke of Northumberland, "yf it had not been wanting in other in these our dayes, at suche time as our souereigne Lord of noble memorie kinge Henry the. viii … it mighte happelye haue comen to passe, that that riche treasurye called *Perularia*, (which is now in Spayne in the citie of Civile, and so named, for that in it is kepte the infinite ryches brought thither from the newe found land of *Peru*) myght longe since haue bene in the towre of London, to the kinges great honoure and welth of this his realme" (sigs. aa4ʳ⁻ᵛ).[50] In the same masculine vein, Florio, in his 1580 translation of Jacques Cartier's account of his first two voyages to Canada (1534–6), calls for English colonies in North America: "Al which oportunities besides manye others, might suffice to induce oure Englishmen, not onely to fall to some traffique wyth the Inhabitants, but also to plant a Colonie in some conuenient place, and so to possesse the Countrey without the gainsaying of any man" (sig. B1ᵛ).[51] With the bravado of Eden, Florio makes it clear in his second translator's epistle that England needs to stand up to other European colonial powers.

Routinely, these calls by early translators for a dramatic increase in English colonial exploration were buttressed by moral arguments and imperatives. Working in the context of Mary I's recent ascension to the English throne, Eden devotes much of his ample prefatory epistle in his translation *The Decades of the New World or West India* (1555) to a defence of the Spanish conversion efforts in the New World.[52] "The Spaniardes," he writes, "as the mynisters of grace and libertie, browght vnto these newe gentyles the victorie of Christes death whereby they beinge subdued with the worldely sworde, are nowe made free from the bondage of Sathans tyrannie, by the myghty poure of this triumphante victourer, whom (as sayth the prophet) god hath ordeyned to be a light to the gentyles, to open the eyes of the blynde, and to delyuer the bounde owt of pryson and captiuitie" (sig. a2ᵛ). Frampton, in his 1579 translation of Barnardino Escalante's *Discurso de la navegacion*, reiterates Eden's moral rationale. "If wee bee not borne to profite our selues but to seeke the aduancement of Gods glory," he asks," how commendable an enterprise is that? how highly to be wished? ... Therefore God hauing decreed to make himselfe knowen as well by our Englishe Nation in some quarters of the vnknowen worlde, as he hath of late yeeres beene by the Spaniarde in West: and by the Portugale in the Easte" (sig. A2ᵛ).[53]

For Eden and his heirs, travel narratives in the vernacular also had the potential of inspiring virtuous action from their audience. That their commendations inspire further good work, argues Eden, is a necessary consequence of heroic narratives written both in the past and in the present. "Such magnanimitie to haue ben in our predicessours, men of noble & stout courage," writes Eden in *A Treatise of the New India*, "that they thought it not sufficiente in their life time to deserue prayse & honour, except the same might also redounde to theyr posteritie, that they might therby bee encouraged to do the like. Whyche thing truely hath ben that cause, that in al ages, noble enterprises haue ben commended" (Münster 1553, sig. aa2ᵛ). As Eden says later in the same epistle, he expects that his readers recognize that their time "is more honourably spent in such attemptes as may be to the glorye of God & commoditie of our countrey, then in soft beddes at home, among the teares & weping of women" (sig. aa4^r).[54] Frampton predicts that his 1578 translation *A Brief Description of the Ports, Creeks, Bays, and Havens of the West India* may "be a meane to keepe [mariners] the more from idlenesse, the Nurce of villany" (Enciso, sig. A2^v).

A majority of these early New World translations were aimed at a specialized audience, one made up of pilots, mariners, and potential patrons/investors (gentlemen and merchants alike). As John Parker has outlined, this was at least partly in response to the emergence in the mid-sixteenth century of English joint-stock companies, founded to underwrite mercantile ventures abroad. "This development," argues Parker, "made it possible for the number of persons interested in voyages of exploration and distant commerce to be considerably increased" (1965, 37).[55] Eden's 1553 and 1555 translations are both directed at such men, at those interested in the potential fame and glory of maritime exploration and in exploration as a potential avenue for economic investment. His Münster translation advertises on its title page that the "diligent reader may see the good successe and rewarde of noble and honeste enterpryses." Likewise, its dedicatory epistle promises that "they which set forth or take vpon them this viage, as also they which shal hereafter attempt the lyke, may in this smal boke as in a little glasse, see some cleare light" (1553, sig. aa3^v). Thomas Nicholas deploys the same figure in *The Pleasant History of the Conquest of the West India* (1578). "[The work] is a Mirrour," he writes, "and an excellent president, for all such as shall take in hande to gouerne nevve Discoueries" (López de Gómara, sig. a2^r). A year before having his translation put to press, the merchant trader Frampton envisions a similar select readership in *A Brief Description* (1578). "This may," he asserts, "for our meere English Seamen, Pilotes, Marriners, &c. not acquaynted with forrayne tongues, bring greate pleasure (if it fortune our Mariners or any other of our Nation, to be driuen by vvinde, tempeste, currents, or by other chaunce to any of the Ilandes, Portes, Hauens, Bayes, or Forelandes mencioned in this Pamphlet)" (Enciso, sig. A2^v).[56] Florio's 1580 translation takes the same tack. His reader's epistle is addressed "To all Gentlemen, Merchants, and Pilots," and in it Florio makes it clear that it is for "the Marchant Venturer, or skilfull Pilot ... for whome especially I haue done it" (Cartier, sig. B1^r). The tract even concludes with a short traveller's dictionary. There, the explorer can find "necessarie to be knowen" words for a "Mans member," for "a Womans member," and for "let vs go to play" (Cartier, sigs. M4^{r-v}).

For the most part, these early translators of travel narratives show little self-consciousness about the semantic and stylistic attributes of their labours. But when they are not glossing over the issue altogether or deploying the usual translators' descriptive refrain – "truly and faithfully" – they inevitably veer towards characterizing their translations as straightforward and unadorned, towards Ascham's *paraphrasis*, what Gordon Braden describes as "stringent literalism."[57] Florio calls his 1580 translation a "simple labour" (Cartier, sig. A2^r) and Frampton in *The Most Noble and Famous Travels of Marcus Paulus* (1579) warns those readers that only have English and are thus forced to read his translation to "seeke onelye for substaunce of matter [in] my playne translation" (Polo, sig. *2^v). While the title page of Nicholas's translation *The Pleasant History of the Conquest of the West India* promises a "pleasant historie ... most delectable to Reade," Nicholas describes his labours as "not decked vvith gallant couloures, nor yet fyled vvith pleasant phrase of Rhetorike, for these things are not for poore Marchant trauellers, but are reserued to learned VVriters" (López de Gómara 1578, sigs. A4^{r-v}). In his later translation *The Discovery and Conquest of the Provinces of Peru*, he similarly laments, "*the stile of this historie in our English tongue is not, nor at the least, I cannot polish as leaned men might require*" (Zárate 1581, sig. A3^r).

Trained at Cambridge in an emergent humanist educational system, Eden, however, appears to have had a more nuanced sense of his translation work, understanding it along the lines of what recent scholars have called "oratorical translation."[58] This sixteenth-century norm was based upon the tenets of Cicero, who in *De optimo genere oratorum* famously imagines the effective translator not as a word-for-word interpreter but as an "orator" who translates according to his main end: to persuade and move his audience.[59] "It is one thing," says Cicero, "to hold an auditor while telling a story, and another to arouse him. ... For the orator who we are seeking must treat cases in court in a style suitable to instruct, to delight, and to move."[60] The Ciceronian conception that the practice of translation should primarily be dedicated to "instructing" and "moving" explains Eden's habit of appending long expository epistles of "reasons and causes" to his 1550s translations. It also might explain Eden's signing his dedicatory epistle to Northumberland in *A Treatise of the New India* with "Your graces poore oratour Rychard Eden" (sig. aa5^r).[61]

Moving Travel Literature

Working within a 1560s print market still largely limited to Eden's 1550s pioneering efforts in the vernacular, Hacket's own translations reproduce a number of the cosmographer-alchemist's penchants.[62] In his first prose translation *The Whole and True Discovery of Terra Florida*, Hacket praises in his dedicatory epistle to Sir Martin Bowes not just the recent colonial forays by English mariners but the financial investment in colonial ventures by a variety of patrons – "noble princes kings and gouernours of realms, as the inferior sorte of subiectes." The bookseller echoes too Eden's concerns about enlarging the Christian faith and enriching the kingdom, as well as the translator's conception of his texts as navigational guides in prose for the aspiring explorer. Five years later in his translation *The New Found World or Antarctic*, Hacket reiterates Eden's moralistic understanding of colonial exploration as an antidote to sloth. "How muche are they to be praised," writes Hacket in his dedicatory epistle to Henry Sidney, "that for their Countrey sake refuse no imminent perill, leauing the Pleasaunt bedde of Delicacie, and the seate or cradle of Sensualitie, their landes and goodes, their Wiues and children, which in dede, are dearest vnto them, to abandon themselues and their swetest liues to the fauoure of the boystrous seas" (Thevet, sigs. *2^v–*3^r).

Even while Hacket appears to borrow much from his predecessor Eden, he at the same time stops short of aggressively targeting pilots and maritime financiers in his 1560s translations.[63] The title page of *The Whole and True Discovery of Terra Florida* makes no direct reference to audience, and though it advertises the "mer | ueylous commodities and treasures of the | country" as well as the "pleasaunt Portes, | Hauens, and wayes therevnto" – elements attractive to prospective explorers – it at the same time trumpets the "wonderfull straunge na- | tures and maners of [Florida's native] people" – provocative details more attractive to London buyers of Italian and Greek romance. In 1563, Hacket was no stranger to this audience. A year earlier he had a published the three-sheet translation of a tale from Boccaccio's *Decameron* entitled *The Most Wonderful and Pleasant History of Titus and Gisippus*. In it, like a portent of the specific direction his publishing career would soon take, Hacket adds a jarringly long marginal note, riffing upon Titus's suicidal wish "that Rhynos with his sharpe horne, /Would rid me of my miserye." Likely drawn from Eden's 1553 translation *A Treatise of the New India* (sigs. C2^v–C3^r), Hacket adds to the margin, "The complaininge of Titus. Rhinos is a certaine beast in the countreise of India hauinge a sharpe horne growing out of the nostrilles of his nose, and an another in his neck, this beast is as big as an Elephant and is naturally an enemye to the Elephant" (sig. A4ᵛ). Here, a wondrous image of the early modern marvel that was the rhinoceros interrupts the narrative at hand (see figure 6).

Like its precursor *The Whole and True Discovery of Terra Florida*, *A True and Perfect Description* contains a variety of topographical, anthropological, and botanic observations useful for the potential Christian explorer. Its title page, however, makes nothing of this. Instead, it focuses only upon the tragic consequences of the voyage, advertising "things as la- | mentable to heare as they | haue bene cruelly | executed."[64] This affective focus is underscored by an ending paragraph that Hacket appears to have added to the work addressing his "gentle Reader."[65] "Here haste thou (gentle Reader)," Hacket writes, "séene the discourse of two sorts of people, wherin thou mayest iudge with indifferencie, and sée what couetousnesse causeth, being both desirous of gaine, and in specially the monstruous crueltie of the one part" (1566, sigs. D8ʳ⁻ᵛ).

The affective takes top billing as well on the title page of *The New Found World or Antarctic*.[66] Promised within are "wonderful and strange | things, as well of humaine crea- | tures, as Beastes, Fishes, Foules, and Ser- | pents, Trees, Plants, Mines of | Golde and Siluer." This is a far cry from Thevet's original 1557 title page which reads "*LES | SINGVLARI- | TEZ DE LA FRAN- | CE ANTARCTIQUE, AU- | trement nommée Amerique & de | plusieurs Terres & Isles de- | couuertes de notre | temps.*" It also is in a different vein than the advertisements on Eden's first translation, which assure that the "diligent reader may see the good | successe and rewarde of noble | and honeste enterpryses, | by the which not only world- | ly ryches are obtayned, | but also God is glo- | rified, & the Chri- | stian fayth en- | larged" (Münster 1553, tp). Where Eden sees New World translations as strictly means to other ends – an increase in English "noble ... enterpryses" – Hacket sees his own efforts as their own ends.[67] This sense of the content of travel narratives as wondrous and pleasurable in and of itself can be seen in Hacket's 1566 publication *A Summary of the Antiquities and Wonders of the World*. There, the translator John Alday describes his material as the "wonderfull & straunge things (unto vs) of the diuersitie of countreyes, the commodities thereof, wyth the most monstrous, and uggly shape of men inhabiting the said countreys" (Pliny, sig. A2ᵛ). Hacket

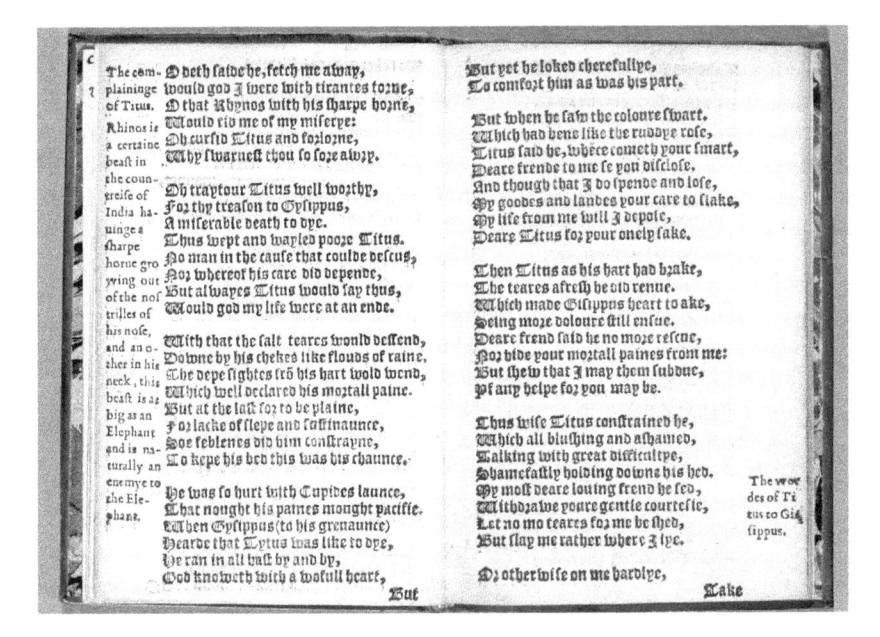

Figure 6 Printed marginalia in *The most wonderful and pleasaunt history of Titus and Gisippus* (1562). By permission of the Huntington Library, San Marino, California.

himself earlier avows a "pleasant experience" for his patron Bowes in *The Whole and True Discovery of Terra Florida*: "Albeit that such attemptes seme paynfull and harde to acheve to. Yet in the end, [these enterprises] be most pleasaunt and profitable" (1563, sig. A1ᵛ). He similarly promises his readers satisfaction in an added dedicatory poem in *The New Found World or Antarctic*: "The Cristall pearle, the Diamond so fayre, / The floting fish of diuers kindes of hew. ... / Hath *Theuet* here through trauell his and payne, / Educted forth, to satisfie thy minde" (sig. *4ᵛ).[68] Eschewing Eden's habit of directing his New World translations at a particular set of readers, Hacket instead fashions his translations to be more versatile commodities, appealing not simply to potential explorers but also to book buyers interested in pleasurable reading.[69]

Hacket's pitch to a broader readership in the 1560s was not an anomaly for the bookseller. It was a common approach in his publications throughout his career. The 1572(?) conversation manual *The Treasury of Amadis of France*, for example, contains a dedicatory poem by

Hacket identifying a wide swathe of possible consumers." According to Hacket, "Euery sort maye imitate and learne here for to write:/To serue their presente vse and tyme, a waye for to indite. .../To euery kynde of wight this booke will serue the turne, /Of Orations fitte, and Pistles pure, themselfe for to adorne" (Paynell, sig. ¶4ᵛ).[70] Thirteen years later in what amounts to an advertisement for his future publications, Hacket in his retitled second edition of Pliny's *The Secrets and Wonders of the World* assures the general "*Reader*" that the present book was "*abstracted out of the sixteene first Bookes of that excellent naturall Historiographer Plinie, for the straungenesse and worthinesse thereof*" (1585, sig. A4ᵛ). Two and one half decades earlier in his only verse translation *The Fable of Ovid Treating of Narcissus*, Hacket imagines a similarly wide reception for his endeavours. In his short dedicatory poem "The prenter to the Booke," he directs his translation to "do thy Indeuoure/to all estates, that vyce doeth refuse. .../In the may the wyse learne vertue in dede/In the maye the stronge manne, of hym selfe knowe/In the maye the ryche manne, of him selfe reed/how to gather his ryches, or them to bestowe" (1560, sig. A1ᵛ). Concluding the work, he signs off, "And thus my simpel trauayle I commende/Unto euery one" (1560, sig. E1ᵛ).

While he attempts to expand the readership for New World travel narratives beyond Eden's mariners and patrons, Hacket at the same time generally shares Eden's humanist conceptualization of translation as a form of oratory. Unlike Frampton or Nicholas, Hacket himself never characterizes his endeavours as "faithful," and this is no oversight. In practice, Hacket frequently makes alterations in rendering his copy into English; most of these changes are small – involving diction and syntax – but some of them are significant and reflect the bookseller's desire to move and instruct his English readership.[71] Hacket's subscription to the tenets of Cicero is most clearly evident in his self-representation in *The New Found World or Antarctic*. There, in his dedicatory epistle, Hacket echoes Eden in addressing Sir Henry Sidney as "Your humble Orator" in his opening address.[72] Four years later in another dedicatory epistle, Hacket explains what such a role entails: "In my mynd this surpasseth all others, that is to say, to be an excellent Oratour, singular in orations, pythie and ingenious in vvriting Epistles, for therby is brought to passe the moste excellent things for publike gouernment, as also for euery mannes priuate cause and vse" (Paynell 1572?, sig. ¶2ᵛ).

It is in Hacket's 1568 translation that a focus upon "publike gouernment" emerges most clearly. There he adds a number of nationalist references in order to corroborate his opening claim that "*this most noble Seignorie and Territorie of England hath of late yeares gotte the fame and renowne, that it hath had in times past, by Nauigation lately atempted by many and sundrie of our countreymen*" (Thevet, sig. *3ʳ).[73] In the translation's second chapter on the Straight of Gibraltar, writing on those nations affected by the piracy of "*Turkes, Moores, and Barbarians*" (sig. B4ʳ). Hacket adds "*Englande* and other places" (sig. B4ʳ) to what in his French source is only "Espagne, q de Frãce" (1557, sig. B4ᵛ). Pages later in Thevet's chapter refuting the ancient claim that parts of the earth are uninhabited, Hacket cuts Thevet's long reference to "Mosieur de Cãbray" (1557, sig. F3ᵛ) as being the explorer who first verified that there be nothing but ice and coldness in the lands near the North pole, the people there forward and brutish; Hacket instead writes, "The which to our Englishe Marchantes is well ynough knowen" (sig. E6). Towards the end of the translation in the seventy-fifth chapter, Hacket refutes Thevet's claim that Canada was first discovered by the Briton James Quartier by adding that the country was "discouered in oure time, first by Sebastian Babat an Englisheman" (sig. R2ᵛ).[74] Together, these alterations produce a travel narrative that seeks to celebrate England and its recent history of exploration, this in contradistinction to the laments of Eden in his 1550s translations which bemoan England's being "decayed and impouerysshed" (Anghiera 1555, sig. b3ᵛ) and its wanting "manlye courage" (Münster 1553, sig. aa4ʳ).

Positivist, nationalist ends can likewise be gleaned in Hacket's decision to cut two long prefatory odes from his Thevet translation, one by the French dramatist and poet Étienne Jodelle and another by the French author, poet, and translator François de Belleforest. In cutting the former poem, Hacket kept his readers from what was Jodelle's focus upon contemporary events in France, and he also shielded them from the poem's potentially unsettling politics, the ode attacking as it does its own readers for sinking below Thevet's savages: "Nous la nostre nous mesprisons, / Pipons, vedons & deguisons" ["We our own despise / Deceive, sell & disguise"] (Thevet 1557, sig. A4ʳ).[75] At the same time, in cutting Belleforest's hyperbolic praise of Thevet in his dedicatory ode "A Monsiegneur Thevet," Hacket tones down what was his copy's praise of France. Gone is Belleforest's "Ainsi l'Europe tributaire /

A ton labeur, t'exaltera:/Pas ne pourra France se taire" ["And so Europe will be dependent/Upon your work and will exalt thee./France will not remain silent"] (Thevet 1557, sig. A6r). In its place is the measured reminder in Hacket's added dedicatory poem that Thevet "well deserues thy thankefull speech to gayne/... So of his worke let iudgement thyne procede" (sig. *4v). Nowhere in the poem's sixteen lines of intertwined rhyme is there any mention of France.

Celebrations of England's emergence as a colonial power notwithstanding, one of Hacket's most pervasive foci in his New World translations is upon "euery mannes priuate cause and vse" (Paynell 1572?, sig. ¶2v), reflecting what was the bookseller's particularly Protestant religious vocation.[76] For Hacket, travel narratives are in essence "histories," works that like poetry educate mankind in virtue, or as Sidney expresses it in *The Defense of Poesy*, teach us "to knowe, and by knowledge to lift vp the mind from the dungeon of the body, to the enioying of his owne diuine essence" (1595a, sig. C4v).[77] They accomplish these ends by demonstrating the work of God in the wide world – in the actions and fate of men, in the strange marvels in the plant and animal kingdom, and in the fantastical varieties of humanity. It falls to the good Protestant both to appreciate and to have faith that all of these wonders are the work of a pervasive deity. Hacket's humanist and Protestant understanding of the travel narrative undergirds his addition to *A True and Perfect Description*, where he closes the work by demarcating its generic and providential workings: "But the Historie suffiseth of it selfe, God is a righteous iudge which séeth the actes of all humaine kinde, and shall rewarde euery one according to their deserts. God kéepe vs from murther and bloudshedde, and giue vs grace to feare him, and honour his holy name aright. Amen" (1566, sig. D8v). Just as a sense of God in the tragic end of Ribaut and his men would translate to a moment of "grace" for Hacket's readers, so too would the appreciation of heroism on the high seas amount to a similar intimation of God. Hacket makes this clear in the dedicatory poem that he added to his 1574(?) publication *The Regiment of the Sea*. "Who trauels Countries gaine," he writes, "is worthy of great prayse:/as those that were before our time & that in sundry ways./Whose actes do so excell, they pierce the loftie skies/that in good artes for common weale, both wit & will applies. .../As Authors old can tell, who list in them to reade/who were inuenters of the same which dayly now procéede/In rule of publike weale, our Ioue it first began/and plast it here in all estates, for the behoofe of man" (sig. B1v). It is, in other words, the admirable "wit & will" of man's leaders from "all estates" that is most evident in the travel narrative; and these leaders' superior skill, argues Hacket, "our Ioue it first began." Ultimately, then, Hacket's invitation in *The New Found World or Antarctic* to "let iudgement thyne procede" amounts to a loaded call to his readers for a particular mode of reading, one that if conducted along the lines of Hacket's own Protestant dictates will truly "further thee, that tooke the same to rede" (Thevet, sig. *4ᵛ).[78]

Of course, Hacket's hermeneutics represent a shift from what were Eden's in the 1550s. As we have seen, Eden was also interested in inspiring virtue in his readership, but for him this virtue would ultimately be manifest in the world, in the good works accomplished abroad by the mariners, soldiers, and patrons interested in his translations. As he argues in *The Decades*, "al good wyttes and honest natures (I doubte not) wyl not onely reioyce to see the kyngedome of God to bee so farre enlarged vppon the face of the earthe, to the confusion of the devyll and the Turkysshe Antichryste, but also do the vttermost of theyr poure to further the same" (Anghiera 1555, sig. a3ʳ). Hacket, by contrast, was more interested in private virtue as manifest in the inspired faith of his readership. As he contends in his epistle "The Printer to the Reader" to his 1574 publication *Theatrum mundi*, "God hath raised in the latter end of thys worlde (dyuers and sundrye wayes) hys worthye instrumentes to publish his knowledge: for truly knowledge did neuer so abound as it doth now in these our dayes, ... neuer more worthier preaching, neuer better of plentifuller writing than is, and hathe bene of late time, and yet sinne did neuer more abounde than it dothe now. ... God graunte that these and such like worthy workes may take suche deepe roote in our hartes, that we maye bring foorthe the worthye fruites of repentaunce and amendment of life, to gods glory, and the comfort of our soules Amen" (sigs. ¶5ʳ⁻ᵛ). Alday reiterates these ends in the prefatory epistle to his translation of Pliny's natural history. "The works of God are maruelous," he insists, "[in] beastes, foules, fishes, trees, plantes, & such like, whose miraculous works, although vnto us some things seeme vncredible; yet if we did consider the omnipotencie of God, vnto whom nothing is vnpossible, doubtlesse we should not runne into so many daungers of sinne as we daily do" (1566, sig. A2ʳ). As both a publisher circulating "knowledge" and an orator translating travel narratives, Hacket saw himself as contributing to his time's "plentifuller writing." He saw it as his vocation in life that his readership be led to "repentaunce and amendment of life, to gods glory."

Such a vocation dominated Hacket's earliest investments. Before publishing his first New World translation in 1563, he financed a number of godly ballads including *Repent o ye England* (Arber, 1.154), *Blessed are they that Die in the Lord* (1.154), and *The Entering of Christ into England* (1.179).[79] In 1562, he published four separate titles having directly to do with reformed Christianity: (1) *The Laws and Statutes of Geneva*, (2) *A Strong Battery against the Idolatrous Invocation of the Dead Saints*, (3) *An Apology Made by the Reverend Father J. Hooper*, and (4) *An Exposition upon the 23 Psalm*. The first of these is a work dedicated to Calvin's theocratic Geneva, "a Citie counted of all godly men singularly well ordered, as well for good policie, as also for the gouernmente of the Churche in all estates, orders, and vocations, where sincere religion is wonderfullye aduaunced" (Fils 1562, sig. *3ʳ). The latter two are by the Protestant martyr John Hooper, bishop of Gloucester and Worcester, who in 1555 was executed at Newgate prison for his radical Protestant beliefs. Hacket's turn to Ribaut's 1562 expedition as his first venture in financing travel narratives appears to have had much to do with his vocation. A Protestant himself born in Dieppe (what has been called the "Norman Geneva" of France), Ribault was commissioned to found an outpost in the Americas that would eventually become a Huguenot colony. On his return after establishing a fort at Parris Island in what is now South Carolina, Ribault spent a year in England looking for Protestant support.[80] Hacket's 1563 translation likely was part of this effort.

Even while he for the most part stopped publishing Protestant tracts after 1562, Hacket consistently advertised his religious vocation in his ample prefatory material written between 1560 and 1590.[81] Most visibly, these pieces invariably end with the religious lexicon of the Anglican godly. A majority of his prefatory epistles conclude with "Amen." And before this requisite signing off, most also contain some version of the prayer that Hacket offers Sir Thomas Gresham and his family in his dedicatory epistle to *The Treasury of Amadis of France*: "I commit you to God, vvith my good Ladie your vvife, vvith all youre familie, praying to God for your prosperous and good successe in all youre affaires and enterprises" (Paynell 1572?, sig. ¶3ʳ). Hacket's prefatory poems also highlight his vocation. His 1560 translation of Ovid, includes his four-line poem on the title page reassuring its potential readers that "God resysteth the proud in euery place/But unto the humble he geueth his grace." And his final lines in praising the author of *A Regiment for the Sea* stress the ubiquity of God: "And thankfulnesse is due, to euery liuing wight, /and doth perteyne to euery man, but yet to God by right./To whom be praise for euermore, which ruleth globe & sphere, /who graunt vs grace to do his will, while we be liuing here" (Bourne 1574?, sig. B1ᵛ). In their intermingling of God's influence over "globe & sphere" with God's gift of "grace," Hacket's lines encapsulate elements of what was his unique fashioning of the New World travel narrative.

It was partially then through the publishing work of Hacket in the 1560s that an English readership continued to be goaded onto the world colonial stage. Like Eden, Hacket appealed repeatedly in his prefatory material to the nationalist impulses of men like Raleigh, Drake, and Frobisher, his translations offering enticing visions of strange lands and strange peoples. Indeed, for his 1576 voyage in search of a northwest passage to fabled Cathay, Frobisher brought with him – along with twenty compasses, twenty hourglasses, various navigational instruments, and "a great globe" – a copy of Hacket's *The New Found World or Antarctic*.[82] In the cultural history of England's slow emergence as a colonial power – between Eden and Hakluyt – stood Hacket and his work as a translator and publisher.

But Hacket's importance goes beyond colonial history. His development of the market for travel literature in the 1560s helped prepare the way for what would be a burgeoning idiom of colonial imagery in poetry collections like *The Paradise of Dainty Devices*, narrative poems like *The Faerie Queene*, and professional plays like *Doctor Faustus*. In labouring to expand the readership of travel narratives in translation, Hacket was possibly the first to articulate an aesthetic of wonder as a desirable end in and of itself for his Protestant bookbuyers. This was not exactly the "wonder" that would emerge as a defining feature of vernacular literature in the 1590s (Brown 2004, 18–26), but its affective workings make it a not-so-distant precursor. More immediately, Hacket's products and ideas – his makings – may have directly influenced the figurative dimension of the 1570s' most popular work of fiction: John Lyly's *Euphues. The Anatomy of Wit* (1578). As is well known, it was in *Euphues* that Lyly first developed his characteristic "euphuistic" prose style, consisting of evenly weighed comparisons drawn from classical mythology and natural history. Pliny's *Naturalis historia* was an important source for Lyly's natural history, providing the content for such euphuistic passages as "And as the Adamant draweth the heauy yron, the harp the fleet Dolphin, so beauty allureth the chast minde to loue and the wisest wit to lust" (sig. D1ᵛ).

For Lyly, sublime and exotic images like these were not simply quaint add-ins; like Hacket, he saw them to be "things" that could have an acute moral impact upon his readers. As *Euphues*'s narrator explains it, "by the terror that the minde of man is stroken into, by lyghtenings, thunderings, tempestes, hayles, snow, earthquakes, pestilence, by the straunge and terrible sightes which cause vs to tremble, as the rayning of bleud, the firie impressions in the Elemente, the ouershadowinge of fluodes in the earth, the prodigious shapes and vnnaturall formes of men, of beastes, of birdes, of fishes, of all creatures ... with these things mortall men beeing afrighted are enforced to acknowledge an immortall & omnipotent God" (sigs. O4^v–P1^r).[83] In the late 1560s and 1570s, both Pliny's imagery of "unnaturall formes of men, of beastes, of birdes, of fishes, of all creatures" and this understanding of the affective moral power of wonder could be had for a few pence near the Royal Exchange, in the bookshops of Thomas Hacket.

Chapter Three

Richard Smith's Browsables: *A Hundreth Sundry Flowers* (1573), *The Fabulous Tales of Aesop* (1577), and *Diana* (1592, 1594?)

Thomas Newman's fraternal 1591 editions of *Astrophel and Stella* stand as landmarks in the history of English literary culture.[1] Not only do the texts represent the first print editions of Sir Philip Sidney's acclaimed volume of poems, but their down-market dissemination in the bookshops of St Paul's quickly sparked what was a 1590s vogue for sonnet sequences and all things Petrarchan. By the middle of the decade, many of England's rising literati like Michael Drayton, Thomas Lodge, and Samuel Daniel had produced sonnet sequences of their own, this as Shakespeare and Spenser were spinning anatomizing offshoots of their Petrarchan sonnets in works like *Titus Andronicus*, *Romeo and Juliet*, and *The Faerie Queene*.[2] But more than simply inspiring a generation of poets, Newman's *Syr P.S. his Astrophel and Stella* worked a kind of cultural magic, conjuring the social capital of a dead aristocratic hero in order to, as Arthur Marotti has put it, "elevate the sociocultural status of lyric poetry and of literary authorship … [and change] the culture's attitudes towards the printing of the secular lyrics of individual writers" (1995, 229).

Sidney's authorial aura is perhaps most obviously manifest in *Astrophel and Stella*'s revised second edition, a version which excises prefatory material by Newman and Thomas Nashe, and a substantial set of appended poems by Daniel, Thomas Campion, Fulke Greville, and others.[3] There, Newman trumpets Sidney's name to both authorize and unify the volume's 117 poems, framing the poetic contents between the title page's possessive exclamation – "SIR P. S. HIS" – and an unambiguous ending signature – "Finis Syr P. S." (1591b, sigs. H4ʳ). This second edition, though, only more explicitly enacts what is implicit in the first: that the title is to be taken as a monument dedicated to

Sidney and his greatness.[4] This is subtly projected in Newman's earlier edition by John Charlewood's use of the title – *Syr P.S. His Astrophel and Stella* – for its running header throughout, on not just the leaves of Sidney's sequence but on those containing the "*other rare Sonnets of diuers Noble | men and Gentlemen*" (tp). It is also underscored by the volume's prefatory material, material that highlights Sidney and his legacy to the exclusion of all else. In his "Somewhat to reade for them *that list*," Nashe is not circumspect in waxing sentimental over Sidney, calling him "so excellent a Poet, (the least sillable of whose name sounded in the eares of iudgement, is able to giue the meanest line he writes a dowry of immortality)" (1591a, sig. A3ʳ). Newman in his own dedicatory epistle matches this effusion, describing Sidney as, among other things, "so rare a man ... whom the works with one vnited griefe bewailed" (1591a, sig. A2ᵛ). In this vein, the publisher is quick too to reassure his patron and his buyers that *Astrophel and Stella* is fully Sidney's, that it has been cleansed of the "corruptions" that it had suffered in manuscript circulation and has been returned to its Edenic "first" state. "I haue beene very carefull in the Printing of it," Newman writes, "and where as being spred abroade in written Coppies, it had gathered much corruption by ill Writers: I haue vsed their helpe and aduice in correcting & restoring it to his first dignitie" (1591a, sig. A2ᵛ). "[H]is first dignitie" may be Newman's mistake for "its first dignitie," but it is an appropriate one, intimating an assumption that his uncorrupted collection mirrors what is essentially Sidney's own apotheosis in the 1580s as ideal patron, soldier, courtier, and writer.

Newman's focus on Sidney in his 1591 editions has been taken as corroboration for the unprecedented rise of the "bibliographic ego" in a variety of printed vernacular genres around the turn of the sixteenth century.[5] To the labours of the playwright Jonson in his 1616 *Works*, of the actors Heminges and Condell in Shakespeare's 1623 First Folio, of the Sidney family in the 1598 folio of Sidney's collected works have been added the efforts of stationers like Newman in the publication of lyric poetry in the 1590s. "In authorizing sonnet sequences," writes Wendy Wall in her cogent assessment of manuscript poetry's transformation in the world of print, "publishers not only appended ... personifying titles, but they also altered the physical presentation of the poems in ways that bolstered the textual unity provided by such figurative titles. In particular, they designed title pages that advertised the writing agent more prominently, arranged the poetic material within a more structured format, and highlighted the typographical features that stabilized the text. As a result, the printed sonnet sequence appeared to be a more stable and fixed artifact than any of its individual poems. ... [The author] became the recipient of the newly emphasized textual authority that different textual producers arrogated to the book" (70). Figurations of authorship and the textual stability that they helped foster, in other words, well served what have been taken to be an early-modern publisher's bottom lines: marketability and profit. In printed sonnet sequences like *Sir P.S. his Astrophel and Stella*, unstable vestiges of aristocratic culture were increasingly being transformed into streamlined commodities, products more easily packaged and sold at bookshops like Newman's in Fleet Street in St Dunstan's churchyard.

It would be misleading, however, to suggest that every Elizabethan publisher was more and more investing in textual "coherence and the rubric of the author" (Wall, 96) in order to transform lyric poetry into marketable literary commodities. As this chapter will demonstrate, the publishing vocation of the little-known draper Richard Smith was defined throughout by an active cultivation of multivocal, capricious texts. Shaped in large part by his own experiences as a bookseller working face-to-face with buyers selling books and other commodities between 1567 and 1597, Smith's publishing consisted not simply of financial risk, speculation, collaboration, and compilation but a significant amount of his own creative mediations as both translator and poet. In George Gascoigne's collected works and the selected fables of Aesop, Smith created titles that would readily appeal to Elizabethan buyers accustomed to *Sammelbände* and commonplacing. His publishing work culminated in the first editions of Henry Constable's sonnet sequence *Diana* in the early 1590s. Arranged and authorized in an altogether different fashion than Newman's second edition of *Astrophel and Stella*, Smith's second revised edition of *Diana* is organized in such a way as to be serviceable to the browsing reader. In this, the collection reprises Smith's earlier conceptions of textuality, authorship, and reading.

The Career of Richard Smith

No records related to Smith's date or place of birth have yet been identified. One small piece of potential evidence comes from his 1577 translation of Henryson's Aesop, where Smith ends with "Finished in the vale of Aylesburie the thirtenth of August. Anno Domini. 1574." (Aesop 1577, sig. H2r).[6] The Vale of Aylesbury is an extensive flatland forty miles northwest of London, and Aylesbury is the county seat of Buckinghamshire. Smith's signature appears to indicate some familial connection to this region. In 1552, Smith was apprenticed in London to the draper Thomas Petyt.[7] In December 1559, his bond was transferred to John Wight. Smith was freed by Wight sometime between 1562 and 1564.[8] Like many drapers in the second half of the sixteenth century, Wight spent much of his career selling commodities other than cloth.[9] Between 1551 and 1589, he ran a bookshop in St Paul's Churchyard, and for four decades regularly published religious and literary texts. Fruit rarely ends up far from the tree; Smith's bookselling and publishing seem no exception.[10]

Smith's whereabouts in the immediate years after his freedom are difficult to track. Records suggest, however, that by the end of the 1560s he had acquired a shop and had likely started a bookselling business. Sometime during the years 1566–7, Smith would make his first and only book entry in the Stationers' Register, for a translation of Boccaccio's *Il filocolo* listed as "the xiiith questions composed in the Italon by master John Bocace" (Arber, 1.337). That he co-published this volume with the stationer Nicholas England and listed the printer Henry Bynneman's shop at the Mermaid as its wholesale location indicates that this may have been a journeyman venture for Smith.[11] Later in 1567, however, the *Minute Book* of the Drapers' Court of Assistants records a dispute between Smith and Christopher Barker (future stationer and Queen's Printer) being settled with Barker agreeing to deliver "upp his Shoppe" to Smith by the following Christmas in exchange for 10 pounds.[12] Barker had apprenticed under Petyt with Smith between 1552 and 1559, and this property dispute was undoubtedly a result of their continued association in the 1560s.

While Barker would within the next two decades be translated to the Stationers' Company and quickly ascend its administrative hierarchy (Kathman 2004a), Smith remained a middling draper for the entirety of his career. He was never taken into the drapers' livery, and he was neither elected to the Drapers' Court of Assistants nor named a Warden in the company. Indeed, other than records related to his own apprenticeship and to his own binding of one or two apprentices, few traces of Smith can be found in the Drapers' Company records.[13] This, though, should not be taken as unusual. The Drapers' Company was a powerful guild with an extensive membership. Only a small number of its members ever rose to power and prominence.

Once established, Smith's own bookselling business appears to have been an idiosyncratic one. As Sidney Thomas observed more than a half-century ago, Smith both published books without paying for entry, and, from 1592 on, had his books entered by their would-be printers, securing his rights to copy through what seems to have been private arrangements between him and men like Charlewood and James Roberts.[14] Smith's places of business are similarly difficult to pin down. Other than the *Minute Book* of the Drapers' Court of Assistants recording what may have been a transaction involving Smith's first shop, we have no record of his bookselling until 1571, when Smith's imprints advertise his selling books wholesale out of a "Corner shoppe, at the North- | weast dore of Paules" (Boccaccio 1571, tp).[15] In 1574, however, Smith rents this shop to Henry Bynneman, and it is not until 1592 that he again advertises his own wholesale bookselling location, this time a "shop, at the | West doore of Paules" (Telin, tp).[16] Whether Smith continued bookselling between 1574 and 1592 is unclear.[17] Smith's 1574 "Aylesburie" note, though, may indicate his temporary departure from London.

H.G.'s 1567 "*English*[ing]" (tp) of Boccaccio's *Il filocolo* was Smith's first publication. The work of what Smith's title page describes as a "Poet Laureat," this collection of framed tales proved a relatively lucrative investment, reaching a fourth edition in 1587.[18] "Poet" work would ultimately become a specialty for Smith in his relatively infrequent publishing ventures over the next three decades. In 1573, Smith published the first edition of George Gascoigne's writings, a fifty-two-sheet, multi-work quarto entitled *A Hundreth Sundry Flowers*. Over the next fourteen years, Smith put out a quarto edition of Gascoigne's *The Steel Glass* (1576) and two further revised and expanded collected editions of his writings: *The Posies of George Gascoigne Esquire* in 1575 and *The Whole Works of George Gascoigne Esquire* in 1587. Smith published a verse translation of Aesop in 1577. The year 1587 saw Smith's publication of Matthew Grove's narrative poem *The Most Famous and Tragical History of Pelops and Hippodamia*.[19] This octavo also includes what Smith's title page describes as "sundrie | pleasant deuises, Epigrams, | Songes and Son- | nettes." Over the next eight years, Smith continued what would be a late-career preoccupation with the sonnet, publishing two radically different editions of Henry Constable's sonnet sequence *Diana* in 1592 and 1594(?), respectively, and George Chapman's *Ovid's Banquet of Sense* in 1595. Chapman's volume includes a "Coronet" of ten sonnets dedicated to "his Mistresse Phi- | losophie" (tp). The year 1595 saw Smith's last literary publication, Gervase Markham's *The Most Honorable Tragedy of Sir R. Grinville*. Together, these literary publications constitute eight of Smith's thirteen titles, and fifteen of his twenty-three editions.

Smith published his first non-literary titles in 1592: *The Masque of the League and the Spaniard Discovered*; the first print edition of Lancelot Andrewes's sermons *The Wonderful Combat (for God's Glory and Man's Salvation) between Christ and Satan*; and Anthony Munday's translation of Guillaume Telin's *Archaioplutos*, subtitled *The Riches of Elder Ages*. A year later, in 1593, he would bring out the first of his four quarto editions of Gervase Markham's popular *A Discourse of Horsemanship*.[20] Smith's last title proved to be an English edition of Luis de Granada's print phenomenon *Of Prayer and Meditation*. He jointly published this title with the bookseller Thomas Gosson.

In his three decades of publishing, Smith appears to have worked closely with a small set of trade printers, possibly establishing a mutually beneficial economic arrangement with each. Between 1567 and 1577, he took his copy exclusively to the printing house of Bynneman at the sign of the Mermaid. Freed in 1566, Bynneman quickly built one of London's busiest printing operations. At his death in 1583, he owned three printing presses and had an estate valued at close to 800£.[21] He also rented bookselling shops in St Paul's Churchyard from Smith and other stationers. After his ten-year hiatus from publishing, Smith initially seems to have preferred the printing house of Abel Jeffes. Jeffes had apprenticed with Bynneman in the 1570s, and it was during this time that he and Smith likely became acquainted. In 1587, Jeffes printed three editions for Smith, and he also may have handled two of these editions' wholesaling.[22] In his final five years of publishing, Smith yet again contracts almost exclusively with one printing house, this time that of Charlewood and his successor Roberts.[23] As he did with Bynneman and Jeffes, Smith appears to have negotiated particular arrangements with Charlewood and Roberts, these stationers both printing and entering a number of his publications.[24]

Throughout these titles, Smith fashioned a pervasive presence as their publisher, frequently underscoring his own agency as compiler and as literary authority. On as many as five occasions, he penned dedicatory pieces for his texts, to court-connected patrons like Richard Stonley, Henry Compton, and Dorothy Edmonds.[25] In these, he speaks in part as convention dictates, wishing his patrons "long health and happines" (Andrewes 1592, sig. ∴3ʳ) and promising "doctrine both pleasant and profitable" (Aesop 1577, sig. ¶2ᵛ). On as many as six occasions, Smith addresses his readers in either short poems or short epistles.[26] Three times, he waxes poetic either as or in conversation with "the Booke." In his translation of Aesop, he both addresses his book in a two-stanza poem entitled "*The bookes passport*" and imagines a conversation between him and Henryson's translation of Aesop in a nineteen-stanza poem "The argument between Esope and the Translatour." In his Gascoigne and Constable collections, Smith also contributed commendatory poems. Of "Gascoignes Posies" in his second edition of Gascoignes's works, Smith writes, "The pleasant plot wherein these Posies grew, / May represent *Parnassus* springs indeede. / Where *Pallas* with hir wise and learned crew, / Did plant great store, and sow much cunning seede" (sig. ¶¶¶3ᵛ). On a following page (sig. ¶¶¶¶3ᵛ), Smith matches this sonnet with another commendatory poem, this time favourably comparing Gascoigne to Chaucer, Gower, Surrey, Wyatt, and George Boleyn. Two decades later in 1594, Smith prefaces his second revised edition of Constable's sonnets with yet another sonnet of his own, "VNTO HER MAIEsties sacred honorable Maydes."

Smith's presence was not just conjured through his ample paratextual material, but it was also reinforced visually by his personalized printer's emblem. Framed by the Latin phrase "Tempore Patet Occulta Veritas" ("Time reveals hidden truth"), the emblem features a winged figure of Time with the body of a satyr, scythe in hand, leading a naked female Truth from a cave. It also contains Smith's initials "R.S." This emblem first appears on the title page of Smith's third edition of *Il filocolo* in 1575. Thereafter, it is inked on a number of Smith's title pages and in some instances on pages within the texts.[27] In 1592, Smith seems to have gone to the trouble of commissioning another version of the emblem, this time with a more finely detailed image and with his initials at the bottom of the frame instead of next to the figure of time (see figure 7).[28]

Frequently in his ventures as a publisher, Smith is forthcoming about his acquiring copy from non-authorial sources. Echoing his emblem, these projects are oft characterized by him as revelations of hidden truth. In his dedicatory poem prefacing *Pelops and Hippodamia*, he compares his 1587 financing of the text to "*Pharaos* daughter['s]" finding and raising of Moses: "*AS Moyses once by law then made / Was taught to swimme*

Figure 7 Richard Smith's redesigned printer's emblem, from *Of prayer and meditation* (1596). By permission of the Houghton Library at Harvard University.

and not to wade/Ariued (by God) at Princes place, /Whom Pharaos *daughter tooke to grace. ... / So I by channce thys Pamphlet here/ Dyd saue sometime from water cleere, /And tooke it vp and brought to light, ..."* (1587, sig. A2ʳ). Five years later, Smith is similarly enthusiatic in his prefatory epistles to the first two editions of Constable's *Diana*. His 1592 prefatory epistle describes Constable's sonnets as "Orphans" who "left desolate ... seeke entertainment" (sig. A4ʳ) from Smith's "*Gentlemen Readers*." Two years later, Smith waxes even more poetic, characterizing his revised edition in epic terms. "OBscur'd wonders (gentlemen)," he writes, "visited me in *Turnus* armor, and I in regard of *Aeneas* honour, haue vnclouded them vnto the worlde" (sig. A2ʳ).[29]

Smith's penchant for publishing orphan texts seems to have led to two significant run-ins with stationer authorities. In 1575, his revised edition of *A Hundreth Sundry Flowers, The Posies of George Gascoigne*, was published with new preliminaries by the author. In a letter "To the reuerende Diuines," Gascoigne alludes to what apparently was the negative reception of this first edition: "It is verie neare tvvo yeares past, since (I beeing in Hollande …) the most parte of these Posies vvere imprinted, and novv at my returne, I find that some of them haue not onely bene offensiue for sundrie vvanton speeches and lasciuious phrases, but further I heare that the same haue beene doubtfully construed, and (therefore) scandalous" (sig. ¶2ʳ). Many have taken Gascoigne's letter to mean that *A Hundreth Sundry Flowers* had been banned by the queen's commissioners for its sexual content.[30] Noting an absence of documents confirming such a ban, however, others have argued that Gascoigne's letter was either an effort to assuage potential offence at his second edition or even a ruse to draw attention away from its potentially libelous material.[31] Whatever the case, *The Posies* was itself recalled in August 1576, when the Stationers' Company Court recorded that "half a hundred of Gascoignes poesies" were "receyued into the hall of R Smithe" (Greg and Boswell, 87). A decade and a half later in 1592, Smith again found himself embroiled in controversy, this time for his publication of a sermon collection without the author's direct approval. As he is in his similar projects, Smith is open about his publishing of *The Wonderful Combat between Christ and Satan* without Andrewes's involvement. In his epistle to the Christian Reader (positioned opposite his printer's emblem), Smith explains that the sermons were "*sent vnto mee by a Gentleman (a friend of mine) … with desire to haue them published to the world. … [A]s the Author to me is not certainly knowen, so am I driuen to let them passe without name: desiring you to suspend your iudgements whose they are*" (sig. ∴4ʳ). In late November, the Stationers' Register bears witness to a flurry of activity surrounding Smith's publication (Arber, 1.561). Together, these four entries suggest that Smith's edition was confiscated at the Archbishop of Canterbury's bidding on behalf of Andrewes.[32]

Stationer troubles notwithstanding, Smith would continue to publish new titles and further editions until 1597. What direction his career takes at this point, though, is again unclear. On 6 November 1598 the Stationers' Register logs the transfer of nine of Smith's rights to copy to the newly freed bookseller William Wood (Arber, 3.131). According to Thomas, this transaction along with a gift of 20 shillings to a "Wydowe Smyth" on the same date by the Stationers' Court suggests the recent demise of Smith (1948, 190–2).[33] This hypothesis, however, is called into question by one further entry in the court records that Thomas does not cite. In 1611, the court "ordered with mʳ Whites consente, that duringe mʳ Smithes life he shall gyue to mʳᵉˢ. Gosson vpon eu'y impression of Granadas meditaconns, xxvᵗⁱᵉ. of those booke And also that he shall presently gyue her xxv^{tie}. booke of that ympression thereof w^{che} he hath now lately printed" (Jackson 1957, 49). Gosson retained a partial right to *Of Prayer and Meditation* when he agreed to work with Smith to bring out a new edition in 1596.[34] Whatever the still-operational terms of their agreement may have been in 1611, this entry might establish that Smith was alive long after 1598.

What might explain Smith's transferring his rights to copy if he were still living in 1598? His decision might have had something to do with the stationers' offensive against publication by men outside of the company in the second half of the 1590s (Johnson 1988, 9–17). This crackdown culminated in January 1598 with a rule passed by the Stationers' Court that forbade "procuringe of Copies and Booke to be entred and allowed vnto [stationers] and then prynting the same for suche persons as be not of this Companye" (Greg and Boswell 1930, 59). This in turn was followed by a number of significant Draper Company capitulations to the Stationers' Company that same year (Johnson 1988, 9–11). Collaborating with Charlewood and then Roberts, Smith had frequently resorted to such "procuringe" practices between 1592 and 1597. With the clear implications of the 1598 rule before him, Smith may have decided to cut his losses by selling many of his rights to copy while he still had the option to do so. Whether Smith continued to sell books from his bookselling "shoppe, at the West ende of Paules" after 1598 is unknown. Wood's own first bookselling shop, though, is advertised "at the West ende of Paules" in his imprints between 1598 and 1601, possibly indicating that he took over Smith's shop at the same time that he acquired Smith's rights to copy. Whichever hypothesis is to be believed, definitive records documenting Smith's death – either in 1598 or after 1611 – have yet to be discovered.

A Hundreth Sundry Flowers (1573)

Of his earliest publication projects, *A Hundreth Sundry Flowers* would prove particularly indicative of Smith's late-sixteenth-century cultural endeavours. Published in 1573, the volume stands out as both the first print edition of Gascoigne's writings and as a provocative window onto the complicated intersection between manuscript and print culture in the Elizabethan era.[35] It at the same time bears witness to vocational practices that were very much the terrain of the bookselling trade in the 1550s and 1560s, specifically to customs of collaboration and to modes of commodity consumption as they were daily rehearsed by Smith and his customers in the bustling bookstalls of London.

A Hundreth Sundry Flowers is a profoundly multifarious, unstable text, or as Matthew Zarnowiecki has recently observed, "among the most miscellaneous of early miscellanies printed in England" (2014, 47). Not only does it include work in a variety of different genres and conclude unfinished, ending mid-stanza in the "*The reporters conclusion vnfinished*," but its "The Printer to the Reader" appears to have been mistakenly placed before *Supposes* and *Jocasta* rather than immediately before *The Adventures Passed by Master F.J.*[36] While the volume's title page advertises different work from a number of different authors, the following "contents of this Booke" outlines a collection dominated by the work of Gascoigne. Simultaneously presenting itself as multivocal, collaborative, anonymous, and penned by "Gascoigne," the collection offers as well a series of textual authorities, from "G.T." (the identified compiler of the source manuscript) to "H.W." (the manuscript's seller) to "A.B." (the publisher as identified by G.T.) to "the Printer" (the publisher as identified in "The Printer to the Reader"). And if that were not dizzying enough, it at various points invites its readers to, as Wall puts it, "assemble and reassemble" the contents according to their pleasure (1993, 244).

This chaos, though, would quickly be tamed. Two years later, a revised edition of the collection was published, this time with the title *The Posies of George Gascoigne Esquire* and an assuring blurb on the title page that the whole was "*Corrected, perfected,* | and augmented by the | Authour." In this 1575 version, the poems that were previously attributed to "sundrie Gentlemen" are ascribed to Gascoigne. Excised are the misplaced printer's epistle, the letters of H.W. and G.T. prefacing *The Adventures Passed by Master F.J.*, and "The Reporter's Conclusion Vnfinished." In their stead is a rationalized tripartite scheme of organization ("*Floures, Hearbes, and Weedes*" [sig. ¶¶4ʳ]), a series of commendatory poems in praise of the author, and three dedicatory epistles by Gascoigne.[37] As almost every commentator has concurred, all of these changes together reveal that the multivocality and instability of *A Hundreth Sundry Flowers* was initially a ruse by Gascoigne, one possibly inspired by print's stigma and potential accusations about the volume's slander and/or vulgarity.

At least some of the volume's initial variability, though, can be linked with Smith. As the volume's publisher and wholesaler, Smith acquired and authorized the collection; licensed it with the Stationers' Company; selected and negotiated with Bynneman's printing house; oversaw its title-page marketing strategies; and answered queries about its content from the Elizabethan authorities. Smith's name appears prominently in the collection's two imprints (tp, sig. X4ᵛ) and in its colophon (sig. Ii3ʳ), and in the collection's later versions, he even contributes as many as two commendatory poems.[38] He was also as the collection's risk-assuming sponsor one of its most motivated readers. Seemingly arbitrary in its constitution and requiring a steep investment to cover its fifty-three sheets per copy, Gascoigne's miscellany was anything but a guaranteed moneymaker. Smith would have had every reason to be fully engaged with all aspects of the title.

Even so, Smith's central role in the publication of *A Hundreth Sundry Flowers* has been routinely misrepresented. In the rare instances when the book trade has been acknowledged at all in the volume's transmission, every commentator has fixated upon Bynneman – the collection's trade printer – as the volume's chief architect besides Gascoigne.[39] Mostly ignored, at times misunderstood, Smith has been called a "stationer" (Marotti 1991, 10); has been entirely disassociated from the title page's preliminaries (Anderson 2003; Staub 2011; Pigman 2000; and Zarnowiecki 2014), and even has been replaced with Gascoigne as the volume's publisher (McCoy, 33). But if Smith's work with *A Hundreth Sundry Flowers* has been overlooked by Gascoigne's editors and critics, it was soundly buried by Adrian Weiss's 1992 bibliographic article on the collection, "Printing, Printer's Copy, and the Text(s) of Gascoigne's 'A Hundreth Sundrie Flowres.'" For close to two decades, this complex article has been taken to prove once and for all that Gascoigne was chiefly responsible both for *A Hundreth Sundry Flowers*'s shape and for its prefatory epistle "The Printer to the Reader."[40] Weiss's article is important because it establishes that Bynneman farmed out portions of *A Hundreth Sundry Flowers* to the printing house of Henry Middleton; that the project was frequently delayed, taking over eight months to complete; and that print copy was delivered "in at least six different manuscript segments" to Bynneman (1992, 96). Throughout, Weiss makes it clear that his ultimate purpose is to use bibliographic methods in order to uncover Gascoigne's "intentions" for the collection. This single-mindedness has much to do with some of Weiss's more significant conclusions.

Towards the end of his article, Weiss argues that delivery delays necessarily point to the fact that Gascoigne was still in the process of composing sections of the collection – particularly "The Printer to the Reader" and *The Adventures Passed by Master F.J.* – when it was being printed by Bynneman and Middleton. As the printer's epistle has an "undeniable" connection to the prose narrative, Bynneman's late separation of them can only mean that he was not the "Printer" in "The Printer to the Reader." And this, proclaims Weiss, establishes that the epistle was written by Gascoigne and no one else. "The 'printer,'" writes Weiss, "obviously is a fictional character with a role in the surreptitious publication subterfuge. Equally obvious is the fact that Bynneman did not write the letter. As printer, he definitely was responsible for organizing and overseeing the printing of the sequence of texts. ... Bynneman did not write the letter, but simply printed it in its proper location as called for by its title: at the beginning of the book despite its undeniable connection to [*The Adventures Passed by Master F.J.*]" (1992, 98–9).[41] Weiss may very well be right that Bynneman was responsible for separating "The Printer to the Reader" from *The Adventures Passed by Master F.J.*, but he is mistaken that this necessarily makes Gascoigne its author. Another candidate – the more likely candidate – is Smith, this because, as was a common practice in most Elizabethan books, the epistle's "Printer" most probably translated to "Publisher" (Blayney 1997, 391).[42] What Weiss, like many other commentators and editors before him, never entertains because he is so focused on Gascoigne is that in 1573 it was Smith – not Bynneman, who was commissioned as the volume's trade printer, not Gascoigne who was in the Low Countries between spring 1573 and autumn 1574 (Pigman 2000, lvii) – that was the collection's most fully present stakeholder at the end of 1573 and as such was in all probability responsible for *A Hundreth Sundry Flowers*'s title page and printer's epistle.[43]

Weiss's failure to recognize Smith's essential role in bringing *A Hundreth Sundry Flowers* to press is in some ways understandable. Other than Sidney Thomas's 1948 article "Richard Smith: 'Foreign to the Company,'" an early article that deals in the main with Smith as a test case of Stationers' Register entries, no accounts have been given of the draper bookseller. Consequently, *A Hundreth Sundry Flowers*'s many commentators could not have readily known about Smith's penchants for publishing poetry collections, for writing his own prefatory material, for penning his own verse, for marking texts with his own brand, and for acquiring copy from non-authorial sources. These vocational tendencies, though, are all relevant in appreciating the full contour of influences that shaped the volume.

Working from Gascoigne's manuscript, it was very likely Smith who promoted *A Hundreth Sundry Flowers* as a multivocal miscellany, and his particular approach appears to have been the product of many influences, some apparently encountered in the draper's own engagement with Gascoigne's slippery paratextual material, some experienced in his work as a bookseller. Particularly evident in its prefatory material and title is the collection's debt to manuscript miscellanies of the period. These books were produced mainly by the elite, and they were made up of transcriptions of what were often anonymous and occasional works that were circulating in a rarified cultural milieu.[44] Halfway into the collection and prefacing *The Adventures Passed by Master F.J.*, Gascoigne's "H.VV. to the Reader" represents *A Hundreth Sundry Flowers* as originally one of these miscellanies.[45] "In August last passed," writes H.W. at the letter's opening, "my familiar friend Master *G.T.* bestowed vpon me the reading of a written Booke, wherin he had collected diuers discourses & verses, inuented vppon sundrie occasions, by sundrie gentlemen (in mine opinion) right commendable for their capacitie" (sig. A1r). Disordered and "diuers," H.W.'s source is defined by its "sundrie[ness]," a quality which is embodied in the title that H.W confers upon it in this same letter. H.W.'s title *A Hundreth Sundry Flowers* gestures towards the restricted elite milieu of textual gathering that produced it. Led by Gascoigne's fictitious prefatory material, Smith alludes to this milieu again and again, both in his amplification of the title's figurative dimension in his many references to the collections' "sauours" and "smellyng noses" (tp), but also in underscoring his readers' power to make of his collection what they will.[46] "The well minded man," writes Smith in the "Printer to the Reader," "may reape some commoditie out of the most friuolous vvorks that are vvritten" (sig. A2v).

A Hundreth Sundry Flowers also bears clear traces of the early printed poetry miscellany. Working as an apprentice in Wight's St Paul's Churchyard bookshop at the sign of the Rose, Smith would have encountered Richard Tottel's groundbreaking verse collection *Songs and Sonnets* as it burst onto the print market in five editions published between 1557 and 1559.[47] *Songs and Sonnets* at first seems to organize itself around the aristocratic celebrity of Henry Howard, Earl of Surrey in qualifying its poetic offerings on the title page as "written by the right honorable Lorde | Henry Haward late Earle of Sur- | rey, and other." What quickly becomes apparent in reading the volume, though, is that "the text ... offers no readily comprehensible generic, authorial, or structural order" (Wall 1993, 24). Modelled itself upon the kinds of manuscript poetic miscellanies alluded to in H.W.'s letter, *Songs and Sonnets* is, in other words, organized less around Surrey than along the lines of what it appropriately describes as "other." The publisher Tottel, of course, is also in this mix. His austere "*Apud Ricardum Tottel*" graces its 1557 imprint, and in his second-leaf prefatory address "To the reder," he stakes out the verse in terms of its learnedness; stateliness; and gentle, restricted origin. He also famously brands his project with nationalism. "That to haue wel written in verse," writes Tottel, "yea and in small parcelles, deserueth great praise, the woorkers of diuers Latines, Italians, & other, doe proue sufficiently. That our tong is able in that kinde to do as praise worthelye as the rest, the honorable stile of the noble earle of Surrey, and the weightinesse of the depe witted sir Thomas Wiat the elders verse, with seueral graces in sondry good Englishe writers, do show abundantly" (1557, sig. A1ᵛ).

If Smith somehow failed to encounter Tottel's protean collection in the 1550s, he certainly had become familiar with it by the early 1570s when he was bringing *A Hundreth Sundry Flowers* to print. This is most clearly evident in the dedicatory poem that Smith contributes to the 1575 revised edition of *A Hundreth Sundry Flowers*. There, in the tetrameter couplets of "The Printer in commendation of Gascoigne and his workes," Smith associates Gascoigne with three of the main poets in Tottel's collection: "Sweete *Surrey*, suckt *Parnassus* springs, / And *Wiat* wrote of wondrous things: / Olde *Rockfort* clambe the stately Throne, / VVhich *Muses* holde, in *Hellicone*. / Then thither let good *Gascoigne* go, / For sure his verse, deserueth so" (sig. ¶¶¶¶iiiᵛ).[48] *A Hundreth Sundry Flowers*'s title-page blurb also echoes Tottel's prefatory epistle, dividing the collection along lines of that which is foreign and "fyne," and that which is English and the product of "fruitefull[ness]": the collection is "*Gathered partely (by transla | tion) in the fyne outlandish Gardins | of Euripides, Ouid, Petrarke, Ariosto, | and others: and partly by inuention, | out of our owne fruitefull Or- | chardes in Englande.*" This nationalist distinction builds upon Tottel while it at the same time provides yet another organizational rubric for the volume.

Smith's investment in a multivocal, collaborative text like *A Hundreth Sundry Flowers*, however, can be situated not simply within the contemporary cultural contexts of the manuscript and printed poetic miscellany. It at the same time can be understood as the product of his own early occupational practices. As a draper bookseller, Smith lived and worked within dual vocational realities, labouring under the hierarchy, rules, and regulations of the long-established Drapers' guild even as he would have frequently reckoned with emergent stationer practices like book wholesaling, marketing, and pricing. From the beginning, Smith's publishing habits were similarly variegated, consistently stamped with the influence of other interested parties. Six years before financing *A Hundreth Sundry Flowers*, Smith shared the risk of bringing Boccaccio's *Il filocolo* to press with two other stationers. Smith entered the translation himself in the Stationers' Register in 1566/7, but the edition's imprint lists him and Nicholas England as the text's publishers. This imprint also advertises Bynneman as printer and his bookshop "in Pater | Noster Rowe, at the signe of the Marmayd" as the wholesale outlet for the volume. Bynneman's investment in the project is underscored on the volume's title page that is conspicuously tattooed with his mermaid printer's emblem.[49] Smith, in other words, was no stranger to differing practices and perspectives, and as such *A Hundreth Sundry Flowers*'s "flexibility and provisionality" (Wall 1993, 245) should come as no surprise.

Smith's imprints tell us that in 1573 he had been operating his own bookshop in St Paul's Churchyard for at least two years, this the realization of his apprenticing in Wright's bookshop in the 1550s.[50] Like the general requirements of his hybrid vocation, the day-to-day demands of running a viable bookshop also seem to have influenced Smith's presentation of *A Hundreth Sundry Flowers*. The most immediate resonance can be found in the occupational connotations of the collection's full title: "*A Hundreth sun | drie Flowres bounde | vp in one small Poesie*" (my emphasis). By the second half of the sixteenth century, bookbinding had mostly become a separate vocation in the early-modern book trade; book buyers bought their various leaves from a bookseller and then were free to bind together whatever title(s) they might choose with a bookbinder. Some bookbinders operated out of their own shops while binders like John Flasket worked in conjunction with a bookseller.[51] Indeed, as Alexandra Gillespie, Seth Lerer, and Jeffrey Todd Knight have shown, sixteenth-century readers even routinely "fractured and recombined works into *Sammelbände* – volumes containing multiple printed texts arranged to suit individual taste."[52] Printed titles, in other words, were one thing. Bound books were quite another. Smith's subtitle smacks of these practices, imagining the full collection as an individually fashioned, bound book.

Smith reinforces this theme towards the end of "The Printer to the Reader." There, he concludes with an extended description of the collection's contents. Imaginatively rendered as a particular "flowre," each work is not simply described as having its own perceptible "sauour"; each is also figured as existing within a marketplace where no buyer is "constreined to smell of the floures therein conteined all at once, neither yet to take them vp in such order as they are sorted" (sig. A2^v). Like any shop full of commodities, in Smith's collection "you may take any one flowre by itselfe, and if that smell not so pleasantly as you wold wish, ... you may find some other which may supplie the defects thereof" (sig. A2^v). Its ability to give its readers the freedom to choose is a significant part of what is supposed to make *A Hundreth Sundry Flowers* "bothe pleasaunt and profitable" (tp). The collection is, in Smith's formulation, a browser's paradise.

Browsing, it should be said, was an essential part of the bustling sixteenth-century bookselling trade in St Paul's Churchyard and other areas of London.[53] Buyers would have begun their inspections of a bookseller's wares outside the shop, glancing over the title pages of the most recent offerings displayed on the "stall-board." More stock and more room to browse could be found inside (Blayney 1997, 413). To browse, in other words, a buyer physically interacted with his (or her) spatial environs, moving through the streets of London, from bookseller's stall to bookseller's stall, into and around the dimly lit room of a bookseller's stored volumes, handling books as he (or she) went along.[54] Smith's spatial, material sense of reading as browsing emerges towards the end of his printer's epistle. There, after listing the many different "floures" that can be had in his bookshop/book – "Tragedie translated out of Euripides," "comedie translated out of Ariosto," "report in verse, made by Dan Bartholmevv of Bathe" – he appeals to "he that vvould see any particuler pang of loue liuely displayed," promising that "[he] may here approue euery Pamphlet by the title, and so remaine contented" (sigs. A2^v–A3^r). In the 1570s, a print "pamphlet" referred exclusively to a material object, a "short printed work[s] of several pages fastened together without a hard cover" (*OED*). Smith's invitation, then, to "approue," or "to put to the test of experience" (*OED*), "euery Pamphlet by the title" was in essence a request born of the bookshop where buyers could actually pick up and leaf through that which they encountered in a bookseller's shop. This sense of *A Hundreth Sundry Flowers* as affording the conditions of space and market comes through in the prefatory epistle's conclusion, where Smith assures his readers that "the worke is so vniuersall, as either in one place or other, any mans mind may therevvith be satisfied" (sig. A3ʳ).

Smith's representation of reading as book browsing in *A Hundreth Sundry Flowers* was not entirely new for the draper. Six years earlier, Smith may have contributed a short prefatory poem "The Booke to the Reader" to his Boccaccio publication that fashions reading in much the same way.[55] Speaking in the guise of "The Booke," the poem imagines readers not curled up with the publication before their fireplaces at home but as potential consumers, browsing their way through the stalls of a bookshop. "*Loke ere thou leape,*" warns the Booke at its poem's beginning, "*dome not by viewe of face/Least hast make wast, in missedoming the case:/For I teach not to Loue, ne yet his lore,/Ne with what salue is cured such a sore*" (sig. A3ʳ). The volume's title that browsers would have first seen in large letters at the top of the book's "*face*," in other words, was not to be taken as code for an Italian discourse on love (in the vein, possibly, of Hoby's 1561 translation of Castiglione). Rather, *A Pleasant Disport* was to be understood as offering various tales of love which Smith's browsing readers were free to "*Compare*" and make "*choise*" of: "*The choise of best, be it of good or lewde,/Compare them so, as domed is the dout,/Thereof, and aye the truth well sifted out.*" Like he does in *A Hundreth Sundry Flowers*'s "The Printer to the Reader," Smith imagines reading as a process of commodity selection, readers as interested consumers.

This theme returns again in a short prefatory poem "To the Reader" that appears on the first leaf of Wilfred Holme's *The Fall and Evil Success of Rebellion*. This title's only edition was published and printed by Bynneman in 1572, but it lists Smith's shop "at the Northwest doore of Paules Churche" as its wholesale location. Smith's initials "R.S." appear at the bottom of the work's prefatory poem "To the Reader," indicating an even further manifestation of his close working relation with Bynneman. Written in five ballad stanzas, Smith's poem offers a relatively straightforward overview of the title in which "haultie Holme in loftie stile/hath paint their [rebels'] doings trim": At its start, however, Smith addresses the reader with language smacking of a bookseller standing outside his shop hawking his wares, asking, "What lookst thou for in this discourse,/(Good Reader) let me know …" Smith answers his own question in the stanza's final lines with "Of loyall Subiectes that doe liue?/No, of Rebels ouerthrow." Here again, reading is represented as a form of browsing, browsing with the assistance of a bookseller.

A Hundreth Sundry Flowers then is most fully understood as a collaborative effort, Gascoigne providing copy, Smith in turn contributing its prefacing "The Printer to the Reader" and possibly the volume's preliminary blurbs on the title page. Recognizing Smith's contributions to the volume does little to dispute what many editors and critics have identified as Gascoigne's own self-conscious engagement with textual transmission and modes of reading in the volume, but it does remind us that Elizabethan authors were in most cases subject to the norms and practices of the book trade and not the other way around. It also demonstrates Smith's own active investment in and contribution to this most miscellaneous of texts.

The Fabulous Tales of Aesop (1577)

Even as he was shepherding *A Hundreth Sundry Flowers* into print in 1573, Smith may have been thinking about Aesop.[56] Less than a year later, we find him fully committed to another large project, this time to "English[ing]" Robert Henryson's *Morall fabillis*.[57] Written in Middle Scottish sometime in the second half of the fifteenth century but first printed in two separate Edinburgh editions in 1570 and in 1571, Henryson's Aesop collection consists of thirteen fables, each with an accompanying moral. With his volume, Henryson developed Aesop's fables in a number of significant ways – lengthening its narratives, expanding and complicating its *moralitates*, and developing its workings as part of a larger collection structure.[58] Smith ultimately translated and published his own octavo English version of the 1571 edition in 1577, retitling it *The Fabulous Tales of Aesop the Phrygian*.[59] This "Englished" (tp) version of Henryson constituted one of only three print translations of Aesop available in England in the sixteenth century; it also represented the first English edition in verse.[60]

Smith's energetic investment in *The Fabulous Tales of Aesop* is apparent not simply in his extensive albeit straightforward work as translator; it is underscored too by his title-page printer's emblem, by his two prefatory poems *"The bookes passport"* and "The argument betweene Esope and the Translatour," by his dedicatory epistle to "Master Richard Stonley," by his expanded table of contents, and by his three-stanza epilogue.[61] Even as they all can readily be ascribed to him, though, these paratextual additions serve more to destabilize rather than unify the volume. Like *A Hundreth Sundry Flowers*, *The Fabulous Tales of Aesop* is framed by an account of artistic production that is as collaborative as it is profoundly unstable, one emerging from and geared towards the variable conditions of St Paul's book stalls.[62]

Straight away, *The Fabulous Tales of Aesop* highlights what will be its triumvirate of voices in its full title "The Fabulous tales of | Esope the Phrygian, Compiled | moste eloquently in Scottishe | Metre by Master Robert | Henrison, & now lately | Englished." The source of its "tales," the "first inuenter" in its dedicatory epistle, and cross-dressed "Scottish guise" in its "argument," Aesop is finally given top billing in the volume's epilogue, where Smith instructs "Behold ye men) Esope that noble clerke. ... But marke his Sawes, and ye finde him no noddy, / But perfect aye, as perfect loe may be, / Who lendes you light good virtuous wayes to see./Then loue this worke, and ... reade it at your will, / I but eclipse his tales of so great skill" (sig. H2ʳ). Henryson's own writerly authority is invoked in the volume's dedicatory epistle – there described as "Authour" (sig. ¶2ʳ) – and in the "argument" – there lauded as "This Scottish Orpheus" (sig. ¶4ᵛ). While veiled in the title page's passive "now lately | Englished," Smith's discerning role in selecting the volume and translating it is most clearly promoted in the dedicatory epistle. In this short appeal to Stonley, the draper assures his potential patron that "I thinke, in that language wherein it was written, [it is] verie eloquent and full of great inuention" and that "in [his] conceite there is learning for all sorts of people worthy the memorie" (sigs. ¶2ʳ⁻ᵛ). Later, in the "argument" Smith asks us to imagine that while the "Scottish Orpheus" "fell a sleepe, and or he wooke, /in hand a while his harpe I tooke" (sig. ¶4ᵛ).

In the abstract, Aesop, Henryson, and Smith stand separated in their roles as the fables' Phrygian originator, Scottish adaptor, and Elizabethan translator respectively. But in practice within *The Fabulous Tales of Aesop*'s paratextual material, these roles frequently merge or morph into one another.[63] This is most immediately apparent in "The booke's passport," a two-stanza poem that follows the title page. The prefatory piece is essentially a complaint. "THat man neare wrote," it begins, "whose wryte pleasd all mens mynd, / Nor I as nowe thinke no such place to find:/ For fyndfault he him selfe that no good can, / By slanderous tounge, doth hinder many a man, / Which els would wryte to many a ones content:/ (But Bayard I) cares not for being shent" (sig. ¶1ᵛ). Unlike most of Smith's other prefatory material, "The booke's passport" does not identify its speaker in its title or with an adjoining tag (e.g., "the translators Epilogue" [sig. ¶4ᵛ]); instead "Bayard I" could refer to Henryson, Smith, or Aesop, each of them a potential "he" that "would wryte to many a ones content." A quick look at his 1571 source text confirms that Smith must have been the author of this poem, but making his authorship clear was not a priority for the publisher.

This same fluidity emerges in the "argument." For most of this verse dialogue, Smith represents himself as having a conversation with an "Esope" who is simply "Apparelled … after the Scottish guise" (sig. ¶3ʳ). When the conversation comes to a close, Smith bids his interlocutor adieu by reinvoking Aesop's Turkish origins: "Farewel good Phrygian Poet now, / I may no more soiourne" (sig. ¶4ʳ). Immediately thereafter, however, Smith ends with a short address to his reader that equates Henryson with Orpheus, identifying the Scottish poet as the real source of the collection's power: "This Scottish Orpheus I meane, / that Esops tales hath made to gree/ In Rethoricke both trim and cleane, / that all my wittes bereft hath hee" (sig. ¶4ᵛ). Here, Aesop's clothes do eventually become the man.

Smith's fluid sense of authorship emerges perhaps most clearly in his dedicatory epistle. There, he begins by outlining a system of textual legitimacy that centres around Henryson as its "Authour," one that is only "obscured" by Smith as translator. "There came vnto my hande," explains Smith, "a Scottishe Pamphlet …, a worke, sir as I thinke, … verie eloquent and full of great inuention. And no doubt you shall finde some smatch thereof, although very rudely I have obscured the Authour, and … turned it into Englishe" (sig. ¶2ʳ). Quickly, however, Henryson's authorial responsibility is matched by Aesop's when Smith attempts to account for his being the only "English[ing]" of the pamphlet to yet appear in St Paul's by imagining that "most men" may have been "thinking scorne of the Authour or first inuenter" (sig. ¶2ʳ). Neither Henryson ("the Authour") nor Aesop ("first inuenter"), however, is offered as a textual guarantor at the epistle's end. Instead, Smith makes it clear that it is he that must answer to the text's patron and to its detractors. "Hoping as oft you looke on this booke," entreats Smith, "you will thinke on me, [and that you will] accept this poore Persian water or Iewes mite, which in so doing I care not for all the scoffers and taunters, which will do nought themselues nor suffer others to do that may pleasure or profit the posteritie" (sig. ¶2ᵛ).

This collaborative model of authorship in *The Fabulous Tales of Aesop*'s paratextual material is persistently framed within the conditions of the sixteenth-century print market, one where the buyer not

120 Elizabethan Publishing

only was at liberty to range among commodities laid out in the various stalls but where, as we have seen, he was also free to arrange, rearrange, and bind texts according to his desire. More than any of Smith's prefatory pieces in the volume, the "argument" invokes this market context. It begins with Smith relating his first encounter with Henryson as personified text. He explains,

> LAte passing thorowe Paules Churchyarde,
>   aside I cast mine eye,
> And ere I wist, to me appearde
>   Sir Esope by and by.
> Apparelled both braue and fine,
>   after the Scottish guise,
> I stood then still with ardent eyne,
>   I viewde him twise or thrise.
> Behold quoth he, now am I here,
>   And faine would meete some one,
> To speake English that would me leare.   (sig. ¶3ʳ)[64]

Represented himself as roaming "Paules Churchyarde," Smith begins the poem with what we have seen for him was the familiar practice and motif of book browsing. Here he describes "cast[ing his] eye" among the various books until one draws him in to "view [it] twise or thrise." Henryson's Scottish translation may be described as "braue and fine," but it is the 1571 edition's conspicuous woodcut of Aesop that likely first drew his eye (see figure 8 below). From the perspective of a publisher and bookseller, this commissioned woodcut was a risky expense for what very easily could have turned out to be a one-edition title. Ultimately, weathering Smith's excuse that "At Helicon I neuer came, / the way I do not knowe," Sir Esope laments his own failure to appeal to English readers in what again are the distinct spatial terms of the booksellers' shops. "They do not care for Scottish bookes," he complains, "they list not looke that way: / But if they would but cast their lookes, / some time when they do play, / Somewhat to see perhaps they might, / That then would like them wel" (sigs. ¶3ᵛ–¶4ʳ). Unlike Smith in his "passing thorowe Paules Churchyarde" at the beginning of the poem, most London book buyers, complains Esope, do not "cast their looks" his way. Instead, trained to navigate booksellers' shops by specialties or sections, browsers avoid "Scottish bookes" all together; "they list not looke that way." Such buyer prejudice is,

Figure 8 The title page of Thomas Bassandyne's *The moral fabillis of Esope* (1571). By permission of the National Library of Scotland.

according to Smith in his dedicatory epistle, likely due to the fact that "most men haue that nation in derision for their hollowe hearts and vngratefull mindes" (sig. ¶2ʳ).

A leaf earlier, Smith draws a similar image of book browsing in "The booke's passport," imagining the practice in terms that are reminiscent of those in *A Hundreth Sundry Flowers*. This poem's opening-stanza complaint leads to consequent lines which begrudgingly direct the "booke" out into a dualistic world, filled with the "wyse," and with the "sadde" and "carping": "Goe therefore booke, to eche mans eye to vewe:/To wyse and sadde, and all the carping crewe./The wisest sort, will well accept my skill:/Sir Momus mates, takes all good things as ill" (sig. ¶1ᵛ). For Smith, though, the rejections of "Sir Momus mates" do not simply amount to what he earlier in the poem calls "slaunderous tounge[s]" against him and his "wryte" in the Elizabethan sphere of opinion; rather, these rejections are most immediately imagined to have real economic consequences for him as a bookseller. This becomes clear when at the end of this second stanza, he dismisses these browsing readers out of his shop: "And he that likes not this as I do say:/Here is the dore/and there furth right the way" (sig. ¶1ᵛ). In imagining his booke as being "to eche mans eye to vewe," then, Smith again conjures up readers as potential consumers, as buyers browsing through potential purchases, not purchasers safely at home "occupied" (as Smith's patron Richard Stonley frequently records in his own diaries) "at [their] book[es] in [their] Chamb[e]r[s]."[65] For Smith, in other words, readers are consumers, always capable of walking away from titles of which they do not approve.

This sense of reading as browsing may have had something to do with Smith's substantial additions to the *Morall fabillis*'s table of contents, "The Taillis contenit in this present Buke."[66] There, the 1571 edition of Henryson includes a table listing the thirteen different fables in what is Spartan language.[67] Other than describing each fable as a "Taill," entries are essentially limited to identifying main characters like "the Fox," "the Wolf," "the Mous," and "the Lyoun." Smith's table, "The Contentes of the Booke," is an entirely different matter. Along with "Englishing" Henryson's information, his entries provide more descriptive language along with more polemic. Whereas Henryson's first entry is "The Taill of the Cok, and the Jasp" (sig. A1ᵛ), Smith's is "The tale of the grossehead Chaunteclere the cocke, and the pretious stone: wherein is shewed the wanton liues of Lasciuious maydes, with the litle care we haue of the precious giftes of God" (sig. ∴1ʳ). Likewise, where Henryson has "The Taill of the Scheip, and the Doig" (sig. A1ᵛ), Smith has "The wofull tale of the plaintife dogge, against the poore sheepe before Justice Wolfe, notably shewing the abuses of such Courtes where money & might maketh the poore to begge" (sig. ∴1ʳ). Every one of Smith's entries offers melodrama and morality to prospective buyers, frontloading content for "twise or thrise" browsing in ways that Henryson's edition does not.

Smith's vociferous table entries, though, speak to more than bookseller marketing penchants. They also attest to the draper's collaborative sense of authorship, to his fluid sense of meaning making, and to his citizen, bourgeois buyers.[68] In effect, *The Fabulous Tales of Aesop* offers dual moralizing, that inscribed in Smith's prefacing table and that explicitly outlined by Henryson's Englished "Morall" or "Moralitie" at the end of each fable. In a few cases these bifurcated lessons match up relatively seamlessly. This is the case with the eighth fable, involving the swallow preacher. Smith concludes in his table entry that the fable shows "the office of a preacher and howe they ought to warne vs of Satan hys trappes, lest we be catched in his net" (sig. ∵1ᵛ). This closely echoes the crux of Henryson's "Moralitie" which in its sixth stanza tells us that "This Swallow which scaped is the snare, / the holy preacher well may signifie, / Exhorting folke to walke and ay beware, / From the nettes of our wicked enimie" (sig. E5ᵛ). Such harmony can be seen in the separate dictums of the sixth, ninth, tenth, and twelfth fables as well.

In the majority of cases, though, Smith's table entries sometimes overly simplify, sometimes contradict *The Fabulous Tales of Aesop*'s morals. Smith's above-mentioned first entry, for example, reads the fable as a clear warning about "the wanton liues of Lasciuious maydes," apparently taking the tale's second stanza as the semantic centre of the piece. There "damosels wanton and insolent" are said to be responsible for carelessly sweeping valuables out of their houses (sig. A2ʳ). Henryson's moral, though, makes no mention of such "Lascivious maydes" in its own five-stanza lesson. Instead, it chastises the cock for valuing corn which symbolizes riches more than the jasper which "Betokenith perfect prudence and cunning" (sig. A3ʳ). In effect, this moral takes aim at middling-sort greed. Smith deflects such blame in his own table-of-contents' entry, targeting instead middling-sort women within the domestic sphere. This prejudicial portrait emerges again in his second entry, where Smith recasts Henryson's diatribe against "wanton man, that vsest for to feede / Thy wombs and makes it a God to be" (sig. A8ʳ) in familiar terms. According to Smith, this second "tale of the plaine country mouse and daintie town mouse … display[s] our daintie citizens wiues, which can keepe them selues in no mediocritie" (sig. ∵1ʳ). Citizen misogyny, it seems, is better suited to attract his customers' "ardent eyne[s]."

Smith's table entries also avoid what Denton Fox has described as the frequent ambiguities of the Englished Henryson's morals, especially when proselytizing upon fables having to do with class and political relations. Thus, Smith presents the third fable of the cock and fox – which the "Moralitie" interprets as presenting *both* the vainglorious ambition of the cock and the flattery of the fox (sig. B4ᵛ) – as being in essence about "the craftie circumuentours of the simple men, and yet some time how they meete with their match" (sig. ˙.˙1ʳ). Lawful bourgeois ambition is similarly defended in Smith's eleventh table entry that introduces the fable of the disguised ram that saves his flock but takes his impersonation of his superiors too far. There, Smith glosses over the ram's heroism, instead characterizing him as being of "lusty bloud" and as "com[ing] vp of low degree by unlawfull meanes" (sig. ˙.˙1ᵛ). Henryson's moral, however, offers more ambiguity in presenting a tension between the ram's admirable "seruice" and low "bloud": "Right so in seruice other some exceedes, /And they haue wages, wealth and cherishing, /That they will be lightly Lordes in deedes, /And looke not to their bloud and offspryng" (sig. G2ᵛ). In the same vein, Smith interprets the seventh fable of the mouse and the lion as "shewing what reuerence we owe to the Princes person, yea though he be dead, and howe we ought to venture our liues to do them good" (sigs. ˙.˙1ʳ⁻ᵛ). Henryson's moral, though, offers a much more nuanced interpretation of the lion, pointing out that it signifies "any King with crowne, /Which should be captayne, guyde and gouernour, /Of his people that takes no labour, /To rule, and stere, the land, and iustice keepe, /Without lying still in lustes, slouth, and sleepe" (sig. D7ʳ). In this, bad kings are criticized even as kingship is upheld.

The collection's dual set of morals underscores Smith's predilection for different kinds of collaboration. Bearing no authorial ascription to distinguish them from the Henryson's Englished morals appearing at the end of every fable, the "Contentes of the Booke" helps expand – sources notwithstanding – what Smith describes in his dedicatory epistle as the volume's "learning for all sorts of people worthy the memorie" (sigs. ¶2ʳ⁻ᵛ). Together, table and morals deliver on the title's page's promise that "Euery tale [is] Moralized most aptly to this present time, worthy to be read." At the same time, Smith's prefacing, "Moralized" list also serves to break the collection up into thirteen unique, individually consumable objects. As a number of commentators have suggested, Henryson originally organized his fables as a unified structural and thematic whole, together demonstrating, for example, "the conflict between man's carnal and spiritual sides" (Fox 1962, 356) and "a progression of increasing frustration that finally reposes in despair" (Gopen 1987, 23). Whereas the 1571 edition's "The Taillis contenit in this present Buke" could ultimately be said to reinforce this unity in its homogenized listings of "the Fox" (in five titles) and "the Wolf" (in four titles), Smith's elaborate "Moralized" listings disperse more than they blend, allowing his browsing readers to collaborate in picking and choosing fables in isolation according to their own tastes, truly to "reade [the collection]," as he writes at the very end of his epilogue, "at [their] will" (sig. H2^r).

Diana (1592, 1594?)

A decade would pass before Smith would publish new works, but when he finally did in the late 1580s and 1590s, his attention did not stray far from "Sweete *Surrey* ... *Wiat* ... [and] *Rockfort*," from what he described in the revised edition of *A Hundreth Sundry Flowers* as "the stately Throne" (sig. ¶¶¶¶iii^v) of lyric poetry in the vernacular. In two titles, Smith again fashions flexible products. In these, browsability is favoured over consolidation, heterogeneity takes precedence over uniformity, and multivocality wins out over the textual authority of a single author.

In 1587, Smith brought out, with a new edition of Boccaccio and a reissue of Gascoigne's collected work, his first edition of Matthew Grove's *The Most Famous and Tragical History of Pelops and Hippodamia*, a nine-sheet pamphlet combining the ballad-metre narrative poem of the title with what Smith designates as "sundrie | pleasant deuises, Epigrams, | Songes, and Son- | nettes" (tp).[69] Making up more than half of the volume's leaves, these "sundrie" poems harken back to the printed poetic miscellanies of the 1570s, coupling the more than two dozen consecutive leaves of amatory lyrics between a "Louer," "Ladie," and "friend" with an equal amount of moral, proverbial, and satiric poems. Like Smith's previous publications, *Pelops and Hippodamia* is, in other words, yet another of his browser's paradises.

Grove's authorship of the whole is made clear on the title page with its "Written by Mathewe Groue," by the inclusion of Grove's "*Authors Epistle*" (sigs. A3^r–A4^r), and by the ending tag "FINIS. M.G." (sig. I8^r), this, even as Smith in his five-stanza dedicatory poem to Sir Henry Compton speaks vaguely of "*sau*[ing]" the pamphlet "*from water cleere*" (sig. A2^r), confessing, "*Th' aucthor sure I doe not know, /N*[e] *what*[eu]*er he be high or low, /Or now aliue, or els be dead*" (sig. A2^v). Mystified as quickly as it is conjured, Grove's authority is further compromised by Smith's admission that *"Foure yeere and more I dyd hym [the pamphlet] nurse./Although no whit it cost my purse"* (sig. A2r). What his *"nurs*[ing]" as publisher ultimately consisted of is not outlined at this point, but it eventually becomes apparent among what the running header describes as "Epigrams and Sonets." There, like Tottel did three decades earlier in his own printed miscellany, Smith appears to have added titles to some of the volume's appended poems, establishing his own authority as framing perspective. This prefatory work is perhaps most apparent in the section's second title, "The Author being minded to write, but lacking an argument, made this following, thinking whereof he were best to write" (sig. D5r), a tag which rambles on and on after referring to "The Author" in the third person. But it is also discernable in the unsystematic deployment of definite and indefinite articles in the amatory poems' titles. Though all twenty-one of these poems clearly belong to chronological narrative having to do with a lover, his lady, and his friend, their titles at times refer instead generally to "a Louer" (sigs. E1v, F4r) to "a Gentlewoman" (sig. E4r), and to "a friend" (sig. E6r).[70] To be sure, such titles are misleading, but they also fashion stand-alone, abstract products in the midst of lyrical sequence, multiplying its potential frames of reception rather than delimiting them.

Four years later, in the same month that Newman's *Astrophel and Stella* was recalled by the Stationers' Company, Smith was again planning another volume of amatory poems, this time an edition of Henry Constable's sonnet sequence *Diana*.[71] The first edition of these twenty-three sonnets – a four-sheet book of diminutive size – made it to the stalls of London's bookshops in 1592, months after Constable himself had embarked with the Earl of Essex for France on what would prove to be an unsuccessful military expedition to aid Henry IV.[72] Whether Constable had anything to do with Smith acquiring the sequence remains unknown. What seems clear, however, is that Constable was not involved with the volume's preparation or printing.[73] We know this because Constable had left England before it was entered in the Stationers' Register, but also because its prefatory epistle "*To the Gentlemen Readers*" (a short piece likely penned by Smith), tells us that "these insuing Sonnets ... are now by misfortune left as Orphans," that they have been "left desolate" (sig. A4r).[74]

Set in the light of Newman's first and second editions of *Astrophel and Stella*, Smith's 1592 *Diana* bears traces of these landmark texts' authorizing strategies.[75] Akin to Newman's second edition, this *Diana* is formatted in quarto and is sparsely faced with a title of around a dozen words. The descriptive terms "in certaine sweete Sonnets" of its title page echo Newman's own title-page description of *Astrophel and Stella*: "Wherein the excellence of sweete | Poesie is concluded." Also familiar is *Diana*'s title-page ascription "By H.C.," which echoes in its use of authorial initials Newman's own title *Sir P.S. His Astrophel and Stella*. Both ascription strategies reveal as they at the same time veil, invoking the anonymity of manuscript circulation while they simultaneously brand their products in decipherable, authorial terms. These terms – individuality, singularity, coherence, etc. – emerge again in *Diana*'s prefatory epistle where the volume's author is described as "no partiall Iudge, whose eies were acquainted with Beauties Riches, whose eares frequented to Angelicall sounds, and sense rauished with excellent Science" (sig. A4^r).

Smith's 1592 *Diana*, in other words, smacks of Newman's single-author, second edition of *Astrophel and Stella*, especially in its authorial valences centred around "H.C." At the same time, though, it is marked by elements that tend to destabilize the volume's veneer of authorial sovereignty, elements that are reminiscent of the first edition of *Astrophel and Stella*. Perhaps the most obvious of these is Smith's large printer's emblem on the title page, an icon that brands the volume as one of Smith's many "Time reveals all hidden truths" products. This brand speaks further through the volume's prefatory epistle, which assures its readers that they will find various products infused with the "beautie, ... vtteraunce, ... [and] Art." Indeed, like Newman's epistle to Francis Flower in his first edition of *Astrophel and Stella*, this dedication stresses in its conclusion that *Diana*'s value and meaning is entirely determined not by "H.C." but by its "Gentlemen Readers." "[T]hese ensuing Sonnets ...," it insists, "craue desertfull acceptance of your experienst iudgements; in whom rests what euer Beautie would grace, or Art adorne. Beeing left desolate, they seeke entertainment: farther they will not, how euer you accept them; better they desire not, but as you like to vse them" (sig. A4^r). Such a statement, of course, is anything but unique in an artistic world still dominated by patronage. But its more subtle nuances are also the stuff of Smith's previous publications. In its ending claim that "better they desire not, but as you like to vse them" rests an understanding of the volume as a commodity to be "vse[d]" according to the desires of its readers. This, as we have seen in *A Hundreth Sundry Flowers* and *The Fabulous Tales of Aesop*, is a perspective born of Smith's experiences as a bookseller in St Paul's, where buyers browsed and created *Sammelbände* to serve their individual tastes. Indeed, the epistle's image of the volume "seeke[ing] entertainment" reinforces this model of relationship, in this case imagining book and reader as reproducing the feudal relations between servant and retainer. *Diana*, in other words, is at least, on one level, made to serve at its readers' pleasure.

This tripartite authorization of the 1592 *Diana* – by "H.C.," by its publisher(s), and by its gentlemen readers – helps explain one of the volume's more perplexing textual features: its seemingly incongruous positioning of the sonnets "*To his absent Diana*" and "*A calculation vpon the birth of an honourable Ladies daughter, borne in the yeare, 1588. & on a Friday.*" Rather than immediately preceding the sequence's first sonnet ("*Sonnetto primo*") as one might expect, the former poem is placed between the title page and the prefatory epistle and thus is made to function not as prologue for the sequence but as dedicatory poem.[76] Coupled then with the anonymous dedicatory epistle, Constable's sonnet offers its own interpretive frame, one that asks its own patron Diana to "Review these Sonnets, pictures of thy praise;/Wherein each woe thy wondrous worth doth raise" (sig. A3ʳ). Positioned as it is, in other words, "*To his absent Diana*" amounts to one hermeneutical ante among many, staking the author's end of "[raising Diana's] wondrous worth" with Smith's. Similarly provoking is the volume's placement of the sonnet "*A calculation vpon the birth of an honourable Ladies daughter*" between "*Sonnetto vinti*" and "*Ultimo Sonnetto.*"[77] Addressed not to his beloved but to a newborn child, this poem celebrates the birth of an unidentified "*Ladies daughter,*" predicting that "Thou of a world of harts in time shalt bee/A Monarch great."[78] It is, in effect, more a sonnet of praise than one of lyrical expression, and its interruption of the lyrical sequence is strongly reminiscent of Grove's *Pelops and Hippodamia* where Smith's inconsistent titles similarly disrupt the poems' lyrical thread. Here, as in Grove, the incongruous inclusion speaks to Smith's fashioning of textual flexibility rather than textual coherence, to what was likely his sense of the volume as providing either browsable examples of "beautie, ... vtteraunce, ... [and] Art" and/or "vse" as much as offering any kind of author-oriented lyrical continuity.

Sometime after 1593, Smith financed another useful *Diana*, this a reorganized and greatly expanded edition with the new title *Diana or the Excellent Conceitful Sonnets of H.C. Augmented with Diverse Quatorzains of Honorable and Learned Personages.*[79] This second edition contains twenty-two of the twenty-three sonnets from the 1592 *Diana* along with a further five sonnets from Constable, eight from Sidney and forty-one from other yet-to-be identified poets.[80] Excised from this edition are the prefatory sonnet "*To his absent Diana*" and the dedicatory epistle "*To the Gentlemen Readers*"; in their stead is a new epistle "THE PRINTER to the Reader" followed by a new dedicatory sonnet "VNTO HER MAIEstie's sacred honorable Maydes," both by Smith.[81] Along with an extensive body of added material, this new *Diana* rearranges the sonnets from the previous edition, adds a new title-page Latin blurb "*Vincitur a facibus, qui iacet ipse faces*" ("They shall be overcome by burning, who lie down themselves at the flames of love"), and fashions a new organizational paradigm, advertising on its title page that the whole is "Deuided into viii. Decads" (i.e., eight sets of ten poems each).[82]

Including poems from other assorted "honorable and | lerned personages" and dispersing some of Constable's 1592 *Diana* sonnets among them, this second edition of *Diana* follows a trajectory towards multivocality that Smith initiated in his *A Hundreth Sundry Flowers* and continued to *Diana*'s first edition.[83] Here, H.C.'s poetry is not simply "Augmented" by the products of other poets, but his individual poems – like all of the added sonnets – are not in any way attributed.[84] And while most of Constable's first-edition sonnets are easily found in the first decade, three of them – "*Sonetto sesto*"; *Sonnetto decinoue*"; and "*A calculation vpon the birth of an honourable Ladies daughter*" – are dispersed into the third, fourth, and eighth decades respectively. In this, Smith's augmented *Diana* proves even less authorial than Newman's first multi-author edition of *Astrophel and Stella*. There, Sidney's poetry is distinguished from the other poems by section headers that clearly introduce both: at the beginning of the second gathering ("SIR P.S. HIS ASTROPHEL AND STELLA" [sig. B1ʳ]) and in the third leaf of the ninth ("Poems and Sonets of Sundrie other Noble men and Gentlemen" [sig. I3ᵛ]).[85] Smith's "Augmented" *Diana*, in other words, continues to tout the authorship of H.C. on its title page only to veil it thoroughly in its leaves.

The presence of H.C. is further diminished by Smith's new prefatory material. Whereas the first edition of *Diana* invoked Constable's agency in what is the authorial pathos of "*To his absent Diana*" and in the commendations of its dedicatory "*To the Gentlemen Readers*," the new epistle and dedicatory sonnet of *Diana*'s second edition make almost no reference to H.C. Instead, "THE PRINTER TO the Reader" highlights Smith's own efforts in acquiring and publishing the collection's additional poems. "OBscur'd wonders (gentlemen,) visited me in *Turnus* armor," he announces, "and I in regard of *Aeneas* honour, haue vnclouded them vnto the worlde" (sig. A2ʳ). In turn, Smith's dedicatory "VNTO HER MAIEstie's sacred honorable Maydes" invokes the "*two-fold* CHARITES" so that they – through the workings of the collection as a whole – "*shall moue/All things in* [man]: *and* [man] *in you shall loue*" (sig. A2ᵛ). Constable is never directly invoked in Smith's dedicatory poem; rather – expanding upon his reference to Constable's sonnets as "Orphans" in his first edition – Smith speaks of the collection as a whole, calling upon the "*two-fold* CHARITES" to "*bow* [their] *Sun-rysing eyes, Planets of ioy,/Vpon these Orphan Poems: in whose rights,/Conceit first claym'd his byrth-right to enioy.*"

Just as he diminishes Constable's authorial presence in the volume so that his buyers are free to read the edition according to their own desires, Smith markets and fashions *Diana*'s second edition as a multifaceted affair. Where the previous edition pledges "certaine sweete Sonnets" on its title page, Smith's augmented *Diana* promises "Quatorzains" by "personages" who are both "honorable" and "lerned." Derived from the Middle French, the English term "quatorzain" first appeared in Thomas Watson's *Hekatompathia* (1582) and was deployed during the period to denote any poem of fourteen lines.[86] Frequently used interchangeably with "sonnet," the term was also associated with formal rigidity and with extensive variability in metre and rhyme. Thus Nashe in his prefatory epistle for the first edition of *Astrophel and Stella* distinguishes Sidney's sonnets from the "crazed quaterzayns" of his various contemporaries: "Put out your rush candles, you Poets and Rimers, and bequeath your crazed quaterzayns to the Chaundlers, for loe, here he commeth that hath broēk your legs" (1591a, sig. A3ᵛ).[87] Smith's "diuers | Quatorzains" then doubly underscores the variety of fourteen-line poems that his revised *Diana* has to offer. Comprised of Petrarchan, Shakespearean, and Spenserian sonnets, the volume affords a range of learned allusions to classical myth and natural history along with poems reminiscent of the Continental verse of Du Bellay and Desportes.[88] It at the same time indicates elite poems, verse readily understood as occasional products from a restricted patrician milieu.

The augmented *Diana*, then, is shaped to be of broader interest than its first edition. Adding to the collection's range, the most significant part of this appeal has to do with the collection's new strategy of organization, its being "Deuided into viii. Decads." Offered as more than simply a measure of the its increased size, *Diana*'s "viii. Decads" also advertises sets of poems, each with its own patterns of imagery and themes. To put it in Smith's other terms, what is promised here are clusters of sonnets that are "conceitful" (tp). With a reconstituted group of Constable's sonnets from the 1592 *Diana*, the first decade introduces the new scheme with ten poems all containing imagery of the heart and eye. Here are poems exploring the various courses and consequences of "Mine humble hart, so with thy heauenly eie / drawne vp aloft" (sig. B1^v) and of "mine eye let[ting] in her eye" (sig. B3^v). The third decade then includes quatorzains all connected in one way or another with the conventional Petrarchan themes of illness and pain. This is signalled from beginning to end, its first sonnet beginning with "UNciuill sicknesse, hast thou no regard, / but doost presume my deerest to molest?" (sig. C3^r), its last complaining in its eleventh and twelfth lines, "the wittiest women are to sport inclind, / honor is pride, and pride is naught but paine" (sig. C7^v). Following the fourth decade's focus on exile, power, and despair, the augmented *Diana*'s fifth decade is organized around echo imagery, and around the related theme of the artistic voice. Thus, while the speaker of its fourth sonnet hopes that in death "each tell-tale eccho with a weeping breath, / may both record my trueth, & true loues breaking" (sig. D6^v), the sixth sonnet's speaker similarly imagines himself within the arms of his beloved singing "sad Eligies" (sig. D7^v). In the fifth decade, Smith tracks the interplay of perseverence and disdain, in the sixth he couples the theme of eternity with imagery of the natural world and the cosmos: "drizzling drops" (sig. E3^r); "Marble rock" (sig. E3^r); "one Moone" (sig. E2^v); "eternall Sunne" (sig. E3^v); "fixed stars" (sig. E3^v); "a flame of fire" (sig. E4^r); "the heauens" (sig. E4^v, E6^r); and "My God" (sig. E6^v). The collection moves to a close with another decade exploring perseverence, and concludes appropriately with a short eighth decade on the themes of endings and death. None of this could be said to be perfect. Smith's second decade of Constable sonnets proves more miscellanious than a related group, and in each of the final six decades there are quatorzains that are at best outliers. But even so, it would be wrong to suggest that these sets of ten are entirely random, that there exists no method in them.

Smith's work in publishing a poetical work of decades was undoubtedly aided by his "OBscur'd wonders," the copy that he had at his disposal. Along with the first edition and possibly a manuscript version of

Diana, he possessed a manuscript copy that also contained a number of poem groupings. The first of these new assemblages included eight sonnets from Sidney that Smith deployed to consitute the lion's share of the third decade's study in illness and pain.[89] Along with these are five sets of poems wherein final lines are repeated in subsequent first lines. Though these groupings have yet to be attributed, each was undoubtedly written by the same author. The first of these appropriately occurs in the fifth decade on the echo ("*SONNET. VI.*" to "*SONNET. IX.*"), it successively repeating the lines "But beeing care, thou flyest mee as ill fortune"; "Deere to my soule, then leaue me not forsaken"; "Whilst Eccho cryes, what shal become of me" (sigs. D7^v–D8^v).[90] The next five are all paired sonnets. The first three together occur in the seventh decade on perserverence, the fourth bridges the seventh and eighth decades, and the fifth pairing constitutes the second and third poems of the eight decade, both ruminations on the speaker's desire for death. With the exception of the last poem of the seventh decade and the first of the eight, these groupings of poems are all put in their own decade, suggesting that they may have helped inspire Smith's new organizational strategy.

Though his second edition of *Diana* is the first English collection of printed poetry to be organized around decades, Smith's subscription to them as organizational tools was not without precedent. Generally defined in the early-modern world of books as a "division of a literary work, containing ten books or parts" (*OED*), the term "decade" appears to have had a number of associations by the 1590s. Taking cue from the many classical and Continental works that were so extensive that they were subdivided into dozens of decades, satirists like Nashe employed the term to indicate works of exhausting length.[91] In his list of "waste authors" within *Nashe's Lenten Stuff* (1599), he rails against two contemporary medical writers, accusing both of painful longwindedness: "To these I might wedge in *Cornelius* the brabantine, who was felloniously suspected in 87. for penning a discourse of Tuftmockados, and a countrey gentleman of my acquaintance who is launching forth a treatise as bigge garbd as the french *Academy* of the *Cornucopia* of a cowe. ... Neither of their *Decads* are yet stampt but eare midsummer tearme they will be if their wordes bee sure payment" (sig. E1^r).[92] In other Elizabethan publications, "decade" had strictly enumerative connotations, employed to indicate the breaking up of a work or page into smaller units of ten. In 1577, for example, in one of the more visible instances of "decade" in print during the period, the bookseller Ralph Newbery touted the term in his title *Fifty Godly and Learned Sermons Divided into Five Decades*, a translation by "H.I." of Swiss reformer Heinrich Bullinger's *Sermonum decades quinque*.[93] In his dedicatory epistle to the Anglican ministry, H.I. explains that "*the doctrine of them* [is] *verie plaine* ...: *and in number,* [5]0. *euerie Decade conteining (as the word importeth) tenne: so that they may easily be so diuided, as there may be for euerie Sunday in the yeare one*" (sig. ¶2ᵛ). Here, H.I. ventures no claim about shared content in each group of ten; in effect, for H.I., Bullinger's sermons are "*easily ... diuided*" into five "*Decade*[s]" because 50 is readily divisible by 10.[94] Just as it was used quantitatively as a term of volume division in Newbery's Bullinger, "decade" was employed in other books to indicate sets of ten lines on their pages. Adding to the growing number of collected sermons in the bookshops of St Paul's during the Elizabethan period, Thomas Woodcock brought out his own collection of sermons in 1583, Arthur Golding's translation *The Sermons of M. John Calvin upon the Fifth Book of Moses called Deuteronomy*. In it, each of the sermons' pages is divided into two columns and its lines are numbered, as Abraham Fleming the author of the volume's indexes tells us in his "To the Reader," "by Decads or Tens."

Like those within Smith's second edition of Diana, though, "decades" could also have qualitative connotations, understood not simply to indicate sets of ten within a larger work but sets of ten, each containing an interconnected web of parts. Such is the sense of the term in Francis Markham's *Five Decades of Epistles of War*, a twenty-seven-sheet quarto published by Augustine Mathewes in 1622. In his "Preface," Markham writes of having limited his collection to the "true proportion of *Decads*, & those iumping into a iust *Semi-Centurie* of Epistles," calling the whole the "frame of mine intended building." Markham's *Five Decades* is not just true in its formal proportions; it also contains decades of letters that are each organized around a particular rank. Thus, his first decade is concerned with the common infantry soldiers, the second with lower-middling-rank infantry soldiers, the third with cavalrymen, the fourth with middling-rank officers, and the fifth with upper-rank officers. In this hierarchical structure of ordered decades, Markham imagined the workings of the great chain of being. Writing three years later in *The Book of Honor. Or, Five Decades of Epistles of Honor*, he is explicit about this orthodox perspective:

"We see on earth the infinit varieties of Stones, Hearbes, Trees, Birds, Beasts, Fish, and Men; and all those placed by his Almightie power in such excellent Order to glorifie his Great name" (1625, sig. B2ʳ).

In constructing his "building" out of discrete decades, Markham might well have been thinking about Livy. At the end of the sixteenth century, it was "decade" as it appeared in editions of Livy's *Ab urbe condita* that was hands down the most-cited source of the term in Elizabethan books. Commonly known in Latin as *T. Livii decades* and in the vernacular as *The Decades of Titus Livius*, Livy's mammoth celebration of the Roman Republic was routinely referenced in the body and margins of humanist chronicles, tracts, and treatises. In its original form, the work consisted of 142 books, but only the first and third decades were known in the Middle Ages. Petrarch drove new interest in the Roman historian at the end of the fourteenth century, and by the 1540s, most of the *Decades*'s books had been rediscovered, allowing Livy to become the fourth most read Latin historian in Europe in the second half of the sixteenth century (Burke 1966, 137).[95] The first complete Latin edition of the *Decades* was published by George Bishop in England in 1589, this helping to spark an upsurge of interest in Livy's history in the 1590s (Culhane 2004, 271). Bishop's edition was soon followed by Philemon Holland's abridged English translation in 1600, an edition published by Adam Islip.[96] At the end of his epistle "To the Reader," Holland recommends "unto my countrymen, *Livie* in English habit: *Livie* (I say) who whether he were more honored whiles he lived, than beloved at this day of forrein nations, I cannot easily determine." Here, Holland confirms the widespread popularity of Livy's republican history, this at a time when England was facing the uncertainty of an aged queen and no heir.

Throughout the early-modern period, Livy's history was routinely navigated and understood through what were understood to be its discrete decades.[97] Petrarch confined his interest to Livy's first, third, and fourth decades; Boccaccio to the third and fourth; and Machiavelli in his *Discourses of Livy* to the first. And there were numerous editions of single decades printed in Lyon, Paris, Frankfurt, and other European cities during the sixteenth century. In England in 1544, Anthony Cope produced an abridged edition of the third decade entitled *The History of Two the Most Noble Captains Annibal and Scipio*, a version meant to be used by Henry VIII as a "military manual."[98] Evidence also suggests that the Elizabethans saw each of Livy's decades as having its own particular content and use value. As Lisa Jardine and Anthony

Grafton outlined in their foundational essay "'Studied for Action': How Gabriel Harvey Read His Livy," Gabriel Harvey read Livy's *Decades* in a variety of ways over his lifetime, each reading driven by a specific purpose, "suited for action." Harvey's marginalia in his 1555 Basle folio shows not simply that the Cambridge pedagogue had different "types of analysis" depending upon the purpose for which he was reading but also that he often assumed that each of Livy's decades had its own content and particular use. In late 1577, for example, Harvey turned to Livy's third decade for "content" particularly applicable to the political situation of the Sidney circle at the time. "Each decade is fine," he writes, "but this one should be studied by the best actors. The quality of the content, and its great power; where the virtue of the Romans suffers so much. ... And it is fitting for prudent men to make strenuous efforts to use whatever sheds light on politics: and to increase it as much as they can" (qtd. in Jardine and Grafton 1990, 38). Six years later, Harvey read Livy's first decade along with Machiavelli's commentary on it, gleaning the decade for what Jardine and have described as "diplomatic or political end[s]": "I had reason to take the greater paines in reading the first decad of Liuie, bie meanes of mie dailie & almost howerlie conference with M. Thomas Preston. ... [The] politique discourses [of Michiavelli] wee thorowghly redd-ouer: with diligent & curious obseruations of the notable actions of the Romans, accomplished at home, & abrode, bie publique, & priuate counsell" (qtd. in Jardine and Grafton 1990, 43).

Smith's decision both to organize and to advertise his second edition of *Diana* in terms of decades, then, can be understood as an attempt to appeal to buyers familiar with these sets as discrete units, more interested in interconnected sets of poetry organized around images and themes than in poems arranged in narrative sequences with a single speaker and a single beloved like Sidney's *Astrophel and Stella*, Spenser's *Amoretti*, or the first edition of *Diana*. Though aptly concluding with a set of poems centred around themes of endings and death, this revised edition of *Diana* eschews a readily apparent ordering principle. Instead, it offers its decades as browsable entities, each usable in and of itself according to the designs of readers. That he fashioned his last decade out of six sonnets rather than the requisite ten suggests that Smith was interested in capitalizing upon the qualitative connotations of "decade" and not worried about Markham's "excellent Order." Promised, of course, were not the kinds of political and diplomatic "vses" that men like Harvey made of classical tomes like

Livy; *Diana*, after all, takes love as its object with its power, as Smith writes in his dedicatory sonnet "VNTO HER MAIEsties sacred honorable Maydes," to "*moueth all things*" (sig. A2ᵛ). What Smith fashions in this revised octavo are decades for howsoever his buyers might "like to vse them."

Sometime before November 1598, Smith would finance a third edition of *Diana*.[99] With some minor exceptions involving spelling and punctuation, it was identical to the second. *Diana*, then, proved to be initially more popular than Drayton's *Idea's Mirror*, Lodge's *Phillis*, Spenser's *Amoretti*, and Shakespeare's *Sonnets*, and as popular as Sidney's *Astrophel and Stella*.[100] It attracted readers even as – possibly because – Smith added elements that from a modern perspective undid textual unity and complicated textual authority. Smith, though, proved at the end of his publishing career to be more than simply a fortunate speculator on the 1590s print market for vernacular lyrical poetry. As many of his dedicatory epistles and commendatory poems reveal, his success was closely linked with his being a savvy reader of his own products and an active participant in a burgeoning literary tradition shaped as much as by Tottel's *Songs and Sonnets* as by Sidney's *Astrophel and Stella*. For Smith, this was not a tradition built upon great authors and their makings; rather, it was buoyed by textual elasticity and driven by acquisitive readers.

Chapter Four

Flasket and Linley's *The Tragedy of Dido Queen of Carthage* (1594): Reissuing the Elizabethan Epyllion

Whatever can be said of the course and causes of Christopher Marlowe's rising reputation at the beginning of the nineteenth century, it can be alleged only with tongue firmly in cheek that *The Tragedy of Dido Queen of Carthage* was a necessary vehicle. When Hurst and Robinson included the play in their 1825 collection *The Old English Drama*, their choice was unmistakably the product of a new market for collections of *early* English drama.[1] *Dido*, admitted the two publishers in their short preface to the play, was chosen "for two reasons: first, the early period at which it was written, (before 1592); and secondly, the extreme rarity of it; there being, we believe, only two copies known to exist in England. Possessing very little intrinsic merit as a play, it is now reprinted chiefly for the purposes of illustrating the progress of dramatic art in this country" (Baldwyn 1825, 2.13).[2] Indeed, venturing upon *Dido* in a cultural milieu newly impressed with Marlowe, Hurst and Robinson laid responsibility for the play squarely upon Nashe's shoulders. "Nash," they write in their prefacing biography, "does not appear, from the specimens he has left us, to have possessed much dramatic talent. ... *Dido*, of which [Nash], probably, wrote the greater part, is little more than a narrative taken from Virgil, constructed according to the form of a drama, but containing little of the essence of that species of composition" (1825, xi–xii).[3]

Hurst and Robinson's deliberate reading of the play constitutes one of our earlier records of *Dido*'s reception as a printed book, and it highlights the extent to which publishers could function as uniquely invested readers. Hurst and Robinson read – and predicted that their *Dido* would be read – as an artefact, as something of the "rare" and "old" whose only appeal could be the extent to which it underscored their society's social and artistic "progress." *Dido* was a good read, in other words, only in so far as it was a bad play.

Dido was printed only one time before Hurst and Robinson's 1825 edition, in 1594. As I will show, its reception by those in the Elizabethan book trade both before and after it first came to press underscores how risky and capricious the market for printed professional playbooks continued to be before the turn of the sixteenth century. It highlights too how sophisticated and resourceful publishers could be – as speculators, as readers, and as marketers – when faced with unproven commodities and a largely untested demand for vernacular literature. This particular story has yet to be told. It involves not just a relatively extensive cast of interdependent characters – drapers, printers, bookbinders, booksellers, and the like – but also lesser-known publishing practices, trade collaborations, and a 1590s literary vogue.

Publishing at the Black Bear

When Thomas Woodcock took it upon himself to publish the first printed edition of Marlowe and Nashe's *Dido* around 1594, the London bookseller undoubtedly found himself with a challenge.[4] Even if we agree with Farmer and Lesser that playbooks would become after 1598 "among the most successful books in which an early-modern publisher could choose to invest" (2005a, 6), in 1594 playbooks were at best risky print commodities, texts with a limited track record in London's bookstalls and an uncertain status in the eyes of the buying public.[5] It is unlikely that Woodcock would have been unaware of this. Though he had from the middle of the 1570s peddled a large variety of books in St Paul's Churchyard at the sign of the Black Bear, he never risked financing a professional play text before *Dido*.[6] In 1588, he did bring out an English edition of Terence's *Andria*, but in this quarto, his title page reassures buyers that the play is "[a] furtherance for the attain- | ment vnto the right knowledge, & true proprietie, of the | Latin Tong. And also a commodious meane of help, | to such as haue forgotten Latin, for their | speedy recouering of habilitie, to vn- | derstand, write, and speake | the same." A half-dozen commendatory poems, two dedicatory epistles, two reader's epistles, and an "Argument" energetically reiterate this title-page promise.

Recorded on the title page of his 1594 edition, Woodcock's efforts at marketing *Dido* are – predictably – cautious, multifaceted in their appeals. Like a number of printed professional play texts before it,

Dido highlights its playing-company credentials with the tag "Played by the Children of her | *Maiesties Chappell*," emphasizing with the italicized "*Maiesties Chappell*" the company's royal connections. Allowing for the off-chance, apparently, that one of his buyers might have been looking for amateur theatrical fodder, the title page also includes information about the play's staging requirements – listing in total sixteen parts for "Actors."[7] At the same time, *Dido*'s first page also invokes what would become a predominant title-page legitimizing strategy for playbooks: authorship. The play text announces that it was "Written by Christopher Marlowe, and | *Thomas Nash*"; it also affirms that Nashe is a "*Gent.*" In this, the social status of Nashe trumped not just Marlowe's own class standing but also what some have taken to have been the notoriety of his recent death.[8]

In the end, Woodcock would not live to see the take from his wide net – he died sometime in the early months of 1594, years before he could have realistically hoped to finance a second edition of the play and thereby gleaned a real profit from his initial investment.[9] But had he lived, he apparently would have been disappointed. Most likely, *Dido* never reached a second edition, at least within a century of Marlowe and Nashe's deaths. Indeed, the play seems not to be printed again until Hurst and Robinson's 1825 edition in *The Old English Drama*. When all seems to have been said and done, Marlowe's first play failed to become an early print-market phenomenon like his *Tamburlaine* (four editions between 1590 and 1606), Kyd's *Spanish Tragedy* (as many as six editions between 1592 and 1603), Shakespeare's *1 King Henry IV* (five editions between 1598 and 1608), or Lyly's *Campaspe* (four editions between 1585 and 1591).

But *Dido*'s failure to reach a second early-modern edition does not in fact end the story of the play-as-book's early reception, at least in so far as London's booksellers were concerned. Shortly after his death, Woodcock's business at the Black Bear seems to have been conveyed wholly to the stationer Paul Linley and his partner John Flasket. Such a transaction was made binding in February 1596 when Woodcock's widow Isabel (daughter of the queen's printer John Cawood) is recorded in the Stationers' Register as transferring "all and euery bookes, and partes of [her husband's] bookes whatsoeuer" to Linley (Arber, 3.58), a conveyance that would have included, among other things, Woodcock's unsold copies of *Dido*.

As the relatively close-knit, small community of stationers would have it, this likely would not have been Linley's first encounter with

Woodcock and his *Dido*. Linley began his career as a stationer two decades earlier in 1576. In that year he was entered into a ten-year apprenticeship with the bookseller William Ponsonby. Before this, Linley grew up in Lillingstone Dayrrel, a small Buckinghamshire village about seventy-five miles to the northwest of London. His father William Linley was a yeoman, and he had at least two siblings, sisters Dorothie and Mary.[10] As an apprentice at the Bishop's Head bookshop, Linley would have learned the ins and outs of the bookselling trade from one of the more literary oriented publishers in St Paul's Churchyard. A figure whom McKerrow *Dictionary* describes as "the most important publisher of the Elizabethan age" (217), Ponsonby published the first print editions of Sidney's *Old* and *New Arcadia* and all six books of Spenser's *The Faerie Queene* (1590, 1596) along with editions of Greene, Fraunce, and Chapman. During eight of his years under Ponsonby (1578–86), Linley would also have become well acquainted with his fellow apprentice Edward Blount, the future publisher of a vernacular collection of Seneca, Florio's translation of Montaigne, and Shakespeare's First Folio. As we shall see, the two men continued their professional relationship into the 1590s, even after Linley was admitted to the freedom of the Company of Stationers in 1586. Between 1586 and 1594, Linley likely worked as a journeyman bookseller in London, possibly for Woodcock when *Dido* was first acquired. Such a close working relationship would explain Linley inheriting Woodcock's bookshop and printing patents in 1594 or 1595.

It was during the early 1590s that Linley seems also to have begun his partnership with Flasket, a draper bookbinder who had recently taken his freedom in 1593 after an apprenticeship with John Wight junior.[11] Flasket had his own professional and familial connections to the bookselling trade, all of which having to do with his grandfather John Wight senior. Wight senior had run an active bookselling and publishing business at the Rose and then at the great North door in St Paul's Churchyard from the 1550s into the late 1580s. Wight senior regularly invested in religious and literary texts during this period, and, as he did for Richard Smith in the 1550s, would have passed knowledge of the ins and outs of bookselling and publishing onto his son Wight junior.[12] Wight senior's son-in-law was Thomas Flasket, John Flasket's father.[13] Thomas Flasket had run a haberdashery business in London from as early as 1563 and was clearly a close associate of his father-in-law.[14] Wight senior's 1589 will alludes to personal debts and real-estate dealings between him and Flasket, and it also names Flasket Wight senior's executor.[15] The wills of draper booksellers Anthony Kitson (1577), Thomas Petit (1585), and Abraham Veale (1596) further suggest that the Wights and Flaskets were members of a small community of families engaged one way or another in the trade of bookselling.

Less than a year after becoming free of the Drapers' Company, John Flasket involved himself with the publication of two short texts about recent political events across the channel in France, wholesaling each of these texts "at the | great north dore of Poules" (Anon. 1594a, tp) possibly at his grandfather's old shop.[16] A year later in 1595, he and Linley began advertising their new bookselling and publishing partnership at Woodcock's old shop, first in a translation of Giovanni Nenna's *Nennio, or a Treatise of Nobility*, its imprint reading "for Paule Linley, and Iohn | *Flasket, and are to be sold at their shop in Paules* | churchyard, at the Signe of the | blacke Beare." This would be the first of as many as twelve separate publications that Linley and Flasket together published between 1595 and 1599.[17] Along with *Nennio*, the duo published Luis de Granada's *Sinner's Guide* (translated by Francis Meres) and collected sermons by the Anglican clergyman and nonconformist preacher Edward Dering. They also seem to have made something of a specialty of Marlowe's poetry.[18] In 1598, they released the first edition of *Hero and Leander* coupled with Chapman's continuation of the poem. Also available wholesale at the Black Bear was a 1600 second edition of the volume, one appending Marlowe's translation of Lucan to its end. The collaboration only ended with the death of Linley in the early spring of 1600.[19] Soon after, Flasket, in May 1600, with eleven other drapers including Clement Knight, Thomas Fisher (Richard Smith's former apprentice), and Thomas Pavier, was transferred to the Stationers' Company.[20] Flasket continued to operate out of the Black Bear until at least 1607.[21]

Hero and Leander and Lucan were not the only Marlowe texts that drew Linley and Flasket's attention. The two also appear to have pursued another project to do with Marlowe, this one involving *The Tragedy of Dido*. The evidence of this again comes from the Stationers' Register. Shortly after Linley's death on 26 June, the Register records Linley's rights to a long list of publications being officially transferred to his partner Flasket. Among these, on a separate line, is listed a single transfer of "Cupydes Journey to hell with the tragedie of Dido" (Arber, 3.164–5), *Cupid's Journey to Hell* being the second subtitle of John Dickinson's 1594 pastoral romance *Arisbas, Euphues amidst his*

Slumbers. The partners had obtained *Arisbas*'s right to copy as part of Isabel Woodcock's conveyance in 1596.

Now it is important to understand that in the idiom of the Stationers' Register, entries that link separate titles using the word "with" or more commonly "together with" seem always to treat the linked titles as parts of one single volume, thus only requiring the standard six-pence entrance fee to record right to copy. Moreover, when part of right-to-copy transfers, these entries mostly record multi-text volumes that have already been published. This is the case with a November 1615 entry, where Thomas Purfoot Jr's purchase of the right to copy two titles is entered in the register "The booke of dyeing with The art of Lymnynge" (Arber, 3.576).[22] These two titles (the former by Leonard Mascall) were at first entered and published separately, but they were republished together by Thomas Purfoot in 1605, ten years before Purfoot Jr's transfer entry.[23] In some cases, such transfer entries could conceivably document a publisher's dissemination of a multi-title reissue with cancel title page. This may have been the case when Francis Williams paid to have, among many other texts, the rights to copy of *The Life of Religion* and *A Brief Discourse ... of the Laudable Customs of London* transferred to him from Roger Jackson's widow in 1625, the entry reading "The life of Religion with the laudable Customes of London" (Arber, 4.150). These two texts were published separately in 1615 and 1584; Jackson may have reissued the two together sometime between 1615 and 1625, and this would have led to Williams's multi-title entry. Possibly confirming that it was a common stationer practice for multi-title register entries to be strictly for multi-title rights to copy is an April 1603 register entry. There, Henry Hooke and Simon Stafford are charged six pence "for their Copie his maiesties Lepanto or heroicall songe beinge parte of his poeticall exercises at vacant houres Together with the furies wrytten by Bartas in Frenche and translated into Englishe verse eyther in parte or in wholle" (Arber, 3.232). In its ending addition "eyther in parte or in wholle," this unique entry seems to outline an exception to standard company practice, that in this particular case these two works could be printed jointly or separately under the six-pence entry fee.

In most cases, multi-title entries using "with" or "together with" have to do with copy that brings together multiple titles by the same author, translator, or compiler. Nicholas Breton's multi-text *The Will of Wit* was inscribed in this way when it was transferred from William Wright to

Thomas Creede in 1596, the Stationers' Register recording "Willes witt with ye miseries of Mavilla printed by Thomas Scarlet" (Arber, 3.72). The next year Creede published what was a new edition of the collected volume, one that included a separate title page for *The Miseries of Mavillia* along with a new general title page. Likewise, on 25 November 1601, James Shaw paid the initial entrance fee for "a memorable propose in Englishe with the treasure of vertue" (Arber, 3.196). The following year, Shaw published these two anonymous translations of Gilles Corrozet together under the title *Memorable Conceits of Diverse Noble and Famous Personages of Christendome, of this our Modern Time*, each translation having its own separate index.[24]

There are, however, a few cases in the Stationers' Register where "with" or "together with" is used to link separate titles by different authors under one entrance fee, these titles comprising one volume to be sold. In 1592, the bookseller Thomas Wight published the sixth edition of William Bourne's *A Regiment for the Sea*. This was a newly expanded edition, one corrected by Thomas Hood and appending Hood's own *Mariner's Guide* at the end. Each text retained its own title page and was separately foliated. When the two-title volume was transferred to Edmund Weaver in 1605, it was entered singly as "A Regiment for the Sea &c. by William Bourne with the Mariners guide by Thomas Hood" (Arber, 3.289) and was charged only one entrance fee.[25] Six years later in 1611, Weaver brought out the seventh expanded Bourne-Hood edition. In another case, Henry Holland and George Gibbes paid six pence in 1624 for the entry "A booke called A scurge for paper persecuters by John Davis with a continued inquisicion against paper persecuters by. Abraham Holland" (Arber, 4.134). The next year appeared in print *A Scourge for Paper-Persecutors ... By I.D. With a Continued Just Inquisition ... Against Paper-Persecutors. By A.H.* Ironically, John Davies's "booke" was in fact a partial reprint of his *The Scourge of Folly* (1611), this even as Holland in his satiric contribution to the volume bewails St Paul's pamphlets that never seem to die. "Shall still such fopperie fill vp each Stall," he asks, "And neuer come to a due Funerall?" (sig. A1r).[26] Along with cases like these, there are also two-author, two-text entries in the Stationers' Register for which we unfortunately no longer have a corresponding printed edition. Perhaps the most tantalizing of these is Eleazar Edgar's early 1600 entry of "A booke called Amours by JD. with certen [other] sonnetes by WS" (Arber, 3.153), an entry which some have taken for a now-lost two-title volume of poems by Donne and sonnets by Shakespeare.

Together, these examples from the Stationers' Register indicate that Flasket's 26 June 1600 transfer entry records a stand-alone, multi-text volume consisting of Dickenson's *Arisbas* and Marlowe's *Dido*. This volume was either (1) a nonce edition with only a new general title page, (2) a partial reissue with a new general title page and a cancel title page for *Arisbas*, or (3) a newly reprinted two-text edition.[27] While it is, of course, possible that Linley and Flasket were inspired to finance two new editions of *Arisbas* and *Dido* sometime between 1594 and 1600, it seems much more likely that the entry records a creative attempt to move unsold copies of Woodcock's prior investments in Dickenson and Marlowe-Nashe, commodities that they had inherited when they took over the Black Bear bookshop after 1594. Flasket's 1600 transfer entry seems to indicate that the volume had retitled *Arisbas* and therefore the second explanation seems the most likely. A newly printed general title page advertising both works would have been relatively cheap, and, as we shall see, what appears to have been their new title, *Cupid's Journey to Hell*, would have appealed to a broader set of buyers.

Linley and Flasket's bundling of *Dido* would not have been an anomaly. In their joint publishing gambits between 1595 and 1600, the pair frequently repackaged texts to stimulate sales. Such was the case with their first publishing venture, the 1595 first edition of *Nennio*. This twenty-seven-sheet quarto includes two dedicatory epistles by the translator William Jones (to Essex and to the reader respectively) and four dedicatory sonnets by Spenser, Daniel, Chapman, and Angel Day. In 1600, the work was reissued as *A Discourse Whether a Noble Man by Birth or a Gentlemen by Desert is Greater in Nobility*, the new title a version of its second original subtitle. It was also significantly repackaged in that Jones's two dedicatory epistles were removed and all of its title-page references to him and Nenna were cut. Spenser's and Daniel's sonnets notwithstanding, the reissue is less authorial and less occasional, in the aggregate broader in its potential appeal.

Repackaging also seems to have been the impetus behind Flasket and Linley's two expanded editions of *Hero and Leander*. The poem was first entered in the Stationers' Register by John Wolfe in September 1593 (Arber, 2.636), but it apparently was not published until early 1598, when Edward Blount brought out its first edition.[28] Shortly thereafter, the poem was transferred from Blount to Linley (Arber,

3.105), and by the end of 1598 the Black Bear shop was wholesaling copies of a new edition of the poem, one including Chapman's additions. Whatever the instigation and whatever the arrangements between former Bishop's Head apprentices that led to the transfer, Linley and Flasket's new edition was marketed as a superior product, it being "*finished*" (tp) unlike Blount's.[29] Before two years had passed, Flasket and Linley began planning a third edition of the poem, one that would include a reissue of Marlowe's translation of the first book of Lucan's *Pharsalia*. Like *Hero and Leander*, Marlowe's translation was originally entered into the Stationers' Register by John Wolfe in 1593 but not brought to press until years later by another publisher, in this case Thomas Thorpe in 1600.[30] At some point in the early weeks of 1600, Flasket and Linley seem to have acquired Thorpe's unsold copies of the translation from the bookseller Walter Burre. After Linley's death, Flasket then released yet another expanded edition of *Hero and Leander*, this one including a reissue of Marlowe's Lucan translation at its end. This edition gave the partnership the opportunity to move newly acquired unsold copies, but perhaps more importantly, it also allowed them to repackage the text as essentially a Marlowe volume, its title page cutting any reference to Chapman and instead advertising "HERO AND | LEANDER: | Begunne by *Christopher Marloe:* | Whereunto is added the first booke of | Lucan *translated line for line* | *by* the same Author."[31]

Reissuing Ovid

On the face of it, Flasket and Linley's penchant for reissues and revised products notwithstanding, an *Arisbas-Dido* volume seems either the product of faulty reckoning or desperation brought on by a dearth of space in the Black Bear stockroom. Dickinson's prose tale seems to offer artifice not simply of a different kind but also of a different temper than *Dido*. In its first subtitle, *Euphues amidst his Slumbers*, and its euphuistic prose style, *Arisbas* summons what were the incredibly popular humanist romances of John Lyly, namely, *Euphues. The Anatomy of Wit* (1578) and *Euphues and his England* (1580). And like *Euphues*'s more contemporary heirs Greene's *Menaphon* or Lodge's *Rosalynde*, it is seasoned with close to a dozen poems, which include a sonnet, an elegy, a madrigal, and many different odes. It at the same time is prefaced with an over-the-top epistle "To the Gentlemen-Readers" in praise of "Astrophil." There, Dickinson describes Sidney as "exceed[ing] the praises of al pens, especially of mine, whose slender wit treating such an ample subiect, feeles want in plentie, raunging in a large field of copious matter, and being engulfed in an Ocean of conceit, lies there ouerwhelmed" (sig. A4r). *Arisbas*'s narrative, though, more offers the trappings of Sidney's Arcadian romance than his Petrarchan lyricism, that is, thwarted love, confused identities, fantastic misadventures, and wonderful reunions. It begins with its protagonist the exiled Prince Arisbas arriving in Arcadia after what we learn has been a long search for his lost-love Timoclea, whom Arisbas refuses to believe has been forever lost at sea. Encountering the Arcadian shepherd Damon, Arisbas relates his history and is ultimately told by the shepherd that his love may in fact be in Arcadia and that he will soon be able to find out for himself at the yearly Parthenia feast in honour the beautiful shepherd boy Hyalus. Arisbas goes to the festival and is quickly reunited with his Timoclea; he then returns to his native country to take the throne.

Dido, of course, seems a very different animal. Heavily drawn from books 1, 2, and 4 of *The Aeneid*, the play has long been read by the likes of Hurst and Robinson, and others as more the work of Virgil than that of its adapters, more classical epic than Elizabethan tragedy.[32] Marlowe and Nashe add an Anna-Iarbas subplot and a Jupiter-Ganymede frame, but even so, *Dido*'s action is as undeniably driven by Aeneas's fate and Dido's passion as is the corresponding narrative in the *Aeneid*. *Dido* also resonates with ghostly vestiges of the stage. The product of London's childrens' theatres, the printed text is presented within a theatrical idiom of abbreviated speech headings (i.e., "*Jup.*"; "*Gan.*"; "*Aen.*"; and "*Iar.*") and stage directions (i.e., "*Here the Curtaines draw* [sig. A2r]; "*Enter Aeneas with Ascanius, with one or two more*" [sig. A4r]; and "*Enter Venus at another doore* [sig. C2v]"); it is permeated, too, with the unmistakable aura of theatrical satire, burlesque, even camp.[33] And while one might ultimately be able to forget that Jupiter, Aeneas, Dido, et al. were originally meant to be enacted on stage by pre-adolescent boys, this is only after reckoning with the play's opening overtly meta-theatrical spectacle of Jupiter "dandling" Ganymede on his knee, admitting – as if he were an auditor within Blackfriars – that the face of the "youth" "reflects such pleasure to mine eyes" (sigs. A2r–v).

But to admit striking differences is not also to deny that *Arisbas* and *Dido* have remarkable stylistic and thematic similarities. These likenesses especially emerge when reading the two works within the context of the Ovidian narrative poem – what C.S. Lewis in the 1950s dubbed the "Elizabethan epyllion" – the form of vernacular literature that most came to dominate the London print market during Flasket and Linley's collaboration at the Black Bear. A response at least in part to what had been the Christian moralizing of Ovid and to what had long been seen as the tired conventions of Petrarchan love poetry, Ovidian narrative poems appealed to youthful sensibilities with their quasi-pornographic imagery and their playful, oftentimes ironic, exploration of gender and sexuality.[34] Most of this poetry was written by younger university-educated men often affiliated in one way or another with the Inns of Court, and these minor epics can be usefully understood as vehicles of political and literary ambition.[35] While its roots can be traced to Greene's late romances, to Sidney's *Arcadias*, and most directly to Thomas Lodge's *Scillaes Metamorphosis* in 1589, the literary vogue peaked a few years later in the mid-1590s when Flasket and Linley would have been able to browse well over a dozen different examples of the genre in the surrounding bookshops of St Paul's.[36] The most successful of these poems in terms of sales were undoubtedly Shakespeare's *Venus and Adonis*, which was reprinted at least six times between 1593 and 1600, and Marlowe's *Hero and Leander*, which as we have seen the Black Bear duo reprinted in 1598 and yet again in 1600.

Indeed, *Arisbas* and *Dido* together respond well to this Ovidian interpretive context. What was likely *Arisbas*'s revised title *Cupid's Journey to Hell* in the two-text reissue strongly echoes the title of R.B.'s 1595 epyllion *Orpheus his Journey to Hell*, and Dickinson's romance is not simply full of allusions to both *Venus and Adonis* and *Hero and Leander*, but, like many other Ovidian poems from the 1590s, shows a self-conscious concern with literary writing, with its highest specimens and its social value. At the same time, both texts are ripe with Ovidian ironies (bordering as they are on amorality) and ambivalence towards human sexuality, and display a penchant for stylistic virtuosity (Keach 1977, 4–5), what Jim Ellis has called the epyllion's "wildly digressive and copious style" (2001, 39).

It is, in other words, within a vogue for the epyllion, within this quickly expanding market of cultural commodities that Flasket and Linley's publication of not just an expanded *Hero and Leander* but a two-text reissue of *Arisbas-Dido* is best explained, even if we admit that Marlowe's rising reputation as a poet in print (Kiséry) was likely a contributing factor. Our Black Bear duo would have already been familiar with one of the earliest examples in the genre, having inherited unsold copies of Abraham Fraunce's *The Third Part of the Countesse of Pembroke's Ivychurch* (1592) in the widow Woodcock's 1596 conveyance. And the plethora of erotic narratives appearing in the stalls around them best explains what appears to be the duo's assertive commissioning of Chapman's *Hero and Leander* continuation in 1597 or 1598. The Black Bear's investment in this market would not end with Marlowe and Chapman. The expanded *Hero and Leander*'s brisk sales along with the continued vitality of Ovidian verse in print at the turn of the sixteenth century also appears to have motivated Flasket's publication of Sir John Beaumont's *The Metamorphosis of Tobacco* in 1602. Invoking the paternity of Ovidian verse with its title-word "*Metamorphosis*" and adorned with dedicatory poems by the Ovidian poets Drayton and Francis Beaumont among many others, John Beaumont's poem would ultimately prove (with Francis Beaumont's *Salmacis and Hermaphroditus*) a bookend to what was a vibrant albeit short-lived literary vogue.[37]

Flasket and Linley's speculative venture into Ovidian poetry in the mid-1590s, however, is evidenced by more than just the four epyllia (by Fraunce, by Marlowe, by Chapman, and by Beaumont) stacked in the Black Bear stock room in 1602 and the coincidence of their collaborative years matching up with a late Elizabethan vogue in poetry. It is also shown by Flasket's own strong connection to the Ovidian poet and satirist John Weever at the turn of the century.[38] Having recently graduated from Queen's College Cambridge, Weever had moved to London sometime around 1598. By 1600 he seems to have become well acquainted with the Black Bear operation, because in 1601 the shop published his satiric poem *The Whipping of the Satyr* with Flasket even providing a sixteen-line dedicatory poem of iambic pentameter couplets for the volume entitled "To his friend" (sig. A4^v).[39] Speaking from the position of a bookseller in the poem's opening "*You that come by, and chance this booke to see,*" Flasket goes on, in conventional and straightforward terms, to attack the potential disapproving "*Parasite*" or "*Sicophant*" and then concludes with the promise that those with an "*impartiall eye*" will "*finde Wit, Poetrie, and Arte*" (sig. A4^v).[40]

A year earlier, Flasket had penned another dedicatory poem for his "friend," this time three stanzas for Weever's *Faunus and Melliflora*, what Keach has described as an eclectic, self-conscious Ovidian narrative poem of considerable virtuosity (1977, 162–89).[41] In language strikingly akin to his later dedicatory poem, Flasket addresses the potential St Paul's book buyers who "*shall chance* [Weever's] *booke to see*" (sig. A4ʳ), promising them at the end that "*In it* [they] *shall reade ripe wit, sweete Poetrie.*" Earlier in the poem, he shows himself particularly sensitive to potential accusations that he is deigning to offer another "*shepheards roundelay,*" defensiveness that one would expect from the collector and publisher of *England's Helicon*, an unprecedented volume of pastoral vernacular poetry released the same year as *Faunus and Melliflora*.[42] Flasket worries too that potential denigrators will complain about his publishing of erotic verse. "*More loue-tricks yet?*" he imagines them asking, "*will this geare neuer end, /But slight lasciuious toyes must still bee penned?*" In response, Flasket conjures a canon of English literary authority, that of Chaucer and of the recently deceased Spenser. "*If for to write of Loue and Loues delights,*" muses Flasket, "*Be not fit obiects for the grauer sights, /Then stil admired* Chaucer, *thou maist rue/And write thy auncient stories all anew:/And that same Fayry Muse may rise againe, /To blot those works that with vs do remaine.*" Spenser would very much have been on Flasket's mind in 1600 as the ascribed author of three pastoral poems in the *England's Helicon* venture. And it is Spenser's presumed literary pedigree – the product of a "*Fayry Muse*" – part and parcel with Chaucer and his "*auncient stories*" that ensures the gravity, the worth of Weever's work. Not surprisingly, given his economic bottom line as a bookseller, Flasket ends the poem by arguing for the broad popularity of such poetry, that "*As well in Cottage as in Court Loue raines*" (sig. A3ʳ).

Like Flasket would in his defence of *Faunus and Melliflora*, Dickinson had openly worried about negative reception in his prefatory addresses to *Arisbas*. In his dedicatory epistle to Edward Dyer, he asks the patron to protect him from "vnfriendly readers ... [who] may wrest his meaning by wrong coniectures" and from "the sowre censures of the ouer-curious Moralists of our age" (sig. A2ᵛ). And like Flasket would do in 1600, Dickinson also turns to a vernacular literary authority to justify what he calls the "saplesse frutes of greene youth ... [the] pithlesse blossomes of a simple Authors vnripe wit" (sig. A3ʳ). As he was for many writers in the early 1590s, Dickinson's English hero and guide is Sidney, "the Herauld of ouer-hastie destiny, ... the honour of Art & hope of Armes, Mineuaes nourse-childe, and beloved Secretary to the sacred Muses" (sig. A3ᵛ).[43] Dickinson continues his rumination upon literary authority in recording what he claims are Arisbas's "fancies" used to pass the time before the Parthenia festival.

Entitled "The Worth of Posie" and written in the style of Spenser's *Faerie Queene*, the third of Arisbas's poems imagines "the workes of [Greek and Roman] Laureate pens" being accosted by "three mishaped elues," Envy, Obliuion, and Ignorance, only to be saved by the angel-like appearance of Fame (sigs. G1ᵛ–G3ʳ).[44] Building upon Arisbas's poetic musings, Dickinson broadens the discussion to include "moderne" poetry across Europe, concluding, "In Albion the wonder of Ilands louely Thamesis, fairest of the faire Nereides loues sea-borne Queene adoring, vaunts the glory of her maiden streames, happy harbour of so many Swans, *Apollos* musical birds, which warble wonders of worth, and chaunt pleasures choice in seuerall sounds of sweetnesse, pleasant, passionate, loftie, louely" (sig. G4ʳ).[45] *Arisbas* here is akin to John Weever's *Faunus and Melliflora* and Thomas Edwards's *Narcissus* and *Cephalis and Procris* in combining an interest in "English literary culture and English nationalist sentiment" (Ellis 2003, 109).[46]

Presenting its Ovidian credentials from the start, *Arisbas* opens with the imaginative albeit paradoxical metaphor of the "Sunne soiourning in his winter mansion, [having] disrobed Arcadia of all her pleasures" (sig. B1ʳ). It quickly adds to this an erotically charged, violent image of Phoebus's return in the Spring: "Phoebus renuing his yeerely taske, and denying longer residence to stormy winter, had pierced earthes entrailes with comfortable warmth, opening a fruitfull passage for the issue of her wombe, to cloath Pomonaes branches with Natures bountie, and diapre her owne mantle with Floraes sense-alluring pomp" (sig. B1ᵛ). Once in Arcadia, we quickly encounter an Ovidian world of beautiful youths, slumming gods, and unbounded sexual energy.[47] Arisbas's shepherd companion Damon in his many tales and reported poems paints Arcadia as a land of unleashed desire and god-driven passion, where natural phenomenon like dusk can be seamlessly imagined as "Titan posting to plunge his firie Chariot in Thetis lappe" (sig. D2ʳ). There, the ship-wrecked and cross-dressed Timoclea is passionately and aggressively pursued by shepherd, shepherdess, and pirate alike, and Arcadia's definitive Parthenia festival, we find out, is dedicated to Hyalus, a boy so beautiful that his pursuit by man, woman, god, and goddess could only be resolved by his being magically transformed into a woman and carried away.

Arisbas announces its connection to the 1590s epyllion as well through allusion and parody. Arisbas himself invokes the myth of Hero and Leander when, newly arrived in Arcadia, he laments his lost love. "Aye me," he moans, "what comfort can Arcadia affoord, from whose coasts the windes fury did violently driue her? Hath then the Sea greedie of such rare gaine swallowed her, not satisfied with Helle, nor glutted with Hero?" (sig. B2ᵛ).⁴⁸ Dickenson's pastoral romance is even more insistent in its invocation of *Venus and Adonis*, alluding to the myth on a number of separate occasions. Again it is Arisbas who first invokes the myth in waxing poetic about his love Timoclea's tears at accepting his marriage proposal, comparing them to "such as might beseeme Venus to shead on her deere Adonis" (sig. C3ᵛ). Later, Damon turns again to the myth to describe the goddess Pomona's obsession with Hyalus. "Pomona," he insists, "Goddesse and patronesse of fruit did so deeply affect him, that Venus could not more dote on her Adonis" (sig. E3ᵛ).⁴⁹

Most insistent, though, are sequences within Dickinson's romance that directly parody sequences from these poems. Venus's aggressive wooing of Adonis, for example, is replayed in the goddess Pomona's relentless pursuit of Hyalus and his exasperated resistance:⁵⁰

> She desirous to winne him with ouer-cloying kindnesse, fed him with Apples, gaue him Plums, presented him Peares. Hauing made this entrance into her future solace, she would vse oft his company, kisse him, coll him, check him, chuck him, walke with him, weepe for him, in the fields, neere the fountaines, sit with him, sue to him, omitting no kindes of dalliance to woe him, winne him, feyning to droupe, to dye for him. But he which would not listen to loues loue, nor obey his hests, nor abide his lawes, tooke no pleasure in her passions, loathed her embraces, liked not these amourous combats. (sig. E3ᵛ)

Akin to Venus's plucking of Adonis from his horse at the beginning of Shakespeare's poem, the goddess and patronesse of fruit's pursuit culminates with her taking the resistant Hyalus "by the hand, and [leading] the blushing boy to her mansion, where she locked him vp close prisoner, restraind his former larger libertie, allowed him only to walke in her Orchards, and feede on her fruites" (sig. F1ʳ).⁵¹ *Arisbas*'s parody of *Hero and Leander* is no less apparent. More generally, it can be sensed in the romance's many etiological myths, digressive narratives in the vein of Ovid's *Metamorphosis* and of *Hero and Leander*'s long tale about Mercury and advent of scholarly poverty. To these, *Arisbas* offers myths about Plutus and the "Mercinary affections" (sigs. D3ʳ–D4ᵛ); Hyalus and sexual desire (sigs. E2ᵛ–F2ʳ); and the strife between Cupid and beauty (sigs. F2ᵛ–G1ᵛ). More pointedly, Poseidon's greedy envelopment of Leander as the youth swims across the Hellespont is mirrored in *Arisbas* by Zephyrus's airy penetrations of Hyalus, both when he first encounters the lad – "Zephyrus ... sighed for him: nor did hee only see him, but by oft breathing coole gales into him, felt the many sweetes lodged in that lovely subiect" (sig. E3ᵛ) – and after he steals the shepherd away to the "fortunate Ilands" – "resoluing himself into ayre, he diued into his dearling, on his eyes, on his lips he feazd, he surfeited" (sig. E4ʳ).

Ganymede's suggestive serving of Jupiter at the beginning of *Dido* invokes the epyllion's playful erotic spirit, but only for a brief four pages. Encountered as a book-to-be-read and not as a titillating play presented by the Queen's Children of the Chapel, *Dido*'s playful eroticism diminishes in both scope and kind. Coupled with Dickenson's pastoral romance, however, *Dido*'s opening playfully homoerotic episode takes on a renewed momentum. This is most immediately because *Arisbas* itself insistently alludes to the myth of Jupiter and Ganymede. The myth is first invoked when the shepherd Damon tells Arisbas of the incredible beauty of Hyalus, the shepherd boy whose transformation into a woman is celebrated in the Parthenia. "There liued in Arcadia," says Damon, "a most faire Ladde famous as the rest, I may well terme him faire, a terme too slender to emblazon his beauties woorth. Much I muse (yet I neede not muse, for Iupiter possessed Ganimede alreadie) that he made not him a praie for his pleasure" (sig. E2ᵛ). Pages later, Ganymede is again summoned in Damon's narration of Hyalus's pursuit by Pomona, Pomona chiding Hyalus for his recent absence by telling the youth, "I thought that *Jupiter* misliking *Ganimede* that now growes stale, had taken thee to supply his roome" (sig. E4ᵛ).[52]

But more than this, *Arisbas*'s mélange of allusion, parody, sexual imagery, and erotically charged ironic episodes creates a horizon of readerly expectation within which *Dido* well responds. Along with its opening scene of dandling, *Dido*, of course, possesses its own titillating episodes, most of them having to do with Dido's own aggressive (even outrageous given that she is a woman) wooing of Aeneas. Struck with the arrow of Cupid midway through the play, Dido speaks of Aeneas with a blazon of eroticism and ironic excess that is so characteristic of both Marlowe's mighty line and Ovidian verse. "Ile make me bracelets of his golden haire," Dido tells the disguised Cupid, "His glistering eyes shall be my looking glasse, / His lips an altar, where Ile offer vp / As many kisses as the Sea hath sands ... / His lookes shall be my only Librarie, / And thou *Aeneas*, *Didos* treasurie" (sig. C4ʳ).

These private musings are quickly matched with attempts, in the poetic vein of "The Passionate Shepherd to His Love," to seduce Aeneas with all that Carthage and her imagination can afford: "tackling made of reueld gold, / Wound on the barkes of odoriferous trees" and, ironically, "Oares of massie Iuorie full of holes, / Through which the water shall delight to play" (sig. C4^v).[53] Immediately before the consummation of their love, her invitation to the incaved Trojan that he "in [her] armes make thy *Italy*, / Whose Crowne and kingdome rests at thy commande" (sig. E1^r) is coupled with the kinds of sexual images that were the coin of the Elizabethan epyllion. Aeneas, Dido provocatively insists, is "The man that I doe eye where ere I am, / Whose amorous face like *Pean* sparkles fire, / When as he buts his beames in *Floras* bed, ..." (sig. D4^v). And she then thanks the "Kind clowdes that sent forth such a curteous storme, / As made disdaine to flye to fancies lap" (sig. E1^r). Once threatened with rejection, Dido's language becomes more desperate, more potentially violent in its sexual imagery. "O that I had a charme to keepe the windes / Within the closure of a golden ball," she tells Anna and company, "Or that the Tyrrhen sea were in mine armes, / That he might suffer shipwracke on my breast" (sig. E4^v). This provocative language of sex, scale, and strength are most obviously reprised in *Venus and Adonis*.

Dido's impassioned pursuit of Aeneas is itself parodied by the Nurse's appeals to the disguised Cupid, invitations that like Venus's seductions of Adonis in Shakespeare's poem comically destabilize the boundaries between motherly love and sexual desire. "[T]hou shalt goe with me vnto my house," the Nurse tells Cupid who she believes to be Aeneas's son Ascanius, "I haue an Orchard that hath store of plums, / Browne Almonds, Seruises, ripe Figs and Dates, / ... a garden where are Bee hiues full of honey, / ... And in the midst doth run a siluer streame, / Where thou shalt see the red gild fishes leape" (sig. F1^v). What seem at first to be maternal ruses to move an unmovable child, however, quickly take on an effusive energy of their own and are clearly reminiscent again of the erotic language in Marlowe's "Passionate Shepherd to his Love." Not surprisingly, then, to Cupid's acquiescence, the Nurse both asks that he "call [her] mother" and at the same time wishes that she "might liue to see this boy a man, / How pretilie he laughs" (sig. F1^v). At the end of the scene, the Nurse is continuing to indulge in desire, musing, "I may liue a hundred yeares, / Fourescore is but a girles age, loue is sweete" (sig. F2^r). Together, these scenes of unbounded female desire take on a new immediacy in the context of *Arisbas*, constituting a textual web of playful eroticism to be enjoyed by Flasket and Linley's readers.

Where Hurst and Robinson in 1825 saw *Dido* as Virgil veneered with drama, then, Flasket and Linley in the late 1590s saw Ovid. In this, they were the first to acknowledge *Dido's* sexual energy and irrepressible ironies, elements that today have made the play a favourite among readers and audiences alike. Over fifty years ago, Douglas Cole in *Suffering and Evil in the Plays of Christopher Marlowe* was one of the first in the twentieth century to make the observation that while "the matter [of *Dido*] is Virgilian, the spirit is Ovid's" (85).[54] Since then, it has become essentially routine to read the play in terms of Ovid, as – among other things – a 1580s manifestation of the "rival tradition" of Aeneas and Dido inaugurated by Ovid, as a joint product of Ovid and Virgil, and as an Ovidian rewriting of Virgil.[55] In repackaging *Dido* with *Arisbas*, however, the Black Bear duo did not simply recognize the Ovidian resonances in Marlowe's earliest play; they also invested in them, speculating that a two-title volume – joined together by theme rather than by a singular author – would find a motivated cadre of Elizabethan bookbuyers. These were "the younger sort" who, as Gabriel Harvey lamented in the margin of his personal copy of Chaucer, were taking "much delight in Shakespeare's *Venus and Adonis*" (Hyland 2003, 64) along with women like Mistress Harebrain in *A Mad World My Masters* (1608), whom Middleton armed with a store of "wanton Pamphlets, as Hero and Leander, Venus and Adonis" (sig. B1ᵛ).

Dido's early reception also indicates that the market for printed professional playbooks continued to be uncertain in the late 1590s. Faced with largely untested commodities and an ever-changing print market, publishers had ample motivation to be flexible in reading play-text copy and agile in responding to its intial reception in print. For Flasket and Linley at the Black Bear, this dexterity was manifest in a publication strategy of reissues amidst commissioning and specialization. Their two-title edition of *Arisbas* and *Dido* may never have reached London's bookstalls to vie with the sixth edition of *Venus and Adonis*, but the project – abortive as it may have been – marks a provocative moment in *Dido's* early fortunes as a book to be read.

Chapter Five

Reading *Hamlet* (1603): Nicholas Ling, Sententiae, and Republicanism

he laboured in the common-wealth, /And sought their good, by gouerning the King
> *The Legend of Humphrey Duke of Gloucester* (1600)

I holde my duetie as I hold my life, / Both to my God, and to my soueraigne King
> *The Tragical History of Hamlet Prince of Denmark* (1603)

Since the mid-1980s, historians have undertaken a broad reconsideration of the roots of the English Civil War.[1] Dissatisfied with the assumption that a republican political temper emerged spontaneously in the late 1630s, that various social practices and customs kept sixteenth-century Englishmen from conceiving of either themselves as active citizens or of the "commonwealth" as potentially a republican state, Patrick Collinson, Quentin Skinner, and Markku Peltonen among others have together identified a number of different republican strands of thought and action in Tudor England.[2] Collinson has even gone so far as to characterize late Elizabethan England as a "monarchical republic," arguing that it "was a republic which happened also to be a monarchy: or vice versa" (1997, 119). According to him, Tudor England's governing practices, shaped as they were by recurring crises of succession, ultimately helped constitute a self-sustaining political system that was doubly ensured both by an empowered citizenry and by a monarch.

These reappraisals have inspired the work of a number of literary scholars. David Norbrook has shown how the various imaginings of republican political practice before the Civil War produced a distinctively republican poetics in the 1630s and 1640s, and Patrick Cheney has called for a rethinking of the politics of Christopher Marlowe's work through the framework of what he describes as "the representational phase" of English republicanism.[3] Like Norbrook and Cheney, Andrew Hadfield has identified elements of republican thought in the work of many different Elizabethan writers, most recently in the early plays and poetry of Shakespeare.[4] In *Shakespeare and Republicanism*, Hadfield contends that a number of Shakespeare's 1590s works can productively be read within the contemporary contexts of republican-inflected political discourse and an ongoing crisis of succession. One of his more compelling arguments concerns *Hamlet*. Tracking allusions to Belleforest's *Histoires tragique* (1570) and to the various works of George Buchanan, Hadfield illustrates how "*Hamlet* stands as a distinctly republican play" (189) both in its implicit comparison of its protagonist to Lucius Junius Brutus and more generally in its rumination upon government and legitimate forms of political action.

In this final chapter, I contend that this reading of *Hamlet* is not as original as it might at first appear, that it may in fact echo the reception of Q1 *Hamlet* by one of its first readers: the bookseller and publisher Nicholas Ling.[5] As underscored throughout this book, early-modern publishers were themselves "actual readers (among the first and most crucial)" in that they had to have their own sense of a potential publication's meaning and had to "understand [a] text's position within all the relevant discourses, institutions, and practices, in order to speculate on the meanings his imagined customers might make of it."[6] In advertising on Q1 *Hamlet*'s title page in 1603 that the play "hath beene diuerse times acted by his Highnesse ser- | uants" and is "By William Shake-speare," Ling casts a reliable net, understanding his text as a potential commodity for both playgoers and for buyers of respectable reading material, literary or otherwise.[7]

Yet Q1 *Hamlet*'s title page only begins to tell the full story of Ling's early speculative reading of the play. His initial decision to finance an edition seems also to have been motivated by his late-career publishing specialties.[8] In general outline, Ling's early publications between 1580 and 1584 were religious in subject matter. In the 1590s, he expanded his offerings to include works in both verse and prose by the likes of Michael Drayton, Thomas Lodge, and Robert Greene. During the last ten years of his career, he put out more than a half-dozen collections of "wise sayings."[9] Ling also began to brand many of his publication's

Figure 9 The printer's emblem of Nicholas Ling, from the title page of *Rosalynde* (1596). By permission of the Huntington Library, San Marino, California.

title pages with his own conspicuous printer's emblem: a ling fish enwrapped by and supporting a climbing flower (see figure 9).[10]

Ling's late publications also can be grouped according to their political content. Beginning in the mid-1590s, Ling invested a significant amount of his energy in texts that engage in substantial ways with republican themes having to do with governance, counsel, and political virtue. These texts are *Cornelia* (1594); *Politeuphuia Wit's Commonwealth* (1597, 1598 [2], 1604); *The Legend of Humphrey Duke of Gloucester* (1600); *Utile-dulce: or, Truth's Liberty* (1606); *The Commonwealth of England* (entered 22 January 1607 to Ling); and *A Commonwealth of Good Counsel* (1607).[11] As I will show, Ling's publishing penchants at the turn of the sixteenth century – particularly his direct and speculative engagements with late sixteenth-century conceptions of counsel, office holding, and political resistance – provide oblique evidence of how the 1603 edition of *Hamlet* was first read as a literary product during the uneasy final months of Elizabeth's reign, and also an alternative genealogy of early-modern republican discourse, one discernible within the limited constellation of a bookseller's publishing specialties, editing practices, reprints, procurements, and marketing strategies.

Vending the Republic

Ling was baptized in Norwich on 4 April 1553.[12] His father John Ling was a successful parchment maker in the large East Anglia city, and it was from an ample paternal legacy that Nicholas likely drew his not insignificant investment capital. By 1570, Ling had moved to London and been indentured to Henry Bynneman, the well-established London printer and publisher. Nine years later in 1579, he was admitted to the freedom of London, but after working only six years as a publisher and bookseller out of shops leased from his old master, he returned to Norwich in 1585.[13] Back in London in 1590, Ling seems to have begun his publishing activities in earnest, financing more than forty different titles in more than seventy editions over the next seventeen years. By 1598, Ling was able to buy into the company livery (Arber, 2.872). Seven months after his death in April 1607, much of his stock was assigned to the stationer John Smethwick (Arber, 3.365).[14]

So far, Ling has attracted bibliographic interest because of a particular habit of business. As Gerald D. Johnson tracked, Ling consistently collaborated with other stationers in his many publishing ventures. Such collaboration took the form of joint entries in the Stationers' Register and/or co-ownership of printing copyrights, along with a collaborative method of procuring copy.[15] "Of the sixty-six titles with which he was involved in his career," writes Johnson, "he entered and published only sixteen alone. ... He entered seven titles with other stationers, published editions of eighteen titles which had been entered to another stationer, and was assigned five copy-rights" (205). Undergirding such practices, surmises Johnson, must have been a number of private "business arrangements" with stationers like Cuthbert Burby, James Roberts, Simon Waterson, and especially John Busby.

Between 1594 and 1607, Ling developed a defining specialty: books engaged implicitly and explicitly with republican political ideas.[16] Gauged in terms of time, money, and energy spent, Ling's most definitive offering in this series was undoubtedly *Politeuphuia*, an extensive collection of aphoristic sayings from classical, scholastic, and contemporary authors.[17] Published solely by the bookseller in 1597 and derived in part from William Baldwin's *A Treatise of Moral Philosophy* and the English translation of Pierre de La Primaudaye's *Academie françoise* (*"The French Academy"*), the work proved to be particularly lucrative, reaching a third edition within one year (1598) and a fourth in 1604.[18] Initially, the compiling of *Politeuphuia*'s aphorisms seems to have been undertaken by John Bodenham, but this labour was apparently at some point energetically taken over by Ling, who in two prefatory epistles represents himself as *both* a compiler and an editor.[19] In his second epistle, Ling refers to the collection as his "trauailes" and "paines," and he concludes by promising to "gather more against the next impression."[20] In this epistle, he makes it clear that he was solely responsible for the collection's section "heades" (or headings). "I haue thus boldly aduentured," he writes, "in gathering of certaine heades or places, that with the more ease thou maist discourse of any subiect tending to vertue or vice" (sig. A3^r). In subsequent editions, Ling would continue to underscore this "gathering." In his second edition, he writes, "Some new heads I haue inserted, corrected many where I found it necessary, and almost euery one in some sort augmented" (1598a, sig. A3^r); in his third, he reiterates, "Some what new I haue inserted, put out many things where I found it necessary" (1598b, sig. A3^r).[21]

Printed in an octavo format with his emblem on the title page, Ling's first *Politeuphuia* divides into 140 different "heades or places," ranging from "Of God" and "Of Heauen" at its beginning to "Of Deuills" and "Of Hell" at its conclusion. Each of Ling's headings includes a "definition" which is then followed by a varying number of "sentences" (aphoristic sayings). The collection can broadly be understood as bridging the gap between the readerly self-fashioning fostered by the manuscript poetic miscellany and the gathering-and-framing reading strategies encouraged by the Elizabethan commonplace book.[22] Along with invoking the elite prerogative of "making it one's own," *Politeuphuia* also appealed to its upwardly mobile readers by assuaging their anxieties about an impoverished and unruly vernacular, offering in its sentences access to a shared cultural code organized under recognizable headings from the religious, political, cultural, and personal realms.

Ling's cultural code, however, proves multivalent if not orthodox. In *Politeuphuia*'s headings, Ling frequently invokes republican ideas about authority.[23] In "Of Treason," for example, Ling defines treason not as a "*damned vice*" perpetuated against a monarch but more vaguely against "Country," "God," or any number of authorities: "*Treason is that damned vice hated of God and man, wherewith periured persons being bewitched, feare not to betray themselues, so they may either betray others or theyr Country; it is the breach of faith and loyaltie, with God, their Gouernours, and Country*" (sig. Kk7ᵛ).²⁴ Indeed, of this heading's twenty-two aphorisms, only two directly allude to treason against a "Prince." This failure to highlight kingly authority can be seen in Ling's other headings as well. In his definition for "Of Oath," Ling makes no reference to oaths made to sovereign kings, only that "*the lawfull oath is that which is taken before authoritie*" (sig. V2ᵛ). Similarly, in "Of Consideration," authoritative judgment is defined as "*that which properly ought to be in euery Magistrate, obseruing the tenor of the law* (sig. N6ʳ).

In these and other sayings, authority is not identified with a monarch but instead assumed to be diffuse, disseminated in a number of possible "*Gouernours*," or, as Ling has it in one of his more unique headings, in a number of possible "offices." *Politeuphuia*'s heading "Of Office" represents a significant departure from its sources. Neither *A Treatise of Moral Philosophy* nor *The French Academy* incorporate it as a heading, and Ling's dedicatee Bodenham does not make it a part of his own later collection *Belvedere*. Even so, office holding was a ubiquitous phenomenon in early-modern England, a significant counterpart to the humanist stress on civic participation. As Marc Goldie has shown, all men, both of the city and the rural parish, would have expected to hold some kind of office during their lifetimes; "the early modern English polity," writes Goldie, "was paradoxically cross-grained in character. People saw themselves as subjects of an anointed monarch who was armed with awesome prerogative powers, yet also saw themselves as citizens of self-governing communities" (2001, 175–6). Early-modern office holding was not just ubiquitous; conceptually, it was often a stake in proto-republican understandings of effective governance. As Collinson has shown, an important strand of the Elizabethan "ideological capacity for resistance" was the conviction found in many mid-century texts that the monarchy was "no more or no less than a public office" (1997, 44), charged to serve the public good. At the same time, works like *A Mirror for Magistrates* (1559) suggested that all office holders were answerable first and foremost to God, morally compelled to resist monarchic tyranny (Lucas 2007).

For Ling, "Office" signifies many things, but his positioning of the term immediately after "Of Lawes," "Of Counsaile," "Precepts and Counsels," and "Of Consideration" demonstrates that he was most concerned with its political connotations. According to Ling's definition,

"*Office ... is the knowledge of man concerning his owne nature, & contemplation of diuine nature, and a labour to benefit our selves and all other men; it is also taken for authoritie or rule*" (sig. N7^v). Of the thirty sentences on "Office" that he includes in the first edition of *Politeuphuia*, half of them have to do explicitly with the governmental connotations of office. Within these, office is equated with "rule" – "He is onley fit to rule & beare office, which comes to it by constraint, & against his will" (sig. N8^v) – and presented in idealized terms – "They which sell offices, sell the most sacred thing in the worlde, euen iustice it selfe, the Common-wealth, subiects, and the Lawes" (sig. N8^v).

In *Politeuphuia*, Ling stresses other activities of active citizenship as well, particularly counsel.[25] As Arthur Ferguson, Peltonen, and others have pointed out, English humanists came to see counsel as a crucial avenue of active civic service in the sixteenth century, essentially adapting the Ciceronian ideal of the *vita activa* to their monarchal context.[26] Indeed, Collinson has demonstrated that the most "clear and coherent" republican-inflected doctrine in Elizabethan times was a belief that it was necessary to control the powers of the crown by establishing a coterie of virtuous advisers who had the constitutional right to advise the monarch (Hadfield 2005, 17). For Ling, "*Counsaile is a most holy thing, it is the sentence or aduice which particulerly is gyuen by euery man for that purpose assembled: it is the key of certaintie, and the end of all doctrine and study*" (sig. I4^v).[27] Ling is so sanguine about the positive value of counsel that in his first edition of *Politeuphuia* he also merges it with "precepts" in his heading "Of Precepts and Counsels." "*Precepts*" – and by extension "counsels" – "*are many rules, orders, or methods, which by instruction leades vs eyther to good conuersation, or to happiness of life, beeing grounded vppon the Grace of God and his word*" (sig. M3^v).[28]

Significantly, in his definitions of "Office" and "Counsaile," Ling does not explicitly associate either with service to a higher political authority; instead, "*Counsaile*" is described as being a product sought by some vague agent ("*gyuen by euery man for that purpose assembled*") and the benefits of "Office" are couched in terms of a larger community ("*all other men*"). Ling pursues a similar line in the consecutive headings "Of Seruing" and "Of Obedience" towards the end of the collection. In the former, he does not mention service to a king, and his negative sentiments towards service in general are barely veiled: "*Seruing, or seruitude is a certaine slauish bond of constraint, by which, eyther for commoditie or loue, men binde themselues to the wil of others; making themselues subiect to controlement*" (sig. T3ʳ).[29] In the latter heading (with a definition that again is taken almost verbatim from *The French Academy* [1594, sig. H2ᵛ]), Ling chooses a more positive slant, but he again is conspicuously silent about any monarchical ramifications of such a "vertue." "*Obedience*," quotes Ling, "*is the end where-unto vertue tendeth, namely, when in all our actions wee obserue honestie & comlines, it is that which bindeth the soule, when fully and willinglie, without force or constraint, we giue to euerie one that which belongeth vnto him: honour to whom honor, reuerence to whom reuerence, tribute to whom tribute, and succour to whom succour belongeth*" (1597, sig. T4ᵛ).[30] In this nebulous vow to give obedience "*to euerie one that which belongeth vnto him*," Ling is very different from Baldwin, who in his *Treatise of Moral Philosophy* clearly connects "obedience" with a king and other sources of "authority": "Gods holy loue & obedience excludeth all shame./Obey thy King, thy parents, all lavves & authority, /Then doubtles thou shalt lead thy life most quietly" (1591, sig. L4ᵛ).

Three years before financing the first edition of *Hamlet*, Ling published another work with strong republican valences: Christopher Middleton's *The Legend of Humphrey Duke of Gloucester* (1600).[31] Stamped with his emblem on the title page and one of 16 works that Ling both entered and published on his own, *The Legend of Humphrey* is prefaced with commendatory poems by familiar Ling authors: Robert Allot, Michael Drayton, and John Weever.[32] Together, these elements underscore what appears to have been Ling's energetic investment in Middleton's 184-stanza poem.

Like Shakespeare's *1 Henry VI* and *2 Henry VI* and a number of other works, *The Legend of Humphrey* is focused upon the fifteenth-century career of Humphrey Duke of Gloucester, Lord Protector during King Henry VI's minority.[33] As J.G.A. Pocock, Anne McLaren, and others have shown, perceptions of monarchical incapacity due to age or gender had had much to do with mid-sixteenth-century calls "to a *vita activa* in the service of the monarchy, to protect and defend the common weal in the absence of a (godly) king."[34] Middleton, in focusing upon the political uncertainty surrounding Henry VI's minority, invokes the terms of this discourse, not insignificantly during the tense years of Elizabeth's later reign. In doing so, he idealizes the office of the counsellor and raises doubts about the extent of kingly authority.

Throughout its stanzas, *The Legend of Humphrey* celebrates the pre-eminent virtue of Humphrey as Henry's protector and counsellor.

Derived from his royal blood, from his "attending the resorts/Of learned Councellors" (sig. B2^v), and from "his matchlesse learning and his wit" (sig. B2^v), Humphrey's virtue is most expressed as a single-minded devotion to his office as Lord Protector. In his infamous confrontation with the Bishop of Winchester, Humphrey "wisht not the Bishops ill"; instead, he "Goes forward in his office, and assayes/To roote vp other weedes, that were as ill, /Though not so mighty; so the weedes being dead, /The flow'rs might sooner grow and better spread" (sig. D1^r). Humphrey's assignation, suggests Middleton, was to involve "all" in governmental affairs. This is most clearly shown when Humphrey refers the "tyranny" of Winchester to the collective will of Parliament: "[Winchester's] tyranny, when Gloster once espies, /Like a good subiect, labours to preuent/The further mischiefe that might else arise, /And in an open Court of Parlament, /Drawes articles; wherein he had exprest/The Bishops wrongs, which all would haue redrest" (sig. C1^r). Because Humphrey, "Medled with nothing, but what did belong/Vnto [his] office" (sig. C1^v), he was "guiltlesse" (sig. C1^v) of England's coming civil broils

Though "the Scepter" "Too heauy was (God knowes) for such a hand" (sig. B2^r), Henry is still shown to wield righteous authority in attempting to mediate between Humphrey and the Bishop of Winchester. As Middleton writes early on in the poem, Henry's "holy life, good workes, and vertuous deedes, /I leaue as subiects fit for greater wits:/For greater are the vertues that proceedes/From Kings, then meaner men" (sig. B2^r). Having said this, however, Middleton continually questions the agency of an unadvised king and insists upon the necessity of law and the political action that it inspires. He makes it clear that one of Henry's greatest mistakes was his "by priuate meanes, without th'consent/Of his Protector Gloster, [being] willing .../To marry" (sig. E4^r). And in lamenting the dispute between Humphrey and Winchester, Henry himself asserts the primacy of law: "But since our first creation, we haue still/Beene subiects vnto sinne, therefore the law/Was first ordain'd .../That those bad men whom no good meanes could mend/For terror of the law, might feare t'offend" (sig. C3^r). It is his strong sense of the necessity and rightness of law that drives Humphrey to intervene often in the early affairs of Henry. As Middleton puts it, Humphrey "laboured in the common-wealth, /And sought their good, by gouerning the King" (sig. F1^v). In so doing, he served his country as an "*Atlas*, abler to sustaine/The heauy burden of his Cousens Raigne" (sig. B2^v).

Six years after publishing Middleton's poetic encomium to Humphrey, Ling added another work to his list of republican-inflected texts: a volume of selected *Colloqiues* by Erasmus. "The first significant presentation of the *Colloquies* in English" (Dodds 2009, 127), this collection was translated by William Burton, an Anglican clergyman.[35] Burton had years earlier occupied a ministry in Norwich in the late 1580s, and it is possible that he and Ling had become acquainted during this time.[36] Ling first published the work as *Utile-Dulce or Truth's Liberty*, advertising on its title page: "*Seuen wittie-wise Dialogues, full of | delight, and fitte for. vse: verie appliable to | these times, but seasonable for all ages, till | Roomes idolatrie, and women's de- | licacie, be reformed.*" In the same year, presumably responding to a recent upsurge of anti-Catholic sentiment in London following the Gunpowder Plot (Devereux 1983, 52), he reissued the collection with a new title, *Seven Dialogues Both Pithy and Profitable*, and a new title-page advertisement that three times stresses the collection's anti-"Popish" content. The reissue also includes a short "Printer to the Reader" epistle in which Ling admits that Burton "was absent, and vnaquainted with the sodaine publication of his booke" (sig. a2ᵛ) and an epistle "To the Christian Reader" in which Burton promises familiar Ling commodities: "*doctrines, both sound and substantiall. ... [S]entences, not prettie, but pithie, ... similes and examples, both wittie and weighty*" (1606a, sig. a1ʳ).[37]

From the early sixteenth century, the *Colloquies* had long provided pedagogical fodder for humanist grammar schools; they constituted one pervasive component of Erasmus's wide and sustained dissemination in Tudor England.[38] In his 1606 translation, Burton trades on this ubiquity. "Erasmus," Burton writes in his added epistle, "*hath no need of my commendations. To the learned and iudicious, yea generally to all men, he is so wel knowne for his deepe learning, and profound iudgment: that for the entertainment of these his conferences I needed not but only to haue said* Erasmus *wrote them*" (1606a, sig. a1ʳ). Burton freely redevelops Erasmus's "*conferences*" for his own particular ends. Gregory D. Dodds has demonstrated how the volume, especially its translation of the dialogue between a butcher and fishmonger, manipulates its source material, producing in its pages a political agenda that supports "moderation, peace, the power of civil authority, and the distinction between public and private spheres of religious discourse – all topics that would not have displeased James I" (2009, 128).

Burton's approach to civil authority, however, is more complex than Dodds would have it. His translation – in both its choice of colloquies and its additions to them – forwards a nuanced understanding of what is best *"for the generall good of* [the] *Church and Common-wealth"* (1606a, sig. a1ʳ), suggesting limits to kingly authority and idealizing a proto-republican model of governance.

In his opening dedicatory epistle to "the *Maior, Shiriffes and Aldermen*, together with all that vnfainedly feare God, *and sincerely loue the truth, in that religious and fa*mous Citie of *Norwich*," Burton fondly remembers the provincial capital Norwich as a city state of the godly, where "common assemblies" decided "matters of weight" and were necessarily held in check by the counsel of the "graue and godlie." "Oh the heauenly harmony and sweete amitie," writes Burton, "that then was amongst you from the highest to the lowest! The magistrates and the Ministers imbracing and seconding one an other, and the common people affording due reverence, & obedience to them both. No matter of weight were vsually concluded in your common assemblies for the good of your Citie, before you had first consulted with your graue and godlie Preachers" (sigs. A1ʳ⁻ᵛ). Inviting comparisons between Norwich and republican Rome, Burton goes on to equate the city's magistrates with "Senators" and ignores James's larger authority as monarch and as head of the Anglican church. Burton's idealization of Norwich as a kind of quasi-independent civic republic was not entirely without warrant. In his study of Norwich in the seventeenth century, John T. Evans has shown how Norwich was in many respects an "anomaly" among early-modern English cities, because of its "strong constitutional heritage" (27) and the unrivalled degree of democratic participation in the freemen-dominated civic government.[39] Moreover, says Evans, "During [Elizabeth's and James's reigns] Norwich was a world in itself: urban unrest was limited, the city was capable of handling its own affairs, and communications to and from either Westminster or Whitehall were infrequent" (63–4).

Though ostensibly about Lent and the biblical prohibition against eating flesh, Erasmus's longest colloquy, a dialogue between a butcher and fishmonger, raises serious questions about the limits of monarchic authority. In responding to the Fishmonger's request that he distinguish between the laws of God and the laws of man, the Butcher eventually lists a fundamental republican principle: "mans law is no law, unless it be approued by the consent of the people" (sig. D4ʳ). To this, the Fishmonger vaguely responds, "You heap vp a number of things together, wherof some I like, and som I mislike, and som I understand not" (sig. D4ᵛ). Whether he "mislike[s]" of the Butcher's "approued ... consent" is never made clear. While the Fishmonger may baulk at the Butcher's questioning of the difference between the authority of God and man – responding forcefully that that is "[a] wicked question" (sig. D3ᵛ), he at the same time is not willing to reject the implications of the question entirely:

> I think that the lawes of our Emperours ought to be reuerently embraced, and religiously obserued, euen as proceeding from God, neither doe I holde it safe, or sauouring of godlinesse, sinisterly to conceiue, or suspitiously to speake of publique authoritie. And if there be any thing that may seeme to sauour of tyranny, which yet dooth not compell men to impietie, I doe holde it better to suffer it patiently, then to resist it seditiously. (sigs. D4ᵛ–E1ʳ)

On the face of it, the Fishmonger seems to insist (in the tradition of St Augustine) that we must "suffer [tyranny] patiently" in all cases, but there is fine print veiled in his obedient language. We must so suffer, says the Fishmonger, only if such tyranny "dooth not compell men to impietie." The Fishmonger offers a similar political caveat a few pages later, arguing that "Whatsoeuer Christ did institute, he instituted it to the health both of soule and bodie, neither can any potentate chalenge vnto himselfe so great power, as that by his constitutions he may driue any persons to endaunger their liues" (sig. F1ᵛ). Godliness, here, trumps service, opening the door – in Baldwin's translation of pope as "potentate" – to religious challenges of kingly authority.

Similarly suggesting limits to such authority is Burton's third selection, "A very excellent Dialogue betweene *a good Woman and a Shrew.*" Grounded in the writings of St Paul, Plutarch, Xenophon, and St Jerome, this dialogue between Eulalia and Xantippe offers a significantly expanded version of Erasmus's popular colloquy on marriage (Thompson 1971, 307–9). Burton's two-page expansion is cued by Xantippe's question "Shall I call him husband that taketh me for his seruante?" and is indicated in the margin with "All that followeth after this marke * til you come vnto the like marke again is not in Erasmus" (sig. H3ʳ). In it, Burton's anatomizes wifely "service," ultimately exploring its connotations through the conventional analogy of wife = subject, husband = king:

Eula. ... Though a man bee a noble man, and a Lord, and hath tenants under him, yet is he also a subiect, and must obey his Prince, as one that liueth under a law: and yet though a Lord, or a freeholder are to obey the law, and to doe seruice for their Prince, yet are they not in the nature of the Princes hired seruants, or bond seruants, which are daily about him, and take wages, but are as free subiects, and do enioy their goods and lands, &c. vnder the Princes protection, and liue in great liberty. (sig. H4ʳ)

Reminiscent of *Politeuphuia*'s anxiety about service as a "slauish bond of constraint," Burton's qualifications – expressed here by Eulalia – betray not simply his more enlightened, companionate understanding of marriage, but also his own discomfort with unconditional obedience to a monarch. Though this passage seems to set up an equivalence between law and king, Burton makes it clear earlier on in his addition that husbands (and by extension kings) only enjoy a "certaine soueraigneitie" over their wives, an authority only going so far as they "commaund ... anie honest and lawfull thing" (sig. H3ʳ).

Burton's ideas about collective governance and delimited monarchical power are echoed by Sir Thomas Smith's *De Republica Anglorum*, a text that Ling entered in the Stationers' Register according to its revised title as "The common wealth of England" on 22 January 1607 (Arber, 3.337). Smith originally wrote the work seven years into Elizabeth's reign in 1565. While it was apparently not published until 1583, the tract was widely circulated in manuscript before being entered by John Day in 1581 and published by George Seton two years later. By the time Ling obtained the rights to copy it, the work had gone through four editions. While he apparently did not live long enough to bring his own fifth edition to press, Ling could not have helped but identify a number of compelling themes in Smith's treatise, themes that resonated well with what I have been suggesting were Ling's kinds of books.[40]

As Anne McLaren has well shown, *De Republica Anglorum* should not simply be read as a status-quo portrait of English society and governance, but as a work that actively "theorizes the 'mixed monarchy' inaugurated with Elizabeth's accession" (1999, 914).[41] That Smith's ideas were potentially contentious was recognized by the work's first publisher John Day, who warned in an epistle that "some termes or other matters may seeme to dissent from the vsuall phrase of the common lawes of this Realme."[42] The "matters" that Day might have been referring to include Smith's equation of rank with virtue (McLaren 1999, 929), his conception of civil order maintained through "the collective will of all men" (932), and his unprecedented assertion of Parliament's sovereignty (Hoak 2007). It might also have had to do with his veneration of office holding at all social levels. Indeed, Smith divides men in commonwealths according to those that can and cannot hold office: "The diuision of these which bee participant of the Common-wealth, is one way of them that beare office, the other of them that beare none: the first are called magistrates, the second priuate men" (sig. D2^v). Smith's strong belief in the collective check upon monarchal power can be seen early on in the treatise when he differentiates between kings and tyrants. "A Tyrant they name him," writes Smith, "who by force commeth to the monarchy against the will of the people, breaketh lawes already made, at his pleasure, maketh other without the aduise & consent of the people, and regardeth not the wealth of his Commons, but the aduancement of himselfe, his faction and kindred" (1601, sig. B3^v).

While Ling apparently was not able to bring out an edition of *The Commonwealth of England* before his death, he *was* able that year to reissue – at entirely his own expense – the first edition of *The Counselor*, a work that has been described as a "remarkable continental republican treatise" (Peltonen 1995, 102).[43] An anonymous English translation of the Latin work *De optimo senatore libri duo, The Counselor* was originally written by the Pole Laurentius Grimalius Goslicius and was first published by Richard Bradock in 1598. Goslicius's stated intention in writing his treatise was to outline "the qualities appertaining to an excellent Counsellour" (sig. A2^v), but his work also offers an approving portrait of Poland's mixed monarchical state. As Peltonen maps out, *The Counselor*'s appearance in 1598 had to do with new intellectual curiosity about Poland; it also represented an endorsement of a particular form of mixed monarchy during the fraught final years of Elizabeth's reign (1995, 103–5).

As he did with his reissue of *Cornelia* in 1594, Ling provided a new title page for *The Counselor*, one containing his printer's emblem, his imprint, some emended blurbs, and most importantly a new title: *A Commonwealth of Good Counsel.*[44] Ling's new title distinguishes his books from Bradock's, and, in adding the word "commonwealth" connects them with his *Politeuphuia* and his planned edition of *The Commonwealth of England*. Given that "commonwealth" also connotes a collection of sorts, it at the same time also indicates that the book, like *Politeuphuia*, contains different kinds of counsel to be gathered. Ling makes a more pointed allusion to this in one of his emended blurbs, promising that "all sorts of well affected | *Readers, may furnish themselues with all kind of Philosophicall or* | Morall reading."[45]

Ling's new title alludes as well to the political content of his new publication. In outlining his ideal commonwealth, Goslicius equates true nobility with virtue and endorses legal and collective checks on the power of the monarch (Peltonen, 108–10), ideas that are similarly endorsed in *Politeuphia* and *The Commonwealth of England*. He frequently suggests too that kings, like all magistrates, occupy "offices," and he makes it clear that virtuous counsellors are best able to maintain a commonwealth on their own:

> Those men beeing as a meane betwixt the king and the people, doe on the one side, know the office of the king, and on the other, what are the customes and lawes belonging to the people: thereof conceiuing, what ought be done for preseruation of the kinges honour, and what apperteyneth to the profitt of the commonweale & people. We thereof inferre; that these magistrates or councellors, are of all other most able to stand the commonweale in stead. (sig. D3ʳ)

As in *The Legend of Humphrey*, kingly imperfections make it necessary that a commonwealth boast many able counsellors. According to Goslicius, "A Kinge shall well gouerne all things, not onelye through his owne opinion, which may many waies be deceiued, but also by the common aduise and councell of others, whereby his reason and iudgemente is brought to perfection" (sig. C4ᵛ).

Wise counsellors are also, according to Goslicius, a necessity for a state when facing the inevitable outbreaks of sedition. "The commonweale," says Goslicius, "requireth the Counsell of some notable and diuine man, in whome it may repose the care of hir happines and welldoing. By his directions and gouernment, all perils, seditions, discordes, mutations and inclinations may be suppressed, and therby enioy a happy peace and tranquility" (sig. H5ʳ). Imagining it within what he takes to be the ideal political context of mixed monarchy, Goslicius consistently assumes sedition to be a danger to the larger state, not simply to a king. Though he allows for the possibility that men "apt for sedition" direct their efforts "against the King, the Counsell and all good subiectes" (sig. H2ᵛ), he continually insists that its antidote must be conceived in terms of the commonwealth's "whole bodie." Citing Plato, Goslicius advises the aspiring counsellor or magistrate "to be carefull for the whole bodie of the commonweale, least in taking the protection of part, he doth abandon the rest. For who so defendeth one onely sort of men, doth induce hatred and sedition: which two plagues, doe debilitate and subuert the state. He ought therefore to be as carefull of the people as of the King, of the nobilitie as of the meaner sort, of the rich as of the poore, of the wise, as the simple, and so consequently of all sortes and estates of men" (sig. H3ᵛ).

Speculating with *Hamlet* (1603)

While these texts together represent a defining investment of time, intellectual energy, and capital, Ling nevertheless remains best known today for his involvement with the first two print editions of *Hamlet*.[46] Some version of the play was first entered into the Stationers' Register on 26 July 1602 by James Roberts (Arber, 2.212).[47] In the next year, *The Tragical History of Hamlet Prince of Denmark* ("Q1") was published by Ling and John Trundle. Strangely, Roberts – the printing patent owner – apparently had no direct involvement with this first printed edition.[48] One year later, Ling's name again appeared on a quarto publication of *Hamlet*. This time, Ling is identified as the sole publisher of *The Tragical History of Hamlet, Prince of Denmark. By William Shakespeare* ("Q2"), with James Roberts listed as the printer. Two compelling explanations have been offered for this odd series of textual events. Gerald D. Johnson among others has suggested that the copy text underlying Roberts's 1602 Stationers' Register entry was likely Q2. In 1603, Ling violated Roberts's printing patent in financing an edition of Q1, the copy for which he acquired from Trundle. Ling then secured some "private agreement" with the printing-patent owner Roberts to distribute Q2 (1986, 211–12).[49] David Kastan, however, has countered that Q1 was likely printed from the copy that Roberts entered in 1602.[50] Having neither the time nor the resources to finance an edition of the text, he farmed the copy out to Ling and Trundle, who promptly contracted Valentine Simmes to print Q1. The copy text of Q2 then was acquired later, either by Ling or Roberts.[51] Whatever the circumstances, it was Q1 – not Q2 – that first drew Ling's interest as financial backer and distributor. Ultimately, Ling seems to have been inspired by his two editions of *Hamlet* to pursue other plays associated with Shakespeare. In early 1607, he paid to have the patents for *Love's Labour's Lost* and *Romeo and Juliet* transferred to him from Cuthbert Burby (Arber, 3.337), and later that same year he published the third edition of *The Taming of a Shrew*.[52]

In 1603, however, Ling would have been less sanguine about the potential market for printed playbooks.[53] Unlike they were for some of his publishing peers, plays had not been lucrative commodities for the bookseller during Elizabeth's reign. Since becoming a citizen Stationer in 1579, Ling had three times arranged to publish a single play edition, but none of these projects seems to have proved particularly successful. In 1594, the year of what Farmer and Lesser have described as the first "boomlet" (2005a, 7) in playbook publication, Ling and Thomas Millington together entered Marlowe's *The Jew of Malta* in the Stationers' Register (Arber, 2.650). Whether Ling and Millington ever brought the play to press is not known, but it seems fair to say that if they *did* publish *The Jew of Malta*, it was not successful enough to warrant subsequent editions.[54] That same year, Ling and John Busby co-financed and co-distributed an edition of Garnier's *Cornelia*, which had been translated into English by Thomas Kyd.[55] Directed at an educated audience and likely never performed, Kyd's translated drama apparently sold so poorly that Ling was forced to go to the extra length of reissuing the play a year later with a new title.[56] His reissue, however, never reached a second edition. Sometime around 1600, Ling published the third edition of Jonson's *Every Man Out of His Humour*.[57] Though the play had initially sold well enough to reach two editions within one year – thus attracting Ling's interest – it, like *Cornelia*, apparently never sold well enough for Ling to warrant his financing a subsequent press run.

Ling, then, would not have been unmindful of the financial risk in putting out a print edition of *Hamlet* in 1603, especially since his would have been the purse in a publishing venture with Trundle. What might have provided motivation, however, was Ling's speculative reading of Q1. Not only does the play contain pervasive themes having to do with counsel, office holding, and political resistance, but its particular textual features also demonstrate that Ling was especially drawn to the play's lead figure of counsel, Corambis.[58] Together, these features likely appealed to a publisher invested in republican political themes and in collections of aphorisms.

Traces of Ling's speculative engagement with Q1 *Hamlet* can be found on the play's title page and within its eighteen leaves. Marking Corambis's lines in the play's third scene are a number of double inverted commas (see figure 10).[59] These textual markers (what G.K. Hunter generally identified as "gnomic pointers") together indicate the aphoristic wisdom within Corambis's advice to Ofelia and Leartes.[60]

172 Elizabethan Publishing

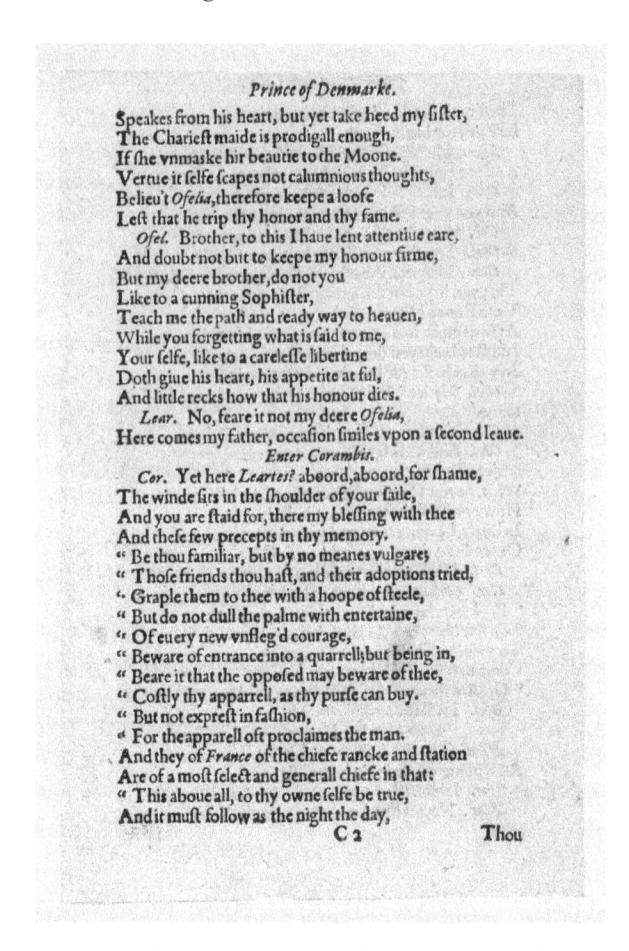

> *Prince of Denmarke.*
> Speakes from his heart, but yet take heed my sister,
> The Charieft maide is prodigall enough,
> If she vnmaske hir beautie to the Moone.
> Vertue it felfe scapes not calumnious thoughts,
> Belieu't *Ofelia*, therefore keepe a loofe
> Left that he trip thy honor and thy fame.
>   *Ofel.* Brother, to this I haue lent attentiue eare,
> And doubt not but to keepe my honour firme,
> But my deere brother, do not you
> Like to a cunning Sophifter,
> Teach me the path and ready way to heauen,
> While you forgetting what is faid to me,
> Your felfe, like to a careleffe libertine
> Doth giue his heart, his appetite at ful,
> And little recks how that his honour dies.
>   *Lear.* No, feare it not my deere *Ofelia*,
> Here comes my father, occafion fmiles vpon a fecond leaue.
>   *Enter Corambis.*
>   *Cor.* Yet here *Leartes?* aboord, aboord, for fhame,
> The winde fits in the fhoulder of your faile,
> And you are ftaid for, there my bleffing with thee
> And thefe few precepts in thy memory.
> " Be thou familiar, but by no meanes vulgare;
> " Thofe friends thou haft, and their adoptions tried,
> " Graple them to thee with a hoope of fteele,
> " But do not dull the palme with entertaine,
> " Of euery new vnfleg'd courage,
> " Beware of entrance into a quarrell, but being in,
> " Beare it that the oppofed may beware of thee,
> " Coftly thy apparrell, as thy purfe can buy.
> " But not expreft in fafhion,
> " For the apparell oft proclaimes the man.
> And they of *France* of the chiefe rancke and ftation
> Are of a moft felect and generall chiefe in that:
> " This aboue all, to thy owne felfe be true,
> And it muft follow as the night the day,
>   C 2   Thou

Figure 10 Gnomic markers in *The tragicall historie of Hamlet Prince of Denmarke* (1603). By permission of the Huntington Library, San Marino, California.

Among these recognizable *sententiae* are "Be thou familiar, but by no meanes vulgare"; "the apparell oft proclaimes the man"; and "louers lines are snares to intrap the heart" (sigs. C2^{r-v}). Ling's Q1 commonplace pointers were not without precedent. They began to appear in classical plays printed on the Continent as early as 1506; in England in the 1570s, they routinely mark printed texts in a variety of literary genres; and by the late 1590s, they seem to have been "systematically" applied to print editions of vernacular poetry.[61] By the end of his career in 1607, Ling himself had distributed at least five different literary works with the markers, and these texts complemented Ling's larger specialization in wise-saying collections represented in the following titles: *A Mirror for English Soldiers* (1595), *The Figure of Four* (1597), *Wit's Trenchmour* (1597), *Politeuphuia* (1597), *Portraiture of the Prodigal Son* (1599), *The Harmony of Holy Scriptures* (1599), *Wit's Theater of the Little World* (1599), *England's Parnassus* (1600), and the second edition of *A Display of Duty* (1602).[62]

It has recently been suggested that Ling's volumes of aphorisms should be understood in terms of a larger sustained project by Bodenham and his circle to valorize vernacular poetry; Q1 *Hamlet*'s commonplace markers were a way for Ling to mark his printed playbook as refined reading material.[63] Ling's selective scoring of Corambis's lines, though, did more than highlight Q1's literary potential; it also helped fashion a particular reading experience, one subtly outlined in the paratextual material of Ling's aphoristic collections.[64] What emerges in this material is that for Ling, "sentences" like Corambis's promised "profit" to an audience interested in what he calls "practice." According to his advertisement on the title page of Leonard Wright's *A Display of Duty* (1602), the work is "*Deckt with sage Sayings, pithie Senten- | ces, and proper Similies. | pleasant to reade, delightful to heare, | and profitable to practice.*" More explicit is Ling's prefatory epistle directed to his readers in *Politeuphuia*. "Euery continued speech," he writes, "is of more force & effecacie to perswade or disswade, being adorned & strengthened vvith graue sentences, then rude heapes of idle wordes, and ... wee ought to haue an especiall regard, not howe much we speake, but howe well" (1587, sig. A3ʳ). Ling understood aphorisms, in other words, to be a particular kind of rhetorical commodity. Indeed, in *The Harmony of Holy Scriptures* (a text which Ling published in 1600), grave sentences are understood to encapsulate the ground of civic authority and are thus essential guides for the aspiring civic statesman. As James Bentley writes in the collection's dedication to London's newly appointed Lord Mayor and Sheriffs:

> *You are chosen in this Citty as chief Magistrates for this yeere ensuing, first, to see that God may be rightly honoured, her Maiesties lawes iustly administered, the people in peace & loue discreetly gouerned, and sin and iniquitie, duly punished ... (as example is the best guide to order, and order cannot bee kept where example wanteth:) euen so this* Harmonie

of holy Scriptures, *(in my poore opinion) doth rightly challenge you as Patrons, being drawne from the true foundation of your seated authoritie.* (sigs. A3ʳ⁻ᵛ)

What is implicit in Bentley is dramatized in Q1 *Hamlet*. Corambis's aphorisms – in both their eloquence and wisdom – help establish the *"foundation"* of his own authority as the king's counsellor. They also, in their early-scene delivery by Corambis, are shown to be profitable tools of "force & effecacie."

Corambis's foundation is different from Bentley's, which is primarily biblical. His, instead, can be identified as classical and humanist, vaguely echoing the parental wisdom of Cato's *Disticha de moribus ad filium*, Isocrates's *Ad demonicum oratio paraenetica*, Burleigh's *Precepts*, and Raleigh's *Instructions to his Son*.[65] Corambis's precepts too, in their latent political pragmatism, invoke the instrumental rationality of Machiavelli.[66] "Beware of entrance into a quarrel," Corambis tells Leartes, "but being in/Beare it that the opposed may beware of thee" (sig. C2ʳ). Or, more famously, "This aboue all, to thy owne selfe be true, / And it must follow as the night the day, / Thou canst not then be false to any one" (sigs. C2ʳ⁻ᵛ). Likewise, in his advice to his daughter, Corambis shows himself to be well attuned to the political realities of language and social hierarchy. Powerful men, Corambis tells Ofelia, "often proue, / Great in their wordes, but little in their love" (sig. C2ᵛ). Machiavelli's work – both his *Discourses* and *The Prince* – was eagerly read by a range of Elizabethans, including those interested in theories of mixed government and political resistance.[67] And as Victoria Kahn points out, "the most insightful readers of Machiavelli in the Renaissance are those who, like Milton, do not simply reject the rhetorical Machiavel for Machiavelli the republican, or the diabolical Machiavelli for the theorist of mixed government, but rather see the inseparability of these two aspect's of Machiavelli's thought" (1994, 12). Corambis's *sententiae*, in other words, likely offered a familiar republican cultural code, one furthered by Corambis's almost universally accepted reputation in the play as a skilled diplomat and, perhaps more than anything else, a wise and active counsellor.

Ling's seeing Elsinore's prime minister as a respectable counsellor/office holder is not entirely unorthodox.[68] In some of the earliest critical engagements with Q2, even Corambis's sibling Polonius was not without his defenders. William Popple, in a long 1735 essay in *The Prompter*, defended Polonius as "a Man of most excellent

Understanding, and great Knowledge of the World, whose Ridicule [on the popular stages] arises not from any radical Folly in the old Gentleman's Composition, but a certain Affectation of Formality and Method, mix'd with a smattering of the Wit of that Age."[69] Responding to William Warburton, who saw him as a "weak, pedant, minister of state" and his character a "satire on Elizabethan courtly rhetoric and stock moralizing," Dr Johnson offered a more generous portrait of Elsinore's elder counsellor: "Such a man excels in general principles, but fails in particular application. He is knowing in retrospect, and ignorant in foresight. While he depends upon his memory, and can draw from his depositaries of knowledge, he utters weighty sentences, and gives useful counsel."[70] At the same time, from the mid-eighteenth century onwards, a number of professional actors like Macklin (1750–1), Baddeley (1772), Munden (1819), and Fechter (1864) were venturing to present a respectable Polonius on stage.[71] J.H. Barnes, playing Polonius at the Lyceum Theatre in 1897, even went so far to describe Polonius as "the *acting* Lord Chamberlain of the court, a splendid father, with a keen eye for the main chance, and a never failing solicitude for the welfare of his son and daughter; far too wise and prudent to make an enemy of the prince whom he firmly believes to be mad – or very nearly so" (qtd. in Hapwood 1999, 55).[72]

Regarding Q1 as a potential investment in 1603, Ling was uniquely positioned to see prudence in Corambis's words and actions, and also laudable devotion in Corambis's dedication to the responsibilities of his position. Such devotion is manifest in the play's seventh scene. To the king's compliment "Thou still hast beene the father of good news," Corambis offers a pregnant reply: "Haue I my Lord? I assure your grace, / I holde my duetie as I hold my life, / Both to my God, and to my soueraigne King" (sigs. D3^{r-v}).[73] For most commentators, Corambis's outlining of a "duetie" to "God" and to "soueraigne King" is innocuous, his compound patrons signifying a seamless whole.[74] For Ling and a host of Elizabethans, however, Corambis's vow may have seemed less redundant. Like Baldwin does in his translation of Erasmus's dialogue between a Fishmonger and a Butcher, sixteenth-century Protestant theologians had long recognized a possible conflict in trying to serve both God and king. Following *The Laws*, where Cicero valorizes the Spartan practice of electing ephors to check monarchic power, Calvinist mid-sixteenth-century thinkers like John Ponet and Christopher Goodman began to argue that it was the office of elected magistrates to uphold the laws of God even against the will of the king.[75] By the end of the century, these arguments would come to be echoed in William Lambard's *Eirenarcha* (1581), one of the best-selling manuals on officeholding in the Elizabethan period.[76] As Helen Hull has recently written, "When Lambard legitimizes the justice's office, he reconfigures the chain of authority. Rather than a vertical hierarchy, in which God's authority is vested in the monarch and the monarch's authority is vested in the officeholder, Lambard depicts a society in which God's authority is vested in monarch and subject alike as ministers of God's law."[77] While he never acquired the rights to copy texts by Ponet, Goodman, or Lambard, Ling's similar conception of office holding is, as we have seen, well encapsulated in his work with *Politeuphuia, The Legend of Humphrey Duke of Gloucester, The Commonwealth of England,* and *A Commonwealth of Good Counsel.*

As Ling may very well have recognized in his speculative reading of the play text, Q1 *Hamlet* frequently presents Corambis's sense of "duetie" as diffuse at best, often more in line with the office-holding tracts of Lambard, Smith, and Goslicius than with Tudor political orthodoxy. At times, of course, Corambis duly shows reverence for the will of his king. In their first exchange, Corambis's request that the king "grant your Highnesse leaue" (sig. B3ᵛ) to Leartes is all humility. At other times, however, such deference is quickly replaced with a single-minded focus on "hunt[ing] ... the traine of policie" (sig. D3ᵛ) through strategies of management and command. In the aforementioned seventh scene, Corambis's ministerial authority is quickly signalled in his passing judgment on the king's handling of Voltemar and Cornelia. "This busines," he tells the King, "is very well dispatched" (sig. D4ʳ). Proceeding then to Hamlet's madness, he not only forcibly sets his plans with respect to Hamlet in motion, but he also issues three separate commands to the king, telling him to "note this letter" (sig. D4ʳ); "Marke [the letter]" (sig. D4ʳ); and "if [his theory] be not true, take this from this" (sig. D4ᵛ). At this point in Q1, Hamlet enters and Corambis quickly choreographs the actions of both Ofelia and the king: "And here *Ofelia,* reade you on this booke, / And walke aloofe, the King shal be vnseene" (sig. D4ᵛ). Ironically, in the face of Corambis's aggressive counsel, the king has already been made to be "vnseene," even before the arrival of his antic nephew. And once Hamlet is gone, things barely change. To the king's vague surmise "Some deeper thing it is that troubles him," Corambis continues his aggressive mode of counsel: "Wel, something it is: my Lord, content you a while, / I will my selfe goe feele him: let me worke, / Ile try him euery way: see where he comes,

/Send you those Gentlemen, let me alone/To finde the depth of this, away, be gone" (sig. E2ʳ). Even more than his order to "Send you those Gentlemen," Corambis's command to the king "away, be gone" may be the most jarring line of the scene, but it is only the penultimate vocative in what in Q1 is an iconic scene of counsel governing king.

Corambis's authoritative mode as counsellor continues as Q1 progresses. Upon hearing of the failed efforts of Rossencraft and Gilderstone in the next scene, Corambis assertively addresses the king and Gertred with his plan to hide "behind [Gertred's] Arras": "Madame, I pray be ruled by me:/And my good Soueraigne, giue me leaue to speake, /... Madam, send you in haste to speake with [Hamlet], /... There question you the cause of all his grief" (sig. F1ᵛ). Even after the queen then promises to "send for him," Corambis quickly nominates himself as her vehicle: "My selfe will be that happy messenger, /Who hopes his griefe will be reueal'd to her" (sig. F1ᵛ). In effect, Corambis continues to be driven more by a devotion to commission than to king. And unlike in Q2, as long as his counsellor survives, Q1's king remains almost entirely overshadowed by him: his suspicions about Hamlet's madness are restricted to two vague lines after the nunnery scene, he has nothing to do with Corambis's arras plans, and he does not decide to ship Hamlet to England until *after* Corambis is dead.[78]

In Q1, Corambis's practices as an assertive counsellor are further highlighted through difference, his practices tellingly juxtaposed against Horatio's subdued, even servile attendance upon Hamlet as the prince's own counsel.[79] When they are first reunited at the beginning of the play, Horatio's response to Hamlet's "(Horatio) or I much forget my selfe" makes his subservient position amply clear: "The same my Lord, and your poore seruant euer" (sig. B4ʳ). Though not entirely the "*slauish bond of constraint*" described by Ling's *Politeuphuia*, Horatio's position as "seruant" is ever conjured in Horatio's obsessive "my Lord"s when addressing Hamlet. It is also apparent in his single-minded devotion to Hamlet over all else. When first confronted with the ghost, Horatio decides only to "acquaint [Hamlet] with it, /As needefull in our loue, fitting our duetie" (sig. B3ʳ), even after suspecting larger political implications (as he says, "some strange eruption to the state" [sig. B2ʳ]). Later, in seeing Hamlet confronted with the ghost, Horatio's one concern is with his immediate patron's safety: "What if it tempt you toward the flood my Lord./That beckles o'er his bace, into the sea, /... And driue you into madnesse" (sig. C3ᵛ). Horatio's bond with Hamlet, of course, also entails counsel, but this advice is invariably dialectical, in response to Hamlet's own actions or ideas. All of this culminates in the final scene, when Horatio contemplates suicide in the face of Hamlet's impending death. "No," he insists to Hamlet, "I am more an antike Roman, /Then a Dane, here is some poison left" (sig. I3ᵛ). Horatio's denial here of his Danish heritage connotes more than his stoicism; it also indicates his disregard for matters having to do with the larger state. Such disregard is further underscored in Q1 when Horatio ultimately imagines a universal audience for his "sad story" of "this tragicke spectacle." "Let there a scaffold be rearde vp in the market place," he cries, "And let the State of the world be there:/Where you shall heare such a sad story tolde, /That neuer mortall man could more vnfolde" (sig. I4ʳ).

Unlike Horatio, Corambis is dedicated to his own particular sense of statecraft before all else, to what Ling's *Politeuphuia* calls "Policie" and broadly defines as *"the order and manner of lyfe, vsed by some politicall person"* (1587, sigs. O6ʳ⁻ᵛ). For Corambis, effectively "hunt[ing] the traine of policie" means having an ability to uncover truth, even "if it were hid/As deepe as the centre of the earth" (sig. D4ᵛ). Believing himself to be a man of policy, Corambis can confidently ask the king if ever "That thing that I haue saide t'is so, positiuely/And it hath fallen out otherwise" (sig. D4ᵛ). In Q2, this same statement is perhaps most belied by Polonius's unwavering certainty that Hamlet's "lunacie" is the result of love. In Q1, however, Corambis is much more circumspect. After the nunnery scene, he does not continue to insist (as Polonius does) that "the origin and commencement of [Hamlet's] greefe, /[is] Sprung from neglected loue" (1604, sig. G3ᵛ); instead, as we have seen, he vaguely asserts, "Wel, something it is." And after his welcoming of the players to Elsinore, Corambis is similarly judicious, admitting that "We cannot yet finde out the very ground/Of [Hamlet's] distemperance" (sig. F1ᵛ). Corambis's policy, in other words, is not as patently questionable as Polonius's. Given all of this, it would have come as no surprise to a reader like Ling that the king, when confronted by a vengeful Leartes in Q1's thirteenth scene, refer to the dead Corambis as "the chiefest piller of our state" (sig. H1ᵛ).

Ling also would not have been surprised by Q1's complex engagement with tyranny and treason. As we have seen, a number of Ling's late publications tacitly participated in what was a widespread contemporary discourse surrounding the issue of political resistance both in England and abroad.[80] *Politeuphia*'s and *A Commonwealth of Good Counsel*'s broad understanding of sedition in terms of commonwealth rather than king, for example, vaguely echoed the French Huguenot treatise *Defense of Liberty Against Tyrants* (1579), a text in which Phillipe de Mornay draws a distinction between officers of the king and officers of the kingdom. Officers of the kingdom, argues Mornay, are "bound, just like the king, to look after the welfare of the commonwealth" (qtd. in Skinner, 317). At the same time, *Utile-Dulce*'s endorsing of resistance to a potentate on religious grounds reaffirmed Calvinist and Catholic tracts alike that used religious conscience to rationalize regicide. "It is in fact possible to claim," writes Calvin towards the end of his life, "that we are not violating the authority of the king [where] ... our religion compels us to resist (*resistere*) tyrannical edicts which forbid us to give Christ and God the honour and worship which is their due" (qtd. in Skinner, 220).

To say that *Hamlet* is broadly concerned with political action in the face of a problematic monarch is anything but a new claim; what is new, however, is to stress that Q1 contains its own particular representation of political resistance, one that likely appealed to a publisher like Ling. Q1 would have drawn Ling's interest not simply because it figures Lucius Junius Brutus in Hamlet and "targets monarchy with unusual frequency, in word and deed" (de Grazia 2007, 69).[81] It also may have attracted Ling because of its multivalent and unorthodox approach to the political problem of treason.

Like Q2 and F, Q1 generally links itself with the discourse of political resistance in a number of scenes – they range from Marcellus, Horatio, and Barnardo offering to "shew" the ghost of the former king "violence" (sig. B2^v) in the opening scene, to the regicidal show of the Mousetrap, to the closing violence against the king in the final scene. Q1's singularity, however, is perhaps most explicitly established in its version of Hamlet's most famous speech – "To be, or not to be, I there's the point." Expanding upon his list of "scornes and flattery of the world," Hamlet lastly imagines "a tirants raigne, / And thousand more calamities besides" (sigs. D4^v–E1^r). As if in response to Hamlet's inclination to "his full *Quietus* make, / With a bare bodkin" (sig. E1^r), Q1 thereafter alludes repeatedly to "treason," uniquely invoking the term's many connotations.[82] The most orthodox of which is delivered by the king in his response to Leartes's heated return from France. Attempting to allay Gertred's fear for his safety, he boldly proclaims, "Let him goe *Gertred*, away, I feare him not, / There's such diuinitie doth wall a king, / That treason dares not looke on" (sig. H1^v). In the king's confident belief that the monarch is divinely ensconced against treason, one can hear

180   Elizabethan Publishing

vague echoes of James VI, who in his *True Law of Free Monarchies* contended that a king should be "acknowledg[ed] ... as a Iudge set by GOD ..., hauing power to judge [men], but to be judged onely by GOD" (1598, sigs. C5[r-v]).

Less orthodox, however, are Q1's other occurrences of the term "treason." When in his delivery of "*Aeneas* tale to *Dido*" the Player refers to Hecuba's appearance and grief, he insists that "Who this had seene with tongue inuenom'd speech, /Would treason haue pronounced, /For if the gods themselues had seene her then, /When she saw *Pirrus* with malitious strokes, /Mincing her husbandes limbs/It would haue made milch the burning eyes of heauen, /And passion in the Gods" (sigs. E4[r-v]). Here, Virgil's Elsinore mouthpiece conjures an image of Hecuba's grief so piteous that it inspires an expanded understanding of political violation, one that includes causing hysteria in a queen. Later in Q1, another queen motivates the play's final deployment of "treason" when Hamlet cries out at Gertred's poisoning "Treason, ho, keepe the gates" (sig. I3[v]). Hamlet's exclamation at the sight of his dying mother constitutes a vague enactment of "the tongue inuenom'd speech" earlier alluded to by the Player. It at the same time similarly widens treason's scope beyond the king's earlier narcissism to include the death of his wife.[83]

What makes this final instance of "treason" in the play so unorthodox, however, is not its being applied to the poisoning of a queen. Since the reign of Edward III in the fourteenth century, "compassing ... the king's death, or that of his wife or eldest son" (*OED*) had been legislated as high treason. What *is* unorthodox is the possibility that Hamlet is accusing the king of treason. Earlier on in Q1, similar accusations are leveled against the king. When Horatio and Gertred meet to discuss Hamlet's circumstances after leaving for England, Horatio confides, "Madame, your sonne is safe arriv'de in *Denmarke*, /This letter I euen now receiv'd of him, /Whereas he writes how he escap't the danger, /And subtle treason that the king had plotted" (sig. H2[v]). To this, Gertred responds, "Then I perceiue there's treason in [the king's] lookes/That seem'd to sugar o're his villanie" (sig. H2[v]).[84] In a straightforward sense, Hamlet's and Gertred's "treason" connotes deception, the king attempting to deceive his adopted son and wife. *Hamlet*'s source – *The History of Hamblet* – offers another way to understand such "treason." As Belleforest's Hamlet explains to his mother, "[his killing the king] will neither be fellonie nor treason, hee being neither my king nor my lord, but I shall justly punish him as my subject, that hath disloyaly behaved himselfe against his lord and soveraigne prince."[85] The king's "treason" in this formulation would be disloyalty to the rightful king Hamlet. Understood within the larger political discourse on lawful resistance, however, Hamlet's and Gertred's use of the term can be read as well to suggest a distinction between king and state, the former not necessarily representing the latter. It is to refute this possible distinction between king and commonwealth that James devotes a number of pages in his *True Law of Free Monarchies*, concluding "No King being, nothing is vnlawfull to none" (1598, sig. D6^v).[86]

In the intervening months between his publication of Q1 and Q2 *Hamlet*, Ling, in collaboration with the bookseller Edward White, entered Michael Drayton's first satiric poem *The Owl* in the Stationers' Register (Arber, 3.252). Reaching four editions by the end of 1604, this heroic-couplet bird fable proved both to be one of Ling's most successful publications and his next-to-last to be offered with gnomic markers.[87] Drayton had the year before published the effusive panegyric "To the Majesty of King James," and he clearly intended the poem as a complimentary sequel, figuring England's new monarch as the "Princely *Eagle*" (sig. D3^v), "so exact and so excellent a King, / So sole and perfect in his gouerning" (sig. G4^r). It is the eagle that empathetically listens to the owl's long tale of past social and political ills, and it is he as well who, at the end of the poem, leads the "applauding" birds "To the great mountaine, to haue all amended" (sig. G4^v). Before exiting, the eagle admonishes these subjects to "Let your wise fathers an example giue, / And by their rules learne thriftily to liue. / Let these weake Birds, that want wher-with to fight, / Submit to those that are of grip and might" (sig. G3^r).

The Owl, however, is more than an ode to absolutism and the great chain of being.[88] It also offers a multivalent text shaped by the particular political vision of Drayton and ultimately by the gnomic and republican gaze of Ling. Along with its compliments to James, the poem at the same time argues for the chief importance of counsel to the new king, for it is only the owl's (and by extension Drayton's) "vigelent eye" that has the power to "Fore-s[ee] the perrill threatened vnto all" (sigs. F4^{r-v}). Without it, the eagle is shown to be blind to the dangers threatening his state. Spurned by James in his bids for patronage, Drayton takes this point even further in his 1619 revision of the poem, imagining "The Princely *Eagle* out of sight was gone, / And left the wise and honest [owl] alone, / To gouerne things, both for his proper heale,

/And for the great good of the publique Weale" (sig. Hhh3ᵛ).[89] In effect, *The Owl* well echoes the sanguine vision of counsel seen in a number of Ling's late publications. And like Q1 *Hamlet*, this vision is reinforced by marked aphorisms, all of which (seventeen in total) delivered by the owl and Drayton as narrator. In *The Owl*, then, Ling continued to finance literary texts with republican themes that were "profitable to practice." Provided with another model of effective aphoristic persuasion, Ling's readers could thus fashion their own speech accordingly, wielding sententiae such as "Least is he marck'd, that doth as most men doo" (1604, sig. B1ʳ) and "So little, fooles good counsell doth regard" (1604, sig. F4ᵛ) as effective tools of their civic-minded ambition.

Notes

Introduction

1 *Axiochus* was first entered in the Stationers' Register on 1 May 1592 (Arber 1875–94 [henceforth Arber], 2.610). Another translation of *Axiochus* was printed in 1607 as part of Matthew Lownes's publication *Six Excellent Treatises of Life and Death Collected (and Published in French) by Philip Mornay* (sigs. A5ʳ–C2ᵛ). Burby apprenticed with the bookseller William Wright and was made free of the Company on 13 January 1592 (Arber, 2.710). His first location was the Middle Shop in the Poultry under St Mildred's Church, and he worked as a bookseller until his death in 1607. For more on Burby, see Johnson 1992. Though advertised by Burby as being originally written by Plato, *Axiochus* was likely written by Aeschines and was a translation of a Latin version by Rayanus Welsdalius (Padelford 1934, 16–18). The printing of the five-sheet quarto was shared by John Charlewood and John Danter, Charlewood printing the preliminaries and sheet D and Danter printing sheets A–C (Jackson 1940, 3.995).
2 In the two years before *Axiochus* was printed, four titles attributed to Spenser were published in London: *The Faerie Queene*; *Complaints*; *Daphnaïda*; and *The Shepheardes Calendar*.
3 Padelford discovered an incomplete copy of the translation in a 1679 folio of Spenser's *Works*. The copy included the title page and preliminaries of the 1592 quarto but not the Whitehall speech. A complete copy of the 1592 quarto was later found in 1936. As he did not have access to it before he published his 1934 edition, Padelford bemoaned its loss because its inclusion might have thrown light both on the translation's date of composition and on the possible authorship of the speech itself.
4 Freyd and Padelford 1935. The piece also includes a rebuttal by Padelford.

Notes to pages 5–8

5 In this, both Padelford and Swan made Burby into a guarantor of Spenser's authorial and cultural status. For a similar use of Shakespeare's printer Richard Field, see Hooks 2011, 2016.
6 Rudolph Gottfried in the Variorum edition of Spenser's prose works (1949), Harold L. Weatherby in *The Spenser Encyclopedia* (1990), and Andrew Hadfield (2012) have sided with Padelford, attributing *Axiochus* to Spenser.
7 Charlewood and Danter have each been the subject of bibliographic studies, but neither has been assessed strictly according to their publishing practices and publishing output; instead, their trade printing has been blended with their publishing, and their company infractions have been given an inordinate amount of attention; see, for example, Rogers 1996 and Provvidera 2002. For more on Burby, see Syme 2013; on Danter, see Melnikoff 2015.
8 According to Swan, Burby included the Whitehall speech as an afterthought – a "scrap," he calls it (1944, 181). Andrew Hadfield in 2012 called the coupling a "mystery."
9 It was, of course, McKenzie who provided the essential warning in 1986 that "any history of the book which excluded study of the social, economic, and political motivations of publishing, the reasons why texts were written and read as they were, why they were rewritten and redesigned, or allowed to die, would degenerate into a feebly digressive book list and never raise to readable history" (1986, 13). Cf. Chartier, 9–16.
10 See, for example, Blayney 1997, esp. 391. The *OED* credits "I.C." with the first use of "publisher" in this sense in 1579. See Anon. 1579d: "I.C. To the Reader." I.C. was a Grays-Inn gentleman and not a member of the book trade.
11 For the percentage of early-modern books published by authors, see McKenzie 2002.
12 For authors, see Erne 2003 and 2013; for readers, see Knight 2013.
13 The *Dictionary* was a collaborative venture between McKerrow, H.R. Plomer, H.G. Aldis, and E.R. McClintock Dix. The entries having to do with London bookmen and bookwomen – the lion's share of the contents – were contributed by Plomer.
14 We have records of Cadman's activities as a publishing bookseller between 1574 and 1589. The Stationers' Register also records him being made free of the company in 1560.
15 Dewes worked as a publishing bookseller in London between 1562 and 1589. He became a liveryman in 1569, and he served as a Renter Warden in 1572–3 and as an Upper Warden in 1581–2 (Tedder 2004c).

16 McKerrow's *Dictionary* also drew from Duff 1905 and Plomer 1903.
17 In 1875, the Court of the Stationers' Company would not allow Arber to transcribe and print these records. It was not until 1930 that they were transcribed and published by Greg and Boswell.
18 See, for example, Pollard 1909 and 1917, 27–54.
19 See McKerrow 1916, 225 and Greg 1956, 84.
20 As Jerome McGann pointed out in 1983 about an editing establishment guided by Bowers and Tanselle, this obsession was born out of a fetishization of the authorial manuscript. Recently, Brian Vickers has re-enacted this obsession in *The One King Lear*, there conjuring an aesthetically perfect, authorial *King Lear* from the flawed printing-house remains of the 1608 quarto and 1623 folio. See Syme 2016 for a detailed report of this book's many failings.
21 Examples are not hard to find. Mark Bland declared in 1999 that "a publisher cared little for the meanings and indirections of a text unless it was likely to cost him his livelihood" (2010b). More recently, Gabriel Egan, in a review of *Shakespeare's Stationers* in 2014, complained, "Straznicky's introduction ... states the collection's premise as the idea that the stationers who invested in Shakespeare 'had motives that were not exclusively financial' ... I would have thought that this was something to be established, not something to start with" (307). Even Ian Green, whose book *Print and Protestantism in Early Modern England* has been part of the recent rethinking of the book trade, maligned revenue as a motive: "For every printer, publisher, or bookseller who on a spectrum of sincerity leant a long way towards principle, there were many, probably a clear majority, who came down on the side of profit" (24).
22 Cf. Rostenburg 1965; Saenger 2006; McCullough 2008; Smith 2012; and Straznicky 2013.
23 For a full overview of Day's long and important career, see Evenden 2008.
24 Aggas worked as a bookseller in London between 1576 and 1616. Along with acting as a translator for his own publications, he also translated for other publishers, especially John Wolfe. For more on Aggas, see chapter 1.
25 See Blayney 1973; Ferguson 1968, 86–9; Blayney 1982; Weiss 1992; and Yamada 1994.
26 The booksellers John Busby and John Trundle routinely acquired titles that they subsequently shared with their publishing peers. See Gerald D. Johnson 1985b and 1986.
27 For dedicatory material, see Holme 1572 and Marlowe 1598; for translating work, see the many collaborations between Edward Aggas and John

Wolfe in the 1580s and 1590s. It should be stressed that the Elizabethan book trade was populated by *both* men and women, and that a number of women worked as publishers during this period. For a list of women in the trade, see Bell 1996, 31–9. For an overview of the many capacities within the trade in which women worked, see Bell 1996, 13–30 and Smith 2012, 87–134.

28 Gaskell 1972, 180–1. For a case study of collaborations within a publishing house, see Kiséry 2012.

29 In one of the more successful partnerships associated with a specific literary title, the printer Thomas East and the bookseller Gabriel Cawood may have collaborated to bring out multiple editions of both *Euphues. The Anatomy of Wit* and *Euphues and His England* between 1578 and 1588. Whatever the arrangement, when Cawood died in 1602, the rights to copy both parts of *Euphues* were transferred to the bookseller William Leake senior (Arber, 3.210), indicating that East had no stake in the venture at this late date.

30 For another example of thin line between one-off jobs and collaboration, see Hooks's work on the printer Richard Field and the bookseller John Harrison (2011, 266–7).

31 In his bestselling *A Quip for an Upstart Courtier* (1592), Greene suggests that wealthy consumers were commonly in debt to booksellers. "For the Printer," Velvet-breeches complains, "by our Lady I think I am some tenne pounds in his debte for bookes" (1592b, sig. F3^r).

32 For examples of this language, see the wills of Abraham Kitson (PRO: PROB 11/60/399) and John Windet (PRO: PROB 11/117/12). Decades before the Elizabethan period, the famed printer Wynkyn de Worde specified in his will that his executors "remytte and forgive vnto the said John Gowgh for his labour all suche monney and debtes as he owith me" (Plomer 1903, 4). Three years earlier, de Worde had printed two books for Gough (Duff 1905, 58).

33 Coldock's dismissal of debt was apparently part of marital arrangements between Ponsonby and Coldock's daughter Joane. It offers a representative example of how familial connections in the trade could sometimes spring from economic obligations.

34 For other examples, see entries on 7 May 1599 (71) and on 12 April 1602 (85).

35 See also the arbitrated dispute between the printer Henry Denham and the printer Thomas Dawson on 10 August 1579 and on 6 December 1585 (Greg and Boswell 1930, 9, 18); and between the bookseller Robert Dexter and the printer Robert Bradock on 7 December 1601. In the latter

case, the court entreated that "said pties to be lovers & freinde as heretofore they haue ben" (Greg and Boswell 1930, 84).
36 See Anon. 1594c; Anon. 1595a (Arber, 2.298); Anon. 1595b (Arber, 3.46); Werdmüller 1595?; and Dickenson 1596? The printing of all these titles is attributed by the STC to Allde. Whatever the terms of their dealings between 1594 and 1596, the two worked together again on a ballad in 1600 (Anon. 1600). Unfortunately, nothing of Allde's dealings with Blackwall is mentioned in McKerrow 1929.
37 The phrase comes from John Sutherland. In his 1988 *Critical Inquiry* article, he compellingly argued that such ignorance about publishing practice had created a significant "hole" in literary sociology.
38 For an excellent account of the wide range of activities that took place at an early-modern bookshop and an overview of contemporary descriptions of these spaces, see Taylor 2008.
39 In Elizabethan books, authors like Thomas Hill (1571, sigs. Hh7^v–Ii4^r), William Bourne (1581, sig. A6^v), and Robert Greene (1590, sig. K3^v), along with publishers like Thomas Hacket (Pliny 1585, "To the Reader"), sometimes advertised their extant or forthcoming titles. For seventeenth-century print advertisements of titles in books, see most recently Hooks 2008; for advertisements of books and of play performances on posts, see Stern 2006.
40 In 1582, Christopher Barker would go even further, characterizing publishing booksellers as in some cases more knowledgeable about printing than the trade printers that they employed. Defending printing patents, he writes, "I speake not this (thoughe it be very true) as wishing any restraynt to Bookesellers, or Bookebinders, but that they may print, and haue printed for them such good bookes, as they can orderly procure: for even some of them, though their skill be little or nothing in the execution of the art, haue more iudgement to governe, and order matters of printing, then some Printers themselves" (Arber, 1.115).
41 Of course, there were many publishing printers who also acted as wholesalers during the Elizabethan period, but their numbers were in decline after 1570 (Lesser 2004, 29). These men also had less of a connection with other wholesalers because most of them did not have bookshops to stock.
42 As Blayney has shown, during Henry VII's reign, master printers in most cases accepted printing jobs from others because of an "inability to procure suitable copy" (2013, 1.652).
43 For introductions to the most prolific of these men, see Blayney 2013, 1.660–7.

44 Tabulating the extent of trade printing during the Elizabethan period is not an easy task. Imprints during the period are notoriously incomplete and the best source for specific information about early-modern stationers, Katherine F. Pantzer's "Printers' and Publishers' Index" (vol. 3 of the STC, 2nd ed.), does not indicate trade printing in its chronological listings. My 1593 and 1599 figures include only vernacular books printed with London imprints, excluding variants and reissues. They are based on ESTC entries checked both against the second edition of the STC and against Arber's *Transcript*. They exclude non-speculative titles (i.e., titles protected by printing patents).
45 Elizabeth confirmed the Stationers' Company charter in November 1559. For examples of such opportunism or "piracy," see Pollard 1978, 18–19 and Kastan 2002, 94. For the various costs associated with publication, see Blayney 1997.
46 The first printing privilege for a specific title (in this case a statute) was granted to Richard Pynson in 1510; the first generic privilege was granted to Pynson in 1518 and lasted for his lifetime (Blayney 2013, 1.161, 168–70).
47 For differing accounts of the 1557 charter, see Arber; Pollard 1978; Blagden, 19–33; and Blayney 2013, 746–842. As Pollard has surmised, licence was probably not restricted to master printers in 1557 because these men were happy to cede the costs and practical difficulties of wholesale distribution to other citizens both within the Stationers' Company and without (1978, 19). It was not until 1598 that the Stationers' Company explicitly restricted licensing to stationers.
48 See Bell and Barnard 1992, 52–3.
49 Though a few non-printers were granted patents, the large majority of patent holders were printers. For overviews of the Stationers' Company during the Elizabethan period along with outlines of Tudor and Stationers' Company ordinances and decrees, see Greg 1956; Blagden; and Kastan 2002.
50 Blagden points out that a "drive against copyright infringers" first appeared in 1576 (65). It was also in this year that the Stationers' Company complained to Lord Burghley about a new privilege for ballads and small books in poetry and prose (Plant, 104). Printers John Wolfe and Roger Ward would ultimately become the most visible of the disputants.
51 As Lesser has pointed out, "These regulations attempted to keep all master and journeyman printers afloat by preventing any one master from becoming too dominant" (2004, 32).

52 Because both orders entailed more company control of printing-house practices, Blagden – seeing company history through a Marxist lens – understood all of this to be part of "a general shifting of economic power away from the craftsmen and towards the dealers in the craftsmen's products" (74), from printers to publishing booksellers. Blagden described this as "a battle among the stationers" (25). Blayney, by contrast, has convincingly countered that a company "battle" between craftsmen and publishers is a myth (2013, 181–3). Rather, from the beginning of printing in England the most economically powerful master printers were also publishers; what began around 1520 and happened more and more after incorporation was that master printers were electing to move away from the industrial side of the trade. Cf. McKenzie 1982, 224.

53 As David Gants has tracked, this trend would generally continue into the Jacobean period, when between 1614 and 1618 only two printing houses out of eighteen published more than half of the edition sheets that they printed. Of these eighteen, almost all of these houses published 30 per cent or less of the edition sheets that they produced (2002, 194).

54 For arguments about the rise of vernacular literature in the Elizabethan period, see Attridge 1989; Brown 2004; Helgerson 1976, 1983; and Knapp 1992. For related arguments, see Hadfield 1994; Matz 2000; Reiss 1992; and Saunders 1964.

55 *The Art of English Poesy* was published anonymously by Richard Field; scholarly consensus is now firmly behind George Puttenham as the author.

56 For other noted conceptualizations of the literary during the period, see Spenser 1579; Nashe 1589; and Meres 1598.

57 See Duncan-Jones and Van Dorsten 1973, 63–70 for an overview of the complicated textual history of Sidney's *Defense*.

58 For Sidney's posthumous canonization as *the* English poet, see Kay 1987.

59 True to his word, a year later, in what proved to be the last publication of his short career as a bookseller, Olney published Richard Linche's sonnet sequence *Diella*.

60 Whigham and Rebhorn initially ascribe the dedication to Field (18), but then hedge that the dedication "was possibly composed by the printer Richard Field, though Puttenham would certainly have welcomed approval from this dedicatee" (50). Cf. I. Bell 2010, 13. Adam Hooks, however, has pointed out that Field, only months earlier, had published French- and English-language versions of Cecil's *The copie of a letter sent ovt of England to Don Bernardin Mendoza*; this does much to explain Field writing such a dedicatory epistle in 1589 (Hooks 2016, 53).

61 For evidence of publishers fashioning title-page blurbs, see Blayney 1982, 259–61.
62 For overviews of Jones's stationer career, see Melnikoff 2001, 2005.
63 For the Horatian binary as an attempt to reconcile a class struggle between an aristocratic courtly culture that valued pleasure and an upwardly mobile middle class that valued work, see Matz. Here I'm suggesting that Jones offers one of the "variations on the trope of 'pleasure and profit'" that Matz points out were "frequent in the sixteenth century" (20).
64 With *The Arbor of Amorous Devices*, these volumes included four poems by Francis Sabie. On the title page of George Whetstone's *Aurelia* (1593), Jones offers a blurb with a more straightforward version of this Horatian binary, calling it "*A worke most sweetely intercoursed (in ciuill and | friendly disputations) with many amorous and | pleasant Discourses, to delight the Reader: and | plentifully garnished with Morall Notes, to make | it profitable to the Regarder.*"
65 In this, I am developing Tzvetan Todorov's point that "it is because genres exist as an institution that they function as 'horizons of expectation' for readers and 'models of writing' for authors" (1990, 18).
66 *A Pleasant Poesy* was transferred to the printer John Charlewood as "A Smellinge Nosegaye" (Arber, 2.406); *All for Money* was originally entered in the Stationers' Register by the printer Roger Ward without a generic tag (Arber, 2.321); Charlewood originally entered *Palmendos* as "The honorable histories of Palmendos and Primaleon of Grece" (Arden 2.513); and *Arden of Feversham* was originally entered by the bookseller Edward White as "The tragedie of Arden of Feuersham and Blackwall" (Arber, 2.607). In these and a number of other cases, revisions to Stationers' Register titles give us strong evidence of publisher interventions.
67 The titles in this volume may have been originally issued separately by Perrin, but they were brought together by the bookseller publisher under a single title page with an added reader's epistle.
68 Another later example of such a juxtaposition occurred in 1657 when the bookseller Philemon Stephens packaged the 7th edition of George Herbert's *The Temple* with the 3rd edition of Christopher Harvey's *The Synagogue*, selling them together as a prayerbook (Birrell 164).
69 For approaches along these lines, see Bednarz 2007 and Erne 2013.
70 During the period, the sonnet form was used to articulate a variety of different content, not simply amatory.
71 See Jauss 1982. Something of this sense of "historical family" is captured in Alistair Fowler's "field of association" (2003, 190).

1 Geldings, "prettie inuentions," and "plaine knauery": Elizabethan Book-Trade Publishing Practices

1 For an account of book-trade retail prices, see Johnson 1950; for acquisition costs, see below.
2 Increasingly popular during the Elizabethan period, the news pamphlet was routinely pieced together by book-trade publishers (Shaaber 1966, 106–68, 320–2). Financed by printers like Bynneman and John Wolfe and by booksellers like Edward Aggas and Thomas Millington and – towards the end of the sixteenth century – often concerning military developments in France and the Low Countries, these offerings usually contained a hodgepodge of accounts, letters, lists, and documents having to do with recent noteworthy events. For an overview of such pamphlets during the period, see Barker 2013. For further examples of such compilations, see Anon. 1579c and Farnese 1590.
3 This constructs a slightly different "communication circuit" than outlined by Robert Darnton in his seminal "What Is the History of Books?" As this book will stress, it was often a member of the book trade – not the author – that generated the "lifecycle" of a printed book.
4 See Muldrew 1998. For booksellers commissioning their publications, see Aldis 1909, 388–9.
5 Conversely, the paratexts of the printer-publishers William Caxton and Wynkyn de Worde have routinely been taken seriously as essential guides to late-fifteenth- and early-sixteenth-century English culture. See, for example, Blake 1973 and Meale 1992.
6 Two years earlier in 1594, John Busby and Nicholas Ling had published the two first editions of which Drayton is complaining. Given that Ling continued to work with Drayton for many years, the author's ire may have been directed at Busby.
7 Daniel was specifically complaining about *The True Description of a Royal Masque* that was published by John Allde earlier the same year. For other author complaints, see Breton 1592; Perkins 1593; Dod 1604; Dallington 1605?; and Heywood 1612.
8 In some cases, copy was intially acquired by a bookman with the express intention of passing it along to a publisher contemporary. See Johnson 1985a, 1985b, and 1986.
9 See also Gascoigne 1575c. There, in his translator's epistle, Gascoigne commends the printer Christopher Barker for "*disburs*[ing] *great summes for the Copies, translations, pictures, and impressions of the same*" (sigs. A2^{r-v}).

10 Robinson's manuscript also records continued dealings with certain publishers.
11 See, for example, Henry Smith 1592 and 1593.
12 See, for example, Arber, 2.300; 2.359; 3.101; and 3.144.
13 Spenser's *Complaints* was entered by Ponsonby into the Stationers' Register on 29 December 1590 (Arber, 2.570); it consists of nine different titles published among four separate volumes, each with its own title page and dedicatory epistle by Spenser.
14 Jugge would bring out his new edition of the Bible in 1575, the same year that he would publish his first edition of Patten's calendar.
15 For more on Patten's scholarly work, see O'Kill 1977. For another example of a title pursued by a publisher, see Best 1578.
16 See Bennett 1965, 229–30.
17 A large number of entries in the Stationers' Register document publishers acquiring copy to be translated; see, for example, Arber, 2.324, 2.353, 2.361, 2.381, 2.384, 2.390, and 2.414. For discussions of publishers commissioning translations, see Hosington 2010, 53; Green 2000, 16–17; and Bennett 1965, 107–11.
18 For other examples of Elizabethan publishers commissioning translations, see Calvin 1561; Calvin 1567; Maisonneufve 1578; Van Marnix van St. Aldegonde 1579; Anon. 1584b; Nicolay 1585; Ortúñez 1586?; Roscio 1590; Ubaldini 1590; Anon. 1594b; Margarite 1597; Anon. 1598a; and Van Linschoten 1598.
19 Two years earlier, Barker's draper acquaintance Richard Smith had brought out Gascoigne's *A Hundreth Sundry Flowers Bound Up in One Small Poesy*.
20 That same year, Barker would bring out Gascoigne's closet drama *The Glass of Government*, a text to which Barker himself contributed a short list of "sentences" upon which Gascoigne's work is "compiled" (1575a, sig. A4^r).
21 See Shaaber 1966, 261–89 and Woodfield 1973.
22 For an example of a publisher as a literary agent, see Johnson 1986. For an example of copy offered to a publisher by a religious official, see Werdmüller 1574? On diplomats as sources for particular kinds of copy, see Parmelee 1994, 862–4.
23 See Smith 2010, 31.
24 "To compile" during the period could mean "To make, compose, or construct (a written or printed work) by arrangement of materials collected from various sources"; "To compose as original work"; or "To heap

together, pile up; to gather or form into a heap or mass" (*OED*). In their prefatory addresses, publishers sometimes referred to their labours as "compiling." Cf. Gascoigne 1575a, A4^r. For authority, licence, and entrance, see Blayney 1997, 396–404. Title pages had become standard parts of English printed books by the late fifteenth century. See Corbett and Lightbrown 1979; Voss, 737–43; Smith 2000; Raven 2007, 55–9; and Bland 2010a.

25 In most cases, Elizabethan imprints identify either the printer-publisher-wholesaler (e.g., "Printed by ——") or the trade printer and the publisher-wholesaler (e.g., "Printed by —— for ——"). W.W. Greg believed wrongly that an imprint was primarily intended to advertise the shop where a book could be bought by individual book buyers. For an essential corrective to this, see Blayney 1997.

26 For further contemporary allusions to this practice, see Hall 1597, sigs. E8^r–F1^r; Nashe 1596, sig. R1^v; Parrot 1615, sig. A4^v; and Davies 1625, sigs. A1^{r-v}.

27 In 1602, Thomas Campion imagined his "put up" title pages to be more like bait. "*Whether thus hasts my little booke so fast?*" he asks in his "Writer to his Booke," "*To Paules Churchyard; what in those cels to stand, / With one leafe like a riders cloke put up / To catch a termer?*" (sig. B4^v).

28 Title-page blurbs could also be produced by publishers. See Blayney 1982, 259–61.

29 The rest of this section is indebted to Gérard Genette's foundational discussion of paratextual material in *Paratexts: Thresholds of Interpretation*, particularly to his sense of the threshold function of this material in shaping reception. However, as Smith and Wilson have recently pointed out, early-modern paratextual material could work as well as "an ever-expanding labyrinth, as likely to lead to a frustrating dead-end as to a carefully built pathway" (2011, 6). This was particularly so because, as I trace, this material was frequently added by book-trade publishers who, as Arthur Marotti and others have underscored, did not necessarily have the same motives as the authors, translators, or collectors whose work they brought to press. See also Hackel 2005.

30 See Kastan 2002, 108–16.

31 For further Elizabethan examples, see Grafton 1565; Barnes 1593; Hasleton 1595; and Hill 1599. For seventeenth-century examples, see Duncon 1606; Symonds 1606; Anon. 1607; Crashaw 1610; and Marston 1633.

32 Crowley believed wrongly that the "prolog" was by John Wycliffe. The printer Robert Wyer, whose career ran from 1529 to 1556, gives us another

early example of a printer who provided new titles for his publications (Neville). Faced with an untitled manuscript copy of Chaucer's *The Prick of Conscience*, for example, Wyer took his title *A New Treatise Divided in Three Parts* (1550?) from the work's prologue (Preston, 312).
33. Drawater first apprenticed with Richard Jones in 1581 (Arber, 2.103); he finished his apprenticeship with Thomas Man in 1593 (Arber, 2.712). Drawater entered the text under this title in the Stationers' Register on 23 January 1595 (Arber, 2.670).
34. For a full account of the dispute between Drawater and Lewkenor, see Kirschbaum 195, 141–3. According to Lewkenor, Drawater assembled his unauthorized edition out of a series of his private letters. Lewkenor took an authorized version of the title to Ponsonby for publication, but because he had established a right to copy with his unauthorized edition, Drawater was able to claim rights to and ultimately bring out Lewkenor's approved edition.
35. See Marotti 1995, 209–38.
36. For Jones's work on *A Handful of Pleasant Delights*, see Melnikoff 2005. For an overview of Jaggard's involvement with *The Passionate Pilgrim*, see Bednarz 2007.
37. For John Wolfe marketing sermons both as transcriptions and as being directly from the author's pen, see Butler 1593 and L.S. 1593 respectively. See also H.B. 1593. For more on the unauthorized publication of Elizabethan sermons, see Bennett 1965, 152–6 and Green 2000, 197.
38. Green 2000, 210–11.
39. For Smith's involvement with Andrewes's sermons, see chapter 3.
40. Ling entered the sermon on 12 September 1591 as "A Sermon preached by master Henrye Smithe vppon the viij Chapter of Luke the 19 20 .21 verses" (Arber, 2.594).
41. Cf. Saenger, 38–54. For publishing-house retitling as part of reissuing unsold copies, see the section "Reissuing" below and chapter 4.
42. We also possess potential manuscript evidence, this printer's copy of a title page from *Scala coeli* (1611). The title offers part of a sermon by Lancelot Andrewes and was published by the London bookseller Francis Burton. On this title page, Burton has crossed out a previous title "Heauen Gate opened" written in a different hand and replaced it with "Scala Caeli." See Blayney 1982, 259–62.
43. In the second edition of *Pierce Penniless*, Nashe rebukes Richard Jones – the publisher of the first edition – for the "long-tayld Title" (sig. ¶2ᵛ). See Hutson, 176–80. For another example of Jones revising a title, see

A New Year's Gift (1569). In his dedicatory epistle to Sir William Garrat, Jones recalls that the work originally came to him "under the title of *An heauenly Acte of Parliament, enacted by our Soueraigne lord God*" (1569, sig. A2^r). For more on Jones's interventions as a publisher, see Melnikoff 2001 and 2005.

44 For Greene's career as a professional writer, see the introduction to Melnikoff and Gieskes 2008.

45 A few bookmen like Robert Crowley also penned forms of "The Book to the Reader" prefatory poems for their publications. All told, close to fifty different examples of these were printed between 1533 and 1603.

46 See Williams 1962. Williams's index is comprehensive but not exhaustive. Cf. Saenger, 55–75.

47 Much of the information here is derived from EEBO copies and from Pollard et al.'s *Short-Title Catalogue*. For a discussion of the ins and outs of the printed dedicatory epistle, see Hackel 2005, 105–14.

48 If we are to believe Williams, this increase in the 1570s and 1580s was largely due to "Grub Street" writers like Thomas Churchyard who helped extend "the practice [of dedications] to slighter 'literary' works of all varieties" (1962, x).

49 In his dedicatory epistle to David Lewes in *The Wellspring of Witty Conceits* (1584), Richard Jones tells readers that the author "committed the dedication of it to bee disposed (by me) to my best liking" (Anon. 1584d, sig. A3^r). For a similar request to a publisher from an author, see C.M. 1596, sigs. A2^{r-v}.

50 "Dedications" include both dedicatory epistles and dedicatory poems. "%" refers to the proportion of STC titles that include dedications. While these figures provide a reasonable starting point of comparison, it should be recognized that certain titles like ballads, almanacs, proclamations, and the like were routinely published without dedicatory material. The total number of titles published each year is taken from Bell and Barnard 1992. See also Blayney 2007. As Blayney points out, Bell and Barnard's numbers are a bit inflated for a number of reasons, but they give us a useful approximation. Figures having to do with dedicatory epistles and poems are based upon my examination of EEBO copies; title figures include reset editions.

51 The epistles listed here do not include those that were reset. Approximately one hundred separate dedicatory epistles were written by London book-trade publishers between 1558 and 1603. While more appeared in both the 1570s and the 1580s than in the 1560s, most of this dedicatory

material was published in the 1590s. This increase reflects the more general growth of dedicatory epistles during the second half of Elizabeth's reign (see table 1).
52 The 1590s also saw growing complaints about the system of literary patronage. For a contemporary account of the situation, see Nashe 1592, sigs. L3^{r-v}.
53 These unsigned addresses have often been attributed by editors and critics alike to agents who were in fact trade printers, not publishers. In the majority of cases, however, such prefatory epistles were in fact penned by publishers who also happened to be booksellers or – in some cases – printers. As Blayney has clarified, "when publishers discussed their activities in prefaces, they generally used the word *print* in the sense of 'caused to be printed.' The formulaic heading, 'The Printer to the Reader,' was therefore commonly used by publishers who were not strictly speaking printers at all" (2007, 391). In the Elizabethan period, more than six dozen "printer to the reader" epistles were added to titles; Richard Jones penned close to a dozen of these. See Williams 1962, 235–7.
54 It has often been mistakenly assumed that trade printers played some role in this process (e.g., Clegg 2007, 250).
55 See Allen 1963 and Williams 1966. For a list of commendatory poems, see May and Ringler 2004.
56 Lodge and Greene together wrote the biblical play *A Looking Glass for London and England*. Most date the play's composition around 1589 or 1590.
57 In his prefatory epistle, Allde suggests that he received a hastily composed version of the work. Each of the four poems refers vaguely to the work's "Author," suggesting that none of the commendatory poets was acquainted with him.
58 Unfortunately, evidence of such commissions remains scarce at best. See Williams 1966, 8. Commendatory poems were also likely written to pay off a previous debt incurred with a bookselling publisher. For the Elizabethan "economy of obligation," see Muldrew 1998.
59 See chapter 2 and Melnikoff 2009. In his dedicatory epistle in *Catharos* (1591), the bookseller John Busby calls Thomas Lodge "my deare friend" (sig. A2^r). Between 1590 and 1596, Busby would publish a number of Lodge's works.
60 For Marshe's early career, see Blayney 2013, 783–4, 979–82.
61 Marshe was taken into the livery in 1562, and he served as a Warden in 1575 and 1581. For more on Marshe's career, see Duff 1905, 100 and Braunmuller 1984, 25–38.

62 Goldwyn 1966. See also Lyne 2004.
63 The Anglican clergyman and translator Thomas Newton also seems to have had a close association with Marshe, as evidenced by Heywood 1577; Lemnius 1576; Osório 1576; and Hunnis 1578. For more on Newton, see Braden 2004.
64 Shakespeare 1594, sig. B3^v and 1599, sig. C1^r.
65 In many cases, even while it is impossible to know whether an author, publisher, or some other agent provided the marginalia, editors and critics have routinely assumed that it was provided by the author. Even Slights, who is willing to recognize the potential role of printing houses in added marginalia, ignores the possibility that a publisher might be responsible for such notes. Discussing the hermeneutics of referential notes, he writes, "Whether added by the author at the time of composition or by printing-house personnel at a later stage of book production, citation deflects the reader's attention from the present text to another" (2001, 64).
66 For other Elizabethan examples of publishers adding marginalia, see Patten 1575 and Harward 1582, sig. K1^v. For an earlier example, see Anon. 1543? and Neville 2014.
67 See Jennett, 273–4 and Day 2011.
68 Though rare, contemporary accounts of headers like these do exist. The prefatory section to Beza's 1576 version of the *Geneva Bible* assures its readers that these devices "may greatly further aswel for memorie, as for the chief point of the page" (sig. ⸫4^r). Decades later, Angel Day in his *The English Secretary* (1586) provides a slightly different rationale for his text's headlines: "Now for the readier finding of those EPISTLES as each of their kindes are suted forth in sundrie EXAMPLES: Peruse but the head of euerie page, and vnder the title of the booke, you shall finde what in the same Page is contained" (sig. 2^v). In separate titles over one hundred pages published between 1574 and 1585, around a dozen employ these kinds of headers.
69 With some significant exceptions, most of the headlines included in the first edition of *The Anatomy* are included in the following three editions.
70 Elizabethan printed books contain a host of other apparatuses. The printer Henry Bynneman, for example, appears to have added what we might describe as a "summative overview" of George Best's account of Frobisher's travels to *A True Discourse of the Late Voyages of Discovery* (sigs. a1^v–a2^r).
71 For an overview of the history and function of print-house correctors in early-modern Europe, see Grafton 2011. For the absence of such learned correctors in English printing houses, see Gaskell 1972, 172.

Notes to pages 50–2

72 George Pettie's collection of romances was heavily influenced by William Painter's *The Palace of Pleasure* (1566). Watkins would publish three further editions of Pettie's collection in 1578(?), in 1585, and in 1590. He had first entered the collection on 8 August 1576 (Arber, 2.301). For such arguments as textual commodities, see the title page of *The Most Delectable and Pleasant History of Clitiphon and Leucippe* (1597).

73 The publishing printer Richard Day similarly added such "headers" to his 1580 Latin publication *De fide, ejusque ortu, & natura, plana ac dilucida explicatio* (Binns 1977, 10). For another example of this type of added textual apparatus in the first half of the seventeenth century, see de Granada 1633.

74 For an example of tables of contents merged with arguments, see Fabyan 1559; Virel 1595; and Gentillet 1602. For examples of ending tables of contents, see Cortés 1561; Anon. 1571; and Boccaccio 1587.

75 Dutton 2008, 34. For medieval examples, see also the work of Richard and Mary Rouse. Tables of contents date from the classical period in works by Pliny, Gellius, and others. See Blair 2010 and Nelson 2013.

76 As early as 1481 in *The History of Reynard the Fox*, Caxton included such tables in his publications.

77 There is evidence that Elizabethan printers employed scholars like Abraham Fleming as press correctors. It stands to reason that these men were also given commissions by publishers to produce apparatuses such as tables of contents and the like. See Donno 1989.

78 See Bèze 1563 and Smith 1594 for other examples of Elizabethan publishers adding tables of contents to titles. See also Gascoigne 1575a (added sentences); Anon. 1633 (added pictures); and Watson 1637 (added pictures).

79 Medieval books also sometimes included indexes; there were also seperate indexes available for some. Unlike in printed texts where they referred to folio and/or page numbers, however, medieval indexes were keyed to book, chapter, and section (Blair 2010, 53). For examples of an index at the beginning of an Elizabethan title, see Plat 1600? and Bullinger 1561. John Wight frequently advertised the inclusion of both tables of content and indices in his publications.

80 Wellisch 1981, 11. In this short article, Wellisch provides a translation of Gessner's practical description of indexing found in his *Pandectarum* (1548).

81 For the latter haphazard method of organization, see Johnson 1595, sigs. S3^v–S4^r.

82 Fleming also contributed a short commendatory poem, "Solertia: non Socordia," to the volume's final leaves. During this period, he produced a number of indices for publishers like Newbery, Henry Denham, and John Harrison, including the long index appearing in Holinshed's *Chronicles*. See Donno 1989, 204.

83 For the earliest examples of errata sheets in English books, see Lerer 2002, 45. My count of printed errata lists in 1560, 1580, and 1600 is based on EEBO copies along with a search for "errata" in the ESTC. As EEBO only provides a partial collection of available copies, these are necessarily rough figures. See also Blair 2007.

84 For other examples of readers being encouraged to correct their own copies according to errata lists, see Luther 1575, sig. **1^v; Bristow 1580, sig. Eee4^v; Hemmingsen 1580, sig. P1^v; Wecker 1585, sig. Z6^r; and Anon. 1594d. For readers being encouraged to correct futher errors not listed in an errata list, see Allen 1600, sig. Ii4^r; Calfhill 1565, sig. DDD2^v; Newton 1580, sig. A3^v; and Whitaker 1585, sig. Dd1^v.

85 See, for example, the British Library copy of Bentley 1600 and the Huntington Library copy of Anon. 1594d (both available on EEBO).

86 For other examples of master-printer publishers adding errata lists, see Norden 1584 and Filippe 1589, sig. A6^r.

87 The "augmentations" that Purfoot refers to on the title page are (1) a list of authors and (2) a short dedicatory poem in the first gathering. The publishing printer Richard Day also provided an errata list for his 1580 Latin publication *De fide, ejusque ortu, & natura, plana ac dilucida explicatio* (Binns 1977, 10).

88 See Hind 1935; Hodnett 1935; Bland 1969; Garrett 1978; O'Connell 1999; and Knapp 2005. James A. Knapp (2003) argues that the first two decades of Elizabeth's reign saw a different kind of book illustration, one that had moved from medieval generalized woodcuts to modern particular ones. He also points to an emerging idealization of the metal engraving over the woodcut at the end of the century because of its fashionability and greater expense. Knapp sees this as an early moment in the commodification of the aesthetic, with the woodcut more and more being described as instrumental by contemporaries.

89 It was of course true that trade printers commissioned woodcuts for publications financed by publishers as well and then maintained ownership of these illustrations. Between 1588 and 1596, for example, Wolfe used a woodcut of St George and the dragon in a number of different titles, first in a quarto published by Francis Coldock and then in eight other titles

brought out by other publishers (Luborsky and Ingram 1998, 311). Cuts also seem to have been routinely shared between printers and publishers. While it is difficult to know from a single title whether the author, printer, or publisher commissioned a woodcut, subsequent editions as well as previous or new titles with the same woodcut give us some evidence to go on.

90 Cf. McCullough 2008, 305–7.
91 For later examples from the 1630s, see Thomas Purfoot's prefatory material in Anon. 1633 and Watson 1637.
92 As Ruth Luborsky has pointed out, members of the book trade routinely used the same woodcuts in a variety of titles; the meanings of these illustrations thus changed depending upon the textual context in which they were used. See Luborsky 1987 and 1992; and Knapp 2003.
   For reuses and migrations of cuts, see Luborsky and Ingram 1998.
93 See Luborsky and Ingram 1998, 714–16. Sir John Harington, in one of the prefatory epistles in his translation of Ariosto's *Orlando Furioso*, praises the "pictures" in "the book of hauking and hunting," but insists that the illustrations in his own volume are superior because they are "metall" engravings (1591, sig. A1ʳ).
94 Barckley's *Discourse* was first printed by Richard Field and then by James Roberts; Spenser's epic by John Wolfe and then by Field. For other examples of woodcuts migrating with publishers to editions set by different printers, see Broughton 1587–91, Broughton 1590?, and Broughton 1596; Anon. 1581a and Anon. 1584a; Monardes 1577a and Monardes 1577b; Browne 1589 and Browne 1590; Roussat 1562? and Roussat 1564; Markham 1593, 1595, 1596, 1597 (and then transferred to Roberts in Markham 1599); Anon. 1592?b and Anon. 1592?c; and Marlowe 1594 and Dickenson 1598.
95 Stationers' Court records can also sometimes document publisher ownership of illustrations. On the 8 January 1577, for example, "all the pictures belonging" to *The Regiment of the Sea* were transferred from Thomas Hacket to John Wight (Greg and Boswell 1930, 1).
96 John Lyly, in his prefatory epistle to "*the Gentlemen Readers*" in *Euphues. The Anatomy of Wit*, complained of the short life cycle of most new titles: "We commonly see the booke that at Christmas lyeth bound on the Stacioners stall, at Easter to be broken in the Haberdashers shop, which sith it is the order of proceding, I am content this winter to haue my doings read for a toye, that in sommer they may be ready for trash. It is not straunge when as the greatest wonder lasteth but nyne days: That a newe worke should not endure but three monethes" (1578, sig.

A4^r). For publishers producing a large edition as a cost-saving measure, see Gaskell 1972, 160–3.

97 McKerrow 1927, 177. For a useful overview of the basic concept of "issue" and "re-issue" as articulated by McKerrow, Bowers, and others, see Tanselle 1975. Cf. Gaskell 1972.

98 For Fredson Bowers, a title page provided by the publisher was requisite for a reissue: "The one firm ground is the arbitrary evidence of the title-page" (1986, 79). See also Bowers 1947 and Gaskell 1949–53, 361–2.

99 Bowers 1959. In *Principles of Bibliographical Description*, Bowers insisted that nonce volumes are *not* to be considered reissues (1986, 90–2).

100 In order to enliven an old title, publishers also commisioned revisions from authors. In 1579, the bookseller Hugh Singleton went to John Foxe to add new material to Foxe's 30-year-old translation of Urbanus Rhegius's *A Necessary Instruction of Christian Faith*. "*I haue now my selfe requested of M. Foxe,*" writes Singleton, "*of whom I fyrste receiued it, that it would please him to reviewe the same, with such profitable additions as to him should seeme meete for the benefite of the godly reader*" (sig. A2^v).

101 A complete picture, of course, is impossible due to lost editions and rebindings. The figures that follow are taken from an inspection of ESTC entries.

102 For slightly later examples of reissuing with revamped titles and title pages, see Muir 1958, 56–7.

103 In the nineteenth century and earlier, it was a common practice for book dealers to break these nonce collections up into single bound editions. As a result, the full extent of the nonce collection as a book-trade offering in the early-modern period will probably never be known. For examples of Elizabethan nonce collections, see Leslie 1571; Malby 1576; Appian 1578; Darell 1578; Lok 1597; Perkins 1597; and Burton 1602.

104 See Gillespie 2004.

105 For Stafford's translation from the Drapers to the Stationers in 1599, see Johnson 1988.

106 For "the Bodenham Circle" and their collections of sententiae, see Marotti 2004; Crane 1993; and Lesser and Stallybrass 2008.

107 Lyons 2011.

108 The new full title was *The Householder's Philosophy. Wherein is Perfectly and Profitably Described, the True Oeconomia and Form of Housekeeping … Whereunto is Annexed a Dairy Book for All Good Housewives*. Hacket

202 Notes to pages 60–1

entered Kyd's translation on 6 February 1588 as "the Philosophicall Discourse of the housholder" (Arber, 2.484). He entered "a Derie booke for huswyfes" five months later on 9 July 1588 (Arber, 2.494). For a full description of these titles, see Freeman 1967, 171–4.

109 Knight in drawing attention to the "malleability of books" (2013, 7) in the early-modern period, almost entirely ignores the book-trade's essential role in this cultural and economic reality.

110 The bookseller Ralph Blower appears to have engaged the surgeon "G.W." to make additions to *A Rich Storehouse, or Treasury for the Diseased*, a quarto that he first published in 1596. John Tap seems to have been engaged by Hugh Astley and the assignees of Richard Watkins to make additions to the fourth edition of Martin Cortes's *The Art of Navigation* (first translated by Richard Eden in the late 1550s). For another example of a publisher commissioning additions, see Gascoigne 1575c.

111 See Budra 2000.

112 In one related example, the bookseller William Ponsonby gathered together a number of Spenser's "smale Poemes" (sig. A2^r) circulating in manuscript and published them together as *Complaints* in 1591. Judith Owens has argued that with *Complaints* Ponsonby was "centering" Spenser's work to make it a more viable print commodity (2002, 31–5).

113 As I discuss at the beginning of chapter 3, such was the case with Thomas Newman's first edition of *Astrophel and Stella* (1591a) which was printed with "*sundry | other rare Sonnets of diuers Noble | men and Gentlemen*" (tp). Similarly, the popular miscellany *The Paradise of Dainty Devices* was first published by Henry Disle in 1576 and was likely initially based on a manuscript compiled by Richard Edwards. As the collection was reprinted over the next few decades, Disle and its second publisher Edward White continued to add poems by other English poets to the volume. William Jaggard's 1599 collection *The Passionate Pilgrim* was not only originally published as "*by W. Shakespere*" even while containing poems by other poets, but it also was "*aug- | mented*" (1612, tp) by Jaggard with further poems not by Shakespeare in its third edition. Thomas Heywood in his *An Apology for Actors* (1612) reports that Shakespeare "was much offended with M. *Jaggard* (that altogether vnknowne to him) presumed to make so bold with his name" (sig. G4^v). For a further example of John Wolfe augmenting a single-authored poetry collection with other poets' work, see Binns 1977, 22.

114 Jones also appears to have added two poems about an "unconstant | ... Mayden" (tp) to two of Isabella Whitney's own poems in his

1567(?) octavo *The Copy of a Letter, Lately Written in Meter, by a Young Gentlewoman.*
115 Jones, of course, may have acquired a manuscript volume of poetry that contained the full miscellany of poems he published as *Breton's Bower.*
116 Michael Brennan has suggested that the composite volume was possibly in the works for a number of years and may have benefited from the direct involvement of the Pembroke group (1983, 99). For another example of a text augmented by a publisher, see Anon. 1585, sig. F4^v.
117 Much of the following paragraph is drawn from Blayney 1997, 396–400.
118 There are many examples in the Stationers' Register of both instances. For the former, see Arber, 2.428, 2.620, and 3.91; for the latter, see Arber, 3.161, 3.163, and 3.216.
119 Clegg 1997 has argued that there was a real distance between the enactment of mechanisms of control in the Elizabethan period and the employment of these censorship mechanisms.
120 For information on Allde, see Tedder 2004a; on Bynnman, see Plomer 1908; on Carter and Waldegrave, see Clegg 1997, 33 and 175–6 respectively.
121 See Cornwallis 1600–1. For an example of a publisher modernizing the language of an old title, see Fitzherbert 1598.
122 Authors and translators, of course, frequently edited their own works. What is almost always unclear is whether an author brought such a revision to a publisher or whether the publisher approached the author with the editorial work.
123 Richardson 1994. According to Richardson, editorial work and editors began to be advertised at the beginning of the sixteenth century in Italy. By the end of the sixteenth century, the editor was commonly advertised alongside the author. For the most part, Italian printers and publishers commissioned editorial work, but in some rare cases they undertook such editing themselves. Grafton (2011) has recently pointed out that correctors in the great Continental printing houses did more than simply "correct" proof sheets; they also "read authors' copy, composed blurbs, and drew up aids to readers: title pages, tables of contents, chapter headings, and indexes" (16). In some cases, they even took on an editorial role, helping these print houses to produce what were advertised as "corrected" texts.
124 For another publisher-edited work on husbandry, see Leigh 1578.
125 See Rollins 1928, 93–101 and Marotti 1995, 217–19.
126 See Melnikoff 2001.
127 See Ringler 1962 and Marotti 228–33.

128 Woudhuysen has suggested that the first quarto of *Astrophel and Stella* might have been based on a manuscript that was "corrected" by Samuel Daniel and Thomas Nashe (378).
129 For different accounts of this collation, see Warkentin, 480–6 and Woudhuysen, 380–1.
130 The following two paragraphs are both heavily influenced by Massai 2007. For the Italian tradition of editing dramatic texts, see also Peters 2000.
131 See also Peters, who argues that Jones's prefatory epistle suggests an editorial concern not with authorial intention but with "eternal truth" (2000, 132–3). In the forthcoming chapter "Making a Scene; or *Tamburlaine the Great* in Print" (Melnikoff and Knutson 2018), Claire M.L. Bourne argues that Jones edited the plays to read as they had been staged.
132 This information is gleaned from the *DEEP* database (25 May 2013). Though they are both now lost, there were likely previous first editions of both *The Spanish Tragedy* and *Love's Labour's Lost*. See respectively Erne 2001, 59–67 and Murphy 2003, 461n1.
133 Massai 102–5. For another account of Wise's career as a publisher, see Hooks 2013.
134 For a similar observation, see Boutcher 2015, 34. Bennett estimates that "over one thousand items were translated during Elizabeth's reign" and that these "represented at least a fifth of the printers' total output" (1965, 104). J.G. Ebel (1967) comes up with a similar overall figure.
135 See Braden 2010a, 5.
136 Thomas Paynell translated exclusively for Thomas Berthelet between 1528 and 1539, and for John Cawood between 1553 and 1559. See Hosington 2010, 52–3. In a related instance, the Welsh scholar William Salesbury was housed by Humphrey Toy while he produced Welsh translations of the New Testament and Book of Common Prayer for the bookseller (Rees 1998, 3).
137 See Green, 16–17 and Bennett, 105–11. For printing-house work on translated texts as itself a form of translation, see Coldiron 2015. Coldiron argues that early English translators and printers should both be understood as "entrepreneurs, experimenters, and innovators" (3).
138 See Coldiron 2008, 2003. The Antwerp-turned-London bookseller Walter Lynne published more than a dozen of his own translations during Edward VI's reign. Among his productions were translations of religious work by Continental reformers such as Luther, Bullinger, Ochino, and Rhegius. Lynne also enjoyed a seven-year patent on Joachimus's

Beginning and Ending of All Popery which he translated from a German-language copy and first published in London in 1548.
139 See Bennett 1965.
140 For more on Aggas, see Braden, Cummings, and Gillespie 2010; Shaaber 1966; and McKerrow 1910.
141 Aggas also includes a number of translated passages from Seneca at the end of the work. See Byrne 1924.
142 See also Melnikoff 2009.
143 For an overview of the relative popularity of different classes of Elizabethan books, see Farmer and Lesser 2013.
144 For maritime publishing, see Adams 1992; for Millington, see Melnikoff 2013b.
145 This is an incomplete list, as interest in publishing has only really come to the fore in the twenty-first century. For overviews of a small subset of these publishers' careers, see Brennan 1983; Yamada 1994; Smith 2003; Evenden 2008; and Syme 2013.
146 For an overview of these economic developments and company practices, see Lesser 2004, 43–9.
147 For further contemporary allusions to publishers' specialities, see Lesser 2004, 42–3.
148 McKerrow 1913, xii–xiii. See also Ferguson 1958 and Lavin 1968.
149 McKerrow does not account for this surge in devices, but it may have had something to do with the emergence of organized resistance within the Stationers' Company to printing patents in the late 1570s. See Blagden 1960, 63–77.
150 See McKerrow 1913, #83 and #302.
151 For specific examples of these emblems, see Anon. 1581b; Latimer 1575; and Nowell 1571.
152 These publications are *The True Tragedy of Richard Duke of York* (1595) and *Deuoreux Virtue's Tears for the Loss of the Most Christian King Henry, Third of that Name, King of France* (1597).
153 For further examples of Elizabethan emblems possibly resonant with publishing specialties, see McKerrow 1913, #180, #186, #243, #297, #304, and #328.
154 For other accounts of early-modern publishing practices, see Johnson 1985a; Johnson 1985b; Lesser 2006; and the various essays in Straznicky 2013.
155 Neither the pamphlet nor any of the ballads recounting the Merry murders are now extant. Our knowledge of this horrific crime comes

from one of the two intertwined plots in Robert Yarington's play *Two Lamentable Tragedies* (1601).
156 Millington and Ling entered the play in the Stationers' Register on 17 May 1594 (Arber, 2.650). Most believe that they never brought it to press. The earliest extant edition is Nicholas Vavasour's 1633 edition.
157 Much of this discussion is taken from Johnson 1992.

2 Thomas Hacket, Translation, and the Wonders of the New World Travel Narrative

1 The STC has identified Richard Jones as the collection's printer. Edwards had died ten years earlier in 1566, and Disle likely played an important role in readying the collection for the press. For an account of Edwards's life and of *The Paradise of Dainty Devices*, see King 2001. See also *Verse Miscellanies Online*.
2 The nine editions include a now-lost 1577 edition. See Rollins 1927. Tottel's 1557 miscellany *Songs and Sonnets* would reach a tenth and final edition in 1587.
3 See, for example, Edwards's "*Wantyng his desyre, he complayneth*" (sigs. C2^{r-v}); F.K.'s "*All thinges ar Vaine*" (sig. E1^r); Hunnis's "*No paines comparable to his attempt*" (sigs. H4^{r-v}); and Hunnis's "*Beyng troubled in mynde, he writeth as followeth*" (sig. L3^r).
4 Something of this same engagement can be seen in the anonymous "*Oppressed with sorowe, he wysheth death*": "I knowe, there is no fruite, no leafe, no roote, no rynde, / No hearbe, no plant, no iuyce, no gumme, no mettal deeply mind: / No Pearle, no Precious stone, ne Jeme of rare effect, / Whose vertues, learned *Gallens* bookes, at large doo not detect" (sig. E2^r).
5 For the relationship between England's New World colonial endeavours and the emergence of English literature, see Hall 1995; Read 2000; and Knapp 1992.
6 Jugge was a close acquaintance of Eden and published a number of his translations; Dawson published three translations of travel literature by the Bristol merchant trader John Frampton between 1579 and 1581; and Bynneman published maritime works by Frampton, Bourne, and Record. For the early publishing history of navigational aids in England, see Adams 1992, 207–20.
7 For a full overview of Hacket's career, see Melnikoff 2009, 257–71. The next section provides an abridged version of this article. Blayney has

concluded that there were two Thomas Hackets in the early London book trade, father and son (Blayney 2013, 902).

8 The parish registers of St Olave, Hart Street contain the record of Hacket's burial: "Aug. 7 Mr Thomas Hacket, stacion^r" (Bannerman 1916, 123). Because Hacket died intestate, the Archdeaconry Court of London was compelled to appoint his son Ambrose as executor on 6 August. For some unknown reason, though, a day later the same court named Hacket's widow executrix, relieving Ambrose of the responsibility. See Guildhall Library, Archdeaconry Court.

9 Hacket's presentation of Foster in 1557 proves that Hacket was a freeman at incorporation, since 1544 or before (Blayney 2013, 902).

10 The parish registers of St Olave, Hart Street contain the record of Joan's burial: "June 1 Joan d[aughter of]. Thomas Hacket widowe" (Bannerman, 128). Ambrose apparently did not pursue work as a stationer after becoming free of the company as no further record of him exists in the Stationers' Register. There is evidence that suggests, however, that he was working in 1592 as a scrivener (Bannerman, 16) and before that as possibly a schoolteacher in Sandwich (an "Ambrose Hacket lit" being licensed to teach on 15 January 1586 by the Diocese of Canterbury [Willis 1972, 6]). In 1585, Ambrose is listed in *Liber A* with a number of other men as being "trained" and outfitted as a "callyuer" (a soldier armed with a light musket) by the Stationers' Company (Myers 1986, 71, 115–16). In November 1591, the Middlesex Session Rolls list "Ambrose Hacket of St. Olave's parish Hartstrete in London stationer" receiving a recognizance of ten pounds. Ambrose's son George (born 30 November 1592 [Bannerman 1916, 16]) was made free of the Stationers' Company on 21 December 1618 (Arber, 3.684).

11 Lang 1993, 137. For a number of reasons, subsidy assessments and valuations are not good indicators of valued wealth in movable goods and annual income, but they do give us an idea of what a person's community thought a person could afford to pay (Lang 1993, lviii–lix). Hacket's 1582 assessment can also cautiously be compared to those for other booksellers: William Ponsonby was assessed 3s on a £3 valuation (Lang, 229); Richard Tottel was assessed £5 on a £100 valuation (Lang, 236); and Thomas Vautrollier as a "straunger" was assessed 30s on a £15 valuation (Lang, 234).

12 The parish registers of St Olave, Hart Street contain the most likely record of her burial: "[Sep.] 3 Ellin Hacket, widowe, buried at hir pew dore" (Bannerman 1916, 129).

13 See Blayney 1997, 391 and Duff 1905, 63. Some have assumed that Hacket was also a printer. This seems based upon a small number of Hacket's early imprints in which he is the sole stationer listed. Of these, however, only *The Most Wonderful and Pleasant History of Titus and Gisippus* (1562) cannot readily be connected to a trade printer working for or with Hacket. He definitely did not own a press as of 1583 (Arber, 1.248).
14 In this 1575/6 entry, Hacket is listed first, indicating that he was the Senior Renter. Renter Wardens served two consecutive years, first as Junior Renter and then as Senior Renter. Given this, Hacket must have been named as a Junior Renter Warden in 1574/5 (Blaney, Letter 3).
15 The Court of the Stationers' Company records in 1576 that "the said Thomas Hacket hathe sold and assigned vnto the said Ihon Wight theise ii copies vi[z] The Regiment for the sea. and all the pictures belonging to the same. Item the Theatre or Rule of the world" (Greg and Boswell 1930, 1).
16 Hacket is first referred to as "Master Hacket" in two entrances on 1 August 1583 (Arber, 2.426). To be elected to the Court of Assistants, a stationer had to serve as both Senior and Junior Renter Warden (Blagden 1960, 37–8). For an explanation of the meaning of the prefix "Master" in the Stationers' Record, see Pollard 1937, 237–67, esp. 241.
17 Curiously, after 1 August 1583, Hacket is inconsistently referred to as "Master" in Stationers' Register records. For entries with Hacket as "Master," see, for example, Arber, 2.34, 127, and 499 along with *Liber A*: 71: 126 and 127. For concurrent entries not referring to Hacket as "Master," see, for example, Arber, 2.433; 2.437; 2.526 as well as *Liber A*: 71: 128 and 136. This inconsistency may have had something to do with a Stationers' Court proceeding in June 1588 at which it was "agreed that m^r Hacket shall Enioy his form' place in the lyv'y" (Greg and Boswell 1930, 29). For edition-sheet estimates, see below.
18 One 1566 record states, "The burse of Lombard Street is of longer antiquity than any other burse is known to be of that is within all Europe" (Hopkinson 1915, 61).
19 As John Payne in his *Royal Exchange* attests, decades later in the 1590s, "sum Printers and stationers at certayne tymes haue there meting there [at the Royal Exchange]" (sig. D4^r).
20 "Travel books," says Worms, was a subgenre "long specialized in by the Exchange booksellers" (1997, 218).
21 The specific location of this sign within Paul's Churchyard has yet to be identified. For other signs and bookshop locations, see Pollard et al., 3: 232–59; and Blayney 1990. Two of Hacket's publications with 1568

Notes to pages 81–2   209

dates in their colophons cite this shop at the Key in their imprints: *The Histories of the Most Famous and Worthy Cronographer Polybius* and *The New Found World*. *Theatrum mundi* also cites Hacket's shop at the Key in its imprint. The STC has inferred that this undated first English edition of *Theatrum mundi* was likely published within two to three years of 1566.

22 For a detailed description of the clearing and construction of the Royal Exchange, see Saunders 1997.

23 The earliest extant imprint to advertise the Exchange is Philip Moore's *1571. An Almanac and Prognostication for xxxvii Years*. Not coincidentally, *The Treasury* includes a three-page dedicatory epistle by Hacket addressed to his new landlord Gresham, in which he concludes by "praying to God for [Gresham's] prosperous and good successe in all [his] affaires and enterprises" (sig. ¶3ʳ).

24 See Bennett 1965, 273–5.

25 As many have pointed out, book publishing required a significant initial outlay of investment capital. See Blayney 1997, 405–10 and Lesser 2004, 26–35. The Stationers' Register records a great many joint entrances of copy.

26 W.W. Greg has argued that "the ornaments [which include a printer ornament containing the intitials 'WP'] used point to Pickering as the actual printer" (1939, 110). Hacket's 1561/2 collaboration with Pickering seems to have led to a dispute in which Hacket was fined for "mysvs[ing] hym selfe in vn Curtiss langyshe vnto william pekerynge" (Arber, 1.217); it may also have led to a joint fine a few years later: in 1570, the Stationers' Register lists a "fyne betwene W pekerynge and hym the last yere past" (Arber, 1.444).

27 While the first edition of *An Apology* is dated "Anno.1562" in its imprint, it colophon lists an "Anno. 1561." publishing date. This discrepancy might have something to do with the title page's note that the text is "Newelye set foorth and allowed accor | dinge to the order appoynted in the | Quenes Maiesties iniunc- | tions."

28 *The Laws and Statutes of Geneva* was entered to Hall in 1561/2 (Arber, 1.175) and its first edition advertises Hall's printing house "in Gutter | Lane, at the sygne of the halfe Egle | and the Keye. | 1562" (Fils) in its imprint. Hall had worked in Geneva between 1559 until 1560 (Duff 1905, 64); given this, it seems likely that he provided the copy for this text.

29 The only exception to this seems to have been Pliny's *A Summary of the Antiquities, and Wonders of the World*. Henry Denham printed the first two editions of the book, in 1566 and then in 1585 under Hacket's

new title *The Secrets and Wonders of the World*. Henry Wolfe brought out the text's third edition in 1587. It seems reasonable to assume that Hacket went back to Denham after nineteen years because Denham had printed the first edition of the work; the two may have had some private arrangement that was inherited later by Wolfe. For more on trade relationships in an "economy of obligation," see Muldrew 1998.

30 See Plomer 1909.
31 In 1583, Bynneman is listed in the Stationers' Register as having three printing presses (Arber, 1.248). See Plomer 1908.
32 Because they did not again require outlay for copy, authority, licence, and registration, subsequent editions could be very profitable for a publisher; in fact, they could be anywhere from two to three times more lucrative than a first edition. See Farmer and Lesser 2005 and Blayney 1997, 412–13. Farmer and Lesser have estimated that between 1576 and 1625, 18.1 per cent of all speculative books were reprinted within twenty years of their first edition (18–20); by my calculation, between 1560 and 1590 approximately 13 per cent of Hacket's first published editions were reprinted within twenty years. Of course, all of this needs to be understood in terms of the potential loss of an entire edition; nonetheless, extant editions – especially of more substantial texts – give us a good idea of a work's popularity.
33 *An Apology Made by the Reverend Father J. Hooper* (1562) was in fact the first of Hacket's publications to be reprinted, but this reprinting was packaged as the second part of Hooper's *An Exposition upon the 23 Psalm* (1562).
34 Hacket appears to have published as many as three translations by John Alday: Boaistuau 1566; Pliny 1566; and possibly I.A. 1566.
35 An exception to this is *The Treasury of Health*. In 1585, Thomas East entered and brought out the sixth edition of this work, more than a decade after Hacket had published the work's fifth edition around 1570. *The Treasury*, however, is described as "an old copie extant in print" (Arber, 2.439) in East's Stationers' Register entry, suggesting that Hacket himself may not have had absolute rights to it when he published it years earlier.
36 For recent arguments about the ubiquity and importance of translation in Tudor England, see Morini 2006; Braden 2010b, 89–90; and Schurink 2011. See also "Translating" in chapter 1.
37 For an overview of Paynell's work as a translator, see Moore 2011.
38 See Bennett 1965, 87–112 and Wright 1935, 339–72.
39 Of the forty-six titles that Bynneman published over his four-decade career, twenty-four were translations. See Barnard and Bell 1991.
40 See Melnikoff 2009, 257–71.

41 For more on *The Regiment*, see Worms 1997, 211.
42 The first extant work is Richard Eden's 1553 translation *A Treatise of the New India*.
43 Only two copies of this octavo now exist, one held at the British Library, the other at the Lambeth Palace Library. The epistle to Bowes can only be found in the Lambeth copy.
44 Thevet's narrative was published eleven years earlier in France as *Les singvlaritez de la France antarctiqve* (Paris, 1557). Thevet was criticized both for embellishing his narrative with accounts from other expeditions and for fabricating episodes.
45 The epistle is unsigned; its style, tone, and content together suggest that it was written by Hacket.
46 For an overviews of Eden's life and career, see Gwyn 1984, 13–34 and Parker 1965, 36–53; for Frampton, see Beecher 2006; for Nicholas, see Baldwin 2004; and for Florio, see Starnes 1965.
47 Hadfield 1998a.
48 More's *Utopia* was first published in Latin in 1516. The English translation by Ralph Robinson first appeared in 1551. Subsequent editions appeared in 1556, 1597, 1624, and 1639.
49 For other examples of this strong nationalist bent among early English translators of travel literature, see Anghiera 1555, sigs. d2^r–d3^v; Enciso 1578, sig. A2^v; López de Gómara 1578, sigs. A2^v–A4^r; Medina 1581, sig. ¶2^r; and Zárate 1581, sig. A4^v.
50 Eden's motivations here also had something to do with his recent debasement of English coinage. See Gwyn 1984.
51 Florio's text was the first publication to be financed by Richard Hakluyt and was based on Giovanni Baptista Ramusio's Italian translation of Cartier's narratives; they were first published in Ramusio's *Delle navigationi e viaggi* (Venice, 1556).
52 The work drew from Peter Martyr's *De orbe novo decades*, and Gonzalo Oviedo's *Natural hystoria de las Indias*, among others. It reached a second edition in 1577.
53 See also López de Gómara 1578, sigs. b1^{r-v}.
54 Something of the same note is struck in Stephan Gosson's dedicatory poem in *The Pleasant History of the Conquest of the West India* (1578). There Gosson praises Nicholas "for his toyle, / Who strings the Lute that putteth us in minde, / How doting dayes haue giuen vs all the foyle. / Whilst learned wittes in forrayne landes doe finde, / That labour beares away the golden fleece, / And is rewarded with the flower of Greece" (López de Gómara, sig. b2^r).

55 This trend in marketing also corresponded with the appearance of the first English-language navigational books in St Paul's Churchyard in the 1550s and 1560s. See Adams 1992, 208.

56 Beecher calls Frampton's translations a "School for English seamen and traders" (2006, 105). Frampton's more pragmatic sense of his vocation as a translator of travel literature emerges as well in *The Most Noble and Famous Travels of Marcus Paulus* (1579) and *A Discovery of the Countries of Tartaria, Scithia, & Cataya, by the Northeast* (1580); in his dedicatory epistle for the latter he claims that he translated the work so that the mariners on the expedition for Rowland Hayward and George Barne may better have avoided perils and "take the benefite of the place the better" (sig. ¶4^r).

57 Braden 2010b, 89–90. For the refrain "truly and faithfully," see, for example, Monardes 1577a, sig. *2^v.

58 Householder has characterized Eden's translations as "for the most part consistent with the original" (2007, 34). Hadfield, however, has pointed out that Eden often uses marginal glosses "to lead the reader away from … criticism of European values" (1995/6, 16). Eden himself, in his poem "Thinterpretours excuse" at the end of *The Decades of the New World*, writes, "I am not eloquent I knowe it ryght well, /If I be not barbarous I desyre no more, /I haue not for euery woorde asked counsell/Of eloquent Eliot or syr Thomas Moore" (Anghiera 1555, sigs. AAAAa5^v–AAAAa6^r).

59 See Braden 2010b, 92–3 and Boutcher 2000. Explaining the practice, Boutcher points out that "the point the translator wanted to make, or the meditation he or she wished to offer regarding a particular issue on a given occasion, from a particular place, by *means* of a translation, … prevailed over any desire to offer a textually accurate version of a noted author's work" (2000, 51). For developments in the Elizabethan understanding of translation work, see Morini 2006 and Belle 2013.

60 Cicero 1949.

61 A large number of Elizabethan authors, translators, and publishers signed off as "daily orators" in their dedicatory epistles. The expression was primarily used to mean "one who ever prays for." In the cases of Eden, Hacket, and others, I will be suggesting a secondary meaning of "one who pleads or argues on behalf of a … cause" (*OED*).

62 Other 1550s travel narratives printed in the vernacular include William Prat's translation *The Description of the Country of Aphrique* (1554); William Waterman's translation *The Fardle of Fashions* (1555); Robert Record's *Castle of Knowledge* (1556); and William Cunningham's *The Cosmographical Glass* (1559). See Parker 1965, 245–6.

63 Parker argues that Hacket's 1563 translation was essentially subsidized "English propaganda to support an overseas settlement" (1965, 58).
64 Hacket seems to have drawn this from the original Dieppe title page that included the line "qu'elle a esté produitoirement & cruellement executee par lesdits Espagnols" ["what hath been (...) & cruelly executed by the said Spaniards"].
65 This ending paragraph is not to be found in Hacket's 1566 Dieppe copy. Parker has suggested that Hacket's inconsistent attitude towards colonial exploration in his three 1560s translations was the product of these projects being "subsidized" and driven by "interests close to court" (1965, 60).
66 Four years later in 1572, Eden responded to the market demand to which Hacket appealed in the 1560s. In *A Brief Collection and Compendious Extract of the Strange and Memorable Things, Gathered Out of the Cosmography of Sebastian Munster*, Eden says in his prefatory epistle that he is offering the book to readers interested in novelty, to "myndes desyrous to heare of straunge things" (sig. *2^v).
67 Hacket's dual focus can be seen in the subtitle of his 1585 publication *The Work of Pomponius Mela The Cosmographer*, where he advertises the book as "right plesant and pro | fitable for all sortes of men: but speciallie | for Gentlemen, Marchants, Mariners, | and Trauellers" (tp).
68 As it is not in Thevet's 1557 French original, this unascribed poem has been ascribed to Hacket. The *OED*, for example, credits Hacket with the first use of the verb "educt."
69 Hacket's pursuing readers interested in travel narratives as pleasurable reading material helps explain his ending apology to Sidney, where he calls his translation of Thevet "*a token of* [his] *good will, the which after your great & waighty affaires, it may please you to vse*" (1568, sig. *3^v).
70 Titled "*T.H. in praise of the booke*," this poem ends with what was a familiar publisher's refrain: "Till other things come to my hands / I bid thee to adewe."
71 In *The New Found World or Antarctic* Hacket also cuts a significant number of marginal notes found in his copy.
72 Hacket may also have been echoing John Alday, the translator of Hacket's 1566(?) publication *Theatrum mundi*. Alday signs his dedicatory epistle to the London alderman Sir William Chester "Your daily orator / Iohn Alday" (Boaistuau, sig. A3^r).
73 This claim echoes Hacket's earlier nationalist deliberations. In his dedicatory epistle to *The Whole and True Discovery of Terra Florida*, he had mused, "when I cal to my remembraunce the great viages & nauigations from time to time, of manye and sundry worthy men as well at the charges

of noble princes kings and gouernours of realms, as the inferior sorte of subiectes. I cannot but amongst the rest reioyce to see the forwardness in these late yeares of Englyshe men" (Ribaut, sig. A1ʳ).
74 Hacket's other additions having to do with England can be found in the chapter "Of Ethiopia," where he changes what in his copy is "les Gaulois" ["the Gauls"] (Thevet 1557, sig. E5ᵛ) to "Englishmen, and those that are vnder the North Pole, which contrary are cold without, but maruelous hot within, to be hardy, courageous, & ful of great boldness" (sig. E1ʳ). In the 38th chapter, Hacket translates "Leurs arcs sont la moitié plus longs que les arcs Turquois" ["their bows are half as long as Turkish bows"] (Thevet 1557, sig. K6ᵛ) as "[the Amazons] bowes are as long as oure bowes in Englande" (Thevet 1568, sig. I2ʳ).
75 See Hart 2005, 75–6.
76 In this, Hacket's specialty could be described as propagandist.
77 See Rackin 1990, 18–21. Hacket would reiterate the equivalent ends of poetry and historiography in his 1587 *The True and Perfect News of the Exploits Performed by Sir F. Drake: at Santo Domingo*. There, he writes, "for there is nothing can more profitte thy posteritie heereafter, then the leauing in memory so worthy a thing, for how shoulde we know the woorthy deedes of our Elders, if those learned Poets and Historiographers had not sette them downe in wryting" (sig. A3ʳ).
78 In all of this, Hacket's work can usefully be connected to what Listrengant and Blair have identified in the 1560s and 1570s as the French Huguenot response to their recent colonial failures in the Americas. Faced with a number of disasters, the Huguenots moved away from colonial projects, describing native peoples as "others" who could not be reformed (1995, 286–7).
79 Like most early-modern ballads, none of these titles is now extant.
80 See Lestringant 1993, and Lestringant and Blair 1995. Ironically, Thevet's subsequent publication *La cosmographie universelle* (1575) included an aggressive attack upon Huguenot colonists.
81 Hacket did publish a handful of Prostestant tracts after 1562: *A Letter Sent by the Maidens of London* (1567); *A Touchstone for This Time Present, Declaring Such Abuses as Trouble the Church and Commonwealth* (1574); *The Third Step of the Ladder to Repentence* (1585); and *A Mirror of Monsters* (1587).
82 McGhee 2001, 36–7.
83 Thomas Churchyard would express a similar idea in *A Warning for the Wise* (1580). There in his "admonition to the Reader," he writes, "The straunger the things are that our eyes behold, the more the impression

of the minde is earnestly occupied about the understanding of a wonder. And the oftener we see maruelles, the more is Gods might made manifest, & we the more affrayed to offend" (sig. A2ᵛ).

3 Richard Smith's Browsables: *A Hundreth Sundry Flowers* (1573), *The Fabulous Tales of Aesop* (1577), and *Diana* (1592, 1594?)

1 Likely motivated by William Ponsonby's publishing of *The Arcadia* in 1590, Newman published *Astrophel and Stella* twice in 1591, John Charlewood printing the first edition and John Danter the second. In September 1591 the title was ordered "tak[en] in" by the Stationers' Company, apparently by Lord Burghley at the instigation of the Sidney family (Arber, 1.555). A third undated edition of the poem was published by Mathew Lownes, possibly in 1597. For differing accounts of the complicated textual history of *Astrophel and Stella* in print, see Ringler 1962; Warkentin 1985; and Woudhuysen 1996.
2 For sonnet sequences in Elizabethan England, see Roche 1989; Dubrow 1995; and Warley 2005.
3 Newman also seems to have corrected textual errors in the first 95 sonnets, possibly with the assistance of Daniel. See Ringler 1962 and Woudhuysen 1996.
4 Marotti argues that Newman delivers a "double message" (232) with his augmented first edition of *Astrophel and Stella*: (1) that Sidney is a great author and (2) that lyric poetry in manuscript should be publically circulated in print.
5 See Loewenstein 1985; Wall 1993; Marotti 1995, 209–90; and Erne 2003.
6 In the volume's dedicatory epistle to Richard Stonley, Smith confirms this date, writing that it has been "two yeres since [he] turned it into Englishe" (sig. ¶2ʳ).
7 Drapers' Hall, Wardens' Accounts: W.A. 4, f. 2ᵛ. The most direct evidence for Smith's career as a draper comes from Henry Bynneman's 1583 inventory. It records that Bynneman acquired a ten-year lease from Smith (starting in 1574) for a bookshop at the west end of St Paul's Churchyard. In this entry, Smith is referred to as a "citizen and draper." See Eccles 1957.
8 Drapers' Hall, Minute Book: M.B. 1/C, fol. 210ʳ. Likely because the Wardens' Accounts between 1562 and 1564 do not list individual freedoms, we do not have the record of Smith's being made free of the Drapers' Company in these years.
9 See Hentschell 2008; Girtin 1964; and Johnson 1914–22. In the late 1590s, the practice was being met with significant resistance from the Stationers'

Company. See Johnson 1988. Wight's connection to the Stationers' Company is underscored by his bequeathing forty shillings to "the pore men of the company of the stationers in London" in his will (PRO, PROB 11/74/150).
10 Wight, it seems, made a habit of training his draper apprentices in bookselling. See Johnson 1988, 6.
11 England worked between 1557 and 1568, publishing many translations, including those of Virgil and Machiavelli.
12 Drapers' Hall, Minute Book: M.B. 8, fol.14^r. Three years later, Barker signed a "21-year lease for part of the residence of the junior cardinal of St Paul's" (Kathman 2004a).
13 In 1596, Thomas Fisher is listed as having been freed by a "Smithe Rich" in the Drapers' Hall Freedom Lists (F.A. 1, 87). Given that Fisher would go on to be one of the twelve drapers who were transferred into the Stationers' Company in May 1600 (Johnson 1988, 2), it seems likely that our Richard Smith was his master. In 1602, John Syde is listed as having been freed by a "Smith Richard" (Drapers' Hall, Freedom Lists: F.A. 2, 180). A "Richard Smith" is also listed as being granted a surety by the company wardens in 1598 (Drapers' Hall, Minute Book: M.B. 11, fol. 235^v).
14 Thomas 1948. Even while a number of his publications have drawn recent critical interest, this remains the sole article dedicated to the career of Smith.
15 Bynneman leased Smith's shop between 1574 and 1584. As a consequence of what may have been a private arrangement between him and Bynneman, Smith seems to have continued to advertise in his 1575 imprints that his books could be bought wholesale out of this shop.
16 In 1587, Smith seems to have reinstituted his Bynneman shop arrangement with Abel Jeffes and with Thomas Woodcock, as two of Smith's imprints from this year advertise Jeffes's shop and one Woodcock's shop.
17 Smith does turn up in the records of the Stationers' Company in 1577. There, he is listed with Wight among "all suche as do lyue by bookselling being free of other Companies" (Arber, 1.111) who objected to Elizabeth's printing privileges.
18 The 1571 second edition only cites Smith, suggesting that he solely possessed the work's right to copy at that time.
19 See Thomas 1948, 187–8.
20 A revised edition of *The Discourse* came out in 1595, with subsequent editions each of the next two years.
21 See Eccles 1957; Barnard and Bell 1991; and Bell 2004.

22 See Thomas 1948, 187–8.
23 The only exception to this was Smith's fourth edition of *A Discourse of Horsemanship*, which was printed by John Windet in 1597. Roberts married Charlewood's widow in 1593 and took over Charlewood's printing house at the Half Eagle and Key. See Tedder 2004b and McKerrow 1910, 229.
24 See Thomas 1948, 188–90.
25 Smith's dedicatory epistle addressed to Stonley appears in *The Fabulous Tales of Aesop* (sigs. A2^{r-v}); to Compton in *History of Pelops and Hippodamia* (sigs. A2^{r-v}); and to Edmunds in *The Masque of the League* (sig. A2^r). Smith may also have written the unsigned dedicatory epistle addressed to John Puckering in *The Wonderful Combat* (sigs. ∴2^r–∴3^r) and to Julius Caesar in *Of Prayer and Meditation* (sigs. A3^r–A4^r).
26 See Gascoigne 1573, sigs. A2^r–A3^r, Ii3^r; Andrewes 1592, sig. ∴4^r; Constable 1592, sig. A4^r; and Constable 1594?, sig. A2^r. As we shall see, Smith may also have been the "R.S." who addresses the reader on the second leaf in Bynneman's 1572 publication *The Fall and Evil Success of Rebellion*.
27 See Andrewes 1592, sig. ∴3^v; Chapman 1595, sig. I3^v; and de Granada 1596, sig. A4^v. McKerrow traces the emblem to the Genevan printer Conrad Badius and to Queen Mary I (1913, 69).
28 In 1592, this new emblem appears in *The Wonderful Combat* (sig. ∴3^v) and *Diana* (tp). Smith may have even commissioned a third version of the emblem around 1598. McKerrow identified a third smaller version of the device in *Dyets Dry Dinner* (1599) (1913, sig. B1^r).
29 For other examples of such acquisitions, see Gascoigne 1573, sig. A3^r; Aesop 1577, sig. ¶2^v; Andrewes 1592, sig. ∴4^r; and de Granada 1596, sig. A4^r.
30 See Prouty 1942 and McCoy 1985.
31 See, respectively, Pigman 2000, liii and Clegg 1997, 103–22.
32 The third of these entries records Smith "appear[ing] at Lambehithe 25 Novembris" (Arber, 1.561; Thomas 1948, 189–90). Lambeth Palace was the official London residence of the Archbishop of Canterbury. According to the Oxford *DNB*, "Throughout his life Andrewes refused to commit his works to print unless commanded to do so by authority" (McCullough 2004). The second edition of these sermons did not appear until 1627, *after* Andrewes's death.
33 Jackson 1957, 65. Wood apparently also acquired Smith's printers' emblems in 1598. These emblems appear in two of Wood's publication thereafter: *Dyets Dry Dinner* (1599) and *The Mirror of Martyrs* (1601).

34 See Arber, 3.130.
35 Foundational criticism treating of the intersections between manuscript poetry and print culture includes Saunders 1951; Wall 1993; and Marotti 1995.
36 "The Printer to the Reader" refers to *A Discourse of the Adventures Passed by Master F.J.* as appearing in "the beginning of this worke" (sig. A2^r).
37 For a complete description of these alterations, see especially Pigman 2000 and Clegg 1997. For differing explanations, see Wall 1993; McCoy; and Clegg 1997 among others. Most commentators, like Wall 1993, Shannon 2004, and Staub 2011, have underscored the various ways in which this edition is reconceived around Gascoigne as author.
38 For a discussion of the first of these poems, see below. The second is entitled "R.S. In prayse of Gascoignes Posies" (sig. ¶¶¶3^v), "R.S." possibly the initials of Smith.
39 See Kerrigan 2001, 123 and Prouty 1942. No record exists of Smith having registered his licence to copy within the Stationers' Register. His ownership of this right to copy, however, is suggested by his being made to return fifty copies of *The Posies* in 1576.
40 The pervasive influence of Weiss's article can be seen in Clegg 1997, 103–22; Kerrigan 1996; and Pigman 2000, lvi. For earlier claims that Gascoigne wrote "The Printer to the Reader," see Marotti 1991 and McCoy 1985.
41 Pigman 2000 follows Weiss's argument in assuming that the "Printer" in this prefatory epistle could only refer to Bynneman.
42 See chapter 1.
43 *A Hundreth Sundry Flowers* also contains a table of contents and an errata sheet in its first gathering. The former was in all likelihood provided by Bynneman, it reproducing the larger collection's separation of the printer's epistle and *The Adventures Passed by Master F.J.* and referring to Gascoigne in the third person ("certayne deuises of master Gascoyne"). As Gascoigne was in the Low Countries when the first edition was completed, the latter could have been put together by Bynneman, Smith, or some other agent.
44 See, for example, the work of Saunders, Marotti, and Wall.
45 Most commentators believe that Gascoigne authored *The Adventures Passed by Master F.J.*'s prefatory letters by "H.W." and "G.T."
46 See Wall 1993, 95–109.
47 Commentators like Wall and Zarnowiecki have connected the title page of Gascoigne's volume with Tottel's earlier miscellany.

48 It is widely believed that a number of poems in Tottel's *Songs and Sonnets* were written by Viscount Rochford, Anne Boleyn's brother. In Smith's 1587 third edition of Gascoigne's works, *The Whole Works of George Gascoigne Esquire*, this dedicatory poem's title is changed to "Richard Smith in commendation of Gascoigne and his workes."

49 See McKerrow 1913, 149. While we cannot be entirely sure that his wholesaling of the *Il filocolo*'s first English-language edition should be understood as his sharing some of the financial risk with Smith, Bynneman did make a habit of such collaborations. See Pollard et al., 3.35.

50 The second edition of his *Il filocolo* was published by Smith in 1571. With the new title *Thirteen Most Pleasant and Delectable Questions*, this edition advertises Smith alone as publisher in its colophon and wholesale copies "at the | Corner shoppe, at the North- | weast dore of Paules" in its imprint.

51 In some cases, buyers might also have been able to purchase pre-bound copies from a bookseller, the larger the book, the more likely that this would be an option. According to Blayney, "pamphlets and other books as slim as most play quartos would usually be sold without bindings, and few purchasers would want them bound individually. Those who bought such books regularly would wait until they had what they considered to be a suitable number, and then would have them bound as a single volume" (1997, 413–15).

52 Knight 2009, 308. See also Lerer 2003; Gillespie 2004; Smyth 2004; and Sherman 2008.

53 For more on book browsing, see Plant 1939, 248; Bennett 1965, 263; Johns 1998, 108–25; Voss 1998, 754–5; and Taylor 2008.

54 Based on Continental accounts, Adrian Johns has speculated that "an assistant was expected to hand [books] over a counter to customers," that book buyers did not have free access to books within a bookseller's shop (1998, 118). Either way, buyers would have encountered other browsers at London's many bookshops, some reading, some conversing (Taylor 2008, 57).

55 No author's name appears with the poem, and as such it could have been penned by the volume's translator "H.G." (thought to have been either Humphrey Gifford or Henry Grantham). However, the poem's content along with its inconsistent metre, awkward phrasing, and convoluted language all seem to point to Smith.

56 Coincidently, Smith began his prefatory epistle in *A Hundreth Sundry Flowers* with a vague allusion to one of Aesop's untranslated fables,

"The Lion, the Bear, and the Fox": "IT hath bin an old saying, that vvhiles tvvo doggs do striue for a bone, the thirde may come and carie it avvay. And this prouerbe may (as I feare) be wel verefied in me which take in hand the imprinting of this poeticall Poesie" (sig. A2^r).

57 As we have already seen, the final page of this translation reports that it was "Finished ... the thirtenth of August. Anno Domini. 1574" (sig. H2^r).

58 See Fox 1962; Gopen 1987; and Wheatley 2000.

59 Smith's version is most likely based upon Thomas Bassandyne's 1571 rather than Henry Charteris's 1570 edition of Henryson's work in that his translation includes four stanzas that can only be found in the former edition (these occur on sigs. A8^r, G6^v, H1^r, and H1^v). H. Harvey Wood argues that Smith's translation may have been based upon a now-lost print edition of the *Morall fabillis* (1933, 223).

60 The other available prose versions of Aesop in the sixteenth century were William Caxton's oft reprinted 1484 translation out of French sources and William Bullokar's 1585 translation out of Latin sources.

61 Smith's "English[ing]" of Henryson mostly involves substituting English words and/or English spellings for Henryson's Middle Scot diction.

62 Smith's translation of Henryson has long been a sore subject for Henryson scholars. Wood complains that "the translator has failed to understand, not only the difficulties and obscurities of his original, but many of the most elementary points of syntax" (1933, 222); Gopen concurs, arguing that the translation is "riddled with inaccuracies and not much help in understanding the original" (1987, 33).

63 For accounts of Henryson's own fashioning of textual authority in the *Morall fabillis*, see Machan 1990 and 1992.

64 Smith indicates dialogue in the poem by using black-letter type for his own narration and comments, and roman type for "Esope."

65 See Folger Shakespeare Library, *Diaries*.

66 For publishers' investments in the tables of contents of Elizabethan printed books, see chapter 1.

67 This table may have been copied from Henry Charteris's 1570 edition.

68 In arguing that Smith's table moralizing endorses bourgeois values, I am suggesting that *The Fabulous Tales of Aesop* can be taken to speak in voices with varying political resonances. For differing senses of the politics of Henryson's Aesop translation, see Patterson 1991 and Fox 1981.

69 Not much is known about Grove except that he likely studied law (Eccles 1982, 57–8).

70 Something of this same will to individuation and abstraction can be seen in the title of the amatory poem "To him that was disappointed of his

woman and louer," a tag which ignores the fact that the speaker is the same "friend" who speaks in the earlier poem "The letter of a friend of a wounded Louer" (sigs. G4^v, E6^r).

71 On 22 September 1591, James Charlewood entered in the Stationers' Register "a little Booke intituled. Dyana the prayses of his mistres in certen sweete Sonnettes &c" (Arber, 2.620). As with his earlier publications, Smith collaborated with a stationer to bring the title to press. Charlewood and Smith chose to make their print editions of *Diana* "little" (5" x 3") like the copy entered in the Stationers' Register, possibly so that these books could be easily kept on buyers' persons.

72 Grundy says that Constable left England a year before the volume's publication, but this is not necessarily true; he very well might have still been in England while the volume was being printed. After converting to Catholicism during the French campaign, Constable did not return to England until 1599. For an overview of the Essex campaign, see Hammer 1999. For Constable's life and career, see Grundy 1960.

73 Grundy has suggested that Constable may have approved of the collection's publication and turned to a friend to see "the volume through the press" while he was in France (1960, 94).

74 In 1594, when Charlewood's licences are transferred to James Roberts, *Diana* is not included in the Stationers' Register list (Arber, 2.651–2). This suggests that Charlewood did not co-publish the first edition of *Diana* with Smith; instead, Smith employed him as the collection's trade printer.

75 Both Newman's first edition of *Astrophel and Stella* and Smith's first edition of *Diana* were printed by Charlewood. It stands to reason that Smith may have been influenced by Charlewood's experience printing the first edition of Sidney's sonnet sequence.

76 Smith's 1592 *Diana* is the only early-modern volume, print or manuscript, which includes Constable's "*To his absent Diana*." Grundy assumes that the poem was meant by Constable to be a "dedicatory sonnet" (94) for the 1592 collection.

77 This sonnet, with slight variations of title, appears in both the 1592 and 1594? editions of *Diana*; it also appears in a number of different contemporary manuscripts.

78 In two contemporary manuscripts, the "Lady" is identified as Lady Rich, Constable's presumed beloved in *Diana*.

79 Printed by James Roberts for Smith, this edition has the date of publication cropped in its copies. As Charlewood had died in 1593 and Roberts had married his widow in September of that year, 1594 would appear to

be the earliest date for this three-sheet octavo. The STC has offered 1594 as the publication date.

80 For attributions, see Grundy 1960.

81 The new epistle is unsigned but in all probability is by Smith. As Charlewood likely was, Roberts was employed by Smith as a trade printer. As Roberts did not co-publish this edition with Smith, it is unlikely that he contributed this new epistle. The new dedicatory sonnet is signed "RICHARD SMYTH" (sig. A2^v).

82 Essentially, the second and third editions of *Diana* print the odd-numbered sonnets of the first edition in their first decade and the even-numbered sonnets in the second decade. This ordering basically follows the arrangement of the Arundel Harington manuscript. Kenneth Muir (1954) suggested that the compositor of the 1592 edition was working from an author's MS that listed the sonnets in two columns; he transcribed one column and then the other when he should have gone left to right. This error was corrected in the order of Constable's sonnets in the first two decades of *Diana*'s second edition.

83 Most scholars and editors have disparaged the aesthetic quality of the additions to Smith's second edition of *Diana* (e.g., Grundy 1960, 51–2) and been unwilling to consider the volume on its own terms. Tom Parker has described the edition as a "willful distortion" by Smith (1998, 150).

84 None of the five new Constable poems that do not appear in the 1592 first edition are given attributions.

85 Some of these "*added*" poems in Newman's first edition are also ascribed: to "*S.D.*" (sig. I3^v); to "Daniel" (sig. L2^v); and to "E.O." (sig. L4^v).

86 The term "quatorzain" occurs three times in the volume which was published by Gabriel Cawood, twice in the commendatory poem by "G. Bucke," and once in the title of Watson's own prefatory poem "A Quatorzain of the Au*thour vnto this his booke of Louepassi*ons" (sig. *4^v).

87 In his *Obseruations* (1602), Thomas Campion complains that the quatorzain's formal rigidity leads to bad poetry. "But there is yet another fault in Rime altogether intollerable," he writes, "which is that it inforceth a man oftentimes to abiure his matter, and extend a short conceit beyond all bounds of arte: for in *Quatorzens* me thinks the Poet handles his subiect as tyrannically as *Procrustes* the thiefe his prisoners, whom when he had taken, he vsed to cast vpon a bed which if they were too short to fill, he would stretch them longer[;] if too long, he would cut them shorter" (sig. A7^v).

88 Of the rhyme schemes in the augmented *Diana*, Grundy writes, "The writer, or writers, avoiding the Italian form in Decads V–VIII shows an

almost feverish interest in the invention of novel rhyme schemes" (1960, 52). A number of the volume's added sonnets have strong connections to Desportes's sonnet sequence *Les Amours de Diana* (1573): the fifth decade's "*SONNET. II.*" is very similar to Desportes's 28th sonnet; the sixth decade's "*SONNET. II.*" seems based on Desportes's 29th sonnet; the seventh decade's "*SONNET. VIII.*" is a translation of Desportes's 47th sonnet; and the seventh decade's "*SONNET. X.*" is a translation of Desportes's 27th sonnet. The fourth decade's "*SONNET. VII.*" is reminiscent of the sonnets in Du Bellay's *Les antiquités de Rome* (1558).

89 These eight sonnets ("*SONNET. II*" to "*SONNET. IX.*") all appeared in William Ponsonby's 1598 edition of Sidney's works, in the section subtitled "CERTAINE SONETS WRITTEN BY SIR PHILIP SIDNEY" (sig. RR2ᵛ).

90 This line structure suggests that these four poems may have originally been part of a sonnet corona or a heroic crown of sonnets.

91 Cintio's *Ecatommiti* and Livy's *Ab urbe condita libri*, to cite two examples, were divided into decades.

92 Nashe similarly employs "decade" in his *Have with You to Saffron-Walden*: "*Benti*: I would our *Gurmo Hidruntum*, were like wise banisht with him, for he can hotch-potch whole Decades vp of nothing, and talks idlely all his lifetime" (1596, sig. K4ʳ).

93 Bullinger appears to have modelled the structure of his *Decades* on the Catholic rosary, which traditionally consisted of five sets of ten beads.

94 This same enumerative sense of a "decade" can be found in Joseph Hall's three volumes of *Epistles* that were first published between 1608 and 1611. Each is divided into two "decads" ("decades" in the third volume) of unconnected letters. See also Anon. 1598a.

95 For an overview of the transmission of Livy's works, see Burke 1966 and Culhane 2004. Livy's regard in the sixteenth century is also attested by Richard Eden's *The Decades of the New World or West India* (1555), his much reprinted translation of Pete Martyr's *De orbe novo decades* (1516). Following Martyr, Eden in his ample prefatory material suggests that "Decades" in the title is an allusion to Pliny, an attempt to put the colonial deeds of the Spaniards on the same level as the republican achievements of the Romans. For more on Eden's *Decades*, see chapter 2.

96 Both Smith and Islip worked extensively with Anthony Munday in the 1590s.

97 As Livy often released his history in sets of ten books, the work came to be copied decade by decade. Over time, each of these decades then took on its own characteristics. Petrarch was among many who pointed out that Livy did not himself divide the books of *Ab urbe condita* into

decades. "I must advertise the Reader," contends Holland in his epistle "To the Reader," "of that vvhich *Petrus Crinitus* hath observed, even against the common opinion approoved by those vvho othervvise are vvell learned, namely that our Author dispensed not this historie into Decades: that is to say, luted and sorted them not into severall Tomes and Sections of ten bookes a peece."

98 Culhane 2004, 270. See also Jardine and Grafton 1990, 57–8.
99 The third edition of the octavo was printed by Roberts for Smith sometime before 6 November 1598, when Smith's licence for *Diana* was transferred to William Wood (Arber, 3.131). The STC has offered 1595 as a publication date. Grundy has limited the publication date to between 1594 and 1596 (1960, 97–100).
100 Before 1640, Drayton's *Idea's Mirror* was printed once in 1594; Lodge's *Phillis* was printed once in 1593; Spenser's *Amoretti* was printed once in 1595; Shakespeare's *Sonnets* was printed once in 1609; and Sidney's *Astrophel and Stella* was printed three times, twice in 1591 and once in 1598. The most popular sonnet sequence of the day was Daniel's *Delia*, which was printed five times, twice in 1592 and once in 1594, 1595, and 1598.

4 Flasket and Linley's *The Tragedy of Dido Queen of Carthage* (1594): Reissuing the Elizabethan Epyllion

1 These collections include *The Ancient British Drama* (1810); *Old English Plays* (1814); and *A Select Collection of Old Plays* (1825–7). For overviews of Marlowe's reclamation in the nineteenth century, see Brooke 1922 and Dabbs 1991.
2 The only other early-nineteenth-century editions of *Dido* were in collected editions of Marlowe: in *The Works of Christopher Marlowe* (1826, ed. Robinson); in *The Dramatic Works of Christopher Marlowe* (1827, ed. Oxberry); and in *The Works of Christopher Marlowe* (1850, ed. Dyce [revised in 1858]). Robinson, in the 1826 edition, argues that *Dido* was written by Marlowe with the assistance of Nashe. His preface to the play laments Nashe's lost elegy on Marlowe because it likely would have established once and for all that Nashe made additions after Marlowe's death.
3 Hurst and Robinson underscore their belief that *Dido* was written by Nashe "assisted by Marlowe" in including a biography of Nashe before the play text, and by printing a running header containing Nashe's name not Marlowe's.

4 William Gager (and possibly George Peele) produced an academic play out of the Dido story in Virgil's *Aeneid*. It was written in Latin iambic pentameter as an entertainment for the Polish ambassador's visit to Oxford in June 1583. It was not printed until Dyce included it in his 1850 *The Works of Christopher Marlowe*. See Sutton.
5 Contra Farmer and Lesser (2005a), Peter Blayney has argued that printed professional plays were not the "bestselling moneyspinners that so many commentators have evidently believed they *should* have been" (1997, 416).
6 Unlike Edward White, Thomas Creede, William Barley, and John Danter, Woodcock also did not involve himself with more than one professional play in 1594.
7 For useful overviews of sixteenth- and seventeenth-century title-page attributes in playbooks, see Saeger and Fassler 1995; Farmer and Lesser 2000; and Erne 2003.
8 See Hopkins 2004; for a more sceptical take on the newsworthiness of Marlowe's demise, see Melnikoff 2013b.
9 For the many factors affecting early-modern publishers' profits, see Blayney 1997.
10 Biographical information about Linley comes from the Stationers' Register (Arber, 2.66) and from Linley's 1599 will (Guildhall Library, Peculiar Court, fol. 92^v).
11 Drapers' Hall, Freedom Lists, F.A. 2, fol. 66^r. Flasket was christened at St Martin's Church, Ludgate in October 1566. He was the eldest son of nine siblings (Mary [b. 1565], Thomas [b. 1567], Humphrey [b. 1569], Leonard [b. 1571], Grace [b. 1572], Susanna [b. 1578], Joseph [b. 1579], and Judith [b. 1583]), and he was buried on 8 August 1616 at St Giles Cripplegate. A number of contemporary sources record Flasket's occupation as a bookbinder: (1) his name appears in the household accounts of the Earl of Northumberland as someone who was paid to bind books (Batho 1960); (2) he is identified as either a bookbinder or as a stationer in the documents related to the Old Joiner case (Erler 2008); and (3) in Sir Julius Caesar's notes concerning this Star Chamber case (British Library, fol. 26^r), it is recorded that John Oswald worked as a bookbinder for Flaskett and his uncle Wight. I am grateful to András Kiséry for sharing this information with me.
12 John Wight junior was freed in 1584 "by patrimony" (Drapers' Hall, Freedom Lists, F.A. 1, fol. 49^r).
13 Thomas Flasket was married to Wight senior's daughter Katherine. Evidence that Wight senior's son-in-law was John Flasket's haberdasher

father and *not* (as some have suggested) his brother Thomas comes from the 1608 will of the draper James Price, the husband of John Flasket's youngest sister Judith. In it, Price calls Wight senior's son Thomas Wight his "louing uncle" (PRO, PROB/11/111/537). Thomas Wight inherited his father's bookselling business in 1589.
14 Haberdashers' Company, Register of Freedom Admission, fol. 62^r.
15 For evidence of a real-estate transaction between Wight and Flasket, see Hertfordshire Archives Estate Papers, DE/FL/17295, 28 July 1579.
16 These 1594 publications are *A Copy of a Letter Sent to Monsieur Beauvoir Lord Ambassador for the French King* and *The Order of Ceremonies Observed in the Annointing and Coronation of the Most Christian King of France*. It is unclear whether Flasket helped finance these texts or whether he simply provided a wholesale location for their respective publishers Peter Short and John Windet.
17 An exact count is difficult because not all Black Bear imprints include both Linley's and Flasket's names. This inconsistency might have had something to do with Flasket's company status as a draper.
18 This is the argument of Kiséry 2012.
19 In his will, Linley calls Flasket his "partner" and names the stationers Gabriel Cawood and Edward Blount executors; he left quarter portions of his personal property to his mother, to each of his two sisters, and to Cawood and Blount (Guildhall Library, Peculiar Court, fol. 92^v).
20 For an overview of the complicated series of company negotiations that preceded this transfer, see Johnson 1988.
21 Flasket's last publications were three sermons by Robert Wilkinson and Drayton's *The Legend of Great Cromwell*, all published in 1607.
22 See as well the following entries: "Gascoynes woorkes with steele glasse" (Arber, 3.131); "Sainct Peters complaint with Mary Magdalens blushe" (Arber, 3.210); "The way to the true Church: 'The defence of the way to the true Church' with two sermons. by John White D.D." (Arber, 4.157); and "Adam Bell with Clim of the Clough" (Arber, 4.182).
23 For *The Book of Dying*'s single entry, see Arber, 2.418; for *The Art of Limming*'s entry, see Arber, 2.419. The former text was first published separately in 1583 as *A Profitable Book Declaring Diverse Approved Remedies, to Take Out Spots and Stains, in Silks, Velvets, Linen and Woollen Clothes*; the latter in 1573 as *A Very Proper Treatise, wherein is Briefly Set Forth the Art of Limming*.
24 For other examples of such multiple-text, single-author entries and editions, see Edward Blount's entry "A panegyrike Congratulatory With a Defence of Ryme" (Arber, 3.235); and Anne Helm's entry "A booke called

The second parte, of the Day lie exercise for ladies and gentlewoemen, with a booke of Cookery, made by john morrell" (Arber, 4.51). For more on publishers retitling their copy, see chapter 1.

25 Thomas East entered *The Mariner's Guide* in December 1592.
26 See also the transfer entry "Master Bradshaws preparacion for receauing Christ body and blood. with master Hylderhams doctrine of the lordes supper" (Arber, 4.269). This volume with texts by William Bradshaw and Arthur Hildersham was originally published in 1609 by Samuel Macham as *A Direction for the Weaker Sort ... By W.B. Whereunto is Adjoined a very Profitable Treatise of the Same Argument, by way of Question and Answer, Written by Another*. For a mid-seventeenth-century example of a multi-title, dual-author volume put together by a publisher, see Birrell, 164.
27 See Bowers 1986. According to Philip Gaskell, a "reissue" "normally involves a new or altered title page, and includes cases such as these: the cancellation of a title page to bring old sheets up to date; a new impression with a new title page; and collections of separate pieces with a new general title" (1972, 316). I will be arguing that Flasket and Linley's two-text edition was essentially an example of the last case. Given the absence of textual evidence, Bowers would certainly disagree. For more on reissuing, see chapter 1.
28 Tucker Brooke, in his 1910 edition of *Hero and Leander*, argues that Blount and Wolfe had reached a private arrangement regarding the poem; W.W. Greg suggests instead that Blount had published his 1598 edition "in defiance of Wolf's five-year-old entrance" (1944, 172–3). Some have further imagined that Wolfe did bring out an edition of the poem before 1598, but it is now lost.
29 Greg (1944) argues that Linley acquired Chapman's continuation of the poem and was thus ultimately able to convince Blount to cede his rights to *Hero and Leander*. It might further have been the case that either Linley or Flasket commissioned Chapman's lines. After all, they had already acquired a dedicatory poem from Chapman for *Nennio* (1595), and Chapman, in his dedicatory epistle to Lady Walsingham in *Hero and Leander*, alludes to some "*strange instigation*" by a "Mony-Monger" (sig. E3^v) as leading to his continuation of the poem. For more on publishers commissioning works, see chapter 1. In 1601, Flasket seems again to have commissioned a work from Chapman, this time a satiric, now-lost play entitled *The Old Joiner of Aldgate*. The play was intended to embarrass Flasket's former fiancée Agnes Howe and led to much litigation. For detailed accounts of all of this, see Sisson 1936 and Erler 2008.

30 The 1600 edition does not name Thorpe in its imprint, only its printer Peter Short and its wholesaler Walter Burre. It does, however, contain a dedicatory epistle to the bookseller Edward Blount from the bookseller Thomas Thorpe (sigs. A2^{r-v}). For an account of the translation's textual history, see Greg 1944, 170–2.
31 What ends up being Flasket's two-title 1600 edition of *Hero and Leander* and Lucan is entered with the multi-volume edition of *Arisbas-Dido* when its rights were transferred to Flasket earlier that same year. Two lines down from the *Arisbas-Dido* entry, it reads, "Hero and Leander with the. j. booke of Lucan by Marlowe" (Arber, 3.165).
32 For readings in this vein, see Kocher 1946 and Potter 2009.
33 See Cope 1974 and Bowers 2002.
34 For the 1590s epyllion as "soft-core pornography," see Merrix 1986.
35 For the formal and thematic conventions of the genre, see Donno 1970; Keach 1977; Hulse 1981; and Ellis 2001. For the political resonances of the genre, see Dubrow 1995; Ellis 2003; and Brown 2004.
36 Lesser-known examples are Richard Barnfield's *The Affectionate Shepheard* (1594); Thomas Heywood's *Oenone and Paris* (1594); Michael Drayton's *Endymion and Phoebe* (1595); R.B.'s *Orpheus his Journey to Hell* (1595); Richard Edwards's *Cephalus and Procis* (1595); George Chapman's *Ovid's Banquet of Sense* (1595); Richard Linche's *Diella* (1596); Henry Petowe's *The Second Part of Hero and Leander* (1598); John Marston's *The Metamorphosis of Pigmalion's Image* (1598); and John Weever's *Fauna and Melliflora* (1600). Many of these poems were first circulated in manuscript. The vogue lost steam after the turn of the century and was essentially over by 1603.
37 In 1606, Flasket and Nicholas Ling jointly published a collected edition of Drayton's works entitled *Poems Lyric and Pastoral*. It included a substantially revised version of Drayton's epyllion *Endymion and Phoebe*. This would be the last Ovidian poem that Flasket would bring to press.
38 For Weever's life and career, see Honigmann 1987 and Kathman 2004b.
39 The poem is signed "I.F." Ringler and May have tentatively assigned it to Flasket (2004, 3.2017). Charles Cathcart (2002) has assigned it to John Fletcher, essentially on the basis of Weever possibly knowing Fletcher or Fletcher's older brother Nathaniel at Cambridge.
40 For other examples of this speaker trope, see chapter 3.
41 The poem is also signed "I.F." Both William Keach (1977, 259 n. 11) and Cathcart have assigned it to Fletcher.
42 The volume contains three "roundelays": Spenser's "Perigot and Cuddies *Roundelay*" (sigs. D2^{r-v}); Greene's "Menaphons *Roundelay*"

(sigs. E2^{r-v}); and Drayton's "*A Roundelay betweene two Sheepheards*" (sigs. L3^v–L4^r).

43 For Sidney's reputation in the 1590s, see Mentz 2000 and Alexander 2006.

44 A more oblique example occurs earlier when Damon comments upon the penchant of Arcadian shepherds for "discoursing on their owne or their fellowes fortunes, Shepheards I meane, men of their owne profession, whether natiue in Arcadia or no: as in memorizing the worth of Astrophell, praising the perfections of Phillis, lamenting the losse, commending the loyaltie of Amyntas, mourning for the death, yet misliking the disdeine and pride of Amaryllis, pitying the distresse of the forlorne Shepheard" (sigs. E3^{r-v}). For the many contemporary literary references in this passage, see Alexander 2006, 267–8.

45 *Arisbas*'s prose is for the most part set in black letter; proper names and place names, however, are set in roman type.

46 Together, *Arisbas* and *Dido* imagine different pasts, presents, and futures for England's nascent vernacular literary tradition. If, as Cheney contends, it is true that *Dido* "re-sounds Queen Eliza's Spenserian woods in order to echo the hideous literary oppression of Elizabethan royal absolutis" (1997, 114), then Dickinson's romance forwards a counter position, one that is more sanguine and more explicit about the situation of the literary under Elizabeth.

47 For a reading of *Arisbas*'s sexual themes in terms of "primary bisexuality," see Whitworth 1999.

48 This and other allusions to the myth of Hero and Leander suggest strongly that Marlowe's poem was circulating in manuscript in the early 1590s.

49 See also sig. C3^v and sig. E4^v.

50 Ellis has pointed out that the "aggressive female wooer and beautiful but reluctant youth" are "the most common couple of the [epyllion] genre" (2001, 42).

51 See Shakespeare 1593, sig. B1^v.

52 Cf. "Ganimede th'Idean boy, / Second glorie of the day: / Phrigiaes wonder fathers joy, / Loues content, Ioues wishful pray" (sig. E2^v).

53 Although first published by William Jaggard in *The Passionate Pilgrim* (in a section titled "SONNETS | To sundry notes of Musicke" [sig. C3^r]), "The Passionate Shepherd" seems to have circulated widely orally and in manuscript years before this date. See Woods 1970.

54 Cole's point, for example, is echoed by Cheney who argues of *Dido*, "As Marlowe manages it … Virgil's sonority never quite succeeds in drowning out Ovid's laughter" (1997, 208).

55 See Singer 1975; Cheney 1997; and Riggs 2005.

5 Reading *Hamlet* (1603): Nicholas Ling, Sententiae, and Republicanism

1 For a shortened version of this chapter, see Melnikoff 2013a.
2 Collinson traces this reconsideration in his "Afterword" (2007). In *Classical Humanism and Republicanism in English Political Thought 1570–1640*, Peltonen has outlined the emergence of classical humanism in the second half of the sixteenth century, particularly its dissemination of ideas about citizenship and the reform of the commonwealth, about mixed constitutions, about the importance of an active life (à la Cicero) as opposed to a life of contemplation, and about merit-based nobility. To this, Skinner, in "Classical Liberty and the Coming of the English Civil War," had added that it was in the Elizabethan age that the major authors of classical civil liberty became available in English: Cicero's *De Officiis*, Tactitus's *Histories* and *Agricola*, and Livy's *History of Rome*. For arguments questioning the emergence of a true republicanism in sixteenth-century England, see Pocock 1975 and, more recently, Worden 2002.
3 Norbrook 1999; Cheney 2009. For a different take on Marlowe's republicanism, see Hadfield 2005, 58–65. For other examinations of literary republicanism, see Shannon 2002 and Walker 2005. "As a sharp counterpoint to the terms understood to hold within the hierarchical relations of monarchical society," argues Shannon, "friendship tropes comprise the era's most poetically powerful imagining of parity within a social form that is consensual" (2002, 7).
4 See Hadfield 1998b; 2003b; 2005; and 2007.
5 Margreta de Grazia, in *Hamlet without Hamlet*, has suggested that *Hamlet*'s earliest readers may have been republican-leaning members of the Essex circle (2007, 69). *Hamlet* exists in three very different forms: in a 1603 quarto ("Q1"), a 1604 quarto ("Q2"), and as part of a collected 1623 volume ("F"). For overviews of their differences, see Jenkins 1982 and Irace 1998. For Q1's earliest readers, see Lull 1992.
6 Lesser 2004, 18, 35–7. See also Massai 2007.
7 For a description of the "overreaching" claims of Ling's Q1 title page, see Menzer 2008, 111–14. For correlations between authorial attributions on play texts and the reception of printed popular drama as literary material, see Wall 1993, 89 and Erne 2003, 43.
8 For specialization as a significant characteristic of early-modern publishing, see Lesser 2004, 37–49 and chapter 1.
9 For an overview of Ling's career and publishing penchants, see Johnson 1985a.

10 Ling first employs this emblem in 1596, on his third edition of Lodge's *Rosalind*. It graces the title pages of both *Hamlet*s that Ling publishes.
11 For *Cornelia*'s strong engagement with republicanism, see Perry 2006. Hadfield has also suggested that Lodge's and Drayton's work contains many characteristics of republicanism (2005, 58–73, 272n175). Of the specific works that Hadfield names, Ling was responsible for publishing editions of Lodge's *Rosalind* (1596, 1604) and Drayton's *The Baron's Wars in the Reign of Edward the Second* (1603). See also Hadfield 2003a, esp. 144.
12 Much of the following biographical information about Ling comes from Johnson 1985a.
13 Arber, 2.679. See also Stoker 1981, 108.
14 Ling was buried on 9 April 1607 at St Dunstan's Church in the West. The parish records state: "Nicholas Lynge Stationer out of Fenton Lane buried" (Guildhall Library, Parish Records). Smethwick is best known as one of the five publishers involved with Shakespeare's First Folio.
15 For more on Busby as a procurer of Ling's copies, see Johnson 1985b, 1–15.
16 It has been suggested that Ling's publications reveal a "commitment to the developing category of English 'literature'" (Lander 2006, 117). For a more developed account of this, see Lesser and Stallybrass 2008.
17 Ling entered "wittes Common wealthe" in the Stationers' Register on 14 October 1597 (Arber, 3.93). Later that same year, Ling published a 34-sheet first edition in octavo format.
18 A number of *Politeuphuia*'s sentences seem to have been derived from Baldwin's *Treatise*, possibly from its 1591 edition. Madaline Shindler has argued that at least forty-nine of the headings in *Politeuphuia* are taken wholly or in part from *The French Academy*. The collection also presents unattributed sentences from contemporary writers like Elyot, Sidney, Lyly, Daniel, Drayton, Lodge, Markham, and Greene. In compiling this work, Ling was shaping an early canon of English literary producers. For a slightly different take on Ling's role in this, see Lesser and Stallybrass 2008, 383–4.
19 For a detailed description of this project and Ling's work as part of what is now described as "the Bodenham circle," see Rollins 1935.
20 Ling 1597, sigs. A3^{r-v}. Unless otherwise indicated, all quotations from *Politeuphuia* are from this first edition.
21 True to his word, Ling in his second edition (1598a) replaces the heading "Of Precepts and Counsels" with "Of Precepts," and inserts "Of

Constancie" after "Of Content" and "Of Country or Commonweale" after "Of Religion." In his third edition (1598b), he cuts "Of Schoole," "Of Counsell," "Of Auncestors," "Of Warre," and "Of Similitudes"; he adds "Of Heresies & Heretiques" after "Of Desperation" as well. In his fourth edition (1604), he reinstates all of the headings that he cut in the 3rd edition.

22 For the elite reading modes encouraged by poetry miscellanies, see Wall 1993; by commonplace books, see Crane 1993.

23 Ling's choice of the term "commonwealth" could also be said to reveal his republican penchants. For discussions of the changing political resonances of the term, see Lowe 1990; Sherman 1997; and McLaren 1999.

24 Like many of his definitions, *The French Academy* is the source for much of this. Ling, though, adds the last sentence about "*God, their Gouernours, and Country*"; he also ignores the *Academy*'s reference to treason against monarchy in its beginning claim that treason is the "pernitious plague of kingdomes and common-wealths" (1594, Dd3^v). Ling begins his overt borrowing immediately after this sentence, lifting "Treason, hated of God and men, wherewith ..." (1594, Dd3^v).

25 From Elyot to Bacon, *consilium* had long been figured in ideal terms in England. As John Guy has pointed out, however, counsel took on new connotations late in Elizabeth's reign, when some political writers "aimed to assimilate the 'inspirational myth' of 'counsel' to practical programmes for limited, responsible, and (in an aristocratic sense) 'representative' government" (2000, 299).

26 On Elizabethan attitudes towards *vita activa* in the 1570s and 1580s, see Ferguson 1965 and Peltonen 1995, 10, 20–36. According to Collinson, counsel loomed large during the reigns of the Tudors when succession was again and again fraught with uncertainty (1997, 129–30).

27 See Baldwin 1591, sig. M6^r.

28 In his second edition of *Politeuphuia*, published the following year in 1598, Ling, possibly recognizing the redundancy of having counsel in two consecutive headings, changes "Of Precepts and Counsels" to simply "Of Precepts."

29 "Of Admiration" is negative as well: Ling writes, "*Admiration is a passion of the soule, which by a suddaine apprehension exalteth the powers, and makes them (as in a traunce) sleep in iudgement of the present obiect, thinking all things to be wonderfull that it beholdeth*" (1587, sig. H5^r). "Admiration" is not explicitly considered in *The French Academy*.

30 Of the twenty-nine sentences in this section, only two explicitly mention obedience with respect to a king.

31 Little is known about Middleton's life. An 1894 entry in the Oxford *DNB* lists his matriculating as a sizar at St John's College, Cambridge in 1587. Before writing *The Legend of Humphrey*, he also had written the poems *The History of Heaven* (1596) and *The Famous History of Chinon of England* (1597), and a two-part translation of *The Nature of a Woman* (1595, 1596). For an overview of Middleton's writing, see Simons 1998.

32 On 15 April 1600, Ling entered "The legend of Humfrey Duke of Gloucester By Christopher Middleton" in the Stationers' Register (Arber, 3.160). Printed by Edward Allde, the poem is in quarto format and is comprised of six edition sheets. Before publishing *The Legend of Humphrey*, Ling had entered and published five separate works by Drayton and two works by Allot. In 1601, Ling published Weever's *An Agnus Dei*, a poem that would reach a third edition in 1606. For more on close working relations between publishers and authors, see chapter 1.

33 For a general overview of the many retellings of Humphrey's life in the early modern period, see Pratt 1965.

34 McLaren 1999, 912. See Pocock 1993.

35 See also Devereux 1983, 51–2. Unless otherwise indicated, all references are to Ling's first edition.

36 See Knighton 2004.

37 The text's printed marginalia often indicates such "similes" and "examples." See sigs. C2^r, D4^v, I1^r, I1^v, N3^r, and N4^r.

38 See McConica 1965; Thompson 1971; Todd 1987; and Dodds 2009, 61–124.

39 See also Pearl 1961, 67.

40 Ling's right to copy this and other works along with his stock was transferred to John Smethwick on 19 November 1607 (Arber, 3.365). Smethwick brought his own revised edition out two years later in 1609.

41 See also Hadfield 2005, 19–25 and Hoak 2007. For more orthodox readings of Smith's treatise, see Wood 1997, 24–42 and Guy 2000, 303.

42 All references to *De Republica Anglorum* are from Smith 1601, the title's 5th edition, the last to be published before Ling obtained rights to copy the text. While Day does not sign this prefatory epistle, his allusion to the obtaining of the "corrupt" (sig. A2^r) manuscript copy suggests that it was he and not Seton who wrote it.

43 For reissuing as an important publishing practice, see chapter 1. Since the middle of the twentieth century, some critics have made more direct connections between Goslicius's treatise and Q2/F *Hamlet*. See Teslar 1960 and Baluk-Ulewiczowa 1993.

44 All references are to Goślicki 1607.

45 *The Counselor*'s title page does not include this assurance; instead, it is described as "REPLENISHED | *with the chiefe learning of the most excellent Philosophers and* | Lawgiuers" for the benefit of "those that be admitted to the administration of a | well-gouerned Common-weale."
46 For an excellent overview of the dominant theories explaining *Hamlet*'s textual transmission, see Thompson and Taylor 2006, 1.500–5.
47 Pollard, Greg, and Kirschbaum all argued that this was in effect a "blocking entry" in the Stationers' Register, made by Roberts on behalf of the Lord Chamberlain's Men in order to keep the play out of print. This, of course, is not the place to rehearse the many theories about *Hamlet*'s textual provenance with regard to Shakespeare. For recent challenges to *Hamlet* Q1 as the product of memorial reconstruction, however, see the work of Paul Werstine and Laurie Maguire among others.
48 For more on Ling's co-publisher John Trundle, see Johnson 1986. Johnson suggests that "Trundle's main interest, or talent, lay in the location of manuscripts which he then published and distributed on a share basis" (1986, 182).
49 See also Jenkins 1982, 15.
50 Kastan 2001.
51 For a persuasive account explaining why wholesaling and selling two different editions of *Hamlet* simultaneously might have been in the best interest of Ling, see Lesser 2015, 64–71.
52 Ling's right to publish *Hamlet* was transferred to John Smethwick in November 1607, a half-year after Ling's death (Arber, 3.365). Shakespeare's name had previously appeared on the 1598 first extant edition of *Love's Labour's Lost*. While neither the 1597 nor the 1599 edition of *Romeo and Juliet* names Shakespeare as author, it is not inconceivable – given that the play had been staged since the mid-1590s – that Ling nevertheless associated Shakespeare's name with the play.
53 Blayney has raised serious doubts about the commercial import of playbooks as compared to other kinds of printed books (1997, 416). Demand, however, seems to have been on the rise for printed playbooks at the end of the sixteenth century, especially for playbooks by Shakespeare, but it was, like demand for most all other printed books, capricious and unpredictable (Taylor 2008).
54 Our first edition of the play is Nicholas Vavasour's 1633 edition. Some have suggested that Ling and Millington *did* bring out an edition that is no longer extant. It is possible that two of their editions are now lost, but this seems very unlikely. For an account of Ling and Millington's collaboration in 1594, see Melnikoff 2013b.

55 Ling and Busby both entered *Cornelia* in the Stationers' Register on 26 January 1594 (Arber, 2.644). The play was printed by James Roberts, the same printer who would eventually print Ling's 1604 edition of *Hamlet*.

56 Ling's new title was *Pompey the Great, His Fair Cornelia's Tragedy*. See Johnson 1985a, 208 n. 13 and Erne 2001.

57 Though its imprint is dated 1600, the editors of the STC believe that Ling's edition of *Every Man Out* was actually printed after 1600. Jonson's play was first entered and published by William Holme in 1600. The play apparently was a good investment, reaching a second edition that same year. No record exists of Holme transferring his right to copy to Ling.

58 In the stage direction marking Polonius's first appearance in Q2, Polonius is described as "Counsaile" (sig. B3^v). In Q6 *Hamlet* (1676), Polonius is described as "Lord Chamberlain" in "The Persons Represented." Critics have read Polonius as a satire on Lord Burghley and on Gozlicki; they have even seen him as a portrait of Seneca. For an overview of these sources, see Jenkins 1982, 421–2.

59 Marked sententiae can also be found in the third scene of Q2 *Hamlet*. There, three bits of Laertes's aphoristic advice to Ophelia are marked. See sig. C3^v.

60 See Hunter 1951.

61 See Lesser and Stallybrass 2008, and Hunter 1951. Because Hunter focused his attention on trade printers rather than publishers, he failed to notice Ling's interest in marked sententiae.

62 These texts are Michael Drayton, *Matilda* (1594); Thomas Kyd, trans., *Cornelia* (1594); Edward Guilpin, *Skialetheia* (1598); Ben Jonson, *Every Man Out of His Humor* (1600); and Michael Drayton, *The Owl* (1604). Although Samuel Gardiner's *Portraiture of the Prodigal Son* does not explicitly advertise sententiae in its title or on its title page, the volume identifies well over one hundred "similitudes" in its margins. The likelihood is that Ling was responsible for these markers.

63 See Lesser and Stallybrass 2008, as well as Stallybrass and Chartier 2007.

64 It seems significant that Ling *only* marks Corambis's sententiae in Q1, even though a number of other characters mouth aphorisms during the course of the play. Lesser and Stallybrass do not account for this selectivity; Hunter generally suggests that such sporadic marking was likely due to compositor oversight (1951, 178). Here, I will be suggesting that Q1 *Hamlet* reflects either Ling's purposeful marking of sententiae for his buyers' consumption or his marking of sententiae for his own use. Neither explanation necessitates recourse to compositor error.

65 See Hunter 1957, 501–6 and Jenkins 1982, 440–3. Alan Fisher has described Polonius in both his words and actions as a "representative humanist" (1990, 46).
66 See Taylor 1968.
67 Kahn 1994. For the Elizabethan reception of the *Discourses*, see Pocock 1975 and Worden 1981.
68 For a different take on Corambis, see Irace 1998, 13–14 and Hadfield 2005, 185.
69 Farley-Hills 1997, 81.
70 Raleigh 1908, 190.
71 Hapwood 1999, 55. According to Hapgood, Polonius was played by "low comedians" in the Restoration and early 1700s.
72 For a thorough, positive reading of Polonius, see Draper 1935. For a less sanguine interpretation, see Falk 1967.
73 In Q2 *Hamlet*, the lines are significantly different: "Haue I my Lord? I assure my good Liege / I hold my dutie as I hold my soule, / Both to my God, and to my gracious King" (sig. E3^r).
74 See, for example, Jenkins 1982, 239 n. 45.
75 Skinner 1978, 2.230–8.
76 *Eirenarcha* reached eight editions by 1602.
77 Hull 2009, 62.
78 By comparison, see sigs. G3^v, E4^v, and G3^v respectively in Q2.
79 Though Horatio has long been primarily interpreted as a foil for Hamlet, he can also be seen as a foil for Corambis/Polonius. Paul M. Edmondson (2000) has described the Q1 Horatio as a man of great "loyalty" to and empathy for Hamlet.
80 For an overview of this discourse, see Skinner 1978 and Frye 1984, 38–70.
81 See Hadfield 2005, 184–204.
82 As we shall see, absent from Q2 are two references to "treason" in Q1's extra scene between Horatio and Gertred (sigs. H2^v–H3^r). Moreover, Hamlet's cry of "Treason, ho" (sig. I3^v) in Q1 is replaced with Q2's general cry of "Treason, treason" *after* Hamlet stabs Claudius, this then referring to Hamlet's action against the king.
83 Q1's connection between these queens also invokes complicated historical and political associations having to do with two other recently executed queens, namely, Elizabeth's mother, Anne Boleyn, and James's mother, Mary Queen of Scots.
84 This scene is only in Q1, in neither Q2 nor F.

85 *The Hystorie of Hamblet* (1608) in Bullough 1978, 7.100. This position is akin to John Hooper's mid-sixteenth-century theory surrounding the right of succession. See Frye 1984, 47–50.
86 James writes, "It is casten vp by diuers, that employ their pennes vpon Apologies for rebellions and treasons, that euery man is borne to carrie such a naturall zeale & dutie to his common-wealth, as to his Mother; that seeing it so rent, & deadly wounded, as whiles it will be by wicked and tyrannous Kings, good Citizens wilbe forced, for the natural zeale and dutie they owe to their owne natiue countrie, to put their hande to work, for freeing their common-welth from such a pest" (1598, sig. D5^v).
87 The poem was in print by 21 April 1604 (Brink 1990, 70). Richard F. Hardin attributes the poem's popularity to its offering "gossip of the great" to "news-hungry Englishmen" (1973, 78). Ling's majority stake in the poem seems indicated by *The Owl*'s right to copy being transferred from Ling to John Smethwick in 1607 (Arber, 3.365). Drayton's revised version of the poem is included in Smethwick's 1619 edition of Drayton's *Poems*.
88 For such readings of the poem, see Hardin 1973, 77–82.
89 See Hadfield 2003a, 125 for a similar argument about these lines.

Works Consulted

Manuscripts

British Library
  A volume of Sir Julius Caesar's Papers, MS. Add 14027

Drapers' Hall
  Freedom Lists, 1567–1656, F.A. 1
  Freedom Lists, 1567–1656, F.A. 2
  Minute Book of the Court of Assistants, 1543–53, Repertory 7, M.B. 1/C
  Minute Book of the Court of Assistants, 1543–53, Repertory E, M.B. 8
  Minute Book of the Court of Assistants, 1543–53, Repertory H, M.B. 11
  Wardens' Accounts, 1547–62, W.A. 4

Folger Shakespeare Library
  Diaries of Richard Stonley, 3 vols., MS. Add. 618

Guildhall Library
  Archdeaconry Court of London Act book, 1564–1807, MS. 9050/2
  Haberdashers' Company Register of Freedom Admission, 1526–1642, MS. 15857
  Parish Records of St Dunstan's-in-the-West, MS. 10342
  Peculiar Court of the Dean and Chapter of St Paul's, Register of Wills, 1535–1608, MS. 25626/3

Hertfordshire Archives and Local Studies
  Estate Papers of the Sebright Family of Beachwood Park, Flamstead, C1150–1937, Court Roll, DE/FL/17295

240 Works Consulted

The National Archives, Public Records Office ("PRO")
Prerogative Court of Canterbury, PROB 11

Printed Primary Sources

A., I., trans. 1566. *The great wonders that are chaunced in the realme of Naples*. London: Thomas Hacket, STC 18358.
Aesop 1577. *The fabulous tales of Esope the Phrygian*. Trans. Richard Smith London: Richard Smith. STC 186.5.
Alison, Richard. 1590. *A plaine confutation of a treatise of Brovvnisme*. London: William Wright. STC 355.
Allen, Robert. 1600. *A treatise of christian beneficence*. London: Thomas Man. STC 367.
Andrewes, Lancelot. 1592. *The wonderfull combate for Gods glorie and mans saluation betweene Christ and Satan*. London: Richard Smith. STC 629.
Anghiera, Pietro Martire d'. 1555. *The decades of the newe worlde or west India*. Trans. Richard Eden London: Edward Sutton et al. STC 647.
Anonymous. 1543? *A newe herball of Macer, translated out of Laten in to Englysshe*. London: Robert Wyer. STC 13175.8c.
– 1561. *A newe enterlude drawen oute of the holy scripture of godly queene Hester*. London: William Pickering and Thomas Hacket. STC 13251.
– 1569. *A New yeres gift*. London: Richard Jones. STC 97.5.
– 1571. *The enemie of idlenesse*. London: Augustine Lawton. STC 11477.
– 1573. *A plaine description of the aunciet petigree of Dame Slaunder*. London: John Harrison. STC 22630.
– 1579a. *A briefe discourse of the most haynous and traytorlike fact of Thomas Appeltree*. London: Henry Bynneman. STC 714.
– 1579b. *Cyuile and vncyuile life*. London: Richard Jones. STC 15589.5.
– 1579c. *A dolorous discourse, of a most terrible and bloudy battel, fought in Barbarie, the fowrth day of August, last past*. London: John Charlewood and Thomas Man. STC 1376.
– 1579d. *A poore knight his pallace of priuate pleasures*. London: Richard Jones. STC 4283.
– 1581a. *A briefe and pleasaunt treatise, intituled, Naturall and artificiall conclusions*. London: Abraham Kitson. STC 13480.5.
– 1581b. *The whole booke of psalmes*. London: John Day. STC 2458.
– 1584a. *A briefe and pleasaunt treatise, entituled: Naturall and artificiall conclusions*. London: Abraham Kitson. 13480.7.
– 1584b. *Cato construed*. London: Andrew Maunsell. STC 4858.

- 1584c. *A most rare and wonderfull tragedy of ... a miserable [u]surer of Fraunce*. London: Thomas Hacket. STC 24167.5.
- 1584d. *The vvelspring of wittie conceites*. London: Richard Jones. STC 5615.
- 1585. *A true and plaine declaration of the horrible treasons, practised by W. Parry*. London: Christopher Barker. STC 19342.
- 1586. *The English courtier, and the cuntrey-gentleman*. London: Richard Jones. STC 15590.
- 1592a. *Axiochus. A most excellent dialogue*. London: Cuthbert Burby. STC 19974.6.
- 1592?b. *Newes from Scotland*. London: William Wright. STC 10841a.
- 1592?c. *Newes from Scotland*. London: William Wright. STC 10842.3.
- 1594a. *The copie of a letter sent to Monsieur de Beauuoir*. London: John Flasket. STC 13130a.
- 1594b. *The present state of Spaine*. London: Richard Sergier. STC 22996.
- 1594c. *The vvarres of Cyrus King of Persia, against Antiochus King of Assyria, with the tragicall ende of Panthaea*. London: William Blackwall. STC 6160.
- 1594d. *Zepheria*. London: Nicholas Ling and John Busby. STC 26124.
- 1595a. *The moste pleasaunt historye of Blanchardine*. London: William Blackwall. STC 3125.
- 1595b. *A students lamentation that hath sometime been in London an apprentice, for the rebellious tumults lately in the citie hapning*. London: William Blackwall. STC 23401.5.
- 1598a. *A treatise paraenetical*. Trans. "I.D. Dralymont." London: William Ponsonby. STC 19838.
- 1598b. *Tyros roring megge*. London: Valentine Simmes. STC 24477.
- 1599. *The passionate pilgrime*. London: William Jaggard. STC 22342.
- 1607. *Mans arraignement, and Gods mercy in deliuering him*. London: John Flasket. STC 17232.5.
- 1612. *The passionate pilgrime*. London: William Jaggard. STC 22343.
- 1633. *The hystorie of the seauen wise maisters of Rome*. London: Thomas Purfoot. STC 21300.

Appian. 1578. *An avncient historie and exquisite chronicle of the Romanes warres, both ciuile and foren*. Trans. W.B. London: Henry Bynneman. STC 713.

Ariosto, Lodovico. 1591. *Orlando furioso in English heroical verse*. Trans. John Harington. London: Richard Field. STC 746.

B., H. 1593. *Moriemini. A verie profitable sermon preached before her majestie*. London: John Wolfe. STC 1034.

Baldwin, William. 1591. *A treatise of morall philosophie containing the sayings of the wise*. London: Thomas East. STC 1263.
Barckley, Sir Richard. 1603. *A discourse of the felicitie of man. Or his summum bonum*. London: William Ponsonby. STC 1382.
Barnes, Barnabe. 1593. *Parthenophil and Parthenophe. Sonnettes, madrigals, elegies and odes*. London: John Wolfe. STC 1469.
Bastard, Thomas. 1598. *Chrestoleros. Seuen bookes of epigrames written by T B*. London: John Broome. STC 1559.
Beaumont, John. 1602. *The metamorphosis of tabacco*. London: John Flasket. STC 1695.
Bentley, James. 1600. *The harmonie of Holie Scriptures vvith the seuerall sentences of sundry learned and vvorthy vvriters*. London: Nicholas Ling. STC 1891.5.
Best, George. 1578. *A true discourse of the late voyages of discouerie, for the finding of a passage to Cathaya, by the Northvveast, vnder the conduct of Martin Frobisher Generall*. London: Henry Bynneman. STC 1972.
Bèze, Théodore de. 1563. *A briefe and piththie summe of the christian faith*. Trans. Robert Fils. London: Roland Hall. STC 2006.7.
– 1576. *The Bible and holy scriptures conteined in the Olde and Nevve Testament*. London: Christopher Barker. STC 2117.
Blake, N.F., ed. 1973. *Caxton's Own Prose*. London: Deutsch.
Boaistuau, Pierre. 1566? *Theatrum mundi, the theatre or rule of the world*. Trans. John Alday. London: Thomas Hacket. STC 3168.
Boccaccio, Giovanni. 1562. *The most wonderful and pleasaunt history of Titus and Gisippus*. London: Thomas Hacket. STC 3184.6.
– 1567. *A pleasaunt disport of diuers noble personages*. Trans. H.G. London: Richard Smith. STC 3180.
– 1571. *Thirtene most plesant and delectable questions*. London: Richard Smith. STC 3181.
– 1587. *Amorous Fiammetta*. London: Thomas Newman and Thomas Gubbin. STC 3179.
Bodenham, John, ed. 1600. *Englands Helicon*. London: John Flasket. STC 3191.
Bourne, William. 1574? *A regiment for the sea*. London: Thomas Hacket. STC 3422.
Breton, Nicholas. 1591. *Brittons bowre of delights*. London: Richard Jones. STC 3633.
– 1592. *The pilgrimage to paradise*. London: Toby Cooke. STC 3683.
Bristow, Richard. 1580. *A reply to Fulke*. East Ham: John Lion. STC 3802.

Brome, Richard. 1652. *A joviall crew: or, The merry beggars*. London: Edward Dod and Nathaniel Ekins. Wing B4873.

Broughton, Hugh. 1587–91. *A concent of Scripture*. Gabriel Simson and William White. STC 3850.

– 1590? *A concent of Scripture*. London: Gabriel Simson and William White. STC 3851.

Broughton, Hugh, trans. 1596. *Daniel his Chaldie visions and his Ebrevv*. London: William Young. STC 2785.

Browne, John. 1589. *The marchants avizo*. London: William Norton. STC 3908.4.

– 1590. *The marchants avizo*. London: William Norton. STC 3908.5.

Bullinger, Heinrich. 1561. *A hundred sermons vpo[n] the Apocalips of Iesu Christe*. Trans. John Daus. London: John Day. STC 4061.

– 1577. *Fiftie godlie and learned sermons*. Trans. H.I. London: Ralph Newbery. STC 4056.

Burton, William. 1602. *The sermons and treatises of maister W. Burton*. London: Thomas Man. STC 4165a.

Butler, [Richard]. 1593. *A learned and notable sermon vpon the text Vos autem non sic. But you not so*. London: John Wolfe. STC 4202.

Calfhill, James. 1565. *An aunswere to the Treatise of the crosse*. London: Lucas Harrison. STC 4368.

Calvin, Jean. 1561. *The institution of Christian religion*. London: Reynolde Wolfe and Richard Harrison. STC 4415.

– 1567. *A little booke of Iohn Caluines concernynge offences*. London: William Seres. Trans. Arthur Golding. STC 4434.

– 1583. *The sermons of M. Iohn Caluin vpon the fifth booke of Moses called Deuteronomie*. Trans. Arthur Golding. London: Thomas Woodcock. STC 4443.5.

Campion, Thomas. 1602. *Obseruations in the art of English poesie*. London: Andrew Wise. STC 4543.

Cardano, Girolamo. 1573. *Cardanus comforte*. Trans. Thomas Bedingfeld. London: Thomas Marshe. STC 4607.

Cartier, Jacques. 1580. *A shorte and briefe narration of the two nauigations and discoueries to the northwest partes called Newe Fraunce*. Trans. John Florio. London: Henry Bynneman. STC 4699.

Castiglione, Baldassarre. 1561. *The courtyer of Count Baldessar Castilio*. Trans. Thomas Hoby. London: William Seres. STC 4778.

Caxton, William, trans. 1481. ... *the myrrour of the worlde*. London: William Caxton. STC 24762.

Chapman, George. 1595. *Ouids banquet of sence*. London: Richard Smith. STC 4985.
Churchyard, Thomas. 1575. *The firste parte of Churchyardes chippes*. London: Thomas Marshe. STC 5232.
– 1580. *A warning for the wise*. London: Nicholas Ling and Henry Bynneman. STC 5259.
Cicero, Marcus Tullius. 1577. *Fovvre seuerall treatises of M. Tullius Cicero*. Trans. Thomas Newton. London: Thomas Marshe. STC 5274.
Clayton, Giles. 1591. *The approoued order of martiall discipline*. London: Abraham Kitson. STC 5376.
Constable, Henry. 1592. *Diana*. London: Richard Smith. STC 5637.
– 1594? *Diana*. London: Richard Smith. STC 5638.
Cornwallis, Sir William. 1600–1. *Essayes*. London: Edmund Mattes. STC 5775.
Cortés, Martín. 1561. *The arte of nauigation*. Trans. Richard Eden. London: Richard Jugge. STC 5798.
Crashaw, William. 1610. *A sermon preached in London before the right honorable the Lord Lavvarre, Lord Gouernour and Captaine Generall of Virginea, and others of his Maiesties Counsell for that kingdome, and the rest of the aduenturers in that plantation*. London: William Welby. STC 6029.
Dallington, Robert. 1605? *A method for trauell Shewed by taking the view of France*. London: Thomas Creede. STC 6203.
Daniel, Samuel. 1604. *The vision of the 12. goddesses*. London: Simon Waterson. STC 6265.
Darell, Walter. 1578. *A short discourse of the life of seruingmen*. London: Ralph Newbery. STC 6274.
Davies, John. 1625. *A scourge for paper-persecutors*. London: Henry Holland and George Gibbs. STC 6340.
Davison, Francis. 1602. *A poetical rapsody*. London: John Bailey. STC 6373.
Day, Angel. 1586. *The English secretorie*. London: Richard Jones. STC 6401.
De Granada, Luis. 1596. *Of prayer and meditation*. Trans. Richard Hopkins. London: Richard Smith. STC 16909.5.
– 1633. *A paradise of prayers*. London: William Sheares. STC 16917.
Dickenson, John. 1594. *Arisbas, Euphues amidst his slumbers*. London: Thomas Woodcock. STC 6817.
– 1598. *Greene in conceipt*. London: William Jones. STC 6819.
Dod, John. 1604. *A plaine and familiar exposition of the Ten commandements*. London: Thomas Man. STC 6968.
Drayton, Michael. 1596. *The tragicall legend of Robert, Duke of Normandy*. London: Nicholas Ling. STC 7232.

- 1604. *The ovvle.* London: Nicholas Ling. STC 7212.
- 1619. *Poems: by Michael Drayton, Esquire.* London: John Smethwick. STC 7222.5.

Duncon, Eleazar. 1606. *The copy of a letter written by E.D. Doctour of Physicke to a gentleman, by whom it was published.* London: Melchisidec Bradwood. STC 6164.

Earle, John 1628. *Micro-cosmographie.* London: Edward Blount. STC 7440.2.

Edwards, Richard. 1571. *The excellent comedie of two the moste faithfullest freendes, Damon and Pithias.* London: Richard Jones. STC 7514.
- 1576. *The paradyse of daynty deuises.* London: Henry Disle. STC 7516.

Enciso, Martin Fernández. 1578. *A briefe description of the portes, creekes, bayes, and hauens, of the Weast India.* Trans. John Frampton. London: Henry Bynneman. STC 10823.

Erasmus, Desiderius. 1606a. *Seven dialogues both pithie and profitable.* Trans. William Burton. London, Nicholas Ling. STC 10457.
- 1606b. *Vtile-dulce: or, truethes libertie.* Trans. William Burton. London: Nicholas Ling. STC 10458.

Escalante, Bernardino de. 1579. *A discourse of the nauigation which the Portugales doe make to the realmes and prouinces of the east partes of the worlde.* Trans. John Frampton. London: Thomas Dawson. STC 10529.

F., T. 1579. *Newes from the north.* London: John Allde. STC 24062.

Fabyan, Robert. 1559. *The chronicle of Fabian.* London: John Kingston. STC 10663.

Farnese, Alexander. 1590. *The thinges which happened vpon the prince of Parmas retire.* London: John Wolfe. STC 336.

Filippe, Bartholomeu. 1589. *The counseller a treatise of counsels and counsellers of princes.* Trans. John Thorie. London: John Wolfe and John Charlewood. STC 10753.

Fils, Robert, trans. 1562. *The lavves and statutes of Geneua.* London: Roland Hall and Thomas Hacket. STC 11725.

Fitzherbert, John. 1598. *Fitzharberts booke of husbandrie.* London: Edward White. STC 11004.

Frampton, John. 1580. *A discouerie of the countries of Tartaria, Scithia, & Cataya.* London: Thomas Dawson. STC 11255.

Garzoni, Tomaso. 1600. *The hospitall of incurable fooles.* Trans. Edward Blount. London: Edward Blount. STC 11634.

Gascoigne, George. 1573. *A hundreth sundrie flowres bounde vp in one small poesie.* London: Richard Smith. STC 11635.
- 1575a. *The glasse of gouernement.* London: Christopher Barker. STC 11643a.

246   Works Consulted

- 1575b. *The posies of George Gascoigne Esquire*. London: Richard Smith. STC 11637.
- Gascoigne, George, trans. 1575c. *The noble arte of venerie or hunting*. London: Christopher Barker. STC 24328.
- Gentillet, Innocent. 1602. *A discourse vpon the meanes of vvel governing and maintaining in good peace, a kingdome, or other principalitie*. Trans. Simon Patericke. London: Adam Islip. STC 11743.
- Gesner, Konrad. 1559. *The treasure of Euonymus*. Trans. Peter Morwying. London: John Day. STC 11800.
- Goślicki, Wawrzyniec. 1598. *The counsellor*. London: Richard Bradock. STC 12372.
- 1607. *A common-vvealth of good counsaile*. London: Nicholas Ling. STC 12373.
- Grafton, Richard. 1565. *A manuell of the Chronicles of Englande*. London: John Kingston. STC 12167.
- Greene, Robert. 1588. *Perimedes the blacke-smith*. London: Edward White. STC 12295.
- 1589. *The Spanish masquerado*. London: Thomas Cadman. STC 12309.
- 1591. *A notable discouery of coosenage*. London: Thomas Nelson. STC 12279.
- 1592a. *Greenes vision*. London: Thomas Newman. STC 12261.
- 1592b. *A quip for an vpstart courtier*. London: John Wolfe. STC 12300.
- Greepe, Thomas. 1587. *The true and perfecte newes of the woorthy and valiaunt exploytes, performed and doone by that valiant knight Syr Frauncis Drake*. London: Thomas Hacket. STC 12343.
- Grove, Mathew. 1587. *The most famous and tragicall historie of Pelops and Hippodamia*. London: Richard Smith. STC 12403.
- H., T. 1560. *The fable of Ouid treting of Narcissus*. London: Thomas Hacket. STC 18970.
- Hake, Edward. 1578. *A ioyfull continuance of the commemoration of the most prosperous and peaceable reigne of our gratious and deare Soueraigne Lady Elizabeth*. London: Richard Jones. STC 12605.5.
- Hall, Joseph. 1597. *Virgidemiarum*. London: Robert Dexter. STC 12716.
- Harward, Simon. 1582. *Two godlie and learned sermons*. London: John Charlewood and Richard Jones. STC 12924.
- Harvey, Gabriel. 1593a. *A nevv letter of notable contents*. London: John Wolfe. STC 12902.
- 1593b. *Pierces supererogation or A new prayse of the old asse*. London: John Wolfe. STC 12903.

Hasleton, Richard. 1595. *Strange and wonderfull things. Happened to Richard Hasleton*. London: William Barley. STC 12925.
Hemmingsen, Niels. 1580. *The epistle of the blessed apostle Saint Paule*. Trans. Abraham Fleming. London: Thomas East. STC 13057.8.
Heywood, John. 1577. *Iohn Heywoodes vvoorkes*. London: Thomas Marshe. STC 13287.
Heywood, Thomas. 1612. *An apology for actors*. London: Nicholas Okes. STC 13309.
Higgins, John. 1574. *The first parte of the Mirour for magistrates*. London: Thomas Marshe. STC 13443.
– 1587. *The mirour for migistrates*. London: Henry Marshe. STC 13445.
Hill, Thomas. 1571. *The contemplation of mankinde contayning a singuler discourse after the art of phisiognomie*. London: William Seres. STC 13482.
– 1599. *The schoole of skil*. London: William Jaggard. STC 13502.
Holme, Wilfrid. 1572. *The fall and euill successe of rebellion from time to time*. London: Henry Bynneman. STC 13602.
Hooper, John. 1562a. *An apologye made by the reuerende father and constante martyr of Christe Iohn Hooper*. London: John Tisdale and Thomas Hacket. STC 13742.
– 1562b. *An exposition vpon the .23. psalme of Dauid*. London: John Tisdale and Thomas Hacket. STC 13752.
Huloet, Richard. 1572. *Huloets dictionarie*. Trans. John Higgins. London: Thomas Marshe. STC 13941.
Hunnis, William. 1578. *A hyue full of hunnye*. London: Thomas Marshe. STC 13974.
James I. 1598. *The true lawe of free monarchies*. Edinburgh: Robert Waldengrave. STC 14409.
Johnson, Francis. 1595. *A treatise of the ministery of the Church of England*. Low Countries? STC 14663.5.
Lanfranco, of Milan. 1565. *A most excellent and learned vvoorke of chirurgerie*. London: Thomas Marshe. STC 15192.
La Noue, François de. 1588. *The politicke and militarie discourses of the Lord de La Nouue*. Trans. Edward Aggas. London: Thomas Cadman and Edward Aggas. STC 15215.
La Primaudaye, Pierre de. 1594. *The French academie*. Trans. Thomas Bowes. London: George Bishop and Ralph Newbery. STC 15235.
Latimer, Hugh. 1575. *Frutefull sermons preached by the tight* [sic] *reuerend father, and constant martyr of Iesus Christ M. Hugh Latymer*. London: John Day. STC 15278.

Le Challeux, Nicolas. 1566. *Discours de l'histoire de la Floride*. Dieppe: Jessé Le Sellier.

– 1566. *A true and perfect description, of the last voyage or nauigation, attempted by Capitaine Iohn Rybaut, deputie and generall for the French men, into Terra Florida*. Trans. Thomas Hacket. London: Thomas Hacket. STC 15347.

Lefèvre, Raoul. 1597. *The auncient historie, of the destruction of Troy*. Trans. William Caxton. London: Thomas Creede and Valentine Simmes. STC 15379.

Leigh, Valentine. 1578. *The moste profitable and commendable science, of surueiyng of landes, tenementes, and hereditamentes*. London: Andrew Maunsell. STC 15417.

Lemnius, Levinus 1576. *The touchstone of complexions*. Trans. Thomas Newton. London: Thomas Marshe. STC 15456.

Leslie, John. 1571. *A treatise concerning the defence of the honour of the right high, mightie and noble Princesse, Marie Queene of Scotland, and Douager of France*. Liège: George Morberium et al. STC 15506.

Lever, Ralph. 1563. *The most noble, auncient, and learned playe, called the Phiosophers [sic] game*. London: James Rowbotham. STC 15542.

Lewkenor, Lewis. 1595a. *A discourse of the vsage of the English fugitiues*. London: John Drawater. STC 15563.

– 1595b. *The estate of English fugitiues vnder the king of Spaine and his ministers*. London: John Drawater. STC 15564.

Ling, Nicholas. 1597. *Politeuphuia wits common wealth*. London: Nicholas Ling. STC 15685.

– 1598a. *Politeuphuia vvits common wealth*. London: Nicholas Ling. STC 15686.

– 1598b. *Politeuphuia wits common wealth*. London: Nicholas Ling. STC 15686.3.

Ling, Nicholas, trans. 1563. *A sum or a brief collection of holy signes, sacrifices and sacraments*. London: Roland Hall. STC 23433.

Lite, Henry. 1588. *The light of Britayne*. London: John Charlewood. STC 17122.5.

Livy. 1600. *The Romane historie vvritten by T. Livius of Padua*. Trans. Philemon Holland London: Adam Islip. STC 166613.

Lodge, Thomas. 1591. *Catharos. Diogenes in his singularitie*. London: John Busby. STC 16654.

– 1592. *Euphues shadow*. London: John Busby. STC 16656.

Lok, Henry. 1597. *Ecclesiastes, othervvise called The preacher*. London: Richard Field. STC 16696.

López de Gómara, Francisco. 1578. *The pleasant historie of the conquest of the VVeast India*. Trans. Thomas Nicholas. London: Henry Bynneman. STC 16807.

Luther, Martin. 1575. *A commentarie of M. Doctor Martin Luther vpon the Epistle of S. Paul to the Galathians*. London: Thomas Vautrollier. STC 16965.

Lydgate, John. 1590. *The serpent of deuision*. London: John Perrin. STC 17029.

Lyly, John. 1578. *Euphues. The anatomy of vvyt*. London: Gabriel Cawood. STC 17051.

– 1601. *Loues metamorphosis*. London: William Wood. STC 17082.

M., C. 1596. *The first part of the nature of a vvoman*. London: Clement Knight. STC 17126.5.

Maisonneufve, Estienne de. 1578. *The gallant, delectable and pleasaunt hystorie of Gerileon of Englande*. Trans. Miles Jennings. London: Miles Jennings. STC 17203.

Malby, Sir Nicholas. 1576. *A plaine and easie way to remedie a horse that is foundered in his feete*. London: Thomas Purfoot. STC 17209.

Map, Walter. 1598. *Phillis and Flora*. London: Richard Jones. STC 19880.

Margarite, Queen. 1597. *The queen of Nauarres tales*. London: John Oxenbridge. STC 17323.

Markham, Francis. 1622. *Fiue decades of epistles of vvarre*. London: Augustine Mathewes. STC 17332.

– 1625. *The booke of honour. Or, Fiue decads of epistles of honour*. London: Augustine Mathewes and John Norton. STC 17331.

Markham, Gervase. 1593. *A discource of horsmanshippe*. London: Richard Smith. STC 17346.

– 1595. *How to chuse, ride, traine, and diet, both hunting-horses and running horses*. London: Richard Smith. 17347.

– 1596. *How to chuse, ride, traine, and diet, both hunting-horses and running horses*. London Richard Smith. STC 17347.5.

– 1597. *How to chuse, ride, traine, and diet, both hunting-horses and running horses*. London: Richard Smith. 17348.

– 1599. *How to chuse, ride, traine, and diet, both hunting-horses and running horses*. London: James Roberts. STC 17349.

Marlowe, Christopher. 1590. *Tamburlaine the Great*. London: Richard Jones. STC 17425. https://doi.org/10.1093/oseo/instance.00000029.

– 1594. *The troublesome raigne and lamentable death of Edward the second, King of England*. London: William Jones. STC 17437.

– 1598. *Hero and Leander: begun by Christopher Marloe; and finished by George Chapman*. London: Paul Linley. STC 17414.

- 1600. *Hero and Leander: begunne by Christopher Marloe: whereunto is added the first booke of Lucan translated line for line by the same author.* London: John Flasket. STC 17415.
Marlowe, Christopher, and Thomas Nashe. 1594. *The tragedie of Dido Queene of Carthage.* London: Thomas Woodcock. STC 17441. https://doi.org/10.1093/oseo/instance.00006675.
Marston, John. 1633. *The vvorkes of Mr. Iohn Marston.* London: William Sheares. STC 17471.
Medina, Pedro de. 1581. *The arte of nauigation.* Trans. John Frampton. London: Thomas Dawson. STC 17771.
Mela, Pomponius. 1585. *The vvorke of Pomponius Mela. the cosmographer.* Trans. Arthur Golding. London: Thomas Hacket. STC 17785.
Meres, Francis. 1598. *Palladis tamia. VVits treasury being the second part of Wits common wealth.* London: Cuthbert Burby. STC 17834.
Middleton, Christopher. 1600. *The legend of Humphrey Duke of Glocester.* London: Nicholas Ling. STC 17868.
Middleton, Thomas. 1608. *A mad vvorld, my masters.* London: John Spencer. STC 17889.
Monardes, Nicolás. 1577a. *Ioyfull nevves out of the newe founde worlde.* Trans. John Frampton. London: William Norton. STC 18006.5.
- 1577b. *The three bookes written in the Spanishe tonge.* Trans. John Frampton. London: William Norton. STC 18005.
Moore, Philip. 1571. *1571. An almanack and prognostication for .xxxvii. yeres, very profitable for all men.* London: Henry Saunderson. STC 485.
Mornay, Philippe de. 1576. *The defence of death.* Trans. Edward Aggas. London: Edward Aggas. STC 18136.
Morwen, Peter, trans. 1558. *A compendious and most marueilous history of the latter tymes of the Iewes commune weale.* London: Richard Jugge. STC 14795.
Münster, Sebastian. 1553. *A treatyse of the newe India.* Trans. Richard Eden. London: Edward Sutton. STC 18244.
- 1572. *A briefe collection and compendious extract of the strau[n]ge and memorable things, gathered oute of the cosmographye of Sebastian Munster.* Trans. Richard Eden. London: Thomas Marshe. STC 18242.
Nashe, Thomas. 1589. *The anatomie of absurditie.* London: Thomas Hacket. STC 18364.
- 1592. *Pierce Penilesse his supplication to the diuell.* London: John Busby. STC 18372.
- 1594. *The terrors of the night or, A discourse of apparitions.* London: William Jones. STC 18379.

- 1596. *Haue vvith you to Saffron-vvalden.* London: John Danter. STC 18369.
- 1599. *Nashes lenten stuffe.* London: Nicholas Ling and Cuthbert Burby. STC 18370.

Nenna, Giovanni Battista. 1595. *Nennio, or A treatise of nobility.* Trans. William Jones. London: Paul Linley and John Flasket. STC 18428.

Newton, Thomas. 1580. *Approoued medicines and cordiall receiptes.* London: Thomas Marshe. STC 18510.

Nicolay, Nicolas de. 1585. *The nauigations, peregrinations and voyages, made into Turkie by Nicholas Nicholay Daulphinois.* Trans. T. Washington. London: Thomas Dawson. STC 18574.

Norden, John. 1584. *A pensiue mans practise.* London: Hugh Singleton. STC 18616.
- 1585. *A sinfull mans solace.* London: Richard Jones. STC 18634.
- 1600. *Vicissitudo rerum. An elegiacall poeme, of the interchangeable courses and varietie of things in this world.* London: Simon Stafford. 18642.
- 1601. *A store-house of varieties, briefly discoursing the change and alteration of things in this world.* London: Simon Stafford. STC 18643.

Nowell, Alexander. 1571. *A catechisme, or first instruction and learning of Christian religion.* London: John Day. STC 18709.
- Ortúñez, Diego. 1586? *The third part of the first booke, of the Mirrour of knighthood.* Trans. R. P. London: Thomas East. STC 18864.

Osório, Jerónimo. 1576. *The fiue bookes of the famous, learned, and eloquent man, Hieronimus Osorius.* Trans. William Blandie. London: Thomas Marshe. STC 18886.

Ovid. 1572. *The thre first bookes of Ouids De tristibus, translated into Englishe.* Trans. Thomas Churchyard. London: Thomas Marshe. STC 18977aa.

Parrot, Henry. 1615. *The mastiue, or Young-whelpe of the olde-dogge. Epigrams and satyrs.* London: Richard Meighen and Thomas Jones. STC 19333.

Partridge, John. 1566. *The worthie hystorie of the most noble and valiaunt knight Plasidas.* London: Thomas Hacket. STC 19438.

Patten, William. 1575. *The calender of Scripture.* London: Richard Jugge. STC 19476.

Payne, John. 1597. *Royall exchange.* Harlem. STC 19489.

Paynell, Thomas, trans. 1572? *The moste excellent and pleasaunt booke, entituled: The treasurie of Amadis of Fraunce.* London: Thomas Hacket. STC 545.

Perkins, William. 1593. *An exposition of the Lords prayer.* London: Robert Bourne and John Porter. STC 19700.5.
- 1597. *The foundation of Christian religion.* London: John Porter et al. STC 19712.

Pettie, George. 1576. *A petite pallace of Pettie his pleasure*. London: Richard Watkins. STC 19819.
Plat, Hugh. 1600? *Delightes for ladies*. London: Peter Short. STC 19977.7.
Pliny. 1566. *A summarie of the antiquities, and wonders of the worlde, abstracted out of the sixtene first bookes of the excellente historiographer Plinie*. Trans. John Alday. London: Thomas Hacket. STC 20031.
– 1585. *The secrets and wonders of the world*. Trans. John Alday. London: Thomas Hacket. STC 20032.
Poleman, John, trans. 1578. *All the famous battels that haue bene fought in our age throughout the worlde*. London: Henry Bynneman. STC 20089.
Polo, Marco. 1579. *The most noble and famous trauels of Marcus Paulus*. Trans. John Frampton. London: Ralph Newbery. STC 20092.
Polybius. 1568. *The hystories of the most famous and worthy cronographer Polybius*. Trans. C.W. London: Thomas Hacket. STC 20097.
Purvey, John. 1550. *The true copye of a prolog wrytten about two C. yeres paste by Iohn Wycklife*. London: Robert Crowley. STC 25588.
Puttenham, George. 1589. *The arte of english poesie*. London: Richard Field. STC 20519.
Rhegius, Urbanus. 1579. *A necessary instruction of christian faith and hope, for Christians to holde fast, and to be bolde vp on the promise of God, & not to doubt of their saluation in Christ*. Trans. John Foxe. London: Hugh Singleton. STC 20848.
Ribaut, Jean. 1563. *The whole and true discouerye of Terra Florida*. Trans. Thomas Hacket. London: Thomas Hacket. STC 20970.
Rich, Barnabe. 1581. *Riche his farewell to militarie profession*. London: Robert Waley. STC 20996.
Robinson, Clement. 1584. *A handefull of pleasant delites*. London: Richard Jones. STC 21105.
Robinson, Richard. 1589. *A golden mirrour*. London: John Proctor. STC 21121.5.
Roscio, Laurentio. 1590. *A double fortresse faith-sacramental*. London: Thomas Purfoot. STC 21319.7.
Roussat, Richard. 1562? *The most excellent, profitable, and pleasant booke of the famous doctour and expert astrologien Arcandam or Aleandrin*. Trans. William Warde. London: James Rowbotham. STC 724.
– 1564. *The most excellent, profitable, and pleasant booke of the famous doctour and expert astrologian Arcandam or Aleandrin*. Trans. William Warde. London: James Rowbotham. STC 724.5.
S., L. 1593. *Resurgendum. A notable sermon concerning the resurrection, preached not long since at the court*. London: John Wolfe. STC 21508.

Schottennius, Hermannus. 1566. *The gouernement of all estates*. Trans. N. Boorman. London: Thomas Hacket. STC 13207.

Segar, Francis. 1582. *The schoole of vertue, and booke of good nurture*. London: Henry Denham. STC 22136.

Shakespeare, William. 1593. *Venus and Adonis*. London: Richard Field. STC 22354.

– 1594. *Lucrece*. London: John Harrison. STC 22345.

– 1599. *The most excellent and lamentable tragedie, of Romeo and Iuliet*. London: Cuthbert Burby. STC 22323.

– 1603. *The tragicall historie of Hamlet Prince of Denmarke by William Shakespeare*. Nicholas Ling and John Trundle. STC 22275.

– 1604. *The tragicall historie of Hamlet, Prince of Denmarke*. London: Nicholas Ling. STC 22276.

– 1623. *Mr. VVilliam Shakespeares comedies, histories, & tragedies. Published according to the true originall copies*. London: William Jaggard, Edward Blount, John Smethwick, and William Aspley. STC 22273.

– 1676. *The tragedy of Hamlet Prince of Denmark*. London: J. Martyn and H. Herringman. Wing S2951.

Sidney, Sir Philip. 1590. *The Countesse of Pembrokes Arcadia*. London: William Ponsonby. STC 22539.

– 1591a. *Syr P.S. His Astrophel and Stella*. London: Thomas Newman. STC 22536.

– 1591b. *Sir P.S. his Astrophel and Stella*. London: Thomas Newman. STC 22537.

– 1595a. *An apologie for poetrie*. London: Henry Olney. STC 22534.

– 1595b. *The defence of poesie*. London: William Ponsonby. STC 22535.

– 1598. *The Countesse of Pembrokes Arcadia*. London: William Ponsonby. STC 22541.

Smith, Henry. 1590. *The vvedding garment*. London: William Wright. STC 22713.

– 1592. *Thirteene sermons vpon seuerall textes of Scripture*. London: Thomas Man. STC 22717.

– 1593. *Gods arrow against atheists*. London: John Danter. STC 22666.

– 1601. *The pride of King Nabuchadnezzer*. London: William Wright. STC 22689.

Smith, Sir Thomas. 1583. *De republica Anglorum. The maner of gouernement or policie of the realme of England*. London: Gregory Seton. STC 22857.

– 1594. *The common-vvealth of England, and maner of gouernment thereof*. London: Gregory Seton. STC 22860.

– 1601. *The common-vvealth of England, and manner of gouernment thereof*. London: Gregory Seton. STC 22861.

Solinus, C. Julius. 1587. *The worthie work of Iulius Solinus Polyhistor.* Trans. Arthur Golding. London: Thomas Hacket. STC 22895a:5.
Spenser, Edmund. 1579. *The shepheardes calendar.* London: Hugh Singleton. STC 23089.
– 1590. *The faerie queene.* London: William Ponsonby. STC 23080.
– 1591. *Complaints Containing sundrie small poemes of the worlds vanitie.* London: William Ponsonby. STC 23078.
– 1595. *Colin Clouts come home againe.* London: William Ponsonby. STC 23077.
– 1596. *The faerie queene.* London: William Ponsonby. STC 23082.
Stellato, Marcello Palingenio. 1576. *The zodiake of life.* Trans. Barnabe Googe. London: Ralph Newbery. STC 19151.
Stow, John. 1598. *A suruay of London.* London: John Wolfe. STC 23342.
Stubbes, Phillip. 1583. *The anatomie of abuses.* London: Richard Jones. STC 23376.
Symonds, William. 1606. *A heauenly voyce.* London: Edmund Weaver. STC 23591.
Tartaglia, Niccolo. 1588. *Three bookes of colloquies concerning the arte of shooting.* Trans. Cyprian Lucar. London: John Harrison. STC 23689.
Tasso, Torquato. 1588. *The housholders philosophie.* Trans. Thomas Kyd. London: Thomas Hacket. STC 23703.
Tatius, Achilles. 1597. *The most delectable and pleasaunt history of Clitiphon and Leucippe.* Trans. William Burton. London: William Mattes. STC 90.
Telin, Guillaume. 1592. *Archaioplutos. Or the riches of elder ages.* Trans. Anthony Munday. London: Richard Smith. STC 23867.
Terence. 1588. *Andria the first comoedie of Terence.* London: Thomas Woodcock. Trans. Maurice Kyffin. STC 23895.
Thevet, André de. 1557. *Les Singvlaritez de la France Antarctiqve.* Paris: Maurice de La Porte.
– 1568. *The new found vvorlde, or Antarctike.* Trans. Thomas Hacket. London: Thomas Hacket. STC 23950.
Tofte, Robert. 1597. *Laura The toyes of a traueller.* London: Valentine Simmes. STC 24097.
Tottel, Richard. 1557. *Songes and Sonettes.* London: Richard Tottel. STC 13861.
Turberville, George. 1575. *The booke of faulconrie or hauking.* London: Christopher Barker. STC 24324.
– 1611. *The booke of falconrie or havvking.* London: Thomas Purfoot. STC 24325.
Ubaldini, Petruccio. 1590. *A discourse concerninge the Spanishe fleete inuadinge Englande in the yeare 1588.* London: Augustine Ryther. STC 24481.

Van Linschoten, Jan Huygen. 1598. *Iohn Huighen van Linschoten. his discours of voyages into ye Easte & West Indies*. London: John Wolfe. STC 15691.
Van Marnix van St. Aldegonde, Philip. 1579. *The bee hiue of the Romishe Church*. Trans. George Gilpin. London: Thomas Dawson. STC 17445.
Virel, Mathieu. 1595. *A learned and excellent treatise containing all the principall grounds of Christian religion*. Trans. Stephen Egerton. London: Robert Dexter. STC 24768.5.
Watson, George. 1582. *The hekatompathia or Passionate centurie of loue*. London: Gabriel Cawood. STC 25118a.
Watson, Henry, trans. 1637. *Valentine and Orson*. London: Thomas Purfoot. STC 24573.
Wecker, Hanss Jacob. 1585. *A compendious chyrurgerie*. Trans. John Banister. London: John Harrison. STC 25185.
Weever, John. 1600. *Faunus and Melliflora*. London: Valentine Simmes. STC 25225.
– 1601. *The vvhipping of the satyre*. London: John Flasket. STC 14071.
Werdmüller, Otto. 1574? *A spirituall, and most precious perle, teaching all men to loue and imbrace the crosse*. Trans. Miles Coverdale. London: Hugh Singleton. STC 25258.3.
– 1595? *A most fruitfull, pithie and learned treatyse, howe a Christian man ought to behaue himselfe in the danger of death*. Trans. Miles Coverdale. London: William Blackwall. STC 25254.
Whetstone, George. 1576. *The rocke of regard diuided into foure parts*. London: Robert Waley. STC 25348.
– 1578. *The right excellent and famous historye, of Promos and Cassandra*. London: Richard Jones. STC 25347.
– 1586. *The enemie to vnthryftinesse*. London: Richard Jones. STC 25341.5.
– 1587. *The censure of a loyall subiect*. London: Richard Jones. STC 25334.
– 1593. *Aurelia*. London: Richard Jones. STC 25338.
Whitaker, William. 1585. *An aunsvvere to a certaine booke*. Cambridge: Thomas Thomas. STC 25364.
Whitney, Geoffrey. 1586. *A choice of emblemes, and other deuises*. Leyden: Francis Raphelengius. STC 25438.
Whitney, Isabella. 1567? *The copy of a letter, lately written in meeter, by a yonge gentilwoman*. London: Richard Jones. STC 25439.
Wither, George. 1615. *The shepheards hunting*. London: George Norton. STC 25922.
Wright, Leonard. 1602. *A display of dutie. Deckt with sage sayings, pithie sentences, and proper similies*. London: Nicholas Ling. STC 26026.

Zárate, Agustin de. 1581. *The discouerie and conquest of the prouinces of Peru.* Trans. Thomas Nicholas. London: Richard Jones. STC 26123.

Secondary Sources

Adams, Thomas R. 1992. "The Beginnings of Maritime Publishing in England, 1528–1640." *The Library*, 6th ser., 14 (3): 207–20. https://doi.org/10.1093/library/s6-14.3.207.

Aldis, H.G. 1909. "The Book Trade: 1557–1625." In *The Cambridge History of English Literature*, vol. 4, 378–414. Cambridge: Cambridge UP.

Alexander, Gavin. 2006. *Writing after Sidney: The Literary Response to Sir Philip Sidney 1586–1640.* Oxford: Oxford UP. https://doi.org/10.1093/acprof:oso/9780199285471.001.0001.

Allen, Peter R. 1963. "Utopia and European Humanism: The Function of the Prefatory Letters and Verses." *Studies in the Renaissance* 10:91–107. https://doi.org/10.2307/2857050.

Anderson, Randall L. 2003. "Metaphors of Books as Garden in the English Renaissance." *Yearbook of English Studies* 33:248–61. https://doi.org/10.2307/3509029.

Arber, Edward, ed. 1875–94. *A Transcript of the Registers of the Company of Stationers of London, 1554–1640 A.D.* 5 vols. London.

Attridge, Derek. 1989. *Peculiar Language: Literature as Difference from the Renaissance to James Joyce.* Ithaca: Cornell UP.

Baldwin, R.C.D. 2004. "Nicholls, Thomas (1532–1601)." In *Oxford Dictionary of National Biography.* Oxford: Oxford UP. Online.

Baldwyn, Charles, ed. 1825. *The Old English Drama.* 2 vols. London: Hurst and Robinson.

Baluk-Ulewiczowa, Teresa. 1993. "Slanders by the Satirical Knave Holding the Mirror up to Nature: The Background for Wawrzyniec Goslicki as One of Shakespeare's Sources for *Hamlet*." In *Literature and Language in the Intertextual and Cultural Context*, ed. Marta Gibinska and Zygmunt Mazur, 27–39. Instytut Filologii Angielskiej UJ.

Bannerman, Bruce, ed. 1916. *The Registers of St. Olave, Hart Street, London. 1563–1700.* London.

Barker, E.K. 2013. "International News Pamphlets." In *The Elizabethan Top Ten: Defining Print Popularity in Early Modern England*, ed. Andy Kesson and Emma Smith, 145–55. Aldershot: Ashgate.

Barnard, John, and Maureen Bell. 1991. "The Inventory of Henry Bynneman (1583)." *Publishing History* 29:5–46.

Batho, Gordon R. 1960. "The Library of the 'Wizard' Earl: Henry Percy Ninth Earl of Northumberland (1564–1632)." *The Library*, 5th ser., 15 (4): 246–61. https://doi.org/10.1093/library/s5-XV.4.246.

Bednarz, James. 2007. "*The Passionate Pilgrim* and 'The Turtle and the Phoenix.'" In *The Cambridge Companion to Shakespeare's Poetry*, 108–24. Cambridge: Cambridge UP. https://doi.org/10.1017/CCOL0521846277.007.

Beecher, Donald. 2006. "John Frampton of Bristol, Trader and Translator." In *Travel and Translation in the Early Modern Period*, ed. Carmine G. Di Biase, 103–22. Rodopi.

Bell, Ilona. 2010. *Elizabeth I: The Voice of a Monarch*. New York: Palgrave Macmillan. https://doi.org/10.1057/9780230107861.

Bell, Maureen. 1996. "Women in the English Book Trade 1557–1700." *Leipziger Jahrbuch zur Buchgeschichte* 6:13–45.

– 2004. "Bynneman, Henry (b. in or before 1542, d. 1583)." In *Oxford Dictionary of National Biography*. Oxford UP. Online.

Bell, Maureen, and John Barnard. 1992. "Provisional Count of STC Titles 1475–1640." *Publishing History* 31:48–64.

Belle, Marie-Alice. 2013. "Elizabethan Defences of Translation, from Rhetoric to Poetics: Harington's and Chapman's 'Brief Apologies.'" In *Elizabethan Translation and Literary Culture*, ed. Gabriela Schmidt, 43–80. Berlin: De Gruyter. https://doi.org/10.1515/9783110316209.43.

Bennett, H.S. 1965. *English Books & Readers 1558 to 1603*. Cambridge: Cambridge UP.

Binns, James. 1977. "STC Latin Books: Evidence for Printing-House Practice." *The Library*, 5th ser., 32 (1): 1–27. https://doi.org/10.1093/library/s5-XXXII.1.1.

Birrell, T.A. 1985. "The Influence of Seventeenth-Century Publishers on the Presentation of English Literature." In *Historical & Editorial Studies in Medieval & Early Modern English*, ed. Mary-Jo Arn and Hanneke Wirtjes, 163–73. Groninghen: Wolters-Noordhoff.

Blagden, Cyprian. 1960. *The Stationers' Company: A History 1403–1959*. Cambridge: Cambridge UP.

Blair, Ann M. 2000. "Annotating and Indexing Natural Philosophy." In *Books and Sciences in History*, ed. Marina Frasca-Spada and Nick Jardine, 69–89. Cambridge: Cambridge UP.

– 2007. "Errata Lists and the Reader as Corrector." In *Agent of Change: Print Culture Studies after Elizabeth L. Eisenstein*, ed. Sabrina Alcorn Baron, Eric N. Lindquist, and Eleanor F. Shevlin, 21–41. Amherst, Boston: U of Massachusetts P.

- 2010. *Too Much to Know: Managing Scholarly Information before the Modern Age*. New Haven: Yale UP.
Bland, David. 1969. *A History of English Book Illustration: The Illuminated Manuscript and the Printed Book*. Berkley: U California P.
Bland, Mark B. 2010a. *A Guide to Early Printed Books and Manuscripts*. London: Blackwell.
- 2010b. "The London Book Trade in 1600." In *A Companion to Shakespeare*, ed. David Scott Kastan, 450–63. London: Blackwell.
Blayney, Peter W.M. 1973. "The Prevalence of Shared Printing in the Early Seventeenth Century." *PBSA* 67:437–42.
- 1982. *The Texts of King Lear and Their Origins: Volume I. Nicholas Okes and the First Quarto*. Cambridge: Cambridge UP.
- 1990. *The Bookshops in Paul's Cross Churchyard*. London: The Bibliographical Society.
- 1997. "The Publication of Playbooks." In *A New History of Early English Drama*, ed. John D. Cox and David Scott Kastan, 383–422. New York: Columbia UP.
- 2003. *The Stationers' Company before the Charter, 1403–1557*. London: The Worshipful Company of Stationers & Newspapermakers.
- 2007. "STC Publication Statistics: Some Caveats." *The Library*, 7th ser., 8 (4): 387–97. https://doi.org/10.1093/library/8.4.387.
- 2013. *The Stationers' Company and the Printers of London, 1501–1557*. 2 vols. Cambridge: Cambridge UP.
Boutcher, Warren. 2000. "The Renaissance." In *The Oxford Guide to Literature in English Translation*, ed. Peter France, 45–55. Oxford: Oxford UP.
- 2015. "From Cultural Translation to Cultures of Translation?" In *The Culture of Translation in Early Modern England and France, 1500–1600*, ed. Tania Demetriou and Rowan Tomlinson, 22–53. New York: Palgrave.
Bowers, Fredson. 1947. "Criteria for Classifying Hand-Printed Books as Issues and States." *PBSA* 41:271–92.
- 1959. "The Function of Bibliography." *Library Trends* 7 (4): 497–510.
- 1986. *Principles of Bibliographical Description*. London: St. Pauls Bibliographies.
Bowers, Rick. 2002. "Hysterics, High Camp, and Dido Queen of Carthage." In *Marlowe's Empery: Expanding his Critical Contexts*, ed. Sarah Munson Deats and Robert A. Logan, 95–106. Newark: U Delaware P.
Braden, Gordon. 2004. "Newton, Thomas (1544/5–1607)." In *Oxford Dictionary of National Biography*. Oxford: Oxford UP. Online.
- 2010a. "An Overview." In *The Oxford History of Literary Translation in English*, vol. 2, ed. Gordon Braden, Robert Cummings, and Stuart Gillespie, 3–11. Oxford: Oxford UP.

- 2010b. "Translation Procedures in Theory and Practice." In *The Oxford History of Literary Translation in English*, vol. 2, ed. Gordon Braden, Robert Cummings, and Stuart Gillespie, 89–100. Oxford: Oxford UP.
Braden, Gordon, Robert Cummings, and Stuart Gillespie. 2010. "The Translators: Biographical Sketches." In *The Oxford History of Literary Translation in English*, vol. 2, 3–11. Oxford: Oxford UP.
Brennan, Michael. 1983. "William Ponsonby: Elizabethan Stationer." *Analytical and Enumerative Bibliography* 7 (3): 91–110.
Brink, Jean. 1990. *Michael Drayton Revisited*. Boston: Twayne.
Brooke, Tucker. 1922. "The Reputation of Christopher Marlowe." *Transactions of the Connecticut Academy of Arts and Sciences* 25 (June): 347–408.
Brown, Georgia. 2004. *Redefining Elizabethan Literature*. Cambridge: Cambridge UP. https://doi.org/10.1017/CBO9780511483462.
Braunmuller, A.R. 1984. "Thomas Marshe, Henry Marshe, and the Roman Emperors." *The Library*, 6th ser., 1 (1): 25–38. https://doi.org/10.1093/library/s6-VI.1.25.
Budra, Paul Vincent. 2000. *The Mirror for Magistrates and the de casibus Tradition*. Toronto: U of Toronto P. https://doi.org/10.3138/9781442670396.
Bullough, Geoffrey, ed. 1978. *Narrative and Dramatic Sources for Shakespeare*, vol. 7: Major Tragedies. London: Routledge.
Burke, Peter. 1966. "A Survey of the Popularity of Ancient Historians, 1450–1700." *History and Theory* 5 (2): 135–52. https://doi.org/10.2307/2504511.
Byrne, M. St Clare. 1924. "An Early Translation of Seneca." *The Library*, 4th ser., 4 (4): 277–85. https://doi.org/10.1093/library/s4-IV.4.277.
Cathcart, Charles. 2002. "John Fletcher in 1600–1601: Two Early Poems, an Involvement in the 'Poets' War,' and a Network of Literary Connections." *Philological Quarterly* 81 (1): 33–51.
Chartier, Roger. 1994. *The Order of Books*. Stanford: Stanford UP.
Cheney, Patrick. 1997. *Marlowe's Counterfeit Profession: Ovid, Spenser, Counter Nationhood*. Toronto: U of Toronto P. https://doi.org/10.3138/9781442677067.
- 2009. *Marlowe's Republican Authorship: Lucan, Liberty, and the Sublime*. New York: Palgrave.
Cicero. 1949. *De Optimo Genere Oratorum*. Trans. H.M. Hubbell. Cambridge: Harvard UP. https://doi.org/10.4159/DLCL.marcus_tullius_cicero-de_optimo_genere_oratorum.1949.
Clegg, Cyndia. 1997. *Press Censorship in Elizabethan England*. Cambridge: Cambridge UP. https://doi.org/10.1017/CBO9780511585241.
- 2007. "'Twill Much Enrich the Company of Stationers': Thomas Middleton and the London Book Trade: 1580–1627." In *Thomas Middleton and Early*

Modern Textual Culture, ed. Gary Taylor and John Lavagnino, 247–59. Oxford: Oxford UP.

Cole, Douglas. 1962. *Suffering and Evil in the Plays of Christopher Marlowe*. Princeton: Princeton UP.

Coldiron, A.E.B. 2003. "Translation's Challenge to Critical Categories: Verses from French in the Early English Renaissance." *Yale Journal of Criticism* 16 (2): 315–44. https://doi.org/10.1353/yale.2003.0015.

– 2008. "William Caxton." In *The Oxford History of Literary Translation in English*: vol. 1, ed. Roger Ellis, 160–70. Oxford: Oxford UP.

– 2015. *Printers without Borders: Translation and Textuality in the Renaissance*. Cambridge: Cambridge UP.

Collinson, Patrick. 1997. "The Monarchical Republic of Queen Elizabeth I." In *The Tudor Monarchy*, ed. John Guy, 110–34. London: Arnold.

– 2007. "Afterword." In *The Monarchical Republic of Early Modern England: Essays in Response to Patrick Collinson*, ed. John F. McDiarmid, 245–61. Aldershot: Ashgate.

Cope, Jackson I. 1974. "Marlowe's *Dido* and the Titillating Children." *English Literary Renaissance* 4 (3): 315–25. https://doi.org/10.1111/j.1475-6757.1974.tb01304.x.

Corbett, Margaret, and Ronald Lightbrown. 1979. *The Comely Frontispiece: The Emblematic Title-Page in England 1550–1650*. London: Routledge.

Crane, Mary Thomas. 1993. *Framing Authority: Sayings, Self, and Society in Sixteenth-Century England*. Princeton: Princeton UP.

Culhane, Peter. 2004. "Philemon Holland's Livy: Peritexts and Contexts." *Translation and Literature* 13 (2): 268–86. https://doi.org/10.3366/tal.2004.13.2.268.

Dabbs, Thomas. 1991. *Reforming Marlowe: The Nineteenth-Century Canonization of a Renaissance Dramatist*. Lewisburg: Bucknell UP.

Darnton, Robert. 1982. "What Is the History of Books?" *Daedalus* 111 (3): 65–83.

Day, Matthew. 2011. "'Intended to Offenders': The Running Titles of Early Modern Books." In *Renaissance Paratexts*, ed. Helen Smith and Louise Wilson, 32–48. Cambridge: Cambridge UP. https://doi.org/10.1017/CBO9780511842429.003.

de Certeau, Michel. 1984. *The Practice of Everyday Life*. Trans. Steven Rendall. Berkeley: U of California P.

DEEP: Database of Early English Playbooks. Ed. Alan B. Farmer and Zachary Lesser. Created 2007. http://deep.sas.upenn.edu.

de Grazia, Margreta. 1991. *Shakespeare Verbatim: The Reproduction of Authenticity and the 1790 Apparatus*. Oxford: Clarendon P. https://doi.org/10.1093/acprof:oso/9780198117780.001.0001.

– 2007. *Hamlet without Hamlet*. Cambridge: Cambridge UP.
Demetriou, Tania, and Rowan Tomlinson, eds. 2015. "Introduction." In *The Culture of Translation in Early Modern England and France*, 1–21. New York: Palgrave. https://doi.org/10.1057/9781137401496_1.
Devereux, E.J. 1983. *Renaissance English Translations of Erasmus, A Bibliography to 1700*. Toronto: U of Toronto P.
Dodds, Gregory D. 2009. *Exploiting Erasmus: The Erasmian Legacy and Religious Change in Early Modern England*. Toronto: U of Toronto P. https://doi.org/10.3138/9781442688056.
Donno, Elizabeth Story. 1970. "The Epyllion." In *English Poetry and Prose 1540–1674*, ed. Christopher Ricks, 57–72. London: Sphere.
– 1989. "Abraham Fleming: A Learned Corrector in 1586–87." *Studies in Bibliography* 42:200–11.
Draper, John. 1935. "Lord Chamberlain Polonius." *Shakespeare Jahrbuch* 71:78–93.
Dubrow, Heather. 1995. *Echoes of Desire: English Petrarchism and Its Counterdiscourses*. Ithaca: Cornell UP.
Duff, Edward Gordon. 1905. *A Century of the English Book Trade*. London: The Bibliographical Society.
Duncan-Jones, Katherine. 2010. *Shakespeare's Sonnets*. London: Arden.
Duncan-Jones, Katherine, and Jan Van Dorsten, eds. 1973. *Miscellaneous Prose of Sir Philip Sidney*. Oxford: Clarendon Press.
Dutton, Elizabeth. 2008. *Julian of Norwich: The Influence of Late-Medieval Devotional Compilations*. Woodbridge, Suffolk: Boydell & Brewer.
Ebel, J.G. 1967. "A Numerical Survey of Elizabethan Translations." *The Library*, 5th ser., 22 (2): 104–27. https://doi.org/10.1093/library/s5-XXII.2.104.
Eccles, Mark. 1957. "Bynneman's Books." *The Library*, 5th ser., 12 (2): 81–92. https://doi.org/10.1093/library/s5-XII.2.81.
– 1982. "Matthew Grove." *Studies in Philology* 79 (4): 57–8.
Edmondson, Paul M. 2000. "Playing Horatio in Q1 *Hamlet*." *Shakespeare Studies* 22:26–39.
Egan, Gabriel. 2014. "Shakespeare: Editions and Textual Studies." *The Year's Work in English Studies* 93 (1): 295–362.
Ellis, Jim. 2001. "Imagining Heterosexuality in the Epyllia." In *Ovid and the Renaissance Body*, ed. Goran V. Stanivucovik, 38–58. Toronto: U of Toronto P. https://doi.org/10.3138/9781442678194-004.
– 2003. *Sexuality and Citizenship: Metamorphosis in Elizabethan Erotic Verse*. Toronto: U of Toronto P.
Erler, Mary C., ed. 2008. *Ecclesiastical London, Records of Early English Drama*. London, Toronto: British Library and U of Toronto P.

Erne, Lukas. 2001. *Beyond the Spanish Tragedy: A Study of the Works of Thomas Kyd*. Manchester: Manchester UP.
– 2003. *Shakespeare as Literary Dramatist*. Cambridge: Cambridge UP.
– 2013. *Shakespeare and the Book Trade*. Cambridge: Cambridge UP.
Evans, John T. 1979. *Seventeenth-Century Norwich: Politics, Religion, and Government, 1620–1690*. Oxford: Clarendon Press.
Evenden, Elizabeth. 2008. *Parents, Pictures and Patronage: John Day and the Tudor Book Trade*. Aldershot: Ashgate.
Falk, Doris. 1967. "Proverbs and the Polonius Destiny." *Shakespeare Quarterly* 18 (1): 23–36. https://doi.org/10.2307/2868060.
Farley-Hills, David, ed. 1997. *Critical Responses to Hamlet 1600–1790*. New York: AMS Press.
Farmer, Alan B., and Zachary Lesser 2000. "Vile Arts: The Marketing of English Printed Drama, 1512–1620." *Research Opportunities in Renaissance Drama* 39:77–165.
– 2005. "The Popularity of Playbooks Revisited." *Shakespeare Quarterly* 56 (1): 1–32. https://doi.org/10.1353/shq.2005.0043.
– 2013. "What Is Print Popularity? A Map of the Elizabethan Book Trade." In *The Elizabethan Top Ten: Defining Print Popularity in Early Modern England*, ed. Andy Kesson and Emma Smith, 19–54. Aldershot: Ashgate.
Ferguson, Arthur. 1965. *The Articulate Citizen and the English Renaissance*. Durham: Duke UP.
Ferguson, W.C. 1958. "Some Additions to McKerrow's Printers' and Publishers' Devices." *The Library*, 5th ser., 8 (3): 201–3. https://doi.org/10.1093/library/s5-XIII.3.201.
– 1968. *Valentine Simmes: Printer to Drayton, Shakespeare, Chapman, Greene, Dekker, Middleton, Daniel, Jonson, Marlowe, Marston, Heywood, and Other Elizabethans*. Charlottesville: Bibliographical Society of the U of Virginia.
Fisher, Alan. 1990. "Shakespeare's Last Humanist." *Renaissance and Reformation* 14 (1): 37–47.
Fowler, Alistair. 2003. "The Formation of Genres in the Renaissance and After." *New Literary History* 34 (2): 185–200. https://doi.org/10.1353/nlh.2003.0017.
Fox, Denton, ed. 1962. "Henryson's Fables." *ELH* 29:337–56.
– 1981. *The Poems of Robert Henryson*. Oxford: Oxford UP.
Freeman, Arthur. 1967. *Thomas Kyd: Facts and Problems*. Oxford: Clarendon Press.
Freyd, Bernard, and Frederick M. Padelford. 1935. "Spenser or Anthony Munday: A Note on the *Axiochus*." *PMLA* 50 (3): 903–13. https://doi.org/10.2307/458225.

Frye, Roland Mushat. 1984. *The Renaissance Hamlet: Issues and Responses*, 38–70. Princeton: Princeton UP.

Gants, David. 2002. "A Quantitative Analysis of the London Book Trade 1614 to 1618." *Studies in Bibliography* 55 (1): 185–213. https://doi.org/10.1353/sib.2005.0004.

Garrett, Albert. 1978. *A History of British Wood Engraving*. Kent: Tunbridge Wells.

Gaskell, Philip. 1949–53. "The Meaning of 'Impression' and 'Issue.'" *Transactions of the Cambridge Bibliographical Society* 1:361–2.

– 1972. *A New Introduction to Bibliography*. New York: Oxford UP.

Genette, Gérard. 1997. *Paratexts: Thresholds of Interpretation*. Cambridge: Cambridge UP. https://doi.org/10.1017/CBO9780511549373.

Gillespie, Alexandra. 2004. "Poets, Printers, and Early English Sammelbände." *Huntington Library Quarterly* 67 (2): 189–214. https://doi.org/10.1525/hlq.2004.67.2.189.

Girtin, Thomas. 1964. *The Triple Crowns: A Narrative History of the Drapers' Company, 1364–1964*. London: Hutchinson.

Goldie, Mark. 2001. "The Unacknowledged Republic: Officeholding in Early Modern England." In *The Politics of the Excluded, c. 1500–1850*, ed. Tim Harris, 153–94. New York: Palgrave. https://doi.org/10.1007/978-1-4039-4030-8_6.

Goldwyn, Merrill Harvey. 1966. "Notes on the Biography of Thomas Churchyard." *Review of English Studies* 17 (65): 1–15. https://doi.org/10.1093/res/XVII.65.1.

Gopen, George D., ed. 1987. *The Moral Fables of Aesop by Robert Henryson*. East Bend: U of Notre Dame P

Grafton, Anthony. 2011. *The Culture of Correction in Renaissance Europe*. London: The British Library.

Green, Ian. 2000. *Print and Protestantism in Early Modern England*. Oxford: Oxford UP. https://doi.org/10.1093/acprof:oso/9780198208600.001.0001.

Greg, W.W. 1939. *A Bibliography of the English Printed Drama to the Restoration*. London: The Bibliographical Society.

– 1944. "The Copyright of *Hero and Leander*." *The Library*, 4th ser., 24 (1–2): 165–74.

– 1956. *London Publishing between 1550 and 1650*. Oxford: Clarendon Press.

Greg, W.W., and E. Boswell, eds. 1930. *Records of the Court of the Stationers' Company 1576 to 1602*. London: The Bibliographical Society.

Grundy, Joan, ed. 1960. *The Poems of Henry Constable*. Liverpool: Liverpool UP.

Guy, John. 2000. "The Rhetoric of Counsel in Early-Modern England." In *Politics, Law and Counsel in Tudor and Early Stuart England*, 299. Aldershot: Ashgate.

Gwyn, David. 1984. "Richard Eden: Cosmographer and Alchemist." *Sixteenth Century Journal* 15 (1): 13–34. https://doi.org/10.2307/2540837.

Hackel, Heidi Brayman. 2005. *Reading Material in Early Modern England: Print, Gender and Literacy*. Cambridge: Cambridge UP.

Hadfield, Andrew. 1994. *Literature, Politics and National Identity: Reformation to Renaissance*. Cambridge: Cambridge UP.

– 1995/6. "Peter Martyr, Richard Eden and the New World: Reading, Experience, and Translation." *Connotations* 5 (1): 1–22.

– 1998a. *Literature, Travel, and Colonial Writing in the English Renaissance, 1545–1625*. Oxford: Oxford UP.

– 1998b. "Was Spenser a Republican?" *English* 47:169–82.

– 2003a. "Michael Drayton's Brilliant Career." *Proceedings of the British Academy* 125:119–47.

– 2003b. "Was Spenser a Republican After All? A Reply to David Scott Wilson-Okamura." *Spenser Studies* 17:275–90.

– 2005. *Shakespeare and Republicanism*. Cambridge: Cambridge UP.

– 2007. "The Political Significance of the First Tetralogy." In *The Monarchical Republic of Early Modern England*, ed. John F. McDiarmid, 149–63. Aldershot: Ashgate.

– 2012. *Edmund Spenser: A Life*. Oxford: Oxford UP.

Hall, Kim. 1995. *Things of Darkness: Economies of Race and Gender in Early Modern England*. Ithaca: Cornell UP.

Hammer, Paul E.J. 1999. *The Polarisation of Elizabethan Politics: The Political Career of Robert Devereux, 2nd Earl of Essex, 1585–1597*. Cambridge: Cambridge UP.

Hapwood, Robert, ed. 1999. *Hamlet, Prince of Denmark*. Cambridge: Cambridge UP.

Hardin, Richard F. 1973. *Michael Drayton and the Passing of Elizabethan England*. Lawrence: U of Kansas P.

Hart, Jonathan. 2005. *Contesting Empires: Opposition, Promotion, and Slavery*. New York: Palgrave. https://doi.org/10.1057/9781403981325.

Helgerson, Richard. 1976. *The Elizabethan Prodigals*. Berkeley: U of California P.

– 1983. *Self-Crowned Laureates: Spenser, Jonson, Milton and the Literary System*. Berkeley: U of California P.

Hentschell, Roze. 2008. *The Culture of Cloth in Early Modern England*. Aldershot: Ashgate.

Hind, Arthur M. 1935. *An Introduction to the History of the Woodcut*. 2 vols. New York: Dover.
Hoak, Dale. 2007. "Sir William Cecil, Sir Thomas Smith, and the Monarchical Republic of Tudor England." In *The Monarchical Republic of Early Modern England*, ed. John F. McDiarmid, 37–54. Aldershot: Ashgate.
Hodnett, Edward. 1935. *English Woodcuts, 1480–1535*. London: The Bibliographical Society.
Honigmann, E.A.J. 1987. *John Weever: A Biography of a Literary Associate of Shakespeare and Jonson*. Manchester: Manchester UP.
Hooks, Adam G. 2008. "Booksellers' Catalogues and the Classification of Printed Drama in Seventeenth-Century England." *Papers of the Bibliographical Society of America* 102 (4): 445–64.
– 2011. "Shakespeare at the White Greyhound." *Shakespeare Survey* 64:260–75.
– 2013. "Wise Ventures: Shakespeare and Thomas Playfere at the Sign of the Angel." In *Shakespeare's Stationers: Studies in Cultural Bibliography*, ed. Marta Straznicky, 47–62. Philadelphia: U of Pennsylvania P.
– 2016. *Vending Shakespeare: Biography, Bibliography, and the Book Trade*. Cambridge: Cambridge UP.
Hopkins, Lisa. 2004. "Marlowe's Reception and Influence." In *The Cambridge Companion to Christopher Marlowe*, ed. Patrick Cheney, 282–96. Cambridge: Cambridge UP. https://doi.org/10.1017/CCOL0521820340.017.
Hopkinson, H.L., ed. 1915. *The Ancient Records of the Merchants Taylors' Company*. London.
Hosington, Brenda M. 2010. "Commerce, Printing, and Patronage." In *The Oxford History of Literary Translation in English*, vol. 2, ed. Gordon Braden, Robert Cummings, and Stuart Gillespie, 47–57. Oxford: Oxford UP. https://doi.org/10.1093/acprof:osobl/9780199246212.003.0006.
Householder, Michael. 2007. "Eden's Translations: Women and Temptation in Early America." *Huntington Library Quarterly* 70 (1): 11–36. https://doi.org/10.1525/hlq.2007.70.1.11.
Hull, Helen. 2009. "Scripting Public Performance: The Representation of Officeholding in Early Modern Literature." PhD diss., U of Maryland.
Hulse, Clark. 1981. *The Elizabethan Minor Epic*. Princeton: Princeton UP.
Hunter, G.K. 1951. "The Marking of *Sententiae* in Elizabethan Printed Plays, Poems, and Romances." *The Library*, 5th ser., 6 (3–4): 171–88. https://doi.org/10.1093/library/s5-VI.3-4.171.
– 1957. "Isocrates' Precepts and Polonius's Character." *Shakespeare Quarterly* 8 (4): 501–6. https://doi.org/10.2307/2867556.
Hutson, Lorna. 1989. *Thomas Nashe in Context*. Oxford: Oxford UP.

Hyland, Peter. 2003. *An Introduction to Shakespeare's Poems*. New York: Palgrave.

Irace, Kathleen O., ed. 1998. *The First Quarto of Hamlet*. Cambridge: Cambridge UP.

Jackson, William A., ed. 1940. *The Carl H. Pforzheimer Library of English Literature 1475–1700*, 3 vols. New York.

– 1957. *Records of the Court of the Stationers Company, 1602 to 1640*. London: The Bibliographical Society.

Jardine, Lisa, and Anthony Grafton. 1990. "'Studied for Action': How Gabriel Harvey Read His Livy." *Past & Present* 129 (1): 30–78. https://doi.org/10.1093/past/129.1.30.

Jauss, Hans Robert. 1982. "Theory of Genres and Medieval Literature." In *Toward an Aesthetic of Reception*, trans. Timothy Bahti, 76–109. Minneapolis: U of Minnesota P.

Jenkins, Harold, ed. 1982. *Hamlet*, 18–74. London: The Arden Shakespeare.

Jennett, Seán. 1951. *The Making of Books*. New York: Pantheon Books.

Johns, Adrian. 1998. *The Nature of the Book*. Chicago: U of Chicago P. https://doi.org/10.7208/chicago/9780226401232.001.0001.

Johnson, A.H. 1914–22. *The History of the Worshipful Company of the Drapers of London*. Oxford: Clarendon Press.

Johnson, F.R. 1950. "Notes on English Retail Book-Prices, 1550–1640." *The Library*, 5th ser., 5 (2): 83–112. https://doi.org/10.1093/library/s5-V.2.83.

Johnson, Gerald D. 1985a. "Nicholas Ling, Publisher 1580–1607." *Studies in Bibliography* 38:203–14.

– 1985b. "John Busby and the Stationer's Trade." *The Library*, 6th ser., 7:1–15.

– 1986. "John Trundle and the Book Trade 1603–1626." *Studies in Bibliography* 39:177–99.

– 1988. "The Stationers versus the Drapers: Control of the Press in the Late Sixteenth Century." *The Library*, 6th ser., 10 (1): 1–17.

– 1989. "William Barley, 'Publisher & Seller of Bookes,' 1591–1614." *The Library*, 6th ser., 11 (1): 10–46.

– 1992. "Succeeding as an Elizabethan Publisher: The Example of Cuthbert Burby." *Journal of the Printing Historical Society* 21:71–8.

Kahn, Victoria. 1994. *Machiavellian Rhetoric: From the Counter-Reformation to Milton*. Princeton: Princeton UP. https://doi.org/10.1515/9781400821280.

Kastan, David Scott. 2001. *Shakespeare and the Book*. Cambridge: Cambridge UP.

– 2002. "Print, Literary Culture, and the Book Trade." In *The New Cambridge History of English Literature*, ed. David Loewenstein and Janel Mueller, 81–116. Cambridge: Cambridge UP.

- 2007. "Humphrey Moseley and the Invention of English Literature." In *Agent of Change: Print Culture Studies after Elizabeth L. Eisenstein*, ed. Sabrina Alcorn Baron, Eric N. Lindquist, and Eleanor F. Shevlin, 105–24. Amherst: U of Massachusetts P.
Kathman, David. 2004a. "Barker, Christopher (1528/9–1599)." In *Oxford Dictionary of National Biography*. Oxford UP. Online.
- 2004b. "Weever, John (1575/6–1632)." In *Oxford Dictionary of National Biography*. Oxford UP. Online.
Kay, Dennis. 1987. "Introduction: Sidney – A Critical Heritage." In *Sir Philip Sidney: An Anthology of Modern Criticism*, ed. Dennis Kay, 3–41. Oxford: Clarendon Press.
Keach, William. 1977. *Elizabethan Erotic Narratives: Irony and Pathos in the Ovidian Poetry of Shakespeare, Marlowe and Their Contemporaries*. New Brunswick: Rutgers UP.
Kerrigan, John. 1996. "The Editor as Reader." In *The Practice and Representation of Reading in England*, ed. James Raven, Helen Small, and Naomi Tadmor, 102–24. Cambridge: Cambridge UP.
- 2001. *On Shakespeare and Early Modern Literature: Essays*. Oxford: Oxford UP.
King, Ros, ed. 2001. *The Works of Richard Edwards: Politics, Poetry, and Performance in the Sixteenth Century*. Manchester: Manchester UP.
Kirschbaum, Leo. 1955. *Shakespeare and the Stationers*. Columbus: Ohio State UP.
Kiséry, András. 2012. "A Shop and an Author: Publishing Marlowe's Remains at the Black Bear." *Philological Quarterly* 91 (3): 361–92.
Knapp, James A. 2003. *Illustrating the Past in Early Modern England*. Aldershot: Ashgate.
- 2005. "The Bastard Art: Woodcut Illustration in Sixteenth Century England." In *Printing and Parenting in Early Modern England*, ed. Douglas A. Brooks, 151–72. Aldershot: Ashgate.
Knapp, Jeffrey. 1992. *A Empire Nowhere: England, America and Literature from Utopia to The Tempest*. Berkeley: U of California P.
Knight, Jeffrey Todd 2009. "Making Shakespeare's Books: Assembly and Intertextuality in the Archives." *Shakespeare Quarterly* 60 (3): 308.
- 2013. *Bound to Read: Compilations, Collections, and the Making of Renaissance Literature*. Philadelphia: U of Pennsylvania P.
Knighton, C.S. 2004. "Burton, William (*c*. 1545–1616)." In *Oxford Dictionary of National Biography*, 9:45–6. Oxford: Oxford UP. Online.
Kocher, Paul H. 1946. *Christopher Marlowe: A Study of His Thought, Learning and Character*. Chapel Hill: U of North Carolina P.

Lander, Jesse M. 2006. *Inventing Polemic: Religion, Print, and Literary Culture in Early Modern England*. Cambridge: Cambridge UP.

Lang, R.G., ed. 1993. *Two Tudor Subsidy Assessment Rolls for the City of London: 1541 and 1582*. London: London Record Society.

Lavin, J.A. 1968. "Additions to McKerrow's *Devices*." *The Library*, 5th ser., 23 (3): 191–205. https://doi.org/10.1093/library/s5-XXIII.3.191.

Lee, Sidney. 1905. *A Life of William Shakespeare*. London: Smith, Elder, and Co.

Lee, Sidney, ed. 1904. *Elizabethan Sonnets*. 2 vols. Westminster: Archibald, Constable, and Co.

– 1905. *Shakespeare's Passionate Pilgrim*. Oxford: Clarendon Press.

Lerer, Seth. 2002. *Error and the Academic Self: The Scholarly Imagination, Medieval and Modern*. New York: Columbia UP.

– 2003. "Medieval English Literature and the Idea of the Anthology." *PMLA* 118 (5): 1251–67. https://doi.org/10.1632/003081203X68018.

Lesser, Zachary. 2004. *Renaissance Drama and the Politics of Publication*. Cambridge: Cambridge UP.

– 2006. "Typographic Nostalgia: Play-Reading, Popularity, and the Meanings of Black Letter." In *The Book of the Play: Playwrights, Stationers, and Readers in Early Modern England*, ed. Marta Straznicky, 99–126. Amherst: U of Massachusetts P.

– 2015. *Hamlet after Q1: An Uncanny History of the Shakespearean Text*. Philadelphia: University of Pennsylvania Press.

Lesser, Zachary, and Peter Stallybrass. 2008. "The First Literary *Hamlet* and the Commonplacing of Professional Plays." *Shakespeare Quarterly* 59 (4): 371–420. https://doi.org/10.1353/shq.0.0040.

Lestringant, Frank. 1993. "The Philosopher's Breviary: Jean de Lery in the Enlightenment." In *New World Encounters*, ed. Stephen Greenblatt, 127–38. Berkeley: U of California P.

Lestringant, Frank, and Ann Blair. 1995. "Geneva and America in the Renaissance: The Dream of the Huguenot Refuge 1555–1600." *Sixteenth Century Journal* 26 (2): 285–95. https://doi.org/10.2307/2542791.

Lievsay, John L. 1969. *The Englishman's Italian Books 1550–1700*. Philadelphia: U of Pennsylvania P. https://doi.org/10.9783/9781512803808.

Loewenstein, Joseph. 1985. "The Script in the Marketplace." *Representations* 12:101–14. https://doi.org/10.2307/3043780.

Lowe, Ben. 1990. "War and Commonwealth in Mid-Tudor England." *Sixteenth Century Journal* 21 (2): 170–92. https://doi.org/10.2307/2541048.

Luborsky, Ruth. 1987. "Connections and Disconnections between Images and Texts: The Case of Secular Tudor Book Illustration." *Word & Image* 3 (1): 74–85. https://doi.org/10.1080/02666286.1987.10435367.

– 1992. "Woodcuts in Tudor Books: Clarifying Their Documentation." *PBSA* 86 (1): 67–81.

Luborsky, Ruth, and Elizabeth Morley Ingram. 1998. *A Guide to English Illustrated Books, 1536–1603*. Tempe, AZ: Medieval & Renaissance Texts and Studies.

Lucas, Scott. 2007. "'Let none such office take, save he that can for right his prince forsake': *A Mirror for Magistrates*, Resistance Theory and the Elizabethan Monarchical Republic." In *The Monarchical Republic of Early Modern England: Essays in Response to Patrick Collinson*, ed. John F. McDiarmid, 91–108. Aldershot: Ashgate.

Lull, Janis. 1992. "Forgetting *Hamlet*: The First Quarto and the Folio." In *The Hamlet First Published (Q1, 1603): Origins, Forms, Intertextualities*, ed. Thomas Clayton, 137–50. Newark: U of Delaware P.

Lyne, Raphael. 2004. "Churchyard, Thomas (1523?–1604)." In *Oxford Dictionary of National Biography*. Oxford: Oxford UP. Online.

Lyons, Tara L. 2011. "English Printed Drama in Collection before Jonson and Shakespeare." PhD diss., U of Illinois.

Machan, Tim William. 1990. "Robert Henryson and Father Aesop: Literary Authority in the *Moral Fables*." *Studies in the Age of Chaucer* 12:193–221.

– 1992. "Textual Authority and the Works of Hoccleve, Lydgate, and Henryson." *Viator* 23:281–99. https://doi.org/10.1484/J.VIATOR.2.301284.

Marotti, Arthur. 1991. "Patronage, Poetry, and Print." *Yearbook of English Studies* 21:1–26. https://doi.org/10.2307/3508476.

– 1995. *Manuscript, Print, and the English Renaissance Lyric*. Ithaca: Cornell UP.

– 2004. "Bodenham, John (c. 1559–1610)." In *Oxford Dictionary of National Biography*. Oxford: Oxford UP. Online.

Massai, Sonia. 2007. *Shakespeare and the Rise of the Editor*. Cambridge: Cambridge UP.

Matz, Robert. 2000. *Defending Literature in Early Modern England*. Cambridge: Cambridge UP. https://doi.org/10.1017/CBO9780511483776.

May, Steven W., and William A. Ringler. 2004. *Elizabethan Poetry: A Bibliography and First-line Index of English Verse 1559–1603*. 3 vols. London: Continuum.

McConica, James. 1965. *English Humanists and Reformation Politics under Henry VIII and Edward VI*. Oxford: Clarendon Press.

McCoy, Richard. 1985. "Gascoigne's 'Poëmata castrata': The Wages of Courtly Success." *Criticism* 27:29–55.

McCullough, P.E. 2004. "Andrewes, Lancelot (1555–1626)." In *Oxford Dictionary of National Biography*. Oxford: Oxford UP. Online.

- 2008. "Print, Publication, and Religious Politics in Caroline England." *Historical Journal* 51 (2): 285–313.
McGann, Jerome. 1983. *A Critique of Modern Textual Criticism*. Chicago: U of Chicago P.
McGhee, Robert. 2001. *The Arctic Voyages of Martin Frobisher: An English Adventure*. Montreal: McGill UP.
McKenzie, D.F. 1982. "Printing in England from Caxton to Milton." In *The Age of Shakespeare*, ed. Boris Ford, 207–26. New York: Penguin.
- 1986. *Bibliography and the Sociology of Texts*. London: The British Library.
- 2002. "Printing and Publishing 1557–1700: Constraints on the London Book Trades." In *The Cambridge History of the Book in Britain*, vol. 4, 553–67. Cambridge: Cambridge UP.
McKerrow, R.B. 1913. *Printers' & Publishers' Devices in England & Scotland 1485–1640*. London: The Bibliographical Society.
- 1916. "Booksellers, Printers, and the Stationers' Trade." In *Shakespeare's England: An Account of the Life and Manners of his Age*, vol. 2, 212–39. Clarendon: Oxford UP.
- 1927. *An Introduction to Bibliography for Literary Students*. Oxford: Clarendon Press.
- 1929. "Edward Allde as a Typical Trade Printer." *The Library*, 4th ser., 10 (2): 121–62.
McKerrow, R.B., ed. 1910. *A Dictionary of Printers and Booksellers in England, Scotland and Ireland, and of Foreign Printers of English Books 1557–1640*. London: The Bibliographical Society.
McLaren, Anne. 1999. "Reading Sir Thomas Smith's *De Republica Anglorum* as Protestant Apologetic." *Historical Journal* (Cambridge, England) 42 (4): 911–39. https://doi.org/10.1017/S0018246X99008730.
Meale, Carol M. 1992. "Caxton, de Worde, and the Publication of Romance in Late Medieval England." *The Library*, 6th ser., 14 (4): 283–98. https://doi.org/10.1093/library/s6-14.4.283.
Melnikoff, Kirk. 2001. "Richard Jones (*fl.* 1564–1613): Elizabethan Printer, Bookseller and Publisher." *Analytical and Enumerative Bibliography* 12 (3): 153–84.
- 2005. "Jones's Pen and Marlowe's Socks: Richard Jones, Print Culture, and the Beginnings of English Dramatic Literature." *Studies in Philology* 102 (2): 184–209. https://doi.org/10.1353/sip.2005.0010.
- 2009. "Thomas Hacket and the Ventures of an Elizabethan Publisher." *The Library*, 7th ser., 10 (3): 257–71. https://doi.org/10.1093/library/10.3.257.
- 2013a. "Nicholas Ling's Republican *Hamlet* (1603)." In *Shakespeare's Stationers*, ed. Marta Straznicky, 95–111. Philadelphia: U of Pennsylvania P.

- 2013b. "*The Jew of Malta* as Print Commodity in 1594." In *The Jew of Malta: A Critical Guide*, ed. Robert Logan, 129–48. London: Arden.
- 2015. "From the Talbot to Duck Lane: The Early Publication History of Robert Wilson's *The Three Ladies of London*." Performance as Research in Early English Theatre Studies: *The Three Ladies of London* in Context, http://threeladiesoflondon.mcmaster.ca.

Melnikoff, Kirk, and Edward Gieskes, eds. 2008. *Writing Robert Greene: Essays on England's First Notorious Professional Writer*. Aldershot: Ashgate.

Melnikoff, Kirk, and Roslyn L. Knutson, eds. 2018. *Christopher Marlowe, Theatrical Commerce and the Book Trade*. Cambridge: Cambridge UP.

Mentz, Steve. 2000. "Selling Sidney: William Ponsonby, Thomas Nashe, and the Boundaries of Elizabethan and Manuscript Culture." *Text* 12:151–74.

Menzer, Paul. 2008. *The Hamlets: Cues, Qs, and Remembered Texts*. Newark: U of Delaware P.

Merrix, Robert P. 1986. "The Vale of Lillies and the Bower of Bliss: Soft-Core Pornography in Elizabethan Poetry." *Journal of Popular Culture* 19 (4): 3–16. https://doi.org/10.1111/j.0022-3840.1986.1904_3.x.

Moore, Helen. 2011. "The 'Profitable' Translations of Thomas Paynell." In *Tudor Translation*, ed. Fred Schurink, 39–57. New York: Palgrave. https://doi.org/10.1057/9780230361102_3.

Moore, J.K. 1992. *Primary Materials Related to Copy and Print of English Books Printed in the Sixteenth and Seventeenth Centuries*. Oxford: Oxford Bibliographical Society.

Morini, Massimiliano. 2006. *Tudor Translation in Theory and Practice*. Aldershot: Ashgate.

Muir, Kenneth. 1954. "The Order of Constable's Sonnets." *Notes and Queries* 199: 424–5.

- 1958. "Elizabethan Remainders." *The Library*, 5th ser., 13 (1): 56–7.

Muldrew, Craig. 1998. *The Economy of Obligation: The Culture of Credit and Social Relations in Early Modern England*. New York: St Martin's Press. https://doi.org/10.1007/978-1-349-26879-5.

Murphy, Andrew. 2003. *Shakespeare in Print: A History and Chronology of Shakespeare Publishing*. Cambridge: Cambridge UP. https://doi.org/10.1017/CBO9780511483820.

Myers, Robin. 1990. *The Stationers' Company Archive: An Account of the Records 1554–1984*. Winchester: St Paul's Bibliographies.

Myers, Robin, ed. 1986. *Liber A*. In *Records of the Worshipful Company of Stationers 1554–1920*. 115 microfilm reels. Cambridge: Cambridge UP.

Nelson, Brent. 5 December 2013. "Tables of Content." *ArchBook: Architectures of the Book*. http://drc.usask.ca/projects/archbook/tableofcontents.php.

Neville, Sarah. 2014. "Re-evaluating the career of Robert Wyer, Salter-Printer." RSA annual convention, New York, 23 March, panel presentation.
Norbrook, David. 1999. *Writing the English Republic: Poetry, Rhetoric and Politics, 1627–1660*. Cambridge: Cambridge UP.
O'Connell, Sheila. 1999. *The Popular Print in England*. London: British Museum Press.
O'Kill, Brian. 1977. "The Printed Works of William Patten (c.1510–c.1600)." *Transactions of the Cambridge Bibliographical Society* 7 (1): 28–45.
Ong, Walter J. 2002. *Orality and Literacy: The Technologizing of the Word*. London: Routledge.
Owens, Judith. 2002. *Enabling Engagements: Edmund Spenser and the Poetics of Patronage*. Montreal: McGill-Queen's UP.
Padelford, Frederick Morgan, ed. 1934. *The Axiochus of Plato Translated by Edmund Spenser*. Baltimore: Johns Hopkins UP.
Parker, John. 1965. *Books to Build an Empire: A Bibliographical History of English Overseas Interests to 1620*. Amsterdam: N. Israel.
Parker, Tom. 1998. *Form in the Sonnets of the Sidney Circle*. Oxford: Clarendon Press.
Parmelee, Lisa Ferraro. 1994. "Printers, Patrons, Readers, and Spies: Importation of French Propaganda in Late Elizabethan England." *Sixteenth Century Journal* 25 (4): 853–72. https://doi.org/10.2307/2542259.
Patterson, Annabel. 1991. *Fables of Power: Aesopian Writing and Political History*. Durham: Duke UP. https://doi.org/10.1215/9780822382577.
Pearl, Valerie. 1961. *London and the Outbreak of the Puritan Revolution*. Oxford: Oxford UP.
Peltonen, Markku. 1995. *Classical Humanism and Republicanism in English Political Thought 1570–1640*. Cambridge: Cambridge UP. https://doi.org/10.1017/CBO9780511598562.
Perry, Curtis. 2006. "The Uneasy Republicanism of Thomas Kyd's *Cornelia*." *Criticism* 48 (4): 535–55. https://doi.org/10.1353/crt.2008.0009.
Peters, Julie Stone. 2000. *Theatre of the Book 1480–1880: Print, Text and Performance in Europe*. Oxford: Oxford UP.
Pigman, G.W., ed. 2000. *George Gascoigne, A Hundreth Sundrie Flowres*. Oxford: Clarendon Press.
Plant, Marjorie. 1939. *The English Book Trade*. London: G. Allen & Unwin.
Plomer, Henry R. 1903. *Abstracts from the Wills of English Printers and Stationers, from 1492 to 1630*. London: The Bibliographical Society.
– 1908. "Henry Bynneman, Printer 1566–1583." *The Library*, 2nd ser., 9 (35): 225–44.
– 1909. "Henry Denham, Printer." *The Library*, 2nd ser., 10 (39): 241–50.

Pocock, J.G.A. 1975. *The Machiavellian Moment: Florentine Political Thought and the Atlantic Republican Tradition.*, 333–60. Princeton: Princeton UP.
- 1993. "A Discourse of Sovereignty: Observations on a Work in Progress." In *Political Discourse in Early Modern England*, ed. Nicholas Phillipson and Quentin Skinner, 377–428. Cambridge: Cambridge UP.
Pollard, A.W. 1909. *Shakespeare's Folios and Quartos: A Study in the Bibliography of Shakespeare's Plays 1594–1685.* London: Methuen.
- 1917. *Shakespeare's Fight with the Pirates and the Problems of Transmission of His Texts.* London: Alexander Moring Limited.
Pollard, A.W., G.R. Redgrave, and Katharine F. Pantzer. 1976–91. *A Short-Title Catalogue of English Books Printed in England, Scotland & Ireland and of English Books Printed Abroad 1475–1640.* 3 vols. London: The Bibliographical Society.
Pollard, Graham. 1937. "The Early Constitution of the Stationers' Company." *The Library*, 4th ser., 18 (3): 235–60.
- 1978. "The English Market for Printed Books." *Printing History* 4:7–48.
Potter, Lucy. 2009. "Marlowe's *Dido*: Virgilian or Ovidian?" *Notes and Queries* 56 (4): 540–4. https://doi.org/10.1093/notesj/gjp201.
Pratt, Samuel M. 1965. "Shakespeare and Humphrey Duke of Gloucester: A Study in Myth." *Shakespeare Quarterly* 16 (2): 201–16. https://doi.org/10.2307/2868270.
Preston, Jean F. 1985. "The *Pricke of Conscience* (Part I–III) and its First Appearance in Print." *The Library*, 6th ser., 7 (4): 303–14. https://doi.org/10.1093/library/s6-VII.4.303.
Prouty, C.T. 1942. *George Gascoigne, Elizabethan Courtier, Soldier, and Poet.* New York: Columbia UP.
Provvidera, T. 2002. "John Charlewood, Printer of Giordano Bruno's Italian Dialogues, and His Book Production." In *Giordano Bruno Philosopher of the Renaissance*, ed. H. Gatti, 167–86. Aldershot: Ashgate.
Rackin, Phyllis. 1990. *Stages of History: Shakespeare's English Chronicles.* Ithaca: Cornell UP.
Raleigh, Walter, ed. 1908. *Johnson on Shakespeare.* London: Henry Frowde.
Raven, James. 2007. *The Business of Books: Booksellers and the English Book Trade 1450–1850.* New Haven: Yale UP.
Read, David. 2000. *Temperate Conquests: Spenser and the Spanish New World.* Detroit: Wayne State UP.
Rees, Eiluned. 1998. "Wales and the London Book Trade before 1820." In *Spreading the Word: The Distribution Networks of Print 1550–1850*, ed. Robin Myers and Michael Harris, 1–20. Winchester: St Paul's Bibliographies.
Reiss, Timothy J. 1992. *The Meaning of Literature.* Ithaca: Cornell UP.

Richardson, Brian. 1994. *Print Culture in Renaissance Italy: The Editor and the Vernacular Text, 1470–1600*. Cambridge: Cambridge UP https://doi.org/10.1017/CBO9780511597510.

Riggs, David. 2005. *The World of Christopher Marlowe*. New York: Henry Holt.

Ringler, William, ed. 1962. *The Poems of Sir Philip Sidney*. Oxford: Oxford UP.

Robinson, Benedict. 2002. "Thomas Heywood and the Cultural Politics of Play Collections." *Studies in English Literature 1500–1900* 42 (2): 361–80. https://doi.org/10.1353/sel.2002.0018.

Roche, Thomas P. 1989. *Petrarch and the English Sonnet Sequences*. New York: AMS Press.

Rogers, Judith K. 1996. "John Danter." In *Dictionary of Literary Biography*, vol. 170, *The British Literary Book Trade, 1475–1700*, ed. James K. Bracken and Joel Silver, 71–7. Detroit: Gale.

Rollins, Hyder, ed. 1927. *The Paradise of Dainty Devices (1576–1606)*. Cambridge, MA: Harvard UP. https://doi.org/10.4159/harvard.9780674435988.

– 1928. *Tottel's Miscellany*. Cambridge, MA: Harvard UP.

– 1935. *England's Helicon*, 2 vols. Cambridge, MA: Harvard UP.

Rostenburg, Leona. 1965. *Literary, Political, Scientific, Religious & Legal Publishing, Printing & Bookselling in England, 1551–1700*. 2 vols. New York: Burt Franklin.

Saeger, James P., and Christopher J. Fassler. 1995. "The London Professional Theatre, 1576–1642: A Catalogue and Analysis of the Extant Printed Plays." *Research Opportunities in Renaissance Drama* 34:63–109.

Saenger, Michael. 2006. *The Commodification of Textual Engagements in the English Renaissance*. Aldershot: Ashgate.

Saunders, Ann. 1997. "The Building of the Exchange." In *The Royal Exchange*, ed. Ann Saunders, 36–47. London: London Topographical Society.

Saunders, J.W. 1951. "The Stigma of Print: A Note on the Social Bases of Tudor Poetry." *Essays in Criticism* 1 (2): 139–64. https://doi.org/10.1093/eic/I.2.139.

– 1964. *The Profession of English Letters*. London: Routledge.

Schurink, Fred, ed. 2011. *Tudor Translation*. New York: Palgrave. https://doi.org/10.1057/9780230361102.

Shaaber, M.A. 1966. *Some Forerunners of the Newspaper in England 1476–1622*. New York: Octagon Books.

Shannon, Laurie. 2002. *Sovereign Amity: Figures of Friendship in Shakespearean Contexts*. Chicago: U of Chicago P.

- 2004. "Poetic Companies: Musters of Agency in George Gascoigne's 'Friendly Verse.'" *GLQ* 10 (3): 453–83. https://doi.org/10.1215/10642684-10-3-453.
Sherman, William H. 1997. "Anatomizing the Commonwealth: Language, Politics, and the Elizabethan Social Order." In *The Project of Prose in Early Modern Europe and the New World*, 104–21. Cambridge: Cambridge UP.
- 2008. *Used Books: Marking Readers in Renaissance England*. Philadelphia: U of Pennsylvania P.
Shindler, Madaline. 1960. *The Vogue and Impact of Pierre de la Primaudaye's The French Academie on Elizabethan and Jacobean Literature*. Ann Arbor, MI: University Microfilms.
Simons, John. 1998. "Christopher Middleton and Elizabethan Medievalism." In *Medievalism in the Modern World: Essays in Honour of Leslie J. Workman*, ed. Richard Utz and Tom Shippey, 43–60. Turnhout: Brepols.
Singer, Irving. 1975. "Erotic Transformations in the Legend of Dido and Aeneas." *Modern Language Notes* 90 (6): 767–83.
Sisson, Charles Jasper. 1936. *Lost Plays of Shakespeare's Age*. Cambridge: Cambridge UP.
Skinner, Quentin. 1978. *The Foundations of Modern Political Thought*. 2 vols. Cambridge: Cambridge UP.
- 2002. "Classical Liberty and the Coming of the English Civil War." In *Republicanism: A Shared European Heritage*. 2 vols. Ed. Martin van Gelderen and Quentin Skinner, 2:9–28. Cambridge: Cambridge UP.
Slights, William W.E. 2001. *Managing Readers: Printed Marginalia in English Renaissance Books*. Ann Arbor: U of Michigan P. https://doi.org/10.3998/mpub.17226.
Smith, Helen. 2010. "The Publishing Trade in Shakespeare's Time." In *A Concise Companion to Shakespeare and the Text*, ed. Andrew Murphy, 59–78. London: Blackwell.
- 2012. *Grossly Material Things: Women and Book Production in Early Modern England*. Oxford: Oxford UP.
Smith, Helen, and Louise Wilson, eds. 2011. *Renaissance Paratexts*. Cambridge: Cambridge UP. https://doi.org/10.1017/CBO9780511842429.
Smith, Jeremy L. 2003. *Thomas East and Music Publishing in Renaissance England*. Oxford: Oxford UP.
Smith, Margaret McFaddon 2000. *The Title-Page: Its Early Development, 1460–1510*. London: Oak Knoll Press.
Smyth, Adam. 2004. "'Rend and teare in peeces': Textual Fragmentation in Seventeenth Century England." *Seventeenth Century* 19:36–52.

Stallybrass, Peter, and Roger Chartier. 2008. "Reading and Authorship: The Circulation of Shakespeare 1590–1619." In *A Concise Companion to Shakespeare and the Text*, ed. Andrew Murphy, 35–56. Oxford: Blackwell. https://doi.org/10.1002/9780470757895.ch2.

Starnes, D.T. 1965. "John Florio Reconsidered." *Texas Studies in Literature and Language* 6:407–22.

Staub, Susan. 2011. "Dissembling his Art: 'Gascoigne's Gardnings'." *Renaissance Studies* 25 (1): 95–110. https://doi.org/10.1111/j.1477-4658.2010.00709.x.

Stern, Tiffany. 2006. "'On each Wall and Corner Poast': Playbills, Title-pages, and Advertising in Early Modern London." *English Literary Renaissance* 36 (1): 57–85.

Stoker, David. 1981. "The Norwich Book Trades before 1800." *Transactions of the Cambridge Bibliographical Society* 8 (1): 79–125.

Straznicky, Marta. 2006. "Introduction." In *The Book of the Play: Playwrights, Stationers, and Readers in Early Modern England*, ed. Marta Straznicky, 1–19. Amherst: U of Massachusetts P.

Straznicky, Marta, ed. 2013. *Shakespeare's Stationers: Studies in Cultural Bibliography*. Philadelphia: U of Pennsylvania P.

Sutherland, John. 1988. "Publishing History: A Hole at the Centre of Literary Sociology." *Critical Inquiry* 14 (3): 574–89. https://doi.org/10.1086/448457.

Sutton, Dana F., ed. *William Gager (and Richard Edes or George Peele?), Dido (1583). The Philological Museum*, http://www.philological.bham.ac.uk/gager/plays/dido/.

Swan, Marshall W.S. 1944. "The Sweet Speech and Spenser's (?) *Axiochus*." *ELH* 11 (3): 161–81. https://doi.org/10.2307/2871698.

Syme, Holger. 2013. "Thomas Creede, William Barley, and the Venture of Printing Plays." In *Shakespeare's Stationers*, ed. Marta Straznicky, 28–46. Philadelphia: U of Pennsylvania P. https://doi.org/10.9783/9780812207385-003.

– 2016. "The Text Is Foolish: Brian Vickers's 'The One King Lear'." *Los Angeles Review of Books*, 6 September 2016. https://lareviewofbooks.org.

Tanselle, G. Thomas. 1975. "The Bibliographical Concepts of *Issue* and *State*." *PBSA* 69 (1): 17–66.

Taylor, Gary. 2004. "Blount, Edward (*bap*. 1562, *d*. in or before 1632)." In *Oxford Dictionary of National Biography*. Oxford: Oxford UP. Online.

– 2008. "Making Meaning Marketing Shakespeare 1623." In *From Performance to Print in Shakespeare's England*, ed. Peter Holland and Stephen Orgel, 55–72. New York: Palgrave.

Taylor, Myron. 1968. "Tragic Justice and the House of Polonius." *Studies in English Literature* 8 (2): 273–81. https://doi.org/10.2307/449659.

Tedder, H.R. 2004a. "Allde, John (*b.* in or before 1531, *d.* 1584)." Rev. I. Gadd. In *Oxford Dictionary of National Biography*. Oxford UP. Online.

– 2004b. "Charlewood, John (*d.* 1593)." Rev. Robert Faber. In *Oxford Dictionary of National Biography*. Oxford UP. Online.

– 2004c. "Dewes, Garrat (*b.* in or before 1533, *d.* 1591)." Rev. I. Gadd. In *Oxford Dictionary of National Biography*, Oxford UP. Online.

Teslar, J.A. 1960. *Shakespeare's Worthy Counsellor*. Rome.

Thomas, Sidney. 1948. "Richard Smith: 'Foreign to the Company.'" *The Library*, 5th ser., 3 (3): 186–92. https://doi.org/10.1093/library/s5-III.3.186.

Thompson, Ann, and Neil Taylor, eds. 2006. *Hamlet*. 2 vols. London: The Arden Shakespeare.

Thompson, C.R. 1971. "Erasmus and Tudor England." In *Actes du Congrès Erasme, Rotterdam, 27–29 Octobre 1969*, 29–68. Amsterdam: North Holland Publishing.

Todd, Margo. 1987. *Christian Humanism and the Puritan Social Order*. Cambridge: Cambridge UP.

Todorov, Tzvetan. 1990. *Genres in Discourse*. Trans. Catherine Porter. Cambridge: Cambridge UP.

Tribble, Evelyn B. 1993. *Margins and Marginality: The Printed Page in Early Modern England*. Charlottesville: U of Virginia P.

Verse Miscellanies Online. Ed. Michelle O'Callaghan. Created 2011. http://versemiscellaniesonline.bodleian.ox.ac.uk.

Vickers, Sir Brian. 2016. *The One King Lear*. Cambridge: Harvard UP. https://doi.org/10.4159/9780674970311.

Vogt, George McGill. 1924. "Richard Robinson's 'Eupolemia' (1603)." *Studies in Philology* 21 (4): 629–48.

Voss, Paul J. 1998. "Books for Sale: Advertising and Patronage in Late Elizabethan England." *Sixteenth Century Journal* 29 (3): 733–56. https://doi.org/10.2307/2543686.

Walker, Greg. 2005. *Writing Under Tyranny*. Oxford: Oxford UP. https://doi.org/10.1093/acprof:oso/9780199283330.001.0001.

Wall, Wendy. 1993. *The Imprint of Gender: Authorship and Publication in the English Renaissance*. Ithaca: Cornell UP.

Warkentin, Germaine. 1985. "Patrons and Profiteers: Thomas Newman and the 'Violent Enlargement' of *Astrophil and Stella*." *Book Collector* 34:461–87.

Warley, Christopher. 2005. *Sonnet Sequences and Social Distinction in Early Modern England*. Cambridge: Cambridge UP.

Watt, Tessa. 1998. "Publisher, Pedlar, Pot-Poet: The Changing Character of the Broadside Trade, 1550–1640." In *Spreading the Word: The Distribution Networks of Print 1550–1850*, ed. Robin Myers and Michael Harris, 61–81. Winchester: St Paul's Bibliographies.

Weatherby, Harold L. 1986. "*Axiochus* and the Bower of Bliss: Some Fresh Light on Sources and Authorship." *Spenser Studies* 6:95–113.

Weiss, Adrian. 1992. "Shared Printing, Printer's Copy, and the Text(s) of Gascoigne's 'A Hundreth Sundrie Flowers.'" *Studies in Bibliography* 45:71–104.

Wellisch, H. 1981. "How to Make an Index – 16th Century Style: Conrad Gessner on Indexes and Catalogs." *International Classification* 8:10–15.

Wheatley, Edward. 2000. *Mastering Aesop: Medieval Education, Chaucer, and His Followers*. Gainesville: U of Florida P.

Whigham, Frank, and Wayne E. Rebhorn, eds. 2007. *The Art of English Poesy by George Puttenham: A Critical Edition*. Ithaca: Cornell UP.

Whitworth, Stephen. 1999. "Far from Being: Rhetoric and Dream-Work in Dickenson's 'Arisbis.'" *Exemplaria* 11 (1): 167–94. https://doi.org/10.1179/exm.1999.11.1.167.

Williams, Franklin B. 1962. *Index of Dedications and Commendatory Poems in English Books before 1641*. London: The Bibliographical Society.

– 1966. "Commendatory Verses: The Rise of the Art of Puffing." *Studies in Bibliography* 19:1–14.

Willis, Arthur James, ed. 1972. *Canterbury Licenses (General) 1568–1646*. London: Phillimore.

Wood, H. Harvey. 1933. *The Poems and Fables of Robert Henryson Schoolmaster of Dunfermline*. Edinburgh: Oliver and Boyd.

Wood, Neal. 1997. "Avarice and Civil Unity: The Contribution of Sir Thomas Smith." *History of Political Thought* 18:24–42.

Woodfield, Denis B. 1973. *Surreptitious Printing in England, 1550–1640*. New York: Bibliographical Society of America.

Woods, Susanne. 1970. "'The Passionate Sheepheard' and 'The Nimphs Reply': A Study of Transmission." *Huntington Library Quarterly* 34 (1): 25–33. https://doi.org/10.2307/3816860.

Worden, Blair. 1981. "Classical Republicanism and the Puritan Revolution." In *History and Imagination: Essays on Honor of H. R. Trevor-Roper*, ed. Hugh Lloyd-Jones, Valerie Pearl, and Blair Worden, 182–200. New York: Homes and Meier.

– 2002. "Republicanism, Regicide, and the Republic: The English Experience." In *Republicanism: A Shared European Heritage,* 2 vols., ed. Martin van Gelderen and Quentin Skinner, 1: 307–27. Cambridge: Cambridge UP.

Worms, Laurence. 1997. "The Book Trade at the Royal Exchange." In *The Royal Exchange*, ed. Ann Saunders, 209–26. London: London Topographical Society.

Woudhuysen, H.R. 1996. *Sir Philip Sidney and the Circulation of Manuscripts 1558–1640*. Oxford: Clarendon Press. https://doi.org/10.1093/acprof:oso/9780198129660.001.0001.

Wright, Louis B. 1935. *Middle-Class Culture in Elizabethan England*. Chapel Hill: U of North Carolina P.

Yamada, Akihiro. 1994. *Thomas Creede: Printer to Shakespeare and His Contemporaries*. Tokyo: Meisei UP.

Zarnowiecki, Matthew. 2014. *Fair Copies: Reproducing the English Lyric from Tottel to Shakespeare*. Toronto: U of Toronto P.

Index

acquisition of copy, 6, 11, 13, 30–6, 81; complaints about, 30–1; payments, 31–2. *See also* Jones, Richard; Ling, Nicholas; Millington, Thomas; Ponsonby, William; Smith, Richard; Wolfe, John
Adams, Thomas (bookseller), 13
advertising, 16, 60, 66, 156, 187n39, 198n79, 203n123. *See also* Hacket, Thomas: pleasurable reading; Smith, Richard: "decades"
Aesop, 117–19, 219–20n56. *See also* Henryson, Robery; Smith, Richard
Aggas, Edward (bookseller and translator), 11, 68–9
Alday, John (translator), 82–3, 90, 95, 213n72
Alison, Richard, 53–4
Allde, Edward (printer), 15, 51, 63
Allde, John (printer), 45, 63
alteration of copy, 61–6; censorship, 62–3; editing (correcting), 63–6, 100; expansion, 61–2, 202n113. *See also* Blower, Ralph; gnomic pointers; Hacket, Thomas; Smith, Richard: *Diana*, *Fabulous Tales of Aesop*; Tap, John

Andrewes, Lancelot: *Wonderful Combat*, 107
Arber, Edward, 79, 185n17; Stationers' Register, 8–9
Askell, James (stationer), 15
authorship, 5, 9, 23, 39, 59, 61, 100–1, 218n37. *See also* Hurst and Robinson; Smith, Richard

Bailey, John (bookseller), 62
Baldwin, William: *Mirror*, 160; *Treatise*, 158–9, 160. *See also* Marshe, Henry
ballads, 4, 32, 47, 71, 96, 188n50
Barker, Christopher (printer), 19, 42, 102, 187n40; *Art of Venery*, 35, 45, 56; *Book of Falconry*, 54
Barley, William (bookseller), 40, 71
Barnes, J.H., 175
Bastard, Thomas: *Chrestoleros*, 31–2
Beaumont, John: *Metamorphosis of Tobacco*, 148
Beecher, Donald, 212n56
de Belleforest, François, 155–6, 180–1
Bennett, H.S., 66, 204n134
Bentley, James: *Harmony*, 173–4

Best, George: *True Discourses*, 63.
    See also Bynneman, Henry
bibliographic ego, 100–1
Blackwall, William (bookseller), 15
Blagden, Cyprian, 188n50, 189n52
Blair, Ann, 52, 53
Bland, Mark, 185n21
Blayney, Peter W.M., 11, 12, 17, 62,
    187n42, 189n52, 196n53, 219n51,
    225n5
Blount, Edward (bookseller and
    translator), 42, 70, 140
Blower, Ralph (bookseller), 202n110
blurbs (title page), 21, 22, 29, 36,
    58, 60, 203n123
Boaistuau, Pierre: *Theatrum mundi*,
    82–3
Boccaccio: *Il filocolo*, 102, 103, 116;
    Titus and Gisippus, 7, 89, 91,
    208n13
bookbinding, 114
"bookseller publisher" (i.e., "publishing bookseller"), 6, 16; rise of,
    16–19
bookshops: as meeting places, 16;
    signs of, 72. *See also* browsing
Bourne, Claire M.L., 204n131
Bourne, William, 187n39; *Regiment*,
    28, 143. *See also* Hacket, Thomas;
    Weaver, Edmund; Wight, Thomas
Boutcher, Warren, 212n59
Bowers, Fredson, 57, 201nn98–9
Braden, Gordon, 88
Brennan, Michael, 70, 203n116
Breton, Nicholas, 61; *Breton's Bower*
    38, 54, 61, 64–5. *See also* Creede,
    Thomas; Jones, Richard: Horatian
    binary
Brooke, Tucker, 227n28
Broome, Joan (bookseller), 31

browsing, 115–17, 120–2, 219n54
Bullinger, Heinrich: *Sermons*, 133
Burby, Cuthbert (bookseller), 3–5,
    6–7, 13, 21, 66, 170; career, 76;
    collaborations, 26, 158
Burton, Francis (bookseller), 194n42
Burton, William (translator). *See*
    Ling, Nicholas: *Seven Dialogues*
Busby, John (bookseller), 26, 43,
    185n26, 196n59; collaborations,
    13, 26, 158, 171, 191n6
Butler, John (bookseller), 17
Bynneman, Henry (printer and
    bookseller), 40, 63, 84, 103, 104,
    158, 197n70, 206n6, 210n39,
    215n7; collaborations, 82, 114,
    116; commissions, 28, 35, 55,
    79; *A Hundreth Sundry Flowers*,
    110–11

Cadman, Thomas (bookseller), 8
Calvin, Jean, 179
Campion, Thomas: *Observations*,
    193n27, 222n87
Carter, William (printer), 63
Castiglione, Balthasar: *The Courtier*,
    42
Caxton, William (printer), 51–2, 64
Chapman, George, 227n29
Charlewood, John (printer), 4, 5,
    100, 190n66, 217n23, 221nn74–5,
    221–2n79; collaborations, 82, 103,
    104, 108, 221n71; commissions,
    55–6
Cheney, Patrick, 54, 155–6, 229nn46
Churchyard, Thomas, 46–8, 214–15n83
Cicero, 67, 88, 161, 175
Clegg, Cyndia, 203n119
Coldiron, A.E.B., 204n137

Coldock, Francis (bookseller), 14, 80
Cole, Douglas, 154
collaborations: between printers, 12–13; between publishers, 13; between trade printers and publishers, 13; *See also* Burby, Cuthbert; Busby, John; Bynneman, Henry; Charlewood, John; debt; Hacket, Thomas; Ling, Nicholas; Linley and Flasket; Smith, Richard; Wolfe, John
Collinson, Patrick, 155, 161
commendatory poems, 40, 43–6, 162, 196n58. *See also* Smith, Richard
commonplace books, 53, 101, 159
compiling, 36–56, 192–3n24
composite packaging (multi-title volumes), 3–5, 27–8, 30, 142. *See also* Linley and Flasket
compositing, 10, 222n82, 235n64
Compton, Sir Henry, 104–5, 125–6
Constable, Henry, 32, 126. *See also* Grundy, Joan; Smith, Richard: *Diana*
counsel, 161–3, 169–70, 181–2, 232n26. *See also* Ling, Nicholas: *Hamlet* (1603); Shakespeare, William: Corambis, Horatio
courtesy manuals, 22, 24
Crashaw, William, 37
Creede, Thomas (printer), 64, 71, 142–3
Crowley, Robert (printer), 37, 40

Daniel, Samuel, 30
Danter, John (printer), 4, 5, 8, 71, 75–6
Darnton, Robert, 191n3

Davison, Francis: *Poetical Rhapsody*, 62
Dawson, Thomas (printer), 13, 71, 186n35, 206n6
Day, Angel: *English Secretary*, 197n68
Day, John (printer), 11, 34, 40, 55, 59, 71, 73–4, 167
debt, 14–15, 31, 46, 140–1, 186nn31–3, 196n58. *See also* Hacket, Thomas
dedicatory epistles, 40–2, 104–5, 195–6n51
Demetriou, Tania, and Rowan Tomlinson, 66
Denham, Henry (printer), 28, 82, 186n35, 209–10n29
Desportes, Philippe, 130, 222–3n88
Dewes, Garrat (bookseller), 8
Dickinson, John: *Arisbas*, 149–50. *See also* Linley and Flasket
Disle, Henry (bookseller), 38, 77, 91, 202n113, 206n1
distribution (wholesaling), 6, 11, 13, 16, 19, 187n41, 188n47
Dodds, Gregory D., 164–5
Drapers' Company, 81, 102–3, 108, 113–14, 141
Drawater, John (bookseller), 37–8
Drayton, Michael, 30, 45–6, 99, 162, 181–2, 231n11
Duncan-Jones, Katherine, 23

Earle, John, 31–2
East, Thomas (printer), 40, 41, 71, 186n29, 210n35
economy of obligation. *See* Muldrew, Craig
Eden, Richard (translator), 85, 93, 213n66; *Decades*, 86, 95, 212n58,

223n95; oratorical translation, 88; *Treatise*, 85, 86–7, 89–90
Edgar, Eleazar (bookseller), 23–4, 143–4
editing. *See* Jones, Richard; Massai, Sonia; Wolfe, John
Edmonds, Dorothy, 104–5
Edmondson, Paul M., 236n79
Edwards, Richard: *Paradise*, 77–8, 202n113
Egan, Gabriel, 185n21
Elizabeth I, 3, 56, 81, 167, 229n46
Ellis, Jim, 147, 229n50
England's Helicon, 149. *See also* Spenser, Edmund
epigraphs, 27, 29
epyllion, 146–7. *See also* Linley and Flasket
Erasmus: *Colloquies*, 163. *See also* Ling, Nicholas: *Seven Dialogues*
errata lists, 53–4, 218n43
euphuistic prose, 4, 50–1, 58, 63, 97–8
Evans, John T., 165

Fabyan, Robert: *Chronicle*, 48, 60
Farmer, Alan, and Zachary Lesser, 138, 171, 210n32
Field, Richard (printer), 20
Fisher, Alan, 236n65
Flasket, John (bookbinder and bookseller), 140–1, 227n29. *See also* Linley and Flasket
Fleming, Abraham (translator), 53, 133, 198n77, 199n82
Florio, John (translator), 85; *New France*, 85–6, 87–8
Fowler, Alistair, 190n71
Fox, Denton, 123–4
Foxe, John, 71; *Acts*, 11, 201n100

Frampton, John (translator), 85; *Brief Description*, 87; *Discourse*, 86; *Discovery*, 212n56; *Marcus Paulus*, 88
Freyd, Bernard, 4
Frobisher, Martin, 97

Gants, David, 189n53
Gardiner, Samuel: *Portraiture*, 235n62
Garnier, Robert: *Cornelia*, 171
Gascoigne, George, 56, 103, 106–7; *Posies*, 109; translator, 35, 45, 191n9. *See also* Smith, Richard: *A Hundreth Sundry Flowers*
Gaskell, Philip, 227n27
Genette, Gérard, 36–9, 193n29
Geneva Bible, 197n68
genre, 22–4, 57, 190n65
Gessner, Conrad, 52
Gillespie, Alexandra, 58
gnomic pointers, 181–2. *See also* Ling, Nicholas
Goldie, Marc, 161
Golding, Arthur (translator), 67, 133
Gopen, George, 220n62
Goslicius, Laurentius Grimalius, 168–70
Gosson, Stephan, 211n54
Gosson, Thomas (bookseller), 104, 107–8
Gough, John (bookseller), 17, 186n32
Grafton, Anthony, 203n123
de Grazia, Margreta, 29, 179, 230n5
Green, Ian, 185n21
Greene, Robert, 45, 140, 147, 231n18; advertisements, 187n39; collaborations, 44, 196n56; *Greene's Vision*, 40–1, 42;

Menaphon, 145; *Morando*, 23; *Notable Discovery*, 39; *A Quip*, 186n31; *Perimedes*, 22; *Spanish Masquerado*, 44
Greg, W.W., 9–10, 57, 193n25, 209n26, 227nn28–9, 234n47
Grove, Mathew, 220n69; *Pelops and Hippodamia*, 103, 125–6
Grundy, Joan, 221nn72, 73, 76, 222–3n88
Guy, John, 232n25

Hacket, Thomas (bookseller and translator), 14–15, 40, 59, 79–83; alteration of copy, 92–4; collaborations, 46, 81, 82; debt, 82; *Last Voyage*, 84, 90, 94; *New Found World*, 84–5, 89–92, 95, 97; oratorical translation, 92–4, 214n74; pleasurable reading (wonder), 89–91; Protestant vocation, 94–7; readership, 91–2; specialties, 71–2, 83–5; translator, 69, 84–5, 89–94; *True Discovery*, 84, 89–91
Hadfield, Andrew, 85, 156, 184n8, 212n58, 231n11
Hall, Roland (printer), 52, 82
Hapwood, Robert, 236n71
Hardin, Richard F., 237n87
Harington, Sir John, 200n93
Harrison, John (bookseller), 43, 48–9
Harrison, Lukas, and George Bishop (booksellers), 67
Harvey, Gabriel, 45–6, 72, 134–5
headings: chapter, 49–52; section, 159–62
headlines, 49, 197n68. *See also* Jones, Richard
Helgerson, Richard, 19

Henryson, Robery: *Morall fabillis*, 117, 121, 122–4. *See also* Smith, Richard
Heywood, Jasper, 77
histories, 24, 94, 214n77
Holland, Henry, and George Gibbs (booksellers), 143
Holland, Philemon (translator), 34, 134, 223–4n97
Holme, Wilfred: *Rebellion*, 116–17
Hooke, Henry (bookbinder), and Simon Stafford (printer), 142
Hooks, Adam, 189n60
Householder, Michael, 212n58
Hull, Helen, 176
humanism, 22, 43, 64, 68, 160, 161, 164, 174, 230n2
Hunnis, William, 77
Hurst and Robinson (publishers): *The Old English Drama*, 137–8

illustrations, 54–7. *See also* Wolfe, John
imprints, 13, 36, 71, 188n44, 193n25
indexes, 52–3, 198n79
Islip, Adam (printer), 34

Jaggard, William (printer and bookseller), 23–4
James VI (I), 164, 179–82, 237n86
Jauss, Hans Robert, 24, 36
Jeffes, Abel (printer), 104
Jennings, Miles (bookseller), 68
Johns, Adrian, 219n54
Johnson, Gerald D., 11, 15–16, 158, 170, 234n48
Johnson, Samuel, 175
Jones, Richard (printer and bookseller), 40, 57; additions by, 61, 202–3n114; dedicatory epistles,

195n49; editing, 64–6; errata, 54; genre, 22–3; headlines, 49–50; Horatian binary, 21–2; poetry miscellanies, 38, 61, 64–5; reissuing, 58–9; specialties, 71; titles, 39, 194–5n43
Jugge, Richard (printer and bookseller), 33, 34, 71

Kastan, David, 170
Kingston, John (printer), 42, 48, 60
Knapp, James A., 199n88
Knight, Jeffrey Todd, 202n109

Lambard, William, 176
de La Primaudaye, Pierre: *Academie françoise*, 159, 160, 162, 232n24
Lawton, Augustine (bookseller), 15
Lee, Sidney, 9
Lesser, Zachary, 7, 11–12, 16, 42–3, 71–2, 156, 188n51
Lestringant, Frank, and Ann Blair, 214n78
Lewkenor, Lewis: *Discourse*, 37–8, 194n34
Ling, Nicholas (bookseller), 39, 156–9; acquisition of *Hamlet*, 170; collaborations, 158, 171; *Counselor*, 168–70; gnomic pointers, 171–3; *Hamlet* (1603), 170–81; *Hamlet* (1604), 170–1, 235n59; *Legend*, 162–3; play publications, 170–1; *Politeuphuia*, 45, 158–62, 173; reading, 171–80; reissues, 164–7, 168–9, 171; *Seven Dialogues*, 164–7; specialties, 71–2, 156, 173; translator, 68
Linley and Flasket (booksellers): *Arisbas-Dido*, 144–54; collaborations, 141, 148–9; epyllion, 147–54; reissues, 144–5; specialties, 141, 148
Linley, Paul (bookseller), 139–40, 226n19. See also Linley and Flasket
literary canon, vernacular, 19–20, 105, 149, 231n18
literary culture, 6, 7, 19–24, 77–8, 97–8, 150, 231n16. See also authorship; epyllion; genre; literary canon; lyric poetry; patrons; plays; poetry miscellanies; sonnets; travel literature
Livy, 134–5. See also Holland, Philemon
Lodge, Thomas, 32, 44, 196nn56, 59, 231n11; *Euphues Shadow*, 44–5
Lydgate, John, 23
lyric poetry, 38, 61–2, 215n4. See also Sidney, Sir Philip: *Astrophel*; Smith, Richard: *Diana*; Spenser, Edmund
Lyly, John: *Euphues*, 97–8, 200–1n96
Lynne, Walter (translator), 204–5n138
Lyons, Tara L., 59

Machiavelli, 174
Man, Thomas (bookseller), 71
Mandeville, Sir John: *Travels*, 78
marginalia, printed, 48–9, 60, 89–90, 91, 135, 212n58, 235n62
mariners, 72, 79, 84, 87, 92, 95, 212n56. See also Bourne, William; Eden, Richard; Frampton, John
Markham, Francis, 133–4
Marlowe, Christopher, 137, 147, 156; *Dido*, 138–9, 141–2, 144–9, 152–4, 224nn2–3, 229n54; *Doctor Faustus*, 97; *Hero and Leander*, 141, 144–5, 147, 151–2; *Jew of Malta*,

76, 171; *Tamburlaine*, 22–3, 39, 65–6, 139
Marotti, Arthur, 62, 99, 110, 215n4
Marshe, Henry (printer), 60
Marshe, Thomas (printer), 46–8, 60, 67
Massai, Sonia, 65–6
Matz, Robert, 22
McGann, Jerome, 185n20
McKenzie, D.F., 5–6, 12
McKerrow, R.B., 9–10, 72–3; *Dictionary* 7–9, 140
McLaren, Anne, 162, 167
Middleton, Christopher: *Legend*, 162–3. *See also* Ling, Nicholas
Millington, Thomas (bookseller), 71, 73–6
de Mornay, Phillipe: *Defense of Death*, 69; *Defense of Liberty*, 178–9
Muir, Kenneth, 222n82
Muldrew, Craig, 14
multivocality, 109, 125, 129
Munday, Anthony, 4–5, 7, 45–6, 104, 223n96

Nashe, Thomas, 100, 137, 139; on commendatory writers, 43, 45–6; on "decades," 132, 223n92; *Pierce Penniless*, 27; on quatorzains, 130; on Sidney, 48, 100, 130; on title pages, 36; on titles, 194–5n43
Nelson, Thomas (bookseller), 39
Newbery, Ralph (bookseller), 14, 42, 52–3, 133, 199n82
New Bibliography, 5, 9–10
Newman, Thomas (bookseller), 40–1; *Astrophel and Stella*, 65, 99–101, 126–7, 202n113, 222n85
Newman, Thomas (translator), 67

news, 16, 71, 74–5, 80, 191n2, 237n87. *See also* Aggas, Edward; Wolfe, John: specialties
Newton, Thomas (translator), 197n63
Nicholas, Thomas (translator), 85, 87, 88
nonce collections, 57–8, 59, 144, 201n103
Norbrook, David, 155–6
Norton, George (bookseller), 38
Norwich, 165

office holding, 160–1, 163, 168, 175–6
Olney, Henry (bookseller), 20
Ovid, 154. *See also* Hacket, Thomas: translator; Linley and Flasket: epyllion; Weever, John
Owens, Judith, 202n112
Oxenbridge, John (bookseller), 44

Padelford, Frederick Morgan, 3–5
paratexts. *See* blurbs; epigraphs; gnomic pointers; headings; headlines; illustrations; indexes; marginalia, printed; running headers; title pages
Parker, John, 87, 213nn63, 65
Parker, Tom, 222n83
Partridge, John (translator), 46
The Passionate Pilgrim, 23, 38, 202n113, 229n53
patrons, 31, 127, 196n52; of maritime ventures, 89, 95; publishers as, 45–6. *See also* dedicatory epistles
Patten, William, 33
Payne, John, 208n19
Paynell, Thomas (translator), 204n136

Peltonen, Markku, 168, 230n2
Perrin, John (bookseller), 23–4
Peters, Julie Stone, 204n131
Pettie, George: *A Petite Palace.* See Watkins, Richard
Petyt, Thomas (printer and bookseller), 102
Phillip, William (translator), 34
Phiston, William (translator), 34, 67
Pickering, William (bookseller), 81
piracy of texts, 4, 9–10
plays, 11, 19, 24, 32, 33, 65–6, 137–8, 225n5, 234n53. See also Ling, Nicholas; Linley and Flasket; Woodcock, Thomas
Pliny, 97–8, 223n95
poetry miscellanies: manuscript, 112, 159; print, 112–13, 125
Poleman, John (translator), 28, 35
Pollard, A.W., 9–10
Pollard, Graham, 188n47
Ponsonby, William (bookseller), 14, 40, 42, 61–2, 140, 202n112, 207n11; acquisition 33, 34; illustrations, 56–7; specialties, 70, 71
Popple, William, 174–5
prefatory epistles ("To the Reader"), 42–4, 105, 111, 195n45, 196n53
prefatory material. See commendatory poems; dedicatory epistles; errata lists; prefatory epistles; tables of contents
"printer publisher" (i.e., "publishing printer"), 6, 16
printers' emblems, 55, 56, 72–4, 105–6, 156–7
printing, 6, 10, 11, 18–19, 53–4, 187n40; Continental, 49–50, 64, 172, 203n123; patents, 17–19, 188nn46, 49, 205n149; shared, 12. See also compositing; trade printing
Proctor, John (bookseller), 27, 61
proofing, 6, 10, 198n77, 203n123
publishing, 184nn9–10; and booksellers, 15–19; financing, 6, 9–10, 17; misconduct, 7–9; and printers, 17–19, 187n41; and profit, 9–10, 185n21; terminology, 6; and women, 185–6n27. See also acquisition of copy; advertising; alteration of copy; collaborations; compiling; composite packaging; debt; distribution; literary culture; New Bibliography; patrons; printers' emblems; reading; reissuing; specialization; translation
Purfoot, Thomas, Jr (printer), 142
Puttenham, George: *Art of English Poesy*, 19–20

Radcliffe, Robert, and Bridget, 44–5
Rastall, John, and William (printers), 65
reading, 7, 12, 22, 48, 50–4, 60, 78, 152, 156, 159. See also Hacket, Thomas; Hurst and Robinson; Jauss, Hans Robert; Lesser, Zachary; Ling, Nicholas
reissuing, 57–60. See also Jones, Richard; Ling, Nicholas; Linley and Flasket
republican political thought, 155–6. See also counsel; office holding; service; treason; tyranny
Ribaut, Jean, 96. See also Hacket, Thomas: *Last Voyage, True Discovery*
Richardson, Brian, 203n123
Roberts, James (printer), 64, 104, 170

Robinson, Benedict, 60
Robinson, George (publisher), 224n2
Robinson, Richard, 61; payments to, 31–2
Robinson, Robert (printer), 8
Rollins, Hyder, 64
Rowbotham, James (bookseller), 43, 71
running headers, 37, 100, 126, 224n3

Salesbury, William (translator), 204n136
Sammelbände, 114–15
Scarlet, Thomas (printer), 13
sententiae, 53, 59, 71, 172–4, 192n20. *See also* Ling, Nicholas: *Politeuphuia*
Seres, William (printer and bookseller), 42
service, 161–2, 166–7
Shakespeare, William, 48; Corambis, 171–8; First Folio, 9; Horatio, 177–8; Polonius, 174–5, 178, 235n58; *The Tempest*, 78; *Venus and Adonis*, 147, 151, 153. *See also* epyllion; Ling, Nicholas; Linley and Flasket; *The Passionate Pilgrim*
Shannon, Laurie, 230n3
Shaw, James (bookseller), 143
Shirley, William, 45
Sidney, Sir Henry, 89, 92
Sidney, Sir Philip, 22, 61–2, 128–9, 132, 145–6, 149, 213n69; *Astrophel and Stella*, 65, 78, 99–101, 126–7, 129; *Defense of Poesy*, 19–20, 94. *See also* Davison, Francis; Nashe, Thomas; Ponsonby, William: specialties

Simmes, Valentine (printer), 8, 13, 21, 64, 170
Singleton, Hugh (bookseller), 15, 79, 201n100
Slights, William, 197n65
Skinner, Quentin, 230n2
Smethwick, John (bookseller), 158, 231n14
Smith, Helen, and Louise Wilson, 193n29
Smith, Henry, 32, 39
Smith, Richard (bookseller), 101–8; acquisition of copy, 105–6, 129–30; and authorship, 118–19, 125–7, 129–30; collaborations, 104, 107–8, 114, 221n71; commendatory poems, 105, 110, 113; "decades," 130–6; *Diana*, 125–36; *Fabulous Tales of Aesop*, 117–25; *A Hundreth Sundry Flowers*, 108–17; specialties, 103–4; translator, 68, 117–18
Smith, Sir Thomas: *De Republica Anglorum*, 167–8
sonnets, 23–4, 99, 100–1. *See also* lyric poetry
specialization, 11–12, 70–6. *See also* Hacket, Thomas; Ling, Nicholas; Linley and Flasket; Smith, Richard; Wolfe, John
Spenser, Edmund, 22, 29, 32, 46–7, 70, 144, 149, 229n46; *Amoretti*, 130, 135–6; *Axiochus*, 3–5, 6–7, 21; *Colin*, 61–2; *Complaints*, 33, 202n112; *England's Helicon*, 228–9n42; *Faerie Queene*, 57, 78, 99, 140, 150; *Shepheardes Calendar*, 19. *See also* Ponsonby, William
Stafford, Simon (printer), 59, 142
Stanley, Margaret, 69

Star Chamber, 225n11; *Decrees* (1587), 18–19
Stationers' Company, 68; charter, 17; Court, 9, 14–15, 108, 200n95; *Orders* (1587), 18–19; printing patents, 18; Register, 8–9, 31, 33, 142–4, 190n66, 192n17
Stonley, Richard, 68, 104, 118, 122
Stow, John, 80
Stubbes, Phillip: *Anatomy of Abuses*, 49
Sutherland, John, 187n37
Swan, Marshall S., 4–5

tables of content, 51–2, 122–5
Tap, John (bookseller), 202n110
Terence. *See* Woodcock, Thomas
Thevet, André, 84–5, 93–4, 211n44. *See also* Hacket, Thomas: *New Found World*
Thomas, Sidney, 103, 107, 111
Tisdale, John (printer and bookseller), 81–2
title pages, 16, 22–3, 36, 52, 60. *See also* imprints; Nashe, Thomas; printers' emblems
titles, 22–3, 36–9; of poems, 126–7, 220–1n70. *See also* Burton, Francis; Jones, Richard; Nashe, Thomas; Wye, Robert
Todorov, Tzvetan, 190n65
Tofte, Robert, 21
Tottel, Richard (printer), 17–18, 64, 71, 112–13, 207n11
trade printing, 6, 17–19, 188n44
translation, 66–70, 192nn17–18; theories of, 88. *See also* Boutcher, Warren; Eden, Richard; Frampton, John; Gascoigne, George; Hacket, Thomas: oratorical translation; Ling, Nicholas; Smith, Richard; Wolfe, John
travel literature, 69, 71, 77–8, 83–8. *See also* Hacket, Thomas
treason, 159–60, 178–81
Tribble, Evelyn, 48
Trundle, John (bookseller), 71, 170, 171, 185n26
tyranny, 160, 163, 165–6, 168, 178–81

Vautrollier, Thomas (printer and bookseller), 207n11

Waldegrave, Robert (printer), 63
Waley, Robert (bookseller), 15, 22, 42
Wall, Wendy, 100–1, 109, 112–13, 114
Warburton, William, 175
Ward, Roger (printer), 7
Watkins, Richard (printer and bookseller), 27, 50–1, 63
Weaver, Edmund (bookseller), 143
Weever, John, 148, 162. *See also* Linley and Flasket: collaborations
Weiss, Adrian, 110–11
Welby, William (bookseller), 37
Whetstone, George, 32; *Promos*, 23, 65; *Rock*, 22
Whigham, Frank, and Wayne E. Rebhorn, 189n60
White, Edward (bookseller), 22, 39, 64, 66, 107–8, 181, 202n113
Wight, John, Jr, 140, 225n12
Wight, John, Sr (bookseller), 15, 101, 140–1, 215–16n9, 216n10
Wight, Thomas (bookseller), 143
Williams, Francis (bookseller), 142
Williams, Franklin B., 44, 45, 195n48
Windet, John (printer), 71

Wise, Andrew (bookseller), 66
Wither, George, 38
Wolfe, John (printer), 7, 40, 45–6, 188n50, 202n113; acquisition, 35; collaborations, 209–10n29, 227n28; dedicatory epistles, 42; editing, 65; illustrations, 199–200n89; specialties, 70, 72, 83–4, 191n2; translation, 34, 67, 69
Wood, H. Harvey, 220nn59, 62
Wood, William (bookseller), 107
Woodcock, Thomas (bookseller), 13, 67, 133, 216n16; *Dido* (1594), 138–9; play publications, 138–9
de Worde, Wynkyn, 186n32
Wormen, Peter (translator), 34
Worms, Laurence, 208n19
Woudhuysen, H.R., 204n128
Wright, William (bookseller), 64
Wyer, Robert (printer), 193–4n34

Zarnowiecki, Matthew, 109

Studies in Book and Print Culture

General Editor: Leslie Howsam

Hazel Bell, *Indexers and Indexes in Fact and Fiction*

Heather Murray, *Come, bright Improvement! The Literary Societies of Nineteenth-Century Ontario*

Joseph A. Dane, *The Myth of Print Culture: Essays on Evidence, Textuality, and Bibliographical Method*

Christopher J. Knight, *Uncommon Readers: Denis Donoghue, Frank Kermode, George Steiner, and the Tradition of the Common Reader*

Eva Hemmungs Wirtén, *No Trespassing: Authorship, Intellectual Property Rights, and the Boundaries of Globalization*

William A. Johnson, *Bookrolls and Scribes in Oxyrhynchus*

Siân Echard and Stephen Partridge, eds, *The Book Unbound: Editing and Reading Medieval Manuscripts and Texts*

Bronwen Wilson, *The World in Venice: Print, the City, and Early Modern Identity*

Peter Stoicheff and Andrew Taylor, eds, *The Future of the Page*

Jennifer Phegley and Janet Badia, eds, *Reading Women: Literary Figures and Cultural Icons from the Victorian Age to the Present*

Elizabeth Sauer, *"Paper-contestations" and Textual Communities in England, 1640–1675*

Nick Mount, *When Canadian Literature Moved to New York*

Jonathan Earl Carlyon, *Andrés González de Barcia and the Creation of the Colonial Spanish American Library*

Leslie Howsam, *Old Books and New Histories: An Orientation to Studies in Book and Print Culture*

Deborah McGrady, *Controlling Readers: Guillaume de Machaut and His Late Medieval Audience*

David Finkelstein, ed., *Print Culture and the Blackwood Tradition*

Bart Beaty, *Unpopular Culture: Transforming the European Comic Book in the 1990s*

Elizabeth Driver, *Culinary Landmarks: A Bibliography of Canadian Cookbooks, 1825–1949*

Benjamin C. Withers, *The Illustrated Old English Hexateuch, Cotton Ms. Claudius B.iv: The Frontier of Seeing and Reading in Anglo-Saxon England*

Mary Ann Gillies, *The Professional Literary Agent in Britain, 1880–1920*

Willa Z. Silverman, *The New Bibliopolis: French Book-Collectors and the Culture of Print, 1880–1914*

Lisa Surwillo, *The Stages of Property: Copyrighting Theatre in Spain*

Dean Irvine, *Editing Modernity: Women and Little-Magazine Cultures in Canada, 1916–1956*

Janet Friskney, *New Canadian Library: The Ross-McClelland Years, 1952–1978*

Janice Cavell, *Tracing the Connected Narrative: Arctic Exploration in British Print Culture, 1818–1860*

Elspeth Jajdelska, *Silent Reading and the Birth of the Narrator*

Martyn Lyons, *Reading Culture and Writing Practices in Nineteenth-Century France*

Robert A. Davidson, *Jazz Age Barcelona*

Gail Edwards and Judith Saltman, *Picturing Canada: A History of Canadian Children's Illustrated Books and Publishing*

Miranda Remnek, ed., *The Space of the Book: Print Culture in the Russian Social Imagination*

Adam Reed, *Literature and Agency in English Fiction Reading: A Study of the Henry Williamson Society*

Bonnie Mak, *How the Page Matters*

Eli MacLaren, *Dominion and Agency: Copyright and the Structuring of the Canadian Book Trade, 1867–1918*

Ruth Panofsky, *The Literary Legacy of the Macmillan Company of Canada: Making Books and Mapping Culture*

Archie L. Dick, *The Hidden History of South Africa's Book and Reading Cultures*

Darcy Cullen, ed., *Editors, Scholars, and the Social Text*

James J. Connolly, Patrick Collier, Frank Felsenstein, Kenneth R. Hall, and Robert Hall, eds, *Print Culture Histories beyond the Metropolis*

Kristine Kowalchuk, *Preserving on Paper: Seventeenth-Century Englishwomen's Receipt Books*

Ian Hesketh, *Victorian Jesus: J.R. Seeley, Religion, and the Cultural Significance of Anonymity*

Kirsten MacLeod, *American Little Magazines of the Fin de Siècle: Art, Protest, and Cultural Transformation*

Emily Francomano, *The Prison of Love: Romance, Translation and the Book in the Sixteenth Century*

Kirk Melnikoff, *Elizabethan Publishing and the Makings of Literary Culture*